Reorienting Global Communication

POPULAR CULTURE AND
POLITICS IN ASIA PACIFIC

Series Editor
Poshek Fu,
University of Illinois
at Urbana-Champaign

*A list of books in the series
appears at the end of this book.*

Reorienting Global Communication

INDIAN AND CHINESE
MEDIA BEYOND BORDERS

Edited by

Michael Curtin and
Hemant Shah

University of Illinois Press

Urbana and Chicago

Chapter 3 was originally published in *New Media and Society* 8, no. 2 (2006): 207–27

Chapter 5 was originally published in *Quarterly Review of Film & Video* 23, no. 2 (2006): 219–38.

Library of Congress Cataloging-in-Publication Data
Re-orienting global communication:
Indian and Chinese media beyond borders /
edited by Michael Curtin and Hemant Shah.
p.   cm. — (Popular culture and politics in Asia Pacific)
Includes bibliographical references and index.
ISBN 978-0-252-03501-2 (cloth : alk. paper)
ISBN 978-0-252-07690-9 (pbk. : alk paper)
1. Mass media—India. 2. Mass media—China.
I. Curtin, Michael. II. Shah, Hemant, 1957–
P92.17R46   2010
302.20954—dc22   2009024502

Contents

Illustrations

Tables

Acknowledgments

This anthology grew out of a series of discussions and endeavors sponsored by the Global Media and Democracy in Asia Research Circle at the University of Wisconsin–Madison. The editors wish to thank Gilles Bousquet, Aili Tripp, and Guido Podestá of the Division of International Studies for supporting this venture as well as other such vital interdisciplinary research collaborations on the Madison campus. We furthermore express our deep appreciation for funding and logistical support provided by the UW Global Studies program under the able guidance of Steve Smith and Natalia Aiello.

Reorienting Global Communication

Introduction

Before its New York opening on April 30, 2007, *Spider-Man 3* had already premiered in nine countries, including Russia, Brazil, and Japan. So important is the global market for Hollywood blockbusters these days that studios now pay substantial attention to international promotion and distribution. During its theatrical run, *Spider-Man 3* raked in more than $500 million from the overseas box office, a figure far exceeding ticket sales in the United States. Consequently, it's somewhat understandable that reflections on the globalization of media often begin and end with reference to the seemingly pervasive presence of Hollywood movies around the world. In dollar figures, the raw power of American movies is undeniable, with films such as *Spider-Man 3* bringing in some $900 million worldwide.

What these numbers don't convey, however, is the relatively modest reach of these blockbusters. Given the premium price of Hollywood movie tickets, the number of people who actually saw *Spider-Man 3* in a movie theater was only 125 million worldwide. Compare this to the Indian superhero movie *Krrish*, which premiered only a few months earlier. In India alone, it sold an estimated 110 million tickets. Worldwide figures are hard to come by, since Indian movie companies have far less control of overseas markets, but one can imagine that audiences in Pakistan, Bangladesh, and the Gulf States were similarly enthusiastic, as were audiences in markets where Hollywood ticket prices are beyond the reach of the average citizen. Based on this comparison, one might reasonably presume that *Krrish*'s cultural impact was on a par with *Spider-Man 3*. In fact, it is quite likely that *Krrish* reached more cinemagoers than its Hollywood counterpart, as is commonly the case with Indian blockbusters these days. The spatial location of Indian movie audiences may differ, but one could certainly argue that *Krrish* is something of a global phenomenon in its own right.

Krrish is also a global movie in another sense, for it was conceived and produced by a Mumbai (a.k.a. Bombay) studio with transnational audiences in mind. This was not always the case with Indian movies, but since the mid-1990s, overseas viewers with familial attachments to the subcontinent have come to figure prominently in the strategies of so-called Bollywood filmmakers and distributors. *Krrish* sold only $1.5 million movie tickets in the United States, but that's largely because it's extremely difficult for foreign movies to get screen time in the crowded American market. Therefore, video sales and online fandom offer a better measure of popularity. According to Yash Raj Films, one of Mumbai's most successful studios, Indian movies generate more $100 million per year in U.S. video and soundtrack sales, making it the most lucrative growth market for the Indian movie industry. It's also estimated that the volume of pirated materials is even larger. In the early 1990s, overseas markets for Indian movies were relatively inconsequential. Today they represent one of the most important parts of the business and, as a result, global perspectives have come to influence the conception and execution of many Indian films.

Chinese movies are undergoing a similar transformation. *Crouching Tiger, Hidden Dragon* is a spectacular example of this shift, but just as intriguing are films such as *Kung-Fu Hustle*, starring Hong Kong's Stephen Chow, which earned more than $100 million in theaters worldwide, and *Hero*, starring China's Jet Li, which earned $177 million. All three of these films not only captured the attention of audiences around the world but were also the product of a multinational collaboration, drawing upon finance, talent, and creative resources from Chinese societies around the world. Again, box-office revenues tell only part of the story, as these films earned much of their income in markets with lower ticket prices than their Western counterparts.

Chinese television is also becoming more transnational. In 1991, Hong Kong entrepreneurs launched Star TV, hoping to create a pan-Asian platform of satellite TV programming, but instead Star helped to spark the deregulation of television industries throughout the region—thereby instigating lively competition for the attention of viewers. Today, Star is owned by a Western conglomerate that competes with other Western conglomerates for a stake in Chinese TV, but just as importantly, Asian media companies that used to operate national or local television stations in Hong Kong, Singapore, and Taipei now run television services that operate throughout the region. Facing growing competition in their deregulated local markets, these companies have been prodded to expand their geographical reach, not only throughout Asia but also to cities in Europe and North America where Chinese audiences can now access tens of thousands of hours of programming via cable, satellite, and home video.

Over the past twenty years, market forces, technological innovation, and government deregulation have engendered new conditions for the production and distribution of commercial Chinese television. Even in the People's Republic of China (PRC), where the state owns all television stations and cable systems, the number of services and the range of competitors have increased dramatically. And although state ownership remains the standard, television institutions have faced dramatic reductions in state subsidies, forcing them to rely on advertising revenues and new entrepreneurial initiatives. This has resulted in joint ventures with commercial television partners from such places as Taipei, Tokyo, and New York, and it has even encouraged the Beijing-based national network, CCTV—which is the only television service officially authorized to operate abroad—to forge distribution agreements that for the first time give it carriage in Europe and North America. Media experts say it's only a matter of time before restrictions loosen further, allowing other PRC broadcasters to extend their reach overseas. Building in part on the success of Star TV, Indian entrepreneurs have likewise established transnational television networks. Networks such Zee TV, Sun TV, and Sahara One now provide a variety of programming in a variety of Indian languages to viewers around the world.

Similar patterns are found in Indian and Chinese music, publishing, and Internet media, where increasingly transnational creativity and circulation foster new cultural forms and new audience affiliations. Yet despite these trends, the globalization of communication still is discussed largely from a Western perspective, positioning Hollywood and New York at the center of analysis. Not only is power seen as emanating from the West to the rest but so too is cultural influence, with media seen as the conduit for Western notions of fashion, taste, politics, and modernity. Global media conglomerates—most of them based in the United States—are portrayed as engines of innovation worldwide, transforming the style, content, and administrative structures of local and national media systems that now must compete with their counterparts from afar. Interestingly, these presumptions have circulated for some time, stretching back as far as modernization theory in the 1950s and 1960s, when it was suggested that exposure to mass media from the West would democratize nations and modernize the economies of Asia, Africa, Latin America, and the Middle East.

Just as influential was the critical counterpart to these arguments, commonly characterized as the media imperialism school, an approach that grew influential during the 1970s by positing that Western media subject populations around the world to an increasingly homogenized set of values that serve the interests of Western capitalist institutions. According to this critique, subordinate countries come to embrace Western media and the values they promote, such as individualism, consumerism, and commodity exchange. Rather than uniting people for positive social change, media imperialism fosters an exploitative global system that offers few opportunities for genuine advancement.

The essays in this volume challenge these approaches, not because they are wholly inaccurate but rather because Western media are now only one element in the increasingly complex global communication order and the movement of content is increasingly multidirectional. Although Hollywood—and the West more generally—are indeed influential forces, we wish to shift attention to other centers of production and other patterns of flow. We are interested in the fact that globalization is not a singular phenomenon that is characterized by cultural homogenization but is rather a trajectory of change that is bringing about new patterns of interconnection and interdependence that are multiple and complex. Since the 1500s, Western images and ideas have indeed circulated far and wide, but today "Chinese" and "Indian" songs, stories, and information flow through communication circuits around the world aimed both at migrant populations and cosmopolitan audiences, enabling new patterns of discussion and exchange. These new flows of imagery are substantially different from the cultural expropriations of the past, when Western powers mined traditional societies for artifacts to serve their own imperial purposes. Such Orientalist projects of the past were explicit and intentional exercises of centralized power that aimed to construct representations of both the modern colonizer and the colorful colonized other. Today, by comparison, the volume and velocity of cultural flows have increased, and the institutions that produce and circulate popular narratives have multiplied. Consequently, new patterns of flow and new relations of influence have emerged in the global cultural economy. Media conglomerates such as News Corporation may have imperial pretensions of their own and may generate billions of dollars in revenue, but, for example, the Indian movie industry serves far more customers in any given year and the Chinese popular music industry reaches far more ears, not just in Asia but worldwide. This is not to say these media are more powerful or more wonderful but rather to suggest that they are worthy of investigation on their own terms.

Furthermore, the social impacts of these media merit attention, since they have helped to foster new values and expectations among their viewers, forcing governments to pay attention to the changing patterns of cultural exchange within nations and across national boundaries. For example, during the SARS crisis of 2003, many citizens of the People's Republic of China were getting their news about the pandemic from Internet sites maintained by Chinese newspapers in Vancouver, London, and Hong Kong. These transnational flows then engendered unauthorized subnational flows within the mainland, as online discussion proliferated and other media chimed in. Within weeks, Chinese officials were forced to reverse their policies and acknowledge the inadequacy of the government's initial response to the crisis. This is but one example of the multiple and complex patterns of media circulation that are increasingly common today, and one that had very little to do with Western media institutions.

When we began this project, we were surprised to find that little had been published regarding the globalization of Indian and Chinese media. Investigation of the popular press turned up some provocative essays, but few authors systematically considered Indian or Chinese media outside of national frameworks or connected their analysis of transnational media flows to larger questions regarding social and cultural change. This is precisely the terrain we hope to stake out in *Reorienting Global Communication*. Our title suggests that we're questioning the cultural presumptions of Orientalism and at the same time presenting a volume of alternative perspectives, hoping to shift or perhaps multiply the starting points for discussions of media and globalization. On the one hand, we wish to disrupt prevailing hierarchies of knowledge so as to privilege that which has been suppressed and thereby reorient the discussion of contemporary media. On the other hand, we believe that attention to the Chinese and Indian spheres of transnational circulation bring into focus a host of issues and dynamics that so far have received little attention. In that sense, we wish to reorient perceptions of cultural flow, offering an alternative mapping of the globe. Critical geographers and postcolonial scholars have sometimes tinkered with Mercator projections that are commonly used to map the world, suggesting other ways of representing geophysical and political relations. Likewise, the chapters in this volume rethink conventional representations of media, suggesting new ways of seeing worldwide patterns of cultural production and exchange.

We focus on globalization because we live in an era where social relations stretch further across space, so that new spheres of activity emerge and existing spheres—domestic, local, and national—are, as Anthony Giddens suggests, interpenetrated by forces from afar. Our project invites an exploration of the ways in which global media are remaking human consciousness in far-flung localities as well as an examination of the structuring forces that shape this process, such as market relations and capital flows. Numerous scholars from diverse perspectives agree that capital organizes the world into centers and peripheries, but too often, the centers are always Euro-American and much of Asia is situated on the periphery. Our project complicates this perspective by examining media institutions and texts that are often overlooked by scholars and by examining the ways in which transnational popular culture provides resources for everyday living and for collective social action. Our interest in globalization does not mean we are leaving the nation-state behind—but neither do we privilege the nation-state, as do most projects in media studies. Moreover, we do not presume that global media relations today can be explained by center–periphery theories from yesteryear. Instead, we wish to embrace prior concerns about media influence by exploring new and intricate patterns of cultural flow and increasingly complex plays of power.

We furthermore aim to elevate the visibility of scholarship about two of the world's largest sociocultural formations, India and China. At the national level, population figures and manufacturing growth are often used to justify attention to these two countries; just as importantly, both countries offer lessons regarding the legacies of colonialism and the enduring power relations of the world system. As they reemerge in positions of world leadership, many observers refer to them as sleeping giants that will influence many aspects of society and culture during the twenty-first century, from energy to ecology to global governance. Likewise, India and China are considered regional leaders, having important and enduring links to such countries as Malaysia, Pakistan, and Uganda where significant populations identify themselves as Indian or Chinese, and where civilizational influences—legends, languages, and religious practices—signify connections that stretch across national boundaries. Moreover, India and China deserve attention because in many ways they represent the return of the repressed, engendering anxieties in the West that have led to brazen attempts to manage and contain them. Such struggles deserve attention, as do the presumptions of civilizational coherence that invite us to perceive India, China, and the West as intelligible and opposed entities.

Additionally, we focus on India and China because they both have been shaped by legacies of colonialism and state socialism. Radically different in their histories and institutions, both countries began experimenting with liberalization of their economies during the 1980s and have subsequently been swept into the tide of trade liberalization, with each becoming an important node on the global assembly line. No longer able to manage their economies internally, they likewise face challenges in the realm of communication, knowing that there may be no road back to a sense of confident, bounded control over the expectations and aspirations of their populations. Their attempts to manage this tumultuous transition have raised numerous concerns regarding creativity, free expression, and cultural identity. Lacking a stable set of external boundaries, both countries are furthermore so vast and diverse that they are experiencing significant internal tensions among and between groups. They are also undergoing noteworthy changes in household economies, gender relations, and generational aspirations. At almost every level—domestic, local, national, and transnational—questions and challenges arise; among the most telling is: What does it mean to be Chinese? or, What does it mean to be Indian?

Within this context of shifting cultural identities, we are keenly interested in media and democracy in the broadest sense. In the case of India, for example, media-intensive electoral politics provide the government with a stamp of legitimacy as it seeks to forge policy on a wide range of pressing issues, such as resource management, women's rights, and the political status of Indians in the diaspora. Meanwhile in China, the single-party state struggles with pressure to loosen its control of the cultural and political realms, while economic institutions grope toward global standards of market transparency. Both China and India in their own ways have been experimenting with degrees of freedom for domestic media and with incorporating foreign media into the mix of available services. This new cultural environment has implications regarding not only the range of available content and the directions of flow but also regarding the ways that media users interact. Debates about "homeland," diaspora, and political efficacy mix with reflections and anxieties regarding location and identity within a very complex transnational cultural geography.

Thus, we acknowledge the importance of formal politics but we also include under the rubric of democracy our interest in the dynamics of inclusion in and exclusion from the cultural formations of "China" and "India" as they intersect with broader questions about transnational flows of media, money, and people. We furthermore interrogate the nature of democracy itself in a world where Indians and Chinese are not contained within singular state boundaries. How does one conceptualize democracy, both in the formal sense and the expanded sense we employ here, within a transnational context? Those designated as Non-Resident Indians may participate in "home-land" politics by sending money and by lobbying foreign institutions and politicians on behalf of India. Yet, their permanent homes—economically and culturally—are outside the subcontinent. Diasporic media may create a transnational sense of cultural connection to "home" through the idioms of Bollywood, but how do diasporic communities of Indians imagine themselves politically in their locations outside India?

This volume furthermore seeks to explore debates regarding "ideologi-cal contamination" and "cultural pollution" within the nations themselves, within migrant communities, and across diverse localities. The intensity of these concerns seems directly related to the fact that Indian and Chinese media are making ever more expansive use of global forms and formats in order to produce their own hybrid popular products. As a result, claims to cultural authenticity grow ever more tenuous, as anxieties and tensions continue to mount, especially among the middle class who most enthusias-tically embrace hybrid cultural forms and who are most likely to travel or migrate. With their societies in motion and their perspectives increasingly cosmopolitan, many nevertheless reach for the flotsam of "Indianness" or "Chineseness," even if these identities may be illusory. How, then, might we locate India and China? Where are the centers of these "civilizations" when the margins have grown so influential? Are these indeed "ungrounded empires?" Do migrations shape contemporary notions of Indianness and Chineseness as much as the exertions and assertions of the nation-state?

Migrations are notoriously difficult to characterize, but "Indian" and "Chinese" diasporas are arguably the world's largest. Though specific con-ditions vary enormously, Indian and Chinese migrants in many parts of the world resist integration by settling in distinctive neighborhood enclaves, setting up their own schools and health-care institutions, and establish-ing media that cater to their linguistic and community needs. Often, such practices generate anxiety and fear among locals. In some cases, Indian and Chinese migrants are reviled for their economic success as well as their per-ceived clannishness. Interestingly, both India and China now energetically claim these migrant populations as their own, hoping to share their success and foster a return flow of innovations and resources. Our focus on these migrants and the cultural connections that sustain them helps to explain as much about transnational formations as it does about the meaning of India and China today. States, homelands, and other imaginary terrains have now been joined by transnational imaginaries that are being put to use by various interests and groups. Media companies are among those who have come to recognize that Indian and Chinese migrant populations may be smaller in number than those in the homeland, but they are avid users of contemporary media and therefore represent important markets.

These diasporas represent not only new markets for media institutions based in the home country that are reimagining themselves as global operators, they also represent resources for politicians who covet the expatriates' money, expertise, prestige, and mobility. Yet interestingly, the migrant who is now hailed as a national hero often constructs a view of "home" based on the media imagery that may bear little relation to the current realities of his or her country of origin. Indeed, the home countries have for many migrants become an imaginary other and therefore relations that have stretched out over space bring to the fore new tensions and contradictions as well as possibilities. Transnational media flows therefore figure prominently in characterizations of what it means to be Indian or Chinese and how that bears on conceptions of the modern states and institutions.

Finally, we direct our attention to India and China because both have significant and distinctive cultural resources: talent, mythologies, and conventions of representation. The religious iconography and traditional folk performances of India have woven their way into movies and music videos, influencing not only contemporary national media but also media in other parts of the world. Likewise, Chinese legends and operatic performance styles infuse the modern martial arts cinema, engendering stylized action-fantasy sequences that have been borrowed by film and television producers around the world. Indian and Chinese media institutions also present interesting case examples and contrasts. Overseas Chinese have operated freewheeling capitalist movie enterprises for almost a century in locations as diverse as Hong Kong, Singapore, and Kuala Lumpur. Meanwhile, media in Mainland China have for more than fifty years been tied tightly to the state and now struggle to discover institutional forms that are both ideologically acceptable and commercially viable. As for Indian media, they too have a tradition of state intervention that is now morphing into state–corporate partnerships in the face of challenges posed by globalization. MTV, for example, not only delivers a cable/satellite service to the subcontinent, it also refashions its South Asian programming for audiences in New York and London. Meanwhile, Zee TV, India's first commercial Hindi-language network, now produces programs for audiences in Europe, North America, and the Middle East, as well as audiences across the subcontinent. Such complexities beg for analyses that interrogate issues of affinity, affect, and power, as well as textual and industrial practice. Accordingly, we have gathered a collection of essays that range across methodologies and theoretical approaches.

When we began to assemble this anthology, we wrestled with various ways to organize the essays. Our original hope was that we might come up with direct connections and affinities between Chinese and Indian media. We thought we might interweave essays about Indian and Chinese media in an evocative manner. We came to see, however, that connections would not be drawn between particular essays so much as between the collective reflections on each realm of transnational culture. That is, the stories of Indian and Chinese media are indeed related, but they are also distinctive, and the essays in the volume reflect those distinctions. Our scholars of Indian media expend a great deal of energy reflecting on the role that the Indian diaspora is playing in media, politics, and culture. Meanwhile, our scholars of Chinese media focus on the role of resurgent nationalism in the increasingly globalized and commercialized realm of Chinese popular culture. Thus, the emphasis differs between the two spheres but, as we shall see, the essays converge around the play between national and global forces and cultural forms.

In chapter 1, Lakshmi Srinivas shows how the growing wealth and prominence of expatriate Indian populations have come to influence the narrative strategies in Hindi-language movies. She contends that since the 1990s, movies produced by Mumbai studios have come to feature a structure of feeling that has less to do with India as a particular place than with a conception of "traditional" social, cultural, and gender relations. Aswin Punathambekar affirms this interpretation in chapter 2 with his study of Indian movie audiences in the United States. He shows how Bollywood films have become cultural unifiers for expatriate populations, but they have also become one of the means by which the state has laid claim to the loyalties and economic resources of so-called Non-Resident Indian (NRI) populations. Both Srinivas and Punathambekar argue that the figure of a "national family" looms large in these transnational texts.

Yet movies aren't the only sites where we find cultural nationalism at work. The online world has exploded with activity among those who consider themselves culturally connected to India. In chapter 3, Madhavi Mallapragada explores the realm of "desktop deities," religious sites that cater to those who are distant from temples and other sacred locations but long to maintain their connections to a spiritual home. Certainly, expatriate populations figure prominently among those who turn to religious solace online—but one also finds second- and third-generation immigrants expressing nostalgia for a home they never knew. The growing prominence of expatriates and their offspring in deliberations about Indian identity also plays out in the world of fashion where wedding plans increasingly revolve around a mixing of Indian and other cultural influences. As Sujata Moorti shows in chapter 4, wedding magazines fuel a copious flow of images and ideas about matrimony, family, and femininity. Whether the wedding is to be staged in India or abroad, planners tap into a common pool of advice and discussion so that the resulting event becomes both a familial ritual and a meditation on what it means to be Indian in a globalizing era.

Behind these cultural phenomena lie the increasingly globalized calculations of Indian media industries. Much attention has been paid to Hindi-language media businesses in Mumbai, but as Shanti Kumar argues in chapter 5, others are globalizing as well. In Andhra Pradesh, Telegu-language media have proliferated since the 1990s and Eenadu media is one of the leaders. Beginning first with publishing and then moving on to film and television, Ramoji Rao has built a media empire that now rivals the scale of its Hindi-language counterparts. Not only has Rao built a massive studio that draws producers and projects from around the world, but he has also extended his reach to audiences worldwide via satellite television. In chapter 6, Divya McMillin elaborates on this trend by delineating the major players in Indian satellite television. Commercial enterprises such as Hindi-language Zee TV and Tamil-language Sun TV now transmit to transnational audiences in South Asia, Europe, Africa, Australia, and North America. Just as interestingly, Doordarshan—the state-owned public service television network that monopolized Indian television before the 1990s—now competes for audiences at home *and* abroad.

This growing emphasis on global India has disrupted prior notions of locality, as Sreya Mitra demonstrates in chapter 7. During the latter half of the twentieth century, the city of Bombay was represented in Hindi-language movies as India's generic big city, a magnet to migrant populations who left the countryside in search of their dreams. For pan-Indian audiences, Bombay came to embody the promise of Nehruvian modernity. Since the 1990s, however, foreign cities such as London and Sydney have become common settings for Bollywood narratives aimed at NRI audiences. Mitra argues that this shift in Bombay's cultural status has opened the door to movies that reflect upon the specific identity of the city that is now called Mumbai.

As with their Indian counterparts, Chinese media are experiencing contradictory pressures and opportunities of globalization. In chapter 8, Yuezhi Zhao describes the emergence of the global Chinese blockbuster movie, showing how economic liberalization in the People's Republic of China has made it possible for global capital and Hollywood studios to play a role in the production of transnational movie projects. *Hero* provides an example of this trend, but it also shows that the state's interest in cinema still plays a major role in such projects. *Hero* is at once a visual spectacle and a historical allegory regarding the value of centralized authoritarian rule. Zhao argues that the film implicitly endorses both the supremacy of the Chinese state and the legitimacy of global neoliberal capitalism. Such paradoxes operate at many levels of the Chinese movie business. As Emilie Yeh explains in chapter 9, "marketization"—a market-oriented managerial approach—has reconnected the mainland with capitalist economies of Asia, but it is an uneasy communion. Movie companies across the region are seeking transnational partnerships and market access, but they find that the price demanded by the PRC is often unreasonably high. Insider deal-making, political privilege, and a lack of transparency undermine potential business and creative ventures in Mainland China. Movie companies from Hong Kong or Seoul find that although the PRC market is a necessary component of their transnational strategies, it is nevertheless fraught with uncertainty and risk.

Yet despite these problems, media in the PRC are undergoing profound changes as they engage with institutional and cultural counterparts from around the world. Joseph Chan explores this dynamic in chapter 10, showing how the structure and practices of the television industry manifest traces of the global at a variety of levels. Although the project of media commercialization has not been fully realized in the PRC, media institutions have adapted to many of the transnational conventions of the industry. As Chan demonstrates, some influence comes from the West, but more substantially, the PRC participates in the television economy of East Asia, drawing upon resources and inspiration from Hong Kong, Taipei, Seoul, and Tokyo.

These transborder flows are also the focus of Chua Beng Huat's discussion of East Asian popular culture in chapter 11, only he focuses specifically at the textual level, showing how film, music, and television trends wend their way across borders and among audiences throughout the region. Writing from Singapore, Chua reflects on the emergence of what he refers to as "Pop Culture China," a realm of cultural exchange that exhibits the active exchange of popular artists and trends. It furthermore engages regularly with cultural influences from Korea, Japan, and other Asian countries. Although this is not an entirely novel development, the speed and intensity of exchange has escalated since the 1990s and has developed into what Chua sees as a nascent East Asian cultural formation.

It is perhaps as a result of these influences that government leaders in Beijing fret about the erosion of their political and cultural authority. Television programs in the PRC often exhibit a tension between the expansive aspirations of global China and the pervasive anxieties about "authentic" Chinese identity. As Zhongdang Pan explains in chapter 12, the annual Spring Festival staged each year by the national CCTV network strives to incorporate viewers into a familial view of the nation, acknowledging differences while also advancing a rhetoric of collective national destiny in an era of globalization. In chapter 13, Chin-Chuan Lee picks up this thread, showing how the discourse of *Global Times*, China's leading foreign-policy newspaper, deliberates upon the state's ambition to rise to the status of a global superpower. Of central concern are China's post–Cold War relations with the United States. What does it mean for China to share the global stage with its old nemesis? Implicit in these debates are both an emergent cosmopolitanism and a resurgent strain of nationalism.

This pattern emerges as well in Jack Qiu's account of Chinese Internet policy in chapter 14. Having developed since the 1990s into the world's leading location for electronics manufacturing, China now aims to upgrade its status from workshop of the world to that of global design center and Internet innovator. Consequently, the state has fostered technology standards that compete directly with Western counterparts, hoping to capture a share of the licensing income that has swelled the coffers of Silicon Valley. Yet in this struggle for global leadership, the state not only must confront its overseas competitors but also must manage a powerful strain of techno-nationalism among Chinese Internet users who have become increasingly vociferous and influential.

Taken together, these essays exhibit many of the paradoxes of globalization. As media flow more freely across national borders, textual representations and institutional practices do indeed begin to share similarities, but those similarities exist in contrast with the enduring specificity of local and national contexts. Moreover, as media look outward, they offer a pretext for reflections on these differences and often lead to impassioned debates about societal and cultural essences. What does it mean to be Indian or Chinese? To be here or there? To be of the nation or outside the nation? Globalization brings new images and ideas from afar, helping to broaden perspectives and engender new ways of thinking, but it also disrupts prevailing social relations and fosters fresh anxieties at home. By moving outside the prevailing Western perspective, these essays persuasively delineate alternative paths to media globalization.

PART ONE

Global India Media

ONE

Nonsense as Sense-Making: Negotiating Globalization in Bombay Cinema

Lakshmi Srinivas

Lakshmi Srinivas shows how globalization and transnationalism have come to influence the narrative strategies of the Bombay film. The films present the impact of these phenomena on everyday life. In the films, foreign locations and Non-Resident Indian (NRI) characters living in the West have become common, and Indians living in India are shown traveling abroad for both business and leisure. The foreign has become been normalized to the extent that "India" as a place is communicated as feeling rather than as geography or territory. In other words, as per the line in a famous Hindi film song, "Phir bhi Dil hai Hindustani" (or "yet the heart is Indian"[1]).

Commercial Indian cinema has enthralled audiences for the past nine decades. The popular films commonly thought of as escapist fiction for the masses have withstood competition from Hollywood and have emerged as a non-Western global cinema to contend with. Characterized by high emotion and predictable plots (or no plot!), the formula films have been criticized as being vulgar and silly, nonsense narratives whose sole purpose is to provide escapist entertainment for the mass audience.

Indian cinema is, however, the largest producer of feature films in the world and reaches more viewers worldwide than Hollywood movies do.

Therefore, it is hardly insignificant as a culture industry. In 2003, 1,100 full-length feature films were produced in India, compared to 593 made in Hollywood. Indian films reached 3.4 billion viewers, while 1.6 billion audiences saw Hollywood movies.[2] Bollywood,[3] or Hindi-language Bombay cinema, is the most widely watched and most visible of India's many film businesses. Not only are the films viewed throughout India where they transcend boundaries of language, regional culture, religion, caste, and class,[4] but they are also exported to over 100 countries.[5]

Given its longevity as well as this global reach, Bombay cinema offers an opportunity for undertaking an examination of cultural flows between and within postcolonial societies and between home or "sending" countries and the diaspora. Although there has been some acknowledgement of non-Western nations as producers of media and popular culture, the literature on cultural globalization has been dominated by a cultural imperialism model considering the global reach and sway of American culture or "soft power."[6] This chapter responds to calls for a model of globalization that challenges the cultural imperialism or homogenization model by requiring a more pluralist understanding of globalization.

Bombay cinema is frequently at the forefront of recognizing social change, often ahead of sociologists and anthropologists in their anticipation of significant societal issues.[7] The films offer a commentary on Indian society recognizable in broad trends: The "social films" of the 1940s and 1950s were followed by action films featuring alienated urban dwellers in the 1970s and early 1980s. In the mid-1990s, a new breed of films variously termed "urban tales," "diaspora films," or "NRI (Non-Resident Indian) films" emerged. Described as "glossy consumerist fantasies" featuring middle-class worlds and transnational lifestyles, these films have captured the imagination of urban moviegoers in India as well as diasporic audiences worldwide and have been commented upon both in news magazines and in academic writing as a significant sociological phenomenon.[8]

NRI films represent a marked shift from earlier films, many of which featured lower-class or lower-middle-class heroes, explored the urban–rural divide or metropolis vs. small-town differences, and in which romance between the hero and heroine played off such differences. In contrast, in recent films the settings are predominantly urban–metropolitan or international and Western; rural areas and villages, when depicted, are highly idealized and stylized. The worlds portrayed in these films are those of the educated, English-speaking, urban middle-class or upper-middle-class

Indian in India and the Non-Resident Indian living in the United States or the United Kingdom. Characters in the films liberally use English phrases and American slang. Representations of a consumer-driven and transnational lifestyle are also taken to new heights: cell phones and computers are taken for granted, characters celebrate Valentine's Day, and they often frequent exercise clubs and shopping malls. The Non-Resident Indian or NRI, symbol of the diaspora, is a fixture in such films and is often the hero, portrayed as part of the familial world and social circle of the urban middle-class Indian.

Globalization as a theme is not new to Bombay films. As early as 1955, the film *Shree 420*, a huge success in India and the Soviet Union, had a song titled "Mera Jootha Hai Japani" (My Shoes Are Japanese) whose lyrics appeared to emphasize an Indian identity in the face of global consumerism. The lyrics went something like this:

My shoes are Japanese
My trousers English
My red hat is Russian
But my Heart [*dil*] remains Indian

For decades, Bombay cinema has used overseas locations to lure audiences. As early as the 1960s, films such as *Sangam* (1964), *Love in Tokyo* (1966), and *An Evening in Paris* (1967) featured scenes abroad. However, in the films made in the 1990s and post 2000, foreign settings have become part of the landscape of everyday life. Popular locations for filming include Switzerland, New Zealand, Mauritius, Scotland, and Australia, as well as destinations such as Los Angeles, Sun City in South Africa, and Niagara Falls in New York. Post 2000, locations such as Egypt (*Kabhi Khushi Kabhie Gham* [or *K3G*], 2001), Greece (*Chalte Chalte*, 2003), Rio (*Dhoom 2*, 2006), and Istanbul (*Guru*, 2007) provide exotica, while an increasing number of films are being shot entirely outside India.[9]

Bollywood movies that are either filmed abroad or that feature storylines situated outside India and the lifestyle of the urban middle-class Indian challenge taken-for-granted notions of what makes a film "Indian." They have been described as "Indian films minus India"[10] and have led to observations that "if you turn off the Hindi language of the soundtrack and if you could forget for a moment the faces of the actors, there is virtually nothing about this movie that would tell you it was set in India."[11] Such understandings of what makes a film Indian highlight the broader problems surrounding the idea of "place" and identity in an era of transnationalism, in which people and goods as well as images and ideas are freely mobile. It is interesting that an Indian film is expected to be "set in India" and that such requirements are not applied to Hollywood films that are set in Europe, Asia, Africa, or outer space—yet are still recognized as American-Hollywood films. Asymmetric critical observations of this nature point to what has been described as "essentialist diffusionism," identified as a "perspective which seriously undermines the analysis of reciprocal transnational diffusion between non-Western and Western parts of the world."[12]

Films portraying Westernized middle-class Indians and transnational lifestyles—while drawing criticism from members of the South Asian intelligentsia, film critics, and scholars, many of whom see such portrayals as irrelevant given the lives of the majority of population—have continued to be popular at the box office in India[13] and more generally throughout South Asia across its linguistic, religious, and other cultural divisions,[14] as well as overseas. In recent years, Bollywood films have enjoyed a renewed popularity with the urban middle classes in India, a popularity that is compounded by the rapid growth of fancy, upscale multiplexes in urban areas. Yet another audience group on the rise is the NRI or diasporic audience, including the children of South Asian immigrants who have grown up outside India and who gravitate toward Bollywood as a product and symbol of Indian culture. Recent evidence suggests that Bollywood cinema is gaining in popularity and is competing with British films in the United Kingdom and moving out of its "specialist niche." Bollywood shows every sign of becoming a world cinema that can provide serious competition for Hollywood.

The popularity of Bombay films in India is not due to the lack of access to and competition from Hollywood fare, which is accessible to audiences throughout India. Habituated audiences[15] of popular cinema have always preferred domestically made movies, which attract over 90 percent of moviegoers in India.[16] Even *Titanic*, which broke box-office records in India as it did worldwide, only managed eighth place in the Indian box office.[17] Various explanations have been offered for the continued popularity and relevance of Bollywood films, the common one being that they provide a fantasy escape for the masses.[18] They are understood to present a moral universe that allows viewers to make sense of events in their own lives[19] and to articulate tensions between (traditional) Indian society and modernity.[20] In what may be an extension of this argument, films made in the 1990s are recognized as a site for the representation of issues related to the urban middle classes and

Indian identity in the context of transnationalism.[21] However, if the films provide audiences with "a mediating space for the negotiation of social life"[22] under conditions of modernization and increasing globalism, it is unclear how they accomplish this.

At the level of everyday life, globalization is experienced in a social and embodied way by individuals and groups who are actively engaged in managing its lived effects, making the ongoing negotiation of the impact of globalization an inevitable part of living in a rapidly globalizing world and, arguably, its universalizing experience. However, globalization's impact on everyday life is frequently overlooked by social science writing that is skewed toward the macro level and the political economy perspective or is programmatic in nature. Few studies have addressed the micro level and the lived social reality of a "world in motion"[23] for ordinary people. An understanding of globalization based on examination of its active mediation—including the sense-making practices people employ, the interpretive and interactional work they do to order their world and function in it—would be an improvement on the cultural imperialism model, which sees subjects as passive recipients of Western culture.

In order to address some of these gaps, I examine the construction and communication of the idea and social reality of globalization and its lived experience in the Bombay film. Based on my study of a selection of films made in the 1990s and post 2000 following the implementation of India's economic liberalization policies, and drawing on anecdotal data drawn from ethnographic research with moviegoers,[24] I identify a framework for the construction of such communication and examine the sense and significance of the films for their audiences.

I argue that Bollywood films assist in transcending the necessarily partial and limited experience of larger social change, perhaps creating a broader understanding of a range of experiences not available firsthand. Films engage in "mapping" the lived experience of globalization and transnationalism, though selectively with focus on the worlds of the urban middle-class Indian and the NRI. Audiences are given a framework for relating the distant and the immediate, the invisible and the visible, and the global, the local, and the national—the last three analytic distinctions intertwined in everyday life. The films function as "bridging narratives" that offer structures of experience and depictions of life worlds that incorporate the known and the familiar with the distant and inaccessible.[25] For the NRI living in self-imposed exile, the films provide experiences of "India" and of being Indian. India is presented through a lens of nostalgia and longing; hence, food, festivities, and familial relations occupy a major portion of such films. Members of India's urban middle classes find their world referenced; for others, the films present this world and attendant lifestyle that is considered emulative and desirable. Aspirants to this world and social class are given a view of a possible future, while those belonging to the lower classes are provided with class voyeurism, a look into a middle-class existence, arguably part of everyday curiosity and desire.

I suggest that the appeal and popularity of recent films lies in their ability to construct and communicate popular understandings of globalization and transnationalism that rest on a phenomenological perspective. Films emphasize lived experience, everyday life, the social relations attendant upon the transnational movement of goods and people, and the significance of place—precisely the considerations that scholars have identified as crucial for an understanding of globalization that is contextual, embodied, and situated in everyday experience.[26] Through the employment of narrative devices familiar to audiences, what I term *feeling rules*, films convey the sensual and emotional experiences—the most immediate and embodied effects of globalization, an aspect of the phenomenology of globalization that is yet to be investigated closely.

Mapping Globalization

In a world where the global and local are intertwined and inseparable, it becomes necessary to rethink their usefulness as categories in making space-based distinctions for an embedded study of globalization.[27] The media cannot be left out of this discussion, as media are powerfully involved in the global circulation of images and messages while at the same time are part of the fabric of everyday life.[28] Mediated spaces may be described as "translocal" since they appear both to transcend locality and at the same time to be lodged in it. Big-budget Bollywood movies with locations abroad and featuring transnational lifestyles are media-produced translocal spaces and therefore concrete instances of these new forms of spatiality.

As Bollywood films attempt to capture a rapidly globalizing world, understandings of place and its experience as specified in the films become important for a negotiation of globalization. Films redefine space and place in seeking to communicate globalization and transnationalism to audiences. In this section, I examine the work done by the Bombay film and the devices it employs to convey the sense and sensibility of globalization and transnationalism through films' depictions of landscapes followed by portrayals of consumer culture and lifestyle. I identify these devices or practices broadly as "mapping" followed by cultural translation.[29] Together, they convey the lived experiences of globalization as they are interpreted by the films and their audiences. Films establish a global iconography, a databank of images and signifiers that are repeated and elaborated in subsequent films. Habitués of the films come to recognize a symbol system (visual and aural codes in the films) that they associate with the urban middle classes in India and with a transnational or NRI lifestyle.

Fantasyscapes and Mindscapes

Similar to cinema of the early 1900s, which delivered travelogue and spectacle to audiences in search of thrills, Bollywood films have always sought to transport their audiences to exotic and picturesque settings. Typically, scenes in snowy Kashmir, beside waterfalls or lakes, and in gardens satisfied audience requirements for fantasy and were part of the formula of the Bombay film and its musical interludes in which dreams are given visual expression and emotions are expressed through song and dance.

In films made after the 1990s, foreign settings have proliferated. Switzerland has replaced Kashmir as a fantasy space, partly due to difficulties of filming in Kashmir; additionally, directors often acknowledge that it is generally easier to film abroad rather than deal with red tape and delays in India. Satisfying audience expectations plays no small part of the decision to film outside India.[30] Audiences today expect an A-grade Bollywood film with top-ranked stars to have "high production value," meaning lavish sets and a mindscape or visuals of America, the United Kingdom, Australia, and Europe. Stars themselves expect to film outside India, an expectation built up at a time when using foreign locations was not that common due to the film's budget and foreign exchange restrictions and when the promise of filming abroad provided a way of attracting stars to a film project. Today global locations are no surprise. The superhit *Kabbie Khushi Kabbie Gham* (2001), for example, was shot in sixteen locations, including Blenheim Palace in England as well as in Wales and Egypt. Stars travel constantly and are as likely to be seen in New York, London, or Boston as in Bombay.[31]

To investigate the significance of foreign locations for a dialogue on globalization, I examine how the setting is incorporated into the film and the grounds on which the film justifies a vast amount of screen time outside

India. Three broad categories emerge: reality sequences, fantasyscapes, and the reconfiguration of India.

REALITY SEQUENCES: TRANSNATIONAL CONNECTIONS   Transnational connections play a pivotal role in structuring the narrative. Foreign settings are made part of the story, as characters travel abroad. The foreign locale becomes part of the experiential realm, or the "scape"[32] of the transnational middle class.

In the recent hit film *Guru* (2007), the hero, a college student, travels to Istanbul for a job; in *Kabhi Khushi Kabhie Gham* (2001), the central characters go to England for "higher studies" and to reunite with family; in *Mujse Dosti Karoge?* (2002), immigration to the United Kingdom is explained in terms of "dot-com" opportunities; and in the earlier *Dilwale Dulhania Le Jayenge* (1995), another superhit, the heroine's parents are immigrants to the United Kingdom and much of the narrative moves between London, Switzerland, and the Punjab. In *Judhwaa* (1997), the hero's parents travel to the United States to obtain expert medical care for his mother, while in *Dil to Pagal Hai* (1998), most of the characters live in India, but there are some who travel abroad: the heroine's childhood friend lives in the West, visits her in India, and spirits her away to Europe for a short holiday. In *Pardes* (1997), the narrative begins with two childhood friends, one of whom has immigrated to the United States, the other having made his home in an Indian village; they reestablish their relationship when they arrange the marriage of their children, following which there is much travel to and from the United States. In the recently released *Thoda Pyar Thoda Magic* (2008), the hero who lives in Delhi goes to Los Angeles to buy an American company, and he and his family vacation in California.

Films present two additional categories of transnational connections and locations: in *Kal Ho Na Ho* (2003), *Kabhi Alvida Na Kehna* (2006), and *Jaan-E-Man* (2007), the narratives are set in New York, the home of the characters; and in the present climate of India's economic boom and the trend of emigrants returning home, the Bollywood film has anticipated such return. India thus becomes another node in the crisscrossing of global flows. As early as 1999, the film *Aa Ab Laut Chalein* (1999) told the story of disillusionment with the West on the part of potential immigrants as the title, which translates to "Now Let's Return [Home]" suggests. In *Kabhi Khushi Kabhie Gham* (2001), the hero's wife is dissatisfied with her life in London and desires to live in India; at the end of the film, the family is reunited and

Scene from *Kal Ho Na Ho*, a Bollywood romance set entirely in New York.

decides to return to India. In *Swades* (2004), the hero is a NASA engineer who travels to a village in North India in search of the woman who took care of him as a child and finds a meaningful life and love there, while the hero in *Guru* gives up a promotion in Istanbul, saying he would rather work in his own country than for the "white man."

None of these situations is "out of this world" for the urban transnational middle class whose lives are intertwined with people and events outside India. The lifestyle of this class has captured the imaginary landscape of the Hindi film; in the films as in real life, the airport is replacing the train station as the site for tearful good-byes.

FANTASYSCAPES: THE DREAM NARRATIVE   Reality sequences are merely one way of using foreign locales. The films freely incorporate reality and fantasy in the form of the dreams, wishes, desires, and emotions of the characters—in short, their "inner world."[33] The musical format facilitates such incorporation, and exotic and foreign locations are used to situate fantasy.

Musical interludes transport characters (and the viewer) to foreign locales—the dreamscape of the narrative. In the film *Yes, Boss* (1997), the hero's romantic musings have him frolicking with the heroine in the Swiss countryside against a background of rolling hills and pastures. The costumes emphasize the fantasy nature of the interlude. The heroine is dressed in a chiffon skirt and blouse with bare midriff; the hero is in brightly colored trousers and shirt. There are several costume changes throughout and props appear magically—sometimes the romantic pair lean against a helicopter or a fancy car. Props seem to be there simply to suggest a lifestyle that is cosmopolitan and wealthy. The scene is pure dream. In the scene immediately prior to the fantasyscape, the hero is seen in his modest home in Bombay. At the end of the dance sequence, he is back in his home and we see him sheepishly snapping out of his romantic reverie. A similar scene in *K3G* has an interlude with the hero and heroine set in Egypt, the pyramids in the background. Egypt does not figure in the story in any way; it is purely a landscape of romance and erotic fantasy. In *Hindustani* (1996), the fantasy-dream is somewhat arbitrarily set in Australia, complete with kangaroos and the Sydney Opera House, while the remainder of the narrative is located in Madras (now Chennai). In *Pukar* (2000), a film that addresses cross-border terrorism in India, song-and-dance sequences transport the audience to a desert landscape resembling the southwestern United States.

RECONFIGURING INDIA: WEST IS EAST   In the third treatment of place, Bombay films creatively use foreign locations without marking them as such, and in the process reterritorialize India in the popular imagination. For example, characters are shown in gardens and arboretums, clearly located in a temperate climate, but the narrative leaves the location unspecified and by default locates it within India. Houses that are recognizably Western or non-Indian are represented as homes in an Indian city. In *K3G* the central characters, a family of wealthy industrialists, live in what appears to be an English manor house that the narrative locates in India. In the film *Main Prem ki Diwani Hoon* (2003), a family lives in the housing locality of "Sundar Nagar," supposedly on the outskirts of Bombay, but the location is rumored to be in New Zealand where part of the filming was done. In this third treatment of foreign locations, India as lived space, as sense of home, is extended to what is outside the geopolitical boundaries of the nation-state.

The India portrayed by the Hindi film is a patchwork constructed out of a combination of locations, some of which are known to Indians in their everyday experience of India, together with fantasyscapes that are culled from a larger global databank. Although the films may not portray an accurate India as per its borders, they do portray a lived reality that is in keeping with globalization and the new spatialities of a world in motion. They see the world as an "interconnected cultural space" where cultural flows are multidirectional rather than from one "core" in the West to a non-Western "periphery," and where at the level of everyday life there is a "heightened entanglement of 'global and local.'"[34] The films deterritorialize and reconfigure India in an exercise in place-making. An imaginary world is constructed, where distinctions between the familiar or the local and the alien or the global are blurred. In doing so, the films comment on the new spatialities of globalization and the need for a perspective that can unpack the production and reconfiguration of lived space.[35]

Everyday Fantasy

Sudhir Kakar expresses his deep understanding of the films and the culture of which they are part when he observes that while Hindi films may be "unreal in a rational sense," they are not "untrue," as they have a "confident and sure-footed grasp on the topography of desire and its vicissitudes." Films express fantasy, a world of the imagination fueled by desire that has its roots in the conflicts of everyday life.[36] The concept of everyday fantasy is useful for an understanding of these three treatments of foreign locales: the global as the local and the known, the global as pure fantasy or dreamscape, and the global as reality, the habitat of the transnational middle class.

Fantasy is present in all three renderings. In the first, it is drawing upon everyday fantasies of millions of Indians for whom travel abroad and to the West is both a dream and an objective, as expressed in a song sequence in the film *Pardes* (1997), which depicts children in a small town in India singing, "I want to go [to] America." In the second, it is the slide into erotic-romantic space and time, which is depicted as non-everyday and nonmundane—and therefore outside India. In the third, it is a reconfiguration of India (and the world) that reflects the possibilities of an interconnected world. The idea and experience of India and of Indians is elaborated, creating an imaginary landscape or "mindscape."

These fantasy worlds are expressions of the curiosity that is part of globalization and are rarely addressed.[37] Curiosity drives audiences to interrogate the reality that informs these fantasy worlds as audiences grapple with the underlying multiple realities of globalization presented to them. Adopting a "documentary mode of viewing,"[38] audiences are heard speculating on the location. In theaters one hears, "Is this Mauritius?" or "This doesn't look like Bombay!" or "This is not America, this is Canada!" The films evoke a desire for travel and firsthand experience of place: "Have you been to Goa? No? You must go!" For the diasporic community watching the films removed from the everyday reality of India—in North America, for example—can be puzzling and lead again to a need for evidentiary confirmation. Women in the audience are frequently overheard commenting on the fashions, "Is that what they are wearing in India these days? So fashionable!" or, looking at the heroine's glamorous outfit, "I'll ask my aunt to get me a suit stitched like that. She lives in Delhi."

This desire to locate the imaginary world of the film in real-life locations, accessible in everyday encounters, is expressed even when the film has few visual depictions of real-world India. The film *Devdas* (2002), a historical saga, was shot on stylized and lavish sets. Much of the story portrayed an upper-class family in Bengal and dealt with interiors. The film became a big hit with audiences in North America. When watching the film in a theater in Boston, I overheard audiences discussing the setting. Younger viewers speculated on whether the film was "like India." Others made plans: "Have you been to Calcutta? We should go there" or "We should go shopping. I want a sari like that" (referring to the heavily embroidered sari worn by the heroine). Material consumption appears to be a way to deal with multiple realities, of situating or grounding them, and of negotiating fantasy and reality.

A striking example of the real-world resonance of the Bollywood film is the rise in tourism to the sites and settings made visible by the films. When overhearing the vacation plans of Indians, one finds the destinations mentioned are often the destinations made visible in the films. Visiting Niagara Falls, for example, where several films have situated romantic song-and-dance sequences, one is struck by the number of South Asian visitors.[39] Following frequent filming in the United Kingdom, Mauritius, and Europe, tourism from India to these places is on the increase. Realizing that Indian tourists seek out travel destinations based on the films, the British Tourist Authority has used Bollywood to promote London by producing a "Bollywood Movie Map" to guide Indian tourists to the exact locations where their favorite movies have been shot.

Bollywood's influence upon shaping such global flows is seen most dramatically in Switzerland, the location most commonly used in the films.

Switzerland has seen a sharp increase in tourists from India. Though the overall increase in foreign visitors between 1995 and 2000 was only 8.3 percent, tourists from India more than doubled in this period. According to a spokesperson for the Bernese Oberland tourist office, "Bollywoood is largely responsible for the fact that a significant number of Indians spend their holidays here."[40] This remark finds support in the greatest number of Indian tourists seen in the areas that are favored by the film romances: central Switzerland, Geneva, Lake Geneva, and the Bernese Oberland. India–Swiss relations themselves are being established anew on the basis of Bombay cinema. The consulate general of Switzerland in Mumbai actively promotes Switzerland and does public relations (PR) work with the film industry; film director Yash Chopra, one of the first to film in Switzerland, was awarded the title of "Honorary Guest of Switzerland for Life" in a ceremony organized by Swiss tourism in Bombay.[41] Following Bollywood's success in filming in Switzerland, Germany is wooing Bollywood both as a venue for filmmaking and with an eye to future profits from tourism.[42]

Consumer Culture and Lifestyle

In his essay on cultural globalization, Peter Berger identifies two of the "four faces" of globalization as, first, Davos culture, an international business culture that extends into lifestyle and leisure activities and involves similarity in dress, speaking English, a technological facility with computers and cell phones, and a familiarity with Westernized fitness culture, and second, McWorld, American popular culture exported everywhere, with its consumer lifestyle of popular music, fast food, convenience goods, and Valentine's Day, complete with cards in English.[43] Watching Bollywood's renditions of globalization, it may appear that the directors have closely read Berger's essay. Films present audiences with settings such as department stores, shopping malls, fitness clubs, upscale restaurants, and airports all seen as spaces where the lifestyle of the urban middle class is sustained and reproduced in the context of an expanding globalist imagination. In contrast to films made in the 1950s–1980s in which characters would meet and interact at the temple or church, at parties and get-togethers at home, in seedy bars or discotheques or on the street, in recent films public places that are associated with international travel (airports) as well as spaces identified as consumer and lifestyle spaces (shopping malls and fitness clubs) for urban middle-class Indians are the sites for significant meetings and sociality.

Global modern symbols are adopted in local or familiar contexts to signify the modern identity of the characters and to display the interconnectedness between everyday life and the global. Characters no longer drive Indian-made Fiats and Ambassadors or Bajaj scooters; the vehicles of choice for both heroes and villains are now BMWs, Mercedes, Porsches, and Ferraris. In the hit film *K3G*, one central character arrives home in a private helicopter (he is heir to an industrial fortune) while another steps out of a fancy Italian sports car. TVs, VCRs, and in more recent films, LCD or DVD players are part of the furniture in middle-class homes and are operated by adults and children. Cell phones and computers are the routine equipment of everyday life and used by both men and women.

Clothing worn by characters is increasingly Western, not simply the generic jeans and T-shirt but brands such as Nike, Reebok, DKNY, Fubu, Ralph Lauren, Tommy Hilfiger, and Gap. In *Judhwaa* the heroine wears a belt with a metallic "New York" buckle, while the hero sports a T-shirt with "Bodytalk" written on it; in *Mujse Dosti Karoge?* the heroine wears shirts and miniskirts with the American flag on them—yet in these narratives, none of these characters has yet stepped out of India. In several films, younger female characters—when they do wear Indian clothing—wear a fashionable *churidar khameez*, or glamorous *ghagra-choli*. Heroines rarely wear saris, which have become an outfit for an engagement or marriage ceremony and symbolize the mature woman (as opposed to the young girl), or the older woman or the mother character.

Films transform certain objects into saturated symbols: the backpack slung on one shoulder and rarely seen in use is a sign of middle-class, college-going educated youth; the cell phone indicates a successful entrepreneur or professional or urban middle-class individual (though in reality in urban India people in many walks of life carry cell phones, and even those who hawk vegetables on the street are seen with cell phones!), the treadmill signifies the emerging health and body culture of the Westernized upper-middle classes. Pepsi and local brand Thums Up soft drinks are scattered throughout the landscape of the co-ed college cafeteria, symbolizing good times and the social world of Westernized youth, while the glass of wine has come to symbolize the cosmopolitan transnational. For the urban middle classes, the films resonate with their lives; with their travel abroad and with NRIs among their extended kin, this class consumes on a global scale. Urban audiences who do not belong to this class may not recognize the brands individually, but they recognize them collectively as symbols of the urban transnational class and of a certain lifestyle.

In the film *Dil to Pagal Hai*, young adults in Bombay are shown drinking tequila shots, enjoying Chinese takeout, and frequenting Western-style restaurants on dates. Characters increasingly speak in English, whether it is phrases or entire sentences. Characters attend private schools where English is spoken, greet one another in English, and liberally use American slang. The amount of English spoken in the films is surprising to those who are unfamiliar with Bombay cinema. Speaking English signals middle-class status for audiences in India, a status many aspire to. Watching the films in darkened theaters in India, non-English-speaking and lower-class audiences "try on" an English-speaking identity, as they repeat lines of English dialogue or talk back to the screen using phrases uttered by the characters. For NRI audiences, especially second-generation immigrants who may not understand much of the Hindi language conversation on screen, dialogue in English brings the film closer to their world and makes the characters more approachable.

Scenes depicting a Western fitness culture have also become part of the formula. The fitness culture conveyed in the films is primarily youth focused. College students are seen in gyms and on playing fields in fashionable Western athletic gear—shoes, leotards for aerobics, sweatbands, and other sports accessories such as towels and bottles of designer water. Visuals of American-style college football are also introduced, along with scenes of cricket matches. Depictions of a fitness culture are seen to extend beyond youth. In *Chachi 420* (1998) and *K3G*, the patriarch who leads, at the very least, an upper-middle-class lifestyle is shown on a treadmill in an exercise-wear uniform. In *Mujse Dosti Karoge?* the NRI visiting relatives in India jogs before his breakfast of cereal and orange juice, while his hosts forgo exercise and enjoy *parathas* and spicy pickles. These scenes are evidence of a growing awareness of fitness and Western-style exercise regimens among middle-class Indians as well as the spread of health clubs and gyms in urban centers that offer aerobics, weight training, and yoga.

In India's postliberalization economy, there is a mushrooming of shopping malls and an explosion of goods. Where earlier foreign brands were not to be seen on store shelves except in "smuggler's markets," it is now possible to buy Hershey's cocoa, Clairol shampoo, and Knorr soups in neighborhood stores that are crammed with local brands as well. While the consumerism and lifestyle changes following upon globalization affect the middle and upper-middle classes in a direct and rapid way, the lower classes are also affected by such change.[44] For example, technology is becoming more affordable and is perceived as a necessity rather than a luxury by many more people.

Certainly for the middle classes, consumption is a means to emphasize globalization locally. Using foreign-made goods, wearing foreign clothes, and watching or listening to foreign media all provide ways of extending experience and making what is geographically distant socially near.[45] Transnational mobility fuels consumption. Even with the ready availability of a range of consumer goods in India, gifts brought for family and friends from travels abroad include not only expensive technological items such as cameras, personal digital assistants (PDAs), and MP3 players but everyday goods that demonstrate a sensual or pragmatic appeal: Fragrant soaps and body lotions, perfumes, aftershave and cosmetics, clothing, chocolate, alcohol, plastic bags, and Reynolds Wrap shape experiences of faraway places.

Ordering Experience: "Worlding" and Hierarchy

Films distinguish between varieties of transnational experience related to the various countries to which Indians have emigrated. NRIs in the United Kingdom are depicted as a mixed group, including shopkeepers as well as industrialists and computer professionals. In *Dilwale Dulhania Le Jayenge*, the heroine's father is a London shopkeeper, while in *K3G* the character played by Shah Rukh Khan is an MBA graduate running his own business in London, and his brother, played by Hritik Roshan, travels to the United Kingdom ostensibly for a college education. NRIs from America are for the most part portrayed as middle to upper-middle class. They live in mansions and are wealthy and successful. In *Kal Ho Na Ho*, a story that is located entirely in New York, Preity Zinta's character and Saif Ali Khan's character are NRIs studying for an MBA. While he is from a wealthy Gujarati family, her background is more modest. In the film *Pardes*, the NRI from America is compared to the returnee from Sri Lanka, who is ridiculed and identified as inferior in status; even the latter's very claim to being an NRI—itself widely recognized as a status label—is questioned.

Films order transnational experience within a larger frame. For instance, class hierarchy and social status are linked to the site of travel and residence. To some degree, this builds on real-world interpretations and experience where immigrants to North America include professionals and members of the educated middle classes. This group of immigrants is more visible and present in sufficiently large numbers to shape the image of immigration to the United States compared to the uneducated or to those who do menial or unskilled work such as immigrants to other parts of Asia or to the Middle East. In the film *Judhwaa*, the Singapore-returned Indian is a stark contrast to the NRI visitor from North America. The Singapore returnee is portrayed as "low class": he dresses loudly and unfashionably, wears flashy gold jewelry, and is uncouth and uneducated. He says he worked as a janitor in Singapore, work that is low status and ritually impure on the purity–pollution scale. He aggressively pushes his suit with the heroine and is dismissed by the heroine's mother. In contrast, NRIs from America are seen as educated, soft-spoken, and civilized, clearly middle-class professionals who are viewed as "cultured." The NRI hero visiting India from America drinks milk, wears suits, is polite to the point of being timid in social interaction, and is diffident with women. He is pursued by the heroine's mother as a suitable match for her daughter.

In ranking immigrants and the immigrant experience in this way, the films order countries and the experience of living in them in a hierarchy. Hierarchies based on local meaning systems, together with the experiences of NRIs, are extended to a global field. Ranking NRIs from various parts of the world, the films impose not only a class ranking but also a castelike hierarchy on the varieties of immigrant experiences.

The bridging narrative of the Bombay film is seen to bring together the disparate experiences and multiple realities attendant to the "world in motion." They present viewers with "contextualised atmospheres of meaning" that the narratives construct as "formed through the continuum of experience."[46] Films construct a transnational space or mindscape where one can glide from a Bombay street to a lake in Switzerland and then to a home in North America. With their practice of "worlding," the films illustrate that "the coming into context of the world, i.e., the formation of environment, at once transcends and extends beyond any characterizations of this or that physical location."[47] Even with large sections of the films depicting landscapes and settings outside India and characters whose lives appear far removed from the majority living in India, films manage to convey a "feeling of India" to their habituated audiences through strategic use of music and dance, aesthetics and style, the placing of well-known stars in repetitive storylines, and the portrayal of a social world and emotional terrain that is familiar and comforting.

Discussion

In a selection of Bollywood films, globalization is framed largely as economic growth and modernization, representing a larger sensibility in postliberalization India where aspirations for upward mobility focus on the Westernized urban middle classes and transnational connections. However, seeking to keep up with ongoing social change, the films present globalization's shifting experiential terrain, which involves more than merely presenting a positive face of globalization; films also address its incoherence, confusion, and disruptions, all parts of globalization's lived experience. In films such as *Aa Ab Laut Chalein*, *K3G*, and *Swades*, for example, critiques of transnationalism have emerged as hints of dissatisfaction with life in the West. Parental anxieties over the loss of Indian culture and values in children growing up in the West is another recognizable theme seen in *K3G*, *Pardes*, and *Dilwale Dulhania Le Jayenge*.

Underlying the popular understandings of globalization that are conveyed is a phenomenological perspective emphasizing lived experience, everyday life, the social relations attendant upon the transnational movement of goods and people, as well as the significance of place—precisely the considerations that scholars have identified as crucial for an understanding of globalization that is contextual, embodied, and situated. Films bring to audiences the sensual experiences and emotions, the most immediate and embodied effects of social change attendant upon globalization. Globalization's "phenomenal worlds"—described by sociologist Anthony Giddens[48] as "simultaneously locally situated yet global"—produce multiple realities in everyday existence; the corresponding need to engage with such multiple realities is the sense-making project of globalization, arguably its universalizing aspect and one that the Bombay film constructs in dialogue with its audience. Films map the lived experience of globalization by (selectively) providing bridging narratives that address these multiple realities; they attempt to address "the intrusion of distant events into everyday consciousness"[49] and to impart some coherence to fragmented and partial experiences of globalization and transnationalism.

The films address broader debates in the study of transnationalism, such as the significance of the local in a postnational world. They offer insights into the production of locality by communicating a sense of place as feeling rather than representations based solely on geography or territory, thereby making a case for a topography of affect as meaningful for a phenomenology of globalization. By deterritorializing the local as feeling, Bollywood films extend the local into the global field, allowing familiar (local) feeling and sensibilities to cloak discrete experiences and events related to globalizing processes. This leads to different understandings of what is "global" and "local" where—in the films as in everyday life—the so-called global and local can be mere moments, experiences of distant and near or strange and familiar that infuse one another. The local as the known and familiar becomes a medium for translating what is unknown and alien, with local idioms coming to the fore whenever globalization leads to encounters with the unknown. Translation then involves a siting of the globalist imagination in the contexts and environments of everyday praxis.

The feeling of India conveys a feeling of the local. Place experienced as feeling—rather than space, geography, or territory—extends the global imaginary, with implications for the textual analysis of media and popular culture products that have typically privileged a detached content analysis of visuals or a decoding or meaning rather than an examination of context and the sensual and emotional frame.

Films are able to communicate with habituated audiences both in India and internationally by drawing on existing local or indigenous and insider dialogue.[50] This "local" dialogue shapes "communities of intelligibility" that are deterritorialized and social rather than spatial.[51] The films are consequently able to outcompete Hollywood within these communities and cultural niches.

Bombay cinema as a cultural narrative offers its audiences a means, limited though it may be, to expand one's cultural repertoire, a possible window onto globalizing processes and phenomena and a world beyond reach. At the same time, films provide an understanding of globalization that sees it linked to the local, rather than as a homogenization project that threatens the local. The model of cultural pluralism offered by the films is an alternative to the model of globalization as the inevitable dominance of Western culture.

Acknowledgments

I would like to thank the editors Michael Curtin and Hemant Shah, Jack Katz, Rukmini Srinivas, Arvind Shah, and Achal Prabhala for comments and feedback on this and earlier versions of this essay. Versions of this essay were presented at the South Asia colloquium at Yale University and at the Newhouse Center for the Humanities at Wellesley College.

Notes

1. The line is from a song in the movie *Shree 420* (1955) titled "Mera Jootha Hai Japani" (My Shoes Are Japanese). It is also the title of a Bollywood film directed by Aziz Mirza and released in 2000.

2. Scott Elder, "The reel world," *National Geographic* (March 2005), Screen Digest. National Geographic Maps, http://soma.sbcc.edu/Users/DaVega/FILMST_101/ FILMST_101_TECHNICAL/WorldFilmoutput.pdf (accessed 21 May 2009).

3. In this chapter, I use the term *Bollywood* interchangeably with *Bombay cinema* or *Hindi cinema*.

4. The films are popular even in the southern states of India where Hindi, the language of the Bombay film, is not spoken. The development of the films in an environment where they have had to reach across linguistic, religious, and regional differences to address heterogeneous and plural audiences in India has led to a narrative formula where language (as in Hindi dialogue) and culture do not become barriers to either an understanding or an appreciation of the films.

5. For decades, Bollywood has been popular in many parts of the non-English-speaking world, including countries of the former Soviet Union, the Middle East, and Turkey. Indian films have been popular in Nigeria for over thirty years. Even though Nigerian audiences were unable to follow the Hindi language dialogue in the unsubtitled films, it did not seem to affect their popularity See Brian Larkin, "Indian films and Nigerian lovers," *Africa* 67, no. 3 (1997): 406. The largest percentage of the films continue to be exported to North America and the United Kingdom, where they are watched by the diasporic community, estimated at 20 million, with a total annual income of $300 billion (*India Today*, 2002). Recently, the films have found audiences in Japan, where the Tamil film *Muthu*—released without subtitles—has achieved cult status. The film was second in box-office takes following *Titanic*. By 1999, the film had become somewhat of a cult sensation in Japan after enjoying a twenty-three-week run in theaters and generating $1.7 million for the Cinema Rise theater in Tokyo. A Japanese film critic reported becoming addicted to the film and having to see it once a day. Following the success of *Muthu*, Bombay films such as *Dilwale* are to be released in Japan. "Dancing maharajas," *Newsweek International*, 10 May 1999; Deepa Deosthalee, "Love in Tokyo—Japanese Yen for Rajni," *Indian Express Newspapers*, 1999, http://www.expressindia.com/news/ie/daily/19990510/ ile10006.html (accessed 21 May 2009).

6. Ien Ang, *Watching Dallas: Soap Opera and the Melodramatic Imagination* (London: Methuen, 1985); Benjamin Barber, *Jihad vs. McWorld* (New York: Random House, 1995); Peter Berger, "Four faces of global culture," *National Interest* 49 (Fall): 23–29; Thomas Friedman, *The Lexus and the Olive Tree* (New York: Farrar, Strauss and Giroux, 1999); Pico Iyer, *Videonight in Kathmandu* (New York: Vintage Books, 1988); Tamar Liebes and Elihu Katz, *The Export of Meaning: Cross-Cultural Readings*

of "Dallas" (New York: Oxford University Press, 1990); John Tomlinson, *Cultural Imperialism* (London: Pinter, 1991).

7. Ashis Nandy, "The popular Hindi film: Ideology and first principles," *India International Center Quarterly* 6, no. 1 (March 1980): 89–96; Patricia Uberoi, "The diaspora comes home: Disciplining desire in DDLJ," *Contributions of Indian Sociology* 32 (1998): 305–36.

8. Rachel Dwyer and Divya Patel, *Cinema India: The Visual Cultural of Hindi Film* (New Brunswick, NJ: Rutgers University Press, 2002); Ron Inden, "Transnational class, erotic arcadia and commercial utopia in Hindi films," in *Image Journeys*, ed. Christine Brosius and Melissa Butcher (New Delhi: Sage, 1999); Uberoi, "The diaspora comes home."

9. The film *Kehtaa Hai Dil Baar Baar*, released in 2002, is reportedly the first full-length Bollywood film shot entirely in the United States; others have followed. *Kal Ho Na Ho* (2003), *Kabhie Alvida Na Kehna* (2006), and *Jaan E Man* (2007) feature stories of NRIs in New York, and much of the shooting was done in North America. In 2007 it was reported that per year an average of forty films are shot in London and the number was expected to rise to sixty in 2008. Adrian Wootten, chief executive of Film London in interview. "London woos Bollywood," *DNAIndia*, November 21, 2007, http://movies.indiainfo.com/2007/11/21/0711210516_london (accessed 21 May 2009).

10. Adam Hochschild, "Globalization and culture," *Economic and Political Weekly*, May 23, 1998, 1235–38.

11. Hochschild, "Globalization and culture," 1238.

12. Sean Chabot and Willem Duyvendak, "Globalization and transnational diffusion between social movements: Reconceptualizing the dissemination of the Gandhian repertoire and the 'coming out' routine," *Theory and Society* 31 (2002): 697–740; see also Jonathan Xavier Inda and Renato Rosaldo, *The Anthropology of Globalization* (Malden, NJ: Blackwell, 2002), 26. In their schema, globalization was seen as an inevitable homogenization and Westernization of the world's cultures and peoples and the consequent erasing of cultural difference arising out of the domination and spread of Western culture, especially American "soft power." There is now recognition of the limitations of this "monolithic core–periphery model," together with an understanding of the world as a "complexly interconnected cultural space, one full of crisscrossing flows and intersecting systems of meaning."

13. While there is some evidence to suggest that audiences in India are differentiating by region (North vs. South India, for example) and by rural and small town vs. urban locations, with audiences in North India and rural areas preferring B- and C-grade movies to the slickly produced urban extravaganzas popular in metropolises in India and with NRIs abroad, there is no consistent evidence that even the latter films are rejected by the mass audience.

14. Officially banned in Pakistan, Bollywood films appear to be accessible to audiences via pirated videos in stores. The same pirated videos are aired on cable television according to some reports by visitors from Pakistan and Pakistani immigrants in the United States (conversational interviews with Pakistani immigrants and visitors

to the United States). Bollywood is popular in Sri Lanka, where the movies are popularizing Hindi language classes for keen viewers who want to sing along with the songs and understand them (again, interviews with visitors from Bangladesh).

15. I refer to audiences who are insiders to the culture of popular cinema who have watched the films over decades and are regulars at the movie theater as "habituated audiences" or habitués. Lakshmi Srinivas, "Active viewing: An ethnography of the Indian film audience," *Visual Anthropology* 11, no. 4 (1998): 323–53; Lakshmi Srinivas, "The active audience: Spectatorship, social relations and the experience of cinema in India," *Media, Culture and Society* 24 (2002): 155–73.

16. Hochschild, "Globalization and culture."

17. Till Brockman, "Planet Bollywood," *Swissair Magazine* (April 2001): 62–67.

18. Indian stars are preferred by audiences and have a loyal following. In a BBC online poll, Bollywood screen legend Amitabh Bachchan was voted the most popular star of the millennium, with Sir Laurence Olivier coming in second; Nasrin Munni Kabir, *Bollywood: The Indian Cinema Story* (London: Macmillan, 2001), 43.

19. Sara Dickey, *Cinema and the Urban Poor on South India* (Cambridge: Cambridge University Press, 1993).

20. Nandy, "The popular Hindi film"; Rosie Thomas, "Melodrama and the negotiation of morality in mainstream Hindi film," in *Consuming Modernity*, ed. Carol Breckenridge (Minneapolis: University of Minnesota Press, 1995); Uberoi, "The diaspora comes home."

21. This last explanation may account for Bombay cinema's popularity in countries other than India that yet have the shared experience of being non-Western societies coping with Western models of growth and development. In northern Nigeria, Bollywood films provide Hausa audiences with "parallel modernities," allowing for a successful negotiation of dilemmas such as speaking English, wearing Western clothes, and enjoying the right to a choice of marriage partner as opposed to an arranged marriage—all issues attendant upon modernization. See Larkin, "Indian films and Nigerian lovers"; see also Arjun Appadurai, *Modernity at Large: Cultural Dimensions of Globalization* (Minneapolis: University of Minnesota Press, 1996; Uberoi, "The diaspora comes home").

22. Larkin, "Indian films and Nigerian lovers," 410.

23. Xavier Inda and Rosaldo, *The Anthropology of Globalization.*

24. This paper draws on several years of watching Indian cinema and participating in its public culture, which includes reading film magazines, watching television programs devoted to the films, and discussing films with audiences and fans. It also draws on ethnographic field research with audiences and filmmakers in South India and the United States, as well as cultural analyses of a selection of films made since the mid-1990s. A majority of the films I have drawn on for this analysis are hits (if not "superhits") and are recognized as significant milestones and trendsetters. Given the tendency of Indian filmmakers to use previously made films as a resource for later films, filmmakers themselves have influenced a spate of subsequent films. The films have therefore entered a public discourse in which audiences, media analysts, academics, and others participate.

25. Alfred Schutz, *The Structures of the Lifeworld* (Evanston, IL: Northwestern University Press, 1973, 1983).

26. Anthony Giddens, *Modernity and Self-Identity: Self and Society in the Late Modern Age* (Cambridge: Polity Press, 1991); Harri Englund, "Ethnography after globalism: Migration and emplacement in Malawi," *American Ethnologist* 29, no. 2 (2002): 261–86.

27. Englund, "Ethnography after globalism"; Michael Kearney, "The local and the global: The anthropology of globalization and transnationalism," *Annual Review of Anthropology* 24 (1999): 547–65.

28. Mike Crang, "Globalization as conceived, perceived and lived spaces," *Theory, Culture and Society* 16, no. 1 (1999): 167–77.

29. Lakshmi Srinivas, "Communication globalization in Bombay cinema: Everyday life, imagination and the persistence of the local," *Comparative American Studies* 3, no. 3 (2005): 319–44.

30. Thomas, "Melodrama and the negotiation of morality in mainstream Hindi film."

31. Recently the engagement of Aishwarya Rai and Abhishek Bachchan was announced when both stars were in New York for the premier of their film *Guru*, and an audience member reported seeing Bollywood stars Karisma and Kareena Kapoor and their mother at Boston's Logan airport.

32. Appadurai, *Modernity at Large*.

33. Sudhir Kakar, "The ties that bind: Family relationships in the mythology of Hindi cinema," *India International Center Quarterly* 6, no. 1 (1980): 11–21.

34. Giddens, *Modernity and Self-Identity*, 21.

35. Crang, "Globalization as conceived, perceived and lived spaces,"

36. Kakar, "The ties that bind."

37. L. Srinivas, "Communicating globalization."

38. Vivian Sobchack, "Toward a phenomenology non-factional experience," in *Collecting Visible Evidence*, ed. Michael Renov and Jane Gaines (Minneapolis: University of Minnesota Press, 1999).

39. Tulasi Srinivas, personal communication, 2001.

40. Brockman, "Planet Bollywood."

41. Brockman, "Planet Bollywood."

42. Vrishali Haldipur, "Achtung! Germany beckons Bollywood," *Times of India*, February 9, 2002.

43. Berger, "The four faces of globalization," 21.

44. Tulasi Srinivas suggests that through consumption of everyday goods the urban poor can imitate the middle classes whose lifestyle they aspire to. She observes that maids working in middle-class homes have shifted to using shampoo available in sachets for a few *paise* where earlier they were using indigenous herbal soap-nut powder; Tulasi Srinivas, "A tryst with destiny," in *Many Globalizations*, ed. Peter L. Berger and Samuel P. Huntington, 89–116 (Oxford: Oxford University Press, 2002).

45. I am paraphrasing "the globalist axiom" that "the socially local is no longer

necessarily the geographically near" (van Binsbergen, quoted in Englund, "Ethnography after globalism," 266).

46. James Ostrow, "Culture as a fundamental dimension of experience: A discussion of Pierre Bourdieu's theory of human habitus," *Human Studies* 4 (1981): 279–97.

47. Ostrow, "Culture as a fundamental dimension," 293.

48. Giddens, *Modernity and Self-Identity*, 187; see also John Tomlinson, *Cultural Globalization* (Chicago: University of Chicago Press, 1999).

49. Giddens, *Modernity and Self-Identity*, 23.

50. L. Srinivas, "Communicating globalization."

51. Ulf Hannerz, *Cultural Complexity* (New York: Columbia University Press, 1992).

TWO

"From Bihar to Manhattan": Bollywood and the Transnational Indian Family

Aswin Punathambekar

There are an estimated 20 million people in the Indian diaspora. While Indians have traveled and lived abroad for centuries, in Bollywood films the diasporic Indian has not always been depicted in a positive light: Travel abroad, particularly to the West, polluted the NRI figure, who could be redeemed only by the ritual purification of denouncing the West and embracing "traditional" Indian values. In the era of globalized Bollywood, however, the NRI figure is now portrayed as a model consumer-citizen who remains connected to the "national family." Based on interviews conducted with a variety of Indian families in the United States and Great Britain, Aswin Punathambekar shows the diverse ways Indians in the diaspora view and interact with a classic NRI film—Kabhi Khushi Kabhie Gham (K3G)—*in ways that help reinforce their valued Indian identity though they live outside India.*

In June 2003, I received an invitation to attend the New York media event of *Main Prem Ki Diwani Hoon* (*MPKDH*, I'm Crazy for Prem, 2003, Sooraj Barjatya). The event was part of Rajshri Productions' promotional campaign and was designed to give journalists and film critics in the United States a glimpse of the film before its worldwide release. Given Rajshri Productions' reputation as having reintroduced the "family film" in India with box-office hits such as *Maine Pyar Kiya* (1989), *Hum Aapke Hain Kaun*

(1995), and *Hum Saath Saath Hain* (1997), and these films' popularity among diasporic audiences, I was excited at the opportunity to attend the event and perhaps even ask Rajat Barjatya, the marketing manager, a few questions.[1]

The event, attended by well over thirty journalists, began with a screening of the trailer of *MPKDH* and three song sequences from the film. Following this, Rajat Barjatya fielded a range of questions about the film's plot, the stars, and the music. Toward the end, he delivered his marketing pitch: "Everyone knows that Rajshri has made family films that appeal to viewers in every strata of society across India. . . . Today, we wish to appeal to families all the way from Bihar to Manhattan. From Bihar to Manhattan, Indian families everywhere."

About half an hour later, I had an opportunity to meet Barjatya and ask him to explain what he meant by saying Rajshri Productions wished to appeal to families "from Bihar to Manhattan." "If you've seen films like *Dilwale Dulhania Le Jayenge, Pardes*, and *Kabhi Khushi Kabhie Gham*, you know exactly what I mean," he began. Pointing out that Bollywood films and film music had become an integral part of life in the Indian-American diaspora and asserting that films such as *K3G* spoke to the sentiments of people in the diaspora who remained "Indian, deep down," Barjatya went on to suggest that viewers in Bihar also enjoyed NRI-centric films partly because they too recognized that NRIs remained "Indian at the end of the day."

Dilwale Dulhania Le Jayenge (*DDLJ*, 1995, Aditya Chopra), *Pardes* (1997, Subhash Ghai), and *Kabhi Khushi Kabhie Gham* (*K3G*, 2001, Karan Johar) are all films that resonated strongly with viewers in India and abroad and count among the most successful films of the past decade. These films, among several others, explored the cultural space of Non-Resident Indians, and as Barjatya observed, affirmed that the expatriate community remained "Indian, deep down." It is this sentiment of remaining "Indian, deep down" and its problematic articulation in Bollywood narratives that I interrogate in this chapter. I do so by exploring what families of Indian origin in North America bring to bear upon their engagement with Bollywood films that grapple with the politics of claiming "Indianness" outside the territorial boundaries of India. Bringing together ethnographic detail and a thematic reading of *K3G*, I demonstrate how narrative and representational strategies, viewing practices, and patterns of socialization in diasporic spaces intersect to create a discursive realm of consensus regarding Indianness.

I focus on *K3G* for two key reasons. First, *K3G* was the film that was referenced most often by the families I interviewed. With one exception, these families had all watched the film multiple times and drew on specific instances in the film to articulate what Indianness meant to them. Second, *K3G*'s narrative marks an important departure from earlier efforts in Bollywood films to recognize and represent the expatriate Indian community. By exploring and cautiously legitimizing the cultural space of Indian life in the diaspora, *K3G* renders the diaspora's version of Indianness less transgressive or impure and more as an acceptable variant at a historical conjuncture when territorially bound definitions of identity in relation to a singular national community have become unimaginable.[2] This process of mediation involving Bollywood, the Indian state, and the diaspora is best understood in terms of a transitive logic involving Bollywood's narrative and representational strategies, first-generation Indian immigrants' emotional investment in the idea of India, and the state's attempts to forge symbolic and material ties with the expatriate community. In other words, I demonstrate how Bollywood's mediation of diasporic life played a crucial role in setting the stage for the state to reterritorialize Non-Resident Indians, position the Non-Resident Indian as a privileged and model citizen-consumer in a global nation space, and remap the sociocultural boundaries of the "national family." It is important to recognize, however, that the Bombay film industry's output in its entirety does not reach or succeed in overseas territories—it is a specific kind of cinema that has, since the mid-1990s, "brought the NRI decisively into the center of the picture as a more stable figure of Indian identity than anything that can be found indigenously" that is at issue here.[3]

Before embarking on the analysis, let me provide a brief outline of *K3G*. *K3G* is the story of an affluent Indian family: Yashvardhan "Yash" Raichand (Amitabh Bachchan), his wife Nandini (Jaya Bachchan), and their two sons, Rahul (Shahrukh Khan), who is adopted, and Rohan (Hrithik Roshan). The family splits when Rahul falls in love with and marries Anjali (Kajol), a girl from the working-class neighborhood of Chandni Chowk in Delhi, instead of marrying the girl his father had chosen. Yashvardhan disowns Rahul, and Rahul and Anjali move to the United Kingdom. Anjali's younger sister Pooja (Kareena Kapoor) and Rahul's nanny (Farida Jalal) accompany them to London. Years later, Rahul's younger brother Rohan learns about these incidents and sets out to London, promising to reunite the family. After graduating from college, Rohan moves to London and manages to make his way into Rahul's family under an assumed name. With Pooja's help, he reconciles the divided family. In the process, Rohan also falls in love with Pooja, and transforms the sassy "Westernized" Pooja into a virtuous "Indian" woman.

Viewing Practices as Rituals of Cultural Citizenship

Preeti Arora and her husband, Kuldip, were one of several enterprising families in North America and the United Kingdom who screened films for the expatriate Indian community during the late 1960s to the 1980s. Screenings were usually held in university halls during the weekend, with films screened off 16 mm, and later, 35 mm reels. These weekend screenings, with an intermission that lasted thirty to forty-five minutes, were an occasion, apart from religious festivals, for people to wear traditional clothes, speak in Hindi or other regional languages, and participate in a ritual that was reminiscent of "home." In cities with a significant concentration of South Asian immigrants, these weekend screenings gradually expanded to include a radio show that broadcast Hindi film songs and various community-related announcements. Families who screened films also organized live shows with film stars from India performing for the community. As one interviewee explained:

> PREETI: We used to inform people by post. They used to come, buy tickets, get *samosas* and a cup of chai, Coke for the kids, and chitchat with their friends, exchange news, gossip, everyday things, you know, that one starts missing when one is away from home. I remember, even when there were snowstorms, people would come and say, we wait the whole week to watch a Hindi film, don't cancel it.

As other families who moved to the United States and the United Kingdom during the late 1960s and early 1970s recalled, there were no cultural

Table 2.1. Profile of Families Interviewed

Family	Migration Path	Annual Income	Occupation	Education
Balwinder & Sukhjit Sodhi	Punjab–Austria–U.S.	$35–45K	B: Doorman at hotel S: Housewife	Middle School
Vinod & Mythili Rao	Bombay–U.K.–U.S.	>$40K	V: Retired doctor M: High school teacher	Degrees in medicine
Ajeet & Aparna Kaura	New Delhi–U.S.	>$80K	Aj: Software analyst Ap: Homemaker	B.S. computer science B.A. liberal arts
Kuldip & Preeti Arora	Punjab–U.S.–Canada	>$60K	Entertainment and travel business	K: Master's engineering P: B.A. liberal arts

institutions in place, and little offered in mainstream media that resonated with their emotions, nostalgic longing, and cultural values, not to mention addressing the difficulties of life in a new cultural space. Importantly, these screenings were marked as an exclusively *Indian* space, away from mainstream society, where families could meet and participate in a ritual of sharing personal and collective memories of life in India. These weekend screenings also became a key ritual in the diaspora because of the difficulties involved in maintaining connections with India. Not only was air travel limited and expensive, but the only means of contact for most families was letter writing and a monthly phone call.

This communal gathering around Hindi cinema was reduced drastically with the entry of the VCR in the early 1980s. Hindi films were available on videocassettes within a week of two of their release and led to dwindling audiences for public screenings. Although this did not happen until the early 1980s in the United States, things changed faster in the United Kingdom. For instance, by the late 1970s, the BBC had begun telecasting Hindi movies as part of a six-week program targeting immigrants from the Indian Subcontinent. In the United States, an important factor was the change in migration patterns. Until 1965, the Asiatic Barred Zone Act of 1917 and the Asian Exclusion Act of 1924 did not allow Asians to immigrate to the United States. In 1965, these laws were changed to permit "occupational migration," primarily to address the shortage of highly educated and skilled labor in the American economy. Thus, the first wave of migration from India was comprised of highly educated professionals and their families. However, by the mid-1980s, people from a less educated, largely merchant-class background also began immigrating to the United States.[4] The spurt in the number of Indian grocery stores all over the country during this period can be attributed, in part, to this demographic shift. And it is these grocery stores that served as initial points of distribution for the videocassettes and, now, DVDs. Grocery-store owners also served as intermediaries as families sought their opinion on the latest films. Further, by this time, both in the United Kingdom and the United States, there were weekly, hour-long television shows comprising film songs, interviews with visiting actors and actresses, movie trailers, and so forth that were broadcast on public access and community television channels. Not only were these shows widely watched, but they determined rental choices as well.

Over the past decade, the establishment of satellite television networks such as Zee TV and B4U (Bollywood for You) has made it easier to access films and television programming from India. Further, with the addition of an India-specific radio station that plays film songs and the establishment of cinema theaters that screen Bollywood films in several cities in the United States, engagement with Bollywood has become, simultaneously, highly diffuse and intense. My intention in tracking changes in viewing practices in terms of access and setting from the late 1960s to present times is twofold. Let me illustrate with an excerpt:

> VINOD: You've grown up watching the movies and you *continue*, that's all. You like the songs, you listen to them here also. You enjoy particular kind of drama . . . you see crowded streets, keeps you in touch with the way of life in India.
>
> MYTHILI: It doesn't matter what the story is like, I like to see the dresses, the *salwar* designs, everyday life, even if it seems like a fantasy, you know.
>
> VINOD: And you see, you want to keep that link with India even if you don't live there. Even though we've lived outside for many years, it's where you're from, isn't it?

It is clear enough that Hindi-language Bombay cinema, as a dominant storytelling institution in postindependence India, has come to possess tremendous cultural and emotional value for expatriate Indians who grew up watching these films. Vinod's comment indicates that the ability to *continue* a cherished ritual that is associated with being Indian is, in and of itself, reason enough to watch Hindi films. Secondly, although advances in communications have facilitated contact with India, over a period of time, work and other social engagements in the diaspora result in most first-generation Indians gradually losing touch with day-to-day developments in India. Vinod's remark about "seeing crowded streets" and Mythili's comments about "seeing India change" and watching films to keep up with the "latest *salwar* designs" thus point to "an everyday, concretized instance of maintaining temporal continuities with the imagined homeland."[5]

Over the years, the act of viewing, Bollywood's role in defining various social rituals, and interactions within sociocultural networks that such viewing practices created have helped sustain expatriate Indians' desire to perform their Indianness and remain, at least culturally, residents of India. Furthermore, it is important to recognize that such need for contact is only a starting point. In shaping *how* the "home" is remembered, Bollywood films reconfigure memory and nostalgia in important ways. It is to this question— of how Bollywood film narratives and first-generation immigrants' emotional investment in the idea of India come together to frame narratives of being and becoming Indian-American—that I shall now turn.

Designer India for Suburban Homes

In newspapers, magazines, and several websites, critics have penned scathing reviews of *K3G*. Paying close attention to the extravagant lifestyles that the characters lead, they have asked: Is this really India? One critic declared: "It is a chilling film. Chilling because here is India, Hinduism, and Jana Gana Mana made into glossy laughable commodities to be purchased for a high price. The film is designed to make NRIs thankful that the Old Country is as beautiful, as backward, and as resoundingly traditional as he wants it to be."[6] Such critiques, exaggerated as they may appear, point to two important sites of negotiation between the film and audiences in the diaspora. The first concerns *K3G*'s not-so-subtle efforts to naturalize a comfortable coexistence of tradition and modernity. In the space of the first few minutes, viewers are left with no doubt as to the transnational-yet-Indian-at-heart status of the Raichand family. In this respect, *K3G* can be situated alongside a series of films such as *Hum Aapke Hain Kaun*, *Dilwale Dulhania Le Jayenge*, and *Kuch Kuch Hota Hai* that "reinvent tradition in easily recognizable terms to suit the exigencies of capitalist production."[7]

Related to this, a second crucial act of reconfiguration is *K3G*'s erasure of class through the rescripting of working-class space (Chandni Chowk) into a commodified sphere of ethnic authenticity.[8] Changes in colors, background music, dialect and mannerisms, the use of "ethnic" clothes, and the presence of street performers all work to mark differences between the upper-class residence of the Raichand family and Chandni Chowk, where Anjali lives. However, for viewers in the diaspora, these encodings function not so much as systematic erasures of class differences but as referents of "tradition" and "home" whose consumption is critical to sustaining and performing ethnicity, particularly at community events. As one interviewee pointed out:

> APARNA: When my friend's daughter graduated high school, she got a dress made in the same design as Madhuri Dixit's . . . so I like to watch out for these designs too for my own daughter. When I go back to Delhi, I just have to tell the tailor that I want a design from such and such movie and he knows exactly what I want. The dress was a great hit in last year's Diwali function here.

In fact, the Chandni Chowk *mela* (carnival) sequence in *K3G* can be read as a tactical response to diasporic viewing practices of the kind that Aparna described. Consumption aside, there is another set of deliberations involved in this mode of viewing. Consider the following excerpt:

> AJIT: It is up to us to keep things Indian here and movies help.
> APARNA: See, we know that Hindi movies are this la-la-land, nothing real-istic about them. I'm from Delhi, I went to college there, but why would I want to see the real Chandni Chowk in a movie? I like to see movies that are well made, that are in foreign locations . . .
> AJIT: Exactly, movies that show the real India are not what we want here . . . we don't want to see the *gandhgi* [filth] all the time . . .

That certain visual elements in films such as *K3G* acquire a materiality that enables the performance of identity in the diaspora is not inherently problematic. What the comments above indicate, however, is the embed-dedness of such practices of consumption and performances of citizenship within two larger discursive terrains. First, they signal the investment that first-generation Indian immigrants have in imagining an India that is no longer associated solely with poverty and corruption but rather an India that is shaping a transnational economic order. As Rajagopal points out, NRIs are acutely conscious of their position as "an apotheosis of the Indian middle class, exemplifying what 'Indians' could achieve if they were not hampered by an underdeveloped society and an inefficient government."[9] I would argue that the visual economy of films such as *K3G* is an important source of cultural capital for NRI families that belong in a particular class bracket, with the requisite education and job opportunities to live and work in countries such as the United States.

Second, Ajit and Aparna's comments also point to middle- and upper-middle-class Indian immigrants' position as racialized minorities in the United States, and the manufacturing and sustenance of a "model minority" image over the years.[10] Ajit's desire for a diasporic India that has no *gandhgi*, that projects an image of success, competence, and cultural stability, also needs to be seen as a refusal to acknowledge the presence of "third world-ness," so to speak, within this picture-perfect world of diasporic Indians.

It is instructive to note that this "naturalization of plenitude" in Bol-lywood films did not go unquestioned by working-class NRIs that I met during the course of my fieldwork.[11] Consider Balwinder Sodhi's experience. Sodhi left his village in Punjab during the early 1980s and first migrated to Vienna, Austria. Working at a newspaper stand in Vienna for nearly five years, he saved enough money to pay an agent who would arrange for his immigration to the United States. Abandoned on the east coast of Mexico instead of the United States, Sodhi made it into southern California after a dangerous and grueling trek. After two more years of living and working in the margins as an "illegal" immigrant, he eventually made his way to Boston. It took him four more years to arrange for his wife to join him in the United States. Sodhi now works at a hotel and supports both his immediate family in Boston and an extended family in India.

Not only did Balwinder Sodhi indicate a deep-rooted dissatisfaction with NRI-centric Hindi films such as *K3G*, he informed me that he had also stopped watching Hindi films altogether. Speaking wistfully of movies such as *Deewar* (1975) and *Zanjeer* (1973), movies in and of a very different social order in 1970s India, he dismissed my questions, saying I would never be able to understand what it meant to be in his position.

> BALWINDER: Whatever they show in movies about people and life, it is always the good aspects, only moments in life that work out well; they hardly show or speak about the hardships and difficulties that one faces and goes through in life. One has to really struggle to experience a good life in America . . . and why do movies not bother to depict the struggles Indians like me go through? Just our everyday life . . . it is not like the families in the suburbs who only think of us when they go to a restaurant or take a cab in the city.

Balwinder Sodhi's story is not just a strikingly different narrative of being "Indian" in the United States. His comments assume great importance when considered in light of the fact that none of the middle- and upper-middle-class families I interviewed mentioned successful films that were not in any way "family-centric." It is not so much that these men and women chose not to watch a diverse range of films. Rather, it is their choice of extravagant family melodramas to speak about their life experiences and notions of *Indianness* that points to how a "designer India" becomes the first step in the transactions between Bollywood and NRI audiences who work to negotiate belonging and circumscribe participation in the new "transnational family."

Rehearsing, Reworking, and Remaining Indian

In a famous sequence in *Dilwale Dulhania Le Jayenge*, the hero (Shahrukh Khan as Raj) and heroine (Kajol as Simran), having missed their train on a trip across western Europe, end up spending the night in a small town, with Simran swilling a bottle of cognac before falling asleep. When Simran wakes up on Raj's bed wearing his clothes, panic-stricken and unable to recall what had transpired, Raj holds her close and growls, "You think I am beyond values, but I am a Hindustani, and I know what a Hindustani girl's *izzat* [honor] is worth. Trust me, nothing happened last night." Mishra recounts this scene to argue that Hindi film consumption in the diaspora speaks to first-generation Indians desperately trying to sustain a value system and inculcate the same in their children in order to set them apart from mainstream society in countries like the United States and the United Kingdom. "These differences," Mishra writes, "are generally about tradition, continuity, family, and often, the importance given to arranged marriages."[12]

K3G is no different from NRI-themed films such as *DDLJ* and *Pardes* in its heavy-handed depictions of a patriarchal family, the upholding of conservative gender norms, and conflicts surrounding the institution of marriage. In *K3G*, several scenes in the Raichand family home clearly establish Yashvardhan's position as the head of the household. Once the narrative moves to London, the role that married women are expected to play in an expatriate context is also detailed in no uncertain terms. In London, Anjali is clearly responsible for maintaining an "Indian" home, including ensuring that the son is well schooled in Indian traditions. In addition to performing an elaborate Hindu *puja* (prayer) at the crack of dawn, she is ready to serve breakfast for her husband and son. As she mills around, she begins singing a patriotic Hindi film song, chastising her son for not being attached enough to India (*"mere desh ki dharti*," the land in my country, from *Upkar*, 1967). The scene borders on the comical, but Kajol's riposte to her son's indifference to all things Indian is worth noting. Turning to her husband, she retorts: "He's already half English (*angrez*), don't complain to me if he becomes completely English."

In every family I interviewed, it is the mothers who watch Bollywood films with their children, translating for them and explaining, as one woman said, "all the Indian customs and traditions." The "woman's question" becomes particularly pronounced in relation to raising daughters in the diaspora. English-language films and music, television programs, and stereotypical assessments of modes of socialization (dating, for instance) and other sociocultural phenomena (divorce rates, single-parent households, and so on) are all marshaled as evidence of a debauched West and situated in sharp contrast to the traditional and morally superior values of Indianness in several Bollywood films and by the families I interviewed. The first-generation immigrants I interviewed were willing to negotiate some common ground with their daughters, without necessarily "reverting to petrified templates of dating and sexual norms in India."[13] However, their discomfort is revealed when they draw parallels to *K3G*, as the following excerpt illustrates.

MYTHILI: You see, the Western community is very different from our culture. Like respect for parents and elders, how to behave, basic things . . . and when children go to school and make friends, you don't know the families that those children come from, what problems they may have. So your child will get influenced by all that.

VINOD: With Hindi movies, there is no question of influence. But they portray nice moral values . . . like *K3G*, we can get lessons for life from it.

MYTHILI: We have to make sure our children do not get too much into this culture. Things like that happen here, and there are parents who are very orthodox and will not accept children making their own choices. But we talk to our daughter and work out things.

VINOD: But you see, things have changed in India also. Like our niece in Bombay, she is very modern. So we have to change with times, but we should still hold on to some values. I think parents everywhere have such concerns and if they are not aware from the beginning, they pay the price in the end.

Vinod and Mythili's comments were partly a function of Neeti, their daughter, opting to move out and live on her own, something first-generation Indian families have had to grapple with in the diaspora. It is revealing to note how *K3G* creates a space for viewers to rehearse and reflect on their hopes and anxieties, particularly through lighthearted moments in the film involving Poo (Pooja, played by Kareena Kapoor), Kajol's younger sister raised in London. Scenes involving Poo echo informants' comments that vividly articulate the difficulties faced by parents wrestling with desires to preserve an authentic "Indian" self, fashioned on the basis of their own upbringing in India, and an acknowledgment of the influences of the starkly different cultural field that their children encounter in schools and colleges in countries like the United States.[14]

This rehearsal and testing of values, ideals, and norms becomes even more pronounced with questions concerning marriage and the imminent threat of interracial marriage.[15] Let me illustrate this point by juxtaposing a comment made by Preeti when I asked what she felt about her son growing up watching Hindi films, and a few lines that Yashvardhan Raichand delivers in *K3G* on hearing about his son's falling in love with Anjali, a woman from Chandni Chowk, a working-class neighborhood.

PREETI: It was very good, he was imbibing his culture. During the week, at school, he was learning the culture of this place and while watching Hindi movies, singing Hindi film songs, he was learning about Indian culture. No one can tell that Sandeep is American, he can speak Hindi so well. It makes it easier as he thinks about marriage, you know. I know Indians married to others, but whatever people say, it will be easier if he marries someone Indian . . . they can share so much . . . they can understand each other's culture. It is important.

YASHVARDHAN: Raichand. The name and respect has been given to us by our ancestors, [and] to honor and respect them is our foremost duty. And I will never tolerate an ordinary girl becoming a hurdle. You didn't think even once about the background of the girl, her status, her upbringing. You didn't spare a single thought . . . whether the girl will be able to understand our culture and our traditions [*sanskar aur sanskriti*].

Will she ever understand our rituals, our rites? [*riti, riwaz*]

Will she understand our ethics and principles?

Will she adhere to the values of our family?

How did you even dare to think that she could be a part of our family?

This scene speaks to first-generation Indian parents' fears that their son or daughter might marry a non-Indian who, in all likelihood, will not possess the cultural capital to participate in and ensure the continuance of the India that they have so assiduously constructed and sustained over the decades. More importantly, *K3G*'s erasure of class, as discussed in the previous section, serves a crucial purpose in terms of how viewers in the diaspora disassociate the dialogue from its context within the film and insert it into their own viewing positionality. While Yashvardhan's dialogue is directed at Anjali's working-class status, for viewers in the diaspora already conditioned to re-code class referents into commodities signifying tradition, such scenes serve as a liminal "talking space" that permit reflection on their own reaction in the eventuality of their children entering into a relationship with a non-Indian, and enable, as we saw with Mythili, Vinod, and Preeti, a rehearsal of values that form the foundation of Indianness.[16] Further, this rehearsal is accompanied by a gradual reworking of ideas and values concerning cultural institutions such as marriage and, in the process, a questioning of India's status as the sole arbiter of Indianness and, most crucially, a sense of confidence in their own diasporic version of Indianness. Consider this argument from Kuldip and Preeti:

KULDIP: Our two married daughters are here, and our son. All our close relatives are here and we have so many close family friends, some we met when we first came to this country.

PREETI: See, people like you, born and raised in India, come and ask us how we are Indian after all these years. But you know, these days we have everything here. Temples, *gurdwaras*, other kinds of cultural places, dance and music school, language classes which our grandchildren attend . . . everything.

KULDIP: Let me tell you something—it is people in India who want to become Western. My grandchildren may not speak Hindi fluently, but they can teach their cousins in India about Indian traditions. I think people like you should stop calling kids here ABCDs [American-Born Confused Desis].

Kuldip and Preeti's comments echo an important narrative departure that sets *K3G* apart from earlier films such as *DDLJ* and *Pardes*. *DDLJ* and *Pardes* sought to fold the diaspora into the nation by insisting on a return to India to resolve familial conflicts, where NRIs were asked to demonstrate their cultural competence to belong in the nation. In contrast to these earlier films, *K3G* inaugurates a new imagination of a transnational family in which the flow of cultural elements that lend authenticity is no longer a heavy-handed one-way flow from India to its expatriate Other. In exploring and legitimizing the cultural space of expatriate Indian families, *K3G* renders the diaspora less of a transgressive Other and more as an acceptable variant within the fold of a "transnational family."

The Nation Seeks Its Citizens

K3G's negotiation of India's relationship with the diaspora is also, as discussed earlier, related to a growing sense within India of the "relocat[ion] of what we might call the seismic center of Indian national identity somewhere in Anglo-America."[17] Hrithik Roshan's character in *K3G*, Rohan, the quintessential cosmopolitan who can navigate multiple cultural spaces with consummate ease, needs to be understood in relation to this. Rohan is, in fact, an embodiment of a "super-Indian" whose Indianness transcends both that of the resident and Non-Resident Indian.

Rohan arrives in London to the strains of a remixed version of *Vande Mataram*—a nationalist song invoked possibly to remind viewers in the diaspora of an irrevocable link that they have with their homeland. Although billboards and storefronts of international labels and chain stores frame the first five to ten seconds of his arrival, in subsequent frames, women wearing saffron-white-green (the colors of the Indian flag) *dupattas* walk by Rohan, he is greeted by a group of Bharatanatyam dancers (the preeminent classical dance form that is highly popular in the diaspora) in the middle of busy traffic intersection, and he sashays down a boardwalk flanked on both sides by a bevy of white English girls also sporting clothes colored saffron, green, and white.

We then see Rohan in a cybercafé, looking up a directory listing for his brother's contact information. As the address is pulled up, and the song in the background changes to *Saare Jahan se Accha, Hindustan Hamara* (Greater Than Any Place in the Universe, Our India), we see Anjali folding her hands in prayer in front of her parents-in-law's framed picture. Not only is the diasporic family rendered inextricable from the nation, it is an explicit acknowledgment, both to viewers in India and the diaspora, of the diaspora's abiding desire to stay in touch with India. In a subsequent scene, we witness Rohan speaking with his parents (in India) on the phone. Sporting a tricolor T-shirt, he assures his parents that he is happy to have found accommodation with an Indian family instead of staying in a hotel: "They're very nice people, papa. When I met them, I felt like I have known them for years, a laughing, happy, contented family, like we used to be." This piece of dialogue needs to be read not just as a reference to the rift within the Raichand family but also as an allusion to commonly held views of NRI families struggling to define a sense of cultural identity, and as a comment that India, as a transnational family, is unimaginable without the inclusion of the diaspora. Although one can point to several other instances that hint at an impending rapprochement between India and the diaspora, it is the singing of the Indian national anthem by Anjali and Rahul's son (Krish) at a school function that serves as the pivotal event that legitimizes and mitigates the "Othered" status of the diaspora's version of Indianness, and reconstitutes the NRI as the ideal citizen-to-be of a transnational family.

Having learned about Krish Raichand's participation in a school function, and Anjali's disappointment at her son not being able to sing the same songs she sang growing up in India, Rohan decides to intervene. As Anjali, Rahul, Pooja, and the rest of the audience wait to hear Krish lead his classmates into "Do Re Mi," he steps up to the mike, says "This one is for you, Mom," and sings the Indian national anthem. A close-up of the visibly moved diasporic family cuts to a long shot of the kids singing, followed by pans and cuts to different parts of a surprised yet respectful audience. Anjali is reduced to tears as she runs down the aisle to embrace her son, and the background

A surprised and overjoyed Anjali (Kajol) embraces her son Krish (Jibraan Khan) after he leads his classmates in a rendition of the Indian national anthem.

music reverts to *Vande Mataram*, finally fading into *Saare Jahan se Accha, Hindustan Hamara*.

This entire sequence functions both as reassurance for a vast majority of first-generation immigrants that they can live in the United Kingdom or the United States yet *belong* and claim cultural citizenship elsewhere, and as a paradigmatic moment of India embracing the diaspora and defining the NRI as one of its own. It does not matter that Anjali's son, a second-generation diasporic Indian who has never experienced life in India, sings the national anthem with a British accent, his mispronunciation toward the end is forgotten (the anthem is completed by Anjali), his being "half-English" is not a concern anymore—every anxiety of negotiating a sense of Indianness is erased in those fifty-two seconds that the national anthem is sung. The diaspora is no longer different and threatening. In Rajat Barjatya's words, the diaspora is "Indian, deep down."

Between Bollywood and the State: Fashioning the Transnational Family

I have shown here that Bollywood's role in reimagining the national family and the diaspora's emotional ties to India can be used to read families' engagement with NRI/family-centric narratives such as *K3G*, the articulation of cultural citizenship as belonging in a "transnational family," and most crucially, the reconstitution of the NRI as a model citizen-consumer in a global and deterritorialized nation-space. This process of mediation is best understood as a transitive logic—that the interactions between the diaspora and Bollywood, and between Bollywood and India, set the stage for India to remap symbolic and material relationships with the diaspora. Such a reading is useful because it allows us to locate our analysis of Bollywood narratives and their reception in diasporic spaces within a broader historical conjuncture and to grapple with the implications of the state's efforts to redefine its relationship with the diasporic community and articulate a new idea of citizenship that is, as Rajadhyaksha puts it, "explicitly delinked from the political rights of citizenship."[18]

It is critical to recognize that the NRI, as a category of selfhood defined in relation to the nation, carries both spatial and temporal dimensions. As Aditya Nigam observed, in inhabiting the space and time of the future in countries in like the United States and the United Kingdom, the NRI did not only come to be seen as someone inhabiting India's present-to-be.[19] The NRI, as someone who inhabited the time and space of global modernity and who played a part in shaping the global information economy in sites like Silicon Valley in the United States, emerged as the model citizen-consumer who could address and bridge the disjunctures and anxieties that lay at the heart of India's efforts to participate fully in a global economy and redefine citizenship in the language of consumption.

To grasp this shift in the terms of Bollywood's mediation of the national family and the figure of the citizen-consumer, consider the differences between Raj Kapoor's articulation of a cosmopolitan self in a newly independent nation in *Shree 420* (1955) and that of Hrithik Roshan in *K3G*. A quintessential 1950s social film, *Shree 420* laid bare the enormous difficulties of sustaining a vision of postcolonial development while a vast majority of the population was struggling to make ends meet. In the film, Raj (Raj Kapoor) migrates to Bombay from the small town of Allahabad, is drawn into a world of deceit and dishonesty, and eventually, regains his innocence and his *imaan* (integrity). Toward the end of the film, we see Raj attired in the same tattered clothes he had on when he first migrated to Bombay, and back on the very same highway he had taken to travel to the city. He begins walking away from the city and his troubles, singing the famous song:

Mera joota hai japani, ye patloon englishstani
Sar pe lal topi rusi, phir bhi dil hai Hindustani
(My shoes are Japanese, these trousers are from England,
A red Russian cap on my head, yet my heart remains Indian)

Raj Kapoor's *Shree 420* is, without doubt, a celebration of a cosmopolitan Indian identity and also one that articulates citizenship to the ideal of sacrifice and the deferral of pleasure through consumption in the interest of nation building. It is this contract between citizenship and consumption that has been rewritten over the past two decades in India and that finds expression in films such as *K3G*, where avowedly "global" NRIs affirm their belonging in the national family and demonstrate that no matter what, their *dil* remains Hindustani (the heart remains Indian).

It is in relation to these imaginative shifts that we need to understand negotiations between the state and the diaspora, and Bollywood's role in setting the stage for these negotiations. Thus, the following quote from Sushma Swaraj, the union minister of broadcasting and information, points to more than just the fact that the importance of the legitimization of diasporic versions of Indianness by cinema is not lost on the Indian state: "Perhaps geographical divisions between Indians in India and the Indian diaspora are blurring if not disappearing altogether. And with the announcement made by the Honorable Prime Minister at yesterday's inaugural session, the dual citizenship will bring the diaspora closer to us not merely due to our cultural bonds but also by a legal system."[20] Lavish transnational rituals such as the *Pravasi Bharatiya Divas* (Day of the Diaspora) signal a qualitative shift in the state's relationship with the NRI. The Indian state is no longer content with wooing foreign currency into nationalized banks, no longer ambivalent about celebrating NRI successes, and no longer hesitant about claiming the NRI as one of its own. What we are witnessing, then, is a state that seeks to capitalize on the work already done by its central mediating institution in reterritorializing the NRI and defining Indianness as a "global *jugalbandi* (fusion) between Bharat *vasi(s)* (those living in India) and Bharat *vanshi(s)* (those who belong to the *civilization* of India)."[21]

It is critical, however, to keep in mind the exclusionary nature of these negotiations, the state's differential response to Indian diasporas worldwide, and the hegemony of this configuration of the NRI as an ideal citizen-consumer that marginalize other imaginations of India and Indianness. As Balwinder Sodhi's comments and *K3G*'s representational strategies indicate, this new "transnational family" is constructed by both "exoticizing" and dispensing with class differences that neighborhoods such as Chandni Chowk in New Delhi or an apartment complex that houses working-class Indian immigrant families in Boston represent.

Citizenship, as critics have pointed out, involves an element of obligation (both material and imagined); in the case of first-generation immigrants, this obligation is worked out in relation to the family and through the family's metonymic relationship with the nation in Bollywood narratives. What emerges in family-centric Bollywood narratives such as *K3G* is an adherence to a social order that normalizes patriarchy and consistently erases class, caste, regional, and religious difference in favor of an upper-class, North Indian, heteronormative, and Hindu way of life. After Balwinder Sodhi refused to talk about *K3G* and expressed his frustration with Bollywood films, I asked if he had heard about the *Pravasi Bharatiya Divas* and the Indian government's plan to offer dual citizenship. He responded: "Do you think I will be able to attend? They don't want NRIs like me." For people like Sodhi and those diasporic Indians who do not inhabit the transnational circuitry that films such as *K3G* and events such as the *Pravasi Bharatiya Divas* celebrate, citizenship in the newly constructed transnational family is deferred.

Although Bollywood films tend to speak for and about Indianness, we need to keep in mind our lack of understanding of how viewers in diverse diasporic contexts (Malaysia, for instance) engage with regional-language films and how the politics and pleasures in those cases intersect with Bollywood's "transnational" narratives. Furthermore, the rapidly expanding space of film culture—online fan communities, new arrangements for distribution and exhibition worldwide, non-Indian audience communities, the performative reception of Bollywood in cultural shows staged by second-generation South Asian youth in different parts of the world, and so on—highlights both the provisional nature of efforts to define and circumscribe the "transnational family" and the need to examine the role of media and communications in enabling and shaping this process.

Notes

1. All three films were directed by Sooraj Barjatya and are generally known for their conservatism and focus on the ideals of a large, joint Hindu family.

2. Arjun Appadurai, *Modernity at Large: Cultural Dimensions of Globalization* (Minneapolis: University of Minnesota Press, 1996).

3. Madhav Prasad, "This thing called Bollywood," *Seminar* 525 (2003), n.p. For

a detailed account of the distinctions between Bombay cinema and Bollywood, see Ashish Rajadhyaksha, "The Bollywoodization of the Indian cinema: Cultural nationalism in a global arena," *Inter-Asia Cultural Studies* 4, no. 1 (2003): 25–39.

4. Migration from India to the United States can be traced to the early 1900s, but the most significant wave of migration can be dated to 1965 following the Immigration Act of 1965, often referred to as the Hart-Cellar Act.

5. Anjali Ram, Mediating Nationalist and Gendered Identities: An Analysis of Asian Indian Immigrant Women's Readings of Popular Indian Cinema, PhD diss., Ohio University, Athens, 1999, 156.

6. Sagarika Ghose, "Email nationalism," *Indian Express* (New Delhi), 28 December 2001.

7. Vamsee Juluri, "Global weds local: The reception of *Hum Aapke Hain Kaun*," *European Journal of Cultural Studies* 2, no. 2 (1999): 236.

8. Chandni Chowk (moonlit square, or silver square), located in central Delhi, is a congested bazaar (marketplace) of narrow lanes packed with shops selling a range of consumer goods. The area dates back to 1650 A.D.

9. Arvind Rajagopal, *Politics after Television: Hindu Nationalism and the Reshaping of the Public in India* (Cambridge: Cambridge University Press, 2001), 241.

10. Vijay Prashad, *The Karma of Brown Folk* (Minneapolis: University of Minnesota Press, 2000).

11. Patricia Uberoi, "The diaspora comes home: Disciplining desire in *DDLJ*," in *Tradition, Plurality and Identity*, ed. Veena Das et al. (New Delhi: Sage, 1999), 164–94.

12. Vijay Mishra, *Bollywood Cinema: Temples of Desire* (New York: Routledge, 2002), 236–37.

13. Sunaina Maira, *Desis in the House: Indian-American Youth Culture in New York City* (Philadelphia: Temple University Press, 2002), 59.

14. Maira, *Desis in the House.*

15. See Patricia Uberoi, "The diaspora comes home," for an analysis of these themes in *DDLJ*.

16. Marie Gillespie, *Television, Ethnicity, and Cultural Change* (London: Routledge, 1995), 184.

17. Prasad, "This thing called Bollywood," n.p.

18. Rajadhyaksha, "The Bollywoodization of the Indian cinema," 32.

19. Aditya Nigam, "Imagining the global nation: Time and hegemony," *Economic and Political Weekly* 39, no. 1 (2004): 72.

20. Nandhini Kaur, "The dreams of a diaspora," *Frontline* (15–21 January 2003), Chennai.

21. Joseph, J., "A global *jugalbandi* between Bharat *vasi* and Bharat *vanshi*," *Rediff* (16 December 2004).

THREE

Home, Homeland, Homepage: Belonging and the Indian-American Web

Madhavi Mallapragada

One of the most important ways of communicating within the Indian diaspora is through the Internet. Madhavi Mallapragada examines the politics of home, homeland, and homepage on the "Indian-American" Web. She shows how the Indian-American Web emerged during the 1990s by targeting Non-Resident Indians (NRIs) and Persons of Indian Origin (PIOs) in the United States. NRI refers to an Indian citizen who resides outside India, while PIO refers to a foreign citizen who claims an Indian origin. The central argument here is that the Web disrupts hegemonic notions of NRI and PIO identities by articulating diverse imaginations of "home," such as household, homeland, and homepage, to the cultural, economic, and political discourses of nation, family, and community. In the process, the Web foregrounds the contestations over "old" and "new" identities within the NRI and PIO communities in the United States.

The World Wide Web is arguably the most dynamic of contemporary communication technologies that are routinely transgressing the "real" and symbolic borders around the "private" household and the "public" homeland. In particular, the digital landscapes of the Web are transforming the meanings of "home" and "homeland" for immigrant and diasporic communities around the world. The cyberworlds of migrant groups participate in the transnational and uneven flows of technology, culture, capital, and communities in this age of globalization; in the process, they disrupt conventional understandings of cyberpractices and migrant politics. At the intersection of the virtual and the diasporic is a riveting narrative about the politics of home, homeland, and homepage in our world today.

This chapter critically examines the politics of home, homeland, and homepage on what it calls the "Indian-American" Web. This term is used here to refer to the section of the Web that targets Non-Resident Indians (NRIs) and Persons of Indian Origin (PIOs) living in the United States and whose institutional architecture is built around a transnational network of cyberentrepreneurs, Web advertisers, and sponsors located in India and the United States. The emergence of the categories "NRI" and "PIO" in the 1970s and 1990s, respectively, is embedded within a complex set of strategic, ambivalent, and often contradictory relations between the Indian state, its legal citizens who live outside the country, and foreign citizens of Indian descent.[1] The politics of the categories NRI and PIO are addressed later in the article; suffice it to mention here that NRI refers to an Indian citizen who resides outside India, while PIO refers to a foreign citizen who claims an Indian origin.

Although these terms came into prominence as part of the official discourse of the Indian state, they have since become central to the migrant sensibilities of the diverse communities that are part of the loosely (and problematically) defined "Indian diaspora in the United States."

Since the 1990s, a network of corporations, nonprofit organizations, and individuals in India and the United States have been forging a set of transnational alliances across the traditional boundaries of the "Indian" and the "American" nation-states to engender the "Indian-American" Web. Although the target users are Indian citizens who reside in America (NRIs) and American citizens who trace their cultural roots to India (PIOs), increasingly the Web has become the site for the construction of official categories of NRI and PIO identities as well as their dismantling. However, central to such practices have been the struggles over issues of identity and belonging in a community shaped in distinct and diverse ways by migration, mobility, dislocation, and relocation.

The central argument of this article is that the Web disrupts hegemonic notions of NRI and PIO identities by articulating diverse imaginations of "home" such as household, homeland, and homepage to the cultural, economic, and political discourses of nation, family, and community. In the process, the Web foregrounds the contestations over "old" and "new" identities within the NRI and PIO communities in the United States. The Web's role in the disruption of the hegemonic definitions of NRI and PIO identities is particularly significant because the emergence of the Web in the 1990s coincided with a dramatic shift in the makeup of NRI and PIO groups, as well as the official discourse about them.

This chapter argues that engaging with the intersecting and overlapping domains of contemporary social life such as the home, homeland, and the homepage within the specific sociohistorical and mediated contexts of the NRI and PIO experience in the United States since the 1990s is absolutely critical to understanding the contemporary cultural practices shaping the discourses of identity and belonging within the Indian diaspora in the United States. It demonstrates the centrality of new media technologies such as the Web to the economic, political, and cultural agendas of Indian immigrants and Indian-Americans as they negotiate their place within official and popular narratives about nation, citizenship, global capital, and transnational labor. It also reveals the strategic use of new media technologies by the Indian nation-state to maintain its relevance and power in an era shaped by the unprecedented emigration of its citizens to the United States, the proliferation of software and information technologies, and the rise of a global network economy.

The examination of the politics of home, homeland, and homepage on the Indian-American Web bears immense significance for rethinking the idea of diaspora and new media in light of current migration and cyberpractices. The predominant conceptualization of the diaspora posits unequivocal nostalgia and desire for the "original" homeland as defining characteristics of the diasporic sensibility; furthermore, the community is rendered into a homogenous, unified entity that demonstrates a strong allegiance to the national culture of its homeland. It is interesting to note in this context that a similar erasure of heterogeneity and complexity occurs in the popular "assimilation or exclusion" framework that has shaped the study of immigrant cultures. In this framework, immigrants—once again read as a unified group—are faced with one of two choices: either total assimilation into or complete exclusion from the host culture. In place of such simplistic readings, the Indian-American Web reveals ambivalence, hybridity, uneven power relations, and strategic alliances as symptomatic of a community shaped by diverse histories of migration and different imaginings of the homeland.

The concept of new media is used often to foreground the unique nature of contemporary media technologies such as the Web—for example, the instantaneity and simultaneity of hypertext-based communication or the unprecedented ways in which notions of time, space, the body, and the real are being reconfigured in virtual contexts. However, the term is problematic in that it renders invisible the key ways in which the practices of new media technologies are shaped by those of the preceding ones, also known as old or traditional media technologies. For example, the institutional practices of advertising, sponsorship, and acquisitions on the Indian-American Web are very similar to that of the television industries in India and the United States. Furthermore, the discursive construction of home, homeland, and home-page on the Indian-American Web point to a critical but neglected aspect of cybercultures—namely, the central role that new media technologies play in reconfiguring discourses of the nation, the family, and the community, medi-ated in past (and present) times through the old technologies of television, film, radio, and print media. It is interesting to note that while scholarship on cybercultures has enthusiastically addressed the issue of community, it has rarely interrogated the politics of nation and family in cyberspace. Yet as the case of the Indian-American Web reveals, the notions of nation and family are absolutely central to the politics of new media technologies, institutions, texts, and users.

In the first section of this chapter, an overview is offered of the contexts shaping the emergence of the NRI and PIO categories within the official discourse of the Indian state. The second section examines four representa-tions on the Indian-American Web that speak to the diverse imaginings of "home" as household, homeland, and homepage. The final section locates the politics of such invocations within the emergent discourses of nation, family, and community in the NRI and PIO constituencies of the United States. These discourses, in turn, participate in the construction as well as disrup-tion of the hegemonic categories of NRI and PIO as representative figures of the migrant sensibility of the Indian diaspora in the United States.

Origins, Locations, and Official Identities

The NRI became part of official parlance when the Indian state created the category of "Non-Resident Indian" in 1975 to enable Indian citizens living abroad to open and maintain foreign-currency nonresident accounts in U.S.

dollars or U.K. sterling. The Indian government at that time hoped that, by creating the NRI category, the country would witness a growth in its foreign exchange reserves. For Indian citizens living abroad, the NRI category was beneficial as it allowed them to repatriate their earnings during a period marking the beginning of a flexible exchange rate.[2] Arguably, NRIs have been valuable to the Indian state primarily for their financial investments. Before India liberalized its economy in the 1990s, its outdated tax laws and regulatory regimes gave NRIs very limited financial options to invest in India. By the end of the 1990s, the Indian state had opened up every sector to NRI investments and extended the same fiscal concessions to NRIs that it granted to its resident citizens.

Unlike the NRI, the PIO has emerged within official state discourse only in recent times. In 1999, the government announced that a PIO card would be extended to those living abroad and holding foreign passports. Not only would it introduce a visa-free regime but it would also confer some special economic, educational, financial, and cultural benefits to foreign citizens of Indian descent. For many, the Indian state's nod was the result of several years of persistent lobbying for greater commitment from the homeland by some of the most prominent members of the global diaspora. For the Indian state, it was a maneuver to demonstrate its desire for parity between the Indian citizen residing abroad and the foreign citizen claiming an Indian origin; this is especially significant in light of the fact that historically the Indian state has been indifferent to the diaspora, for the most part casting its emigrants as unpatriotic and contributing to the brain drain of the nation.[3] However, the shift toward liberalizing its markets in the 1990s as a way to compete in the global economy had led the state to a new realization of its potential ability (or lack thereof) to compete successfully in the global arena. With that has come a newfound love of the financially successful diaspora, many of whose members espouse a cultural allegiance to the nation of India and many others who are keen on playing a key role in the nation's growth. Hence, the PIO card scheme marked a pragmatic measure on the part of the state that was keen to inaugurate a new phase in its relations with the global diaspora.

Having said that, the NRI and PIO are more than idealized figures of the Indian state; they have currency within popular media discourses about the Indian diaspora. The lines between the NRI and PIO categories are often blurred when terms such as "Indian immigrants," "Indian-Americans," and "people of Indian origin" are used fairly interchangeably in the media. The symbolic dismantling of the different categories by using them interchangeably is significant because it foregrounds a pivotal transformation in the makeup of the Indian diaspora since the 1990s, a transformation brought about by a shift in the pace and patterns of migration from India to the United States. In turn, this shift was symptomatic of, and contributed to, the technological, economic, and cultural transformations of the 1990s. A predominant cause for the migration of Indians to America was the dearth of talented technical professionals to meet the rising demands of the high-tech industries in Silicon Valley and elsewhere within the United States. India, which holds the distinction of having the world's largest technical workforce, became an attractive resource for the numerous information technology (IT) firms that needed workers to sustain their rapidly growing ambitions and business interests.[4] As a result, Indian citizens became the dominant group receiving temporary work visas, including the contentious H1–B for the "highly skilled professional," from the U.S. Citizenship and Immigration Services (formerly the INS) during the past decade.[5]

Nonetheless, the high-tech professional on an H1–B visa accounts for only part of the influx of Indian citizens to the United States. Changes in immigration rules, as well university policies, made graduate education in the United States an attractive prospect for Indian students. Record numbers of Indians enrolled in American universities over the course of the decade. It is a trend that seems to be getting stronger, based on the 2003 report that Indian students accounted for the largest contingent of international students to enroll in American universities in 2002.[6] In addition, businesspeople, migrants on seasonal visas, family members, and relatives accounted for the sharp increase in Indian immigration to the United States during the 1990s.

While the 1990s witnessed record numbers of Indians moving to the United States, it also witnessed the maturing of the diaspora as its second and third generations became increasingly visible within the community. By most accounts, the first extended phase of Indian migration to the United States occurred in the years following 1965, when the family reunification clause amended immigration laws and made it easier for single immigrants to be reunited with their family members in America.[7] By the 1990s, the children and grandchildren of that first generation of immigrants were making their presence increasingly felt in the cultural, political, and institutional domains of the diaspora, and they aspired to do so within mainstream America as well. The multigenerational Indian diaspora in the 1990s was witnessing dramatic transformations in the contexts and contours of its community, and "old" and "new" identities were increasingly subject to scrutiny, rethinking, and negotiation. The media's tendency to use the categories of PIO, Indian immigrant, and Indian-American interchangeably was one strategic response to the emergent complexity.

Mobile Homes and Virtual Geographies

This section argues that the concept of home is central to the narratives on nation, family, and community on the Web. Home is invoked in strategic and flexible ways; as a result, it carries many different associations—that of the homepage, virtual home, homeland, the familiar, the intimate, the domestic, and the physical place that one inhabits.

The imaginative use of home on the Indian-American Web echoes David Morley's insightful remark in *Home Territories: Media, Mobility and Identity* that in the contemporary world, the answer to the question "Where is someone at home?" bears less on a geographical than a rhetorical territory. As Morley writes: "Traditional ideas of home, homeland and nation have been destabilized, both by new patterns of physical mobility and migration and by new communications technologies which routinely transgress the symbolic boundaries around both the private household and the nation state. The electronic landscapes in which we now dwell are haunted by all manner of cultural anxieties, which arise from this destabilizing flux."[8]

At the heart of the cultural anxieties in question is the relationship between identity, mobility, place, and belonging. By closely examining the connections between the home, family, household, nation, and community in light of transnational media and migration, Morley contends that media are a crucial force in the construction of "home territories" in our world today. In a similar vein, this chapter argues that the Indian-American Web participates in the construction of spaces of belonging such as the family, the nation, and the community. It does so by articulating the notion of home to the intersecting domains of contemporary social life such as the domestic home, collective homeland, and virtual homepage.

In constructing such spaces of identity and belonging, an individual's gender, class, and religion along with other axes of difference such as age, caste, and ethnicity, are, in the words of Doreen Massey, "the ways in which we inhabit and experience space and place and the ways in which we are located in the new relations of time-space compression."[9] Massey argues that place is formed out of the particular set of social relations that intersect at a particular location. Places, she adds, "are unfixed in part precisely because the social relations out of which they are constructed are themselves by their very nature dynamic and changing."[10]

The Indian-American Web participates in the configuration and reconfiguration of places such the domestic home, homeland, and homepage. In the process, it participates in the discursive construction of family, nation, and community; above all, it speaks to the continuing significance and increasing mobility of what David Morley calls "home territories." In the rest of this section, four key representations of "home" are discussed that illustrate the strategic and flexible invocations of home—as household, homeland, and homepage—on the Indian-American Web.

In the summer of 2000, *Siliconindia*, a print magazine aimed at business and technical professionals in India and the United States, featured a provocative advertisement for the shopping site Namaste.com (www.namaste .com). The headline for the advertisement, which reads "Beauty Secrets of India @ Namaste.com," suggests that by logging onto the site, the user would become part of an exclusive community that knows the secrets about an Indian brand of beauty. However, the fine print sutures the concept of beauty to ideas of culture and consumption, represented here through two of the most popular products of cultural consumption, Indian movies and food: "From *bindis* [application of colored designs on the forehead] to *mehendi* [henna] and from *kangans* [bracelets] to *jhumkas* [earrings], all that you need for the classic Indian look is at your fingertips. So no matter where you live, everything you love about India—movies, snacks, music, and health and beauty products—is just a click away."[11]

Framing the narrative of the advertisement is the visual representation of two women clad in traditional Indian clothes and jewelry, participating in the ritual application of *mehendi* against the blurry backdrop of New York's Times Square. Of the two women, Namaste.com clearly marks the one with the lighter skin, longer hair, the heavily brocaded skirt, elaborate jewelry, and *bindi* as embodying the "classic Indian look." No less significant is the fact that, unlike her companion, the lady in question has her body turned toward the camera as she looks directly into the eyes of the viewers, thereby inviting their gaze on her. Bringing the headline, the fine print, and the visual together is the slogan for the site, which reads: "Bring India Home!"

By framing the women against a classic marker of America in the immigrant imagination—namely, the global city of New York—Namaste.com participates in a troubling narrative of transnational, patriarchal desire—a desire that inscribes the nation on the bodies of its women. The fine print invites us to believe that, thanks to the services of the shopping site, immigrant women can maintain their "Indian" traditions and cultural practices in their transnational locations. However, the fetishized body of the classic Indian woman, when read in conjunction with the slogan "Bring India home," reveals a more complex story. By inviting the gaze of the viewer along with the suggestion that both India and its women are just a click away—from being brought home—the advertisement presents a gendered space of the nation for symbolic consumption. By adorning the women with fine clothes and jewelry, along with traditional markers of Hindu identity such as the *bindi*, in this particular instance Namaste.com inscribes the nation on the bodies of Hindu middle-class women. By literally and figuratively foregrounding the latter in a quintessentially "American" location, the site presents the middle-class, Hindu, female body as symbolically central to NRIs and PIOs in the United States. In this context, the juxtaposition of the leisurely activity of *mehendi* application with the dynamic image of transnational flows of capital, icons, people, and products is particularly significant. Locating women at the site of consumption, leisure, ritual, and the domestic, Namaste.com offers a gender-centered, class-based, and religion-centric discourse of labor, family, and nation in transnational settings. It constructs a homology where middle-class Hindu femininity is articulated to issues of consumption, labor, the private, and national, while middle-class Hindu masculinity is linked to issues of production, capital, the public, and transnational.

Adding another layer of complexity is the play on the word "home" in the slogan "Bring India Home!" On the one hand, there is the implication that India can be brought to one's home, the space of the domestic and familial; on the other hand, there is the suggestion that one can bring India to the new "homeland" of the NRI and PIO—the elite locations of America and the world, symbolized by New York. And last but not least, there is the innovative idea that India can be brought to its new home in cyberspace, thanks to the online community of Namaste.com. In this representation is the promise that India is virtually everywhere, in no small measure due to the success of its "digerati" and diaspora.

The slogan further raises another set of complex questions, such as: What does the idea of home mean? How are notions of the domestic and the "private," traditionally associated with the idea of home, articulated to the "public" domain of the nation? The advertising campaign for NRI banking on the very popular Rediff.com (http://us.rediff.com), a Mumbai-based site owned by Rediff India Ltd., offers some insights on these and related questions.

During 2002–2003, the users of the NRI Finance Channel on Rediff .com were treated to an unusual advertisement when they clicked on a link entitled "Know more about ICICI Bank" on the channel's main page. The advertisement featured Bollywood superstar Amitabh Bachchan, who greeted users with a warm smile and the following words, "You've always been proud of Indian culture, cuisine and heritage. Well, it's time to add banking to the list!"[12] The advertisement was unusual in part because it was arguably the first time that Amitabh Bachchan had been featured on a Web advertisement targeting NRIs, but more so given the fact that he was endorsing "Indian banking" as a fitting addition to the pantheon of the best of India, including its culture, cuisine, and heritage. Bachchan's new avatar on Rediff.com was as the cultural ambassador for the Industrial Credit and Insurance Company of India (ICICI) Bank, a leader within the banking industry.

A central factor shaping the mobility of home territories in present times is the flexible and innovative pattern of transnational capital flows. These patterns demonstrate the limits of nation-states in controlling economic flows across national borders. At the same time, the new configurations of capital flows are engendering flexible strategies within nation-states as they reinvent themselves in an effort to participate more effectively in the competitive global marketplace. One such strategy used by the Indian nation-state in recent times is to extend an unprecedented level of financial and investment incentives to NRIs. Given the Web's potential to target transnational users, it is no surprise that highly competitive private banks in India were the first, and arguably the most successful, institutions to target NRIs with e-banking and financial investment opportunities. And no bank has done it better than ICICI Bank.

ICICI Bank sponsors the NRI Finance Channel on Rediff.com. In the mid-1990s, the site primarily targeted users in India. However, the parent company was quick to take note of the massive number of hits from users in the United States and soon introduced the Rediff USA edition of the site. One of the highlights of the new edition is the NRI Finance Channel sponsored by ICICI Bank. Users are invited to "Come, be a part of the ICICI bank family!"[13] by exploring three services in particular—banking, money2India, and home loans. While the banking service offers NRIs flexible plans for creating and maintaining ICICI money accounts in India, it is the money2India and home loans services that are of particular significance to the present discussion.

In early 2003, the bank launched its money2India e-transfer service. An upgrade from the regular money2India service, which involved time-consuming paperwork, the e-transfer service promised unprecedented convenience and speed in transnational financial services: "A completely online and paperless way of transferring money to India. No branch visits, no posting of cheques. Just issue us your instructions online from your home or office! You can transfer money free to any ICICI Bank account or issue a bank demand draft at more than 670 locations."[14]

For NRIs, e-transfer provides a refreshing change from the antiquated methods of existing money transfer services. More importantly, it allows them to "send money home at express speed." When read in light of the four- to six-week timeframe for earlier transactions, the instantaneity of the cyber-transaction reinvents the very act of repatriating money to one's home.

Furthermore, in place of home as "here" and "there" (invoked by the earlier methods), the "express speed" of e-transfer links the U.S. and Indian homes of the NRI within a narrative of the here and now. It also reinvents the identity of ICICI, India's national bank, within a discourse of the transnational, represented through its cyberhome, U.S.–based clientele, and globally competitive financial practices.

Equally significant is ICICI Bank's advertising campaign for its home loan service, which assures the NRI that "a dream home in your homeland is a definite possibility."[15] While ICICI's home loans are "fast to apply and even easier to get!" its online database of the entire real estate market in India makes the ICICI method "the most convenient way of finding [one's] dream home."[16] The bank's role in this instance is to realize the NRI's dream, which goes beyond fulfilling his financial obligations toward his family in India (the money2India service takes care of that). The dream, we are told, involves a brick-and-mortar structure in the land he once called home. Framing the advertising campaign are the image and caption that appear on the homepage of ICICI's NRI services on Rediff.com—a beaming father–son duo gazing into a computer screen while the caption states, "Welcome back to where you belong: feel at home anywhere in the world with a range of services to meet your every financial requirement."[17]

The image and caption are significant on many levels. On the one hand, the relatively comfortable, wired, living space of the father–son duo who stands in for the NRI family allows for a middle-class, techno-savvy masculinity to be sutured effortlessly to ideologies of familial, national, and migrant identities. In welcoming NRIs "back" to where they belong, ICICI conflates the cybernetic space of ICICI, a veritable institution in India, with the national home. Therefore one can feel at home by entering ICICI Bank's virtual space. More importantly, it implies that, for the Indian who resides abroad, the act of being at home is mediated through the digital worlds of one of India's leading financial institutions. To fulfill his dreams and obligations, the NRI has to return to where he belongs: the ICICI family (where he is welcomed, of course). It is suggested that fulfillment of the NRI's financial obligations toward his home and family in India is possible only when he enters into a different kind of financial commitment with the ICICI "family." Hence, the young man and his progeny can feel at home while residing in the United States because, through their acts of investing in ICICI and their loved ones in India, they experience a sense of belonging. Thus home, homeland, and homepage are entangled in the discourse of belonging on Rediff.com's Finance Channel sponsored by ICICI Bank. By framing NRI familial relationships within a web of financial obligations, Rediff.com's Finance Channel and ICICI offer an economically reductive discourse of nation, family, and the migrant condition.

Offering a very different perspective on the idea of "home" is Drumnation.org (www.drumnation.org), the cyberhome of Desis Rising Up and Moving (DRUM), an organization devoted to the struggles and issues facing working-class and poor South Asian immigrants in New York. "Desi" is South Asian, Hindi terminology that stands for "those from the homeland." Within South Asian communities, it is common to refer to each other as Desis. DRUM grew out of a community education project involving the South Asian youth of Jackson Heights, Queens. Unlike the previously discussed examples from Namaste.com and Rediff.com, Drumnation.org targets members of the Indian diaspora but is not limited to them.

There is an institutional distinction between the sites. Namaste.com and Rediff.com are commercially sponsored. They are supported primarily by their advertising, sponsorship, and tie-in related revenues. Much like the institutional politics of old media where, for example, the commercial aspects of television often shaped its mainstream appeal, the advertising-driven content of Namaste.com and Rediff.com predominantly reinforce the mainstream discourse on nation and migration in the diaspora.

Drumnation.org, however, is an example of a nonprofit community site that foregrounds a marginalized viewpoint within the Indian and South

Asian diaspora, one that reveals rather than erases the key distinctions in class and location within the immigrant community.

The institutional distinctions between the sites have key implications for understanding the politics of the diverse representations of "home" on the Indian-American Web. For example, Rediff.com is a highly visible site within the community. Advertisements for the site are featured regularly in the Indian-American print media. The site's parent company, Rediff India Ltd., recently acquired a leading Indian-American newspaper, *India Abroad*, and what has ensued is a synergistic alliance between Rediff.com and *India Abroad*. Rediff.com also makes itself visible in the community by sponsoring cultural events in the United States. Similarly, Namaste.com is part of larger network enterprise aimed at the "ethnic" market in the United States. The site's parent company, Ethnicgrocer Inc., was started up by a group of Indian-American entrepreneurs in 1998 and also hosts the popular Ethnic-grocer.com (www.ethnicgrocer.com), which targets the ethnic market at large, and Gongshee.com aimed primarily at the Chinese diaspora. While a network of commercial alliances bestows a high visibility and potentially greater reach to Rediff.com and Namaste.com, Drumnation.org relies on local networks of working-class activists to make its political project visible within the community. Drumnation.org clearly lacks the financial clout and high-profile visibility of the commercial sites discussed previously, and as the following discussion reveals, the representation of "home" on its homepage differs greatly from those on the other sites. However, it is precisely the site's relative marginality within the dominant commercial framework of the Indian-American Web as well as its alternative framework of imagining "home" that makes it imperative to include Drumnation.org (and similar sites) within the present analysis of home, homeland, and homepage on the Indian-American Web. The alternative perspective not only makes visible the constructed nature of the hegemonic but also equally importantly reveals the key links between capital, institutions, and ideologies.

For Drumnation.org, it is the idea of the South Asian, rather than Indian, Bangladeshi, or Pakistani, that is pivotal to the identity of a working-class and poor migrant from South Asia. The grassroots organization aims to mobilize "low-income South Asian immigrants for racial, economic and social justice on critical local struggles and their global roots."[18] Drumnation.org's struggle is against the American state and the mainstream that participate in the oppression of working-class immigrants, as well as the "conservative trends particular to South Asian immigrant communities, particularly, the facets of racism, patriarchy, class oppression and communalism."[19] In addition to building alliances with progressive forces in other minority communities, DRUM's strategy includes using media to mobilize support for its agenda.

Although Drumnation.org acknowledges that South Asia includes diverse nations, its dominant perception is that South Asian immigrants share a regional identity and common history that is reinforced under different circumstances within mainstream America; when it comes to the working class, the "Indian immigrant" is not differentiated from his or her Pakistani or Sri Lankan counterpart—both are low-income "brown" folk. In addition, in a neighborhood such as Jackson Heights, it is their common South Asian identity that marks the "Indian" immigrant and the "Bangladeshi" immigrant apart from their neighbors; in other words, it matters little if one is from India or Bangladesh, since it is one's regional affiliation to South Asia that becomes the marker of one's ethnic and racial identity within mainstream America.

Drumnation.org highlights the struggles and the politics of working-class South Asians who labor as immigrants in the United States. The organization's grassroots politics necessitate a shift from the India-centric, middle-class, nationalist discourse of the NRI and PIO to a regional, working-class perspective on "the spaces of belonging" that ultimately constitute the place called home. It is belonging to the same neighborhood—of the South Asian region in the world and the working-class, migrant locations of global cities such as New York—that shapes their sense of being at home. For the members of Drumnation.org, a collective sense of belonging is engendered precisely by their marginalized locations within the national imaginings of the United States and the countries of South Asia.

Mobilizing on similar issues of marginality and conservative nationalist practices is the cyber, membership-based South Asian Women's Network (SAWNET; www.sawnet.org). Through a series of discursive formats, including e-mail, discussion forums, debates, opinions, creative writing, and information pieces, members foreground issues that are relevant to them as South Asian women. As with Drumnation.org, South Asia at large rather than India in particular is the focus of the network; however, in the process of opening up a dialogue about South Asian women's issues, the status and struggles of women in and from India are addressed often. Some of the issues discussed relate to media representation, political activism, legal matters, marriage, divorce, parenting, health, sexuality, domestic violence, and the workplace. The picture that emerges from the diverse viewpoints reveals the complexity of the issues addressed and, equally importantly, highlights the political, legal, domestic, technological, and economic practices that shape the dominant narratives about "Indian" women as well as those that disrupt them.

For example, SAWNET has a link to sakhi.com (www.sakhi.com), the homepage of Sakhi, a New York–based South Asian organization offering support to women facing domestic abuse. Creating a virtual link to organizations addressing the problem of domestic violence, tackling the subject of domestic abuse in middle-class NRI and PIO households, SAWNET participates in the demystification of the ideal "Indian immigrant family."[20] It disrupts the conservative notion that domestic violence occurs only in working-class and poor immigrant households. Highlighting the links between domestic abuse, patriarchy, and the shifting gender roles due to changes such as the growing economic power of women, SAWNET remarks on the ways in which politics, culture, and economics are deeply implicated in the ways in which women experience their everyday lives. It also foregrounds the difficulty of imagining one nation for differently gendered subjects when the immigrant family, a microcosm of the patriarchal "public" nation, writes violence and coercion into the narratives of women's lives in the familiar, intimate space of the "private" home.

The women of SAWNET produce an alternative to the national community by revealing the common thread of gendered nationalisms in South Asia and articulating community to a set of shared practices that transgress national borders and boundaries. Here, exemplifying Morley's insightful remarks in *Home Territories*, South Asia also bears less on a geographical than a rhetorical territory. Furthermore, the very act of creating and maintaining a cyberhome where diverse representations of South Asian women thrive destabilizes the hegemonic discourse of gendered technologies, where passive consumption rather than active negotiation marks the dominant relationship of women to media, communication, and technologies.

Interrogating Nation and Migration

This section locates the politics of the diverse representations of home on the Web within the emergent discourses of nation, family, and community within NRI and PIO groups in the United States. It argues that the discourses in turn destabilize the hegemony of the NRI and PIO as representative figures of a group shaped by different contexts of migration, belonging, and citizenship.

The representations of home in the first two examples discussed—namely, the Namaste.com advertisement and ICICI Bank's services on Rediff.com's NRI finance page—clearly work toward maintaining the hegemony of a middle-class, gendered Indian nationalism in immigrant locales. Common to both representations is the depiction of the immigrants' location within America; while the "Indian" women of Namaste.com are juxtaposed against the transnational capital flows of Times Square, the familial duty-bound NRI of Rediff.com is ensconced within his network-ready home. Both representations present their target users as part of the transnational elite, whose interaction with America is limited to its technological and financial domains. The politics of silencing framing such a representation makes the discourse of the gendered nation and cultural belonging through the idea of "home" all the more significant.

Seen in conjunction with each other, Namaste.com and Rediff.com participate in a discourse of nation and family where women are in charge of maintaining "Indian" culture and tradition in the private space of the household, while the men sustain the nation in its technological and financial domains. Although the women of Namaste.com are framed against the dizzying pace of life in Times Square, they seem impervious to their surroundings. Instead it is leisure, tradition, the private, and the feminine symbolized by the practice of *mehendi* application that has them engrossed. By contrast, Rediff.com's father–son duo at the computer screen are active participants in the public domain of technology networks and transnational capital flows. In this instance, it is the network-ready computer that mediates the location of the NRI men within the "private" household and the "public" homeland.[21] Their participation within technological and financial domains thus sustains both the individual household and the collective homeland. Primarily investing the men with expertise in the technological and financial worlds and the women with a desire for tradition and leisure, Namaste.com and Rediff.com deny the histories of women's participation in the technological and financial realms.

They construct a gendered divide between the "public" masculine worlds of technology and finance and the "private" feminine realm of the household and the private. Further, such a reductive discourse on gender is problematic for denying the complex ways in which the technological and financial are deeply implicated in the realms of the domestic and the social.

While the Rediff.com page is clearly addressed to the NRI, the classic "Indian woman" in the Namaste.com ad[22] targets both NRIs and PIOs. By inviting the viewer to "Bring India Home!" the advertising campaign speaks to a trend where the cybernetworks of matrimonial sites and the social networks of extended family and friends in the "homeland" are mobilized to find suitably "cultured" brides in India for NRI and PIO grooms in the United States.

Furthermore, the gendered discourse on nation, family, and technology is inflected by a middle-class, Hindu bias. While a Hindu identity is subtly suggested through the women's attire, *bindi*, and other embellishments, their class location as well as that of the father–son duo is represented more clearly through their access to technology and capital as well as their upwardly mobile location in a transnational context. On the one hand, the recasting of the women in the diaspora as Indian, arguably Hindu women, speaks to the reworking of hegemonic nationalist thought in transnational locales. It recalls Partha Chatterjee's argument that the hegemonic project of nation building in colonial India relied on the construct of the middle-class Hindu woman in the domestic sphere as a sign for nation in colonial India.[23] On the other hand, the recasting of the men in the diaspora as essentially Indian foregrounds a strategic alliance in the making between the elites in the Indian state and diaspora. Rediff.com speaks to this alliance by casting the male NRI aspiration to be that of financial security for his extended family and a dream home for himself in the homeland. Both ventures involve making a financial investment in India, an idea that is being aggressively promoted by the Indian state. As stated previously, historically the Indian state has been indifferent toward its expatriates; however, in recent years, economic pragmatism above all else has made the state do an about-face and woo the financially powerful sections of the diaspora.[24]

In the wake of its newfound love of diaspora, the Indian state has introduced a series of economic reforms that in effect make it easier for Indian citizens residing abroad as well as foreign citizens of Indian descent to participate in the financial and cultural domains of the nation.[25] Interestingly, many of the elites are more than happy to do so, given their own agendas to shape India's political and economic future. Moving away from the traditional rhetoric about the diaspora's role in draining the nation of its resources, former prime minister of India Atal Behari Vajpayee has on many occasions expressed the nation's pride at the achievements of its "extended family."[26] In 2003, Vajpayee, a member of the staunchly nationalist Bharatiya Janata Party (BJP), announced that January 9 would be celebrated as *Pravasi Bharatiya Divas* (Indians Residing Abroad Day). At the inaugural celebrations in 2003, Vajpayee announced plans to grant dual citizenship to the expatriate community based in seven countries around the world.[27] While those based in Australia, Canada, New Zealand, the United Arab Emirates, the United Kingdom, and the United States are among the chosen few, notable exceptions include those based in Africa, Fiji, and Trinidad. Given the fact that Indians migrated to Fiji long before New York became the center of the Indian migrants' imagination, the state's current stance reeks of economic pragmatism, cultural insensitivity, and little else.[28]

By offering a reductive narrative on a complex and diverse community of people shaped by migration, Namaste.com and Rediff.com participate in the construction of the hegemonic discourse of the NRI and the PIO as representative figures of the community. It is, nonetheless, a discourse that is made vulnerable in light of alternative imaginings of the migrant condition, experience, and context.

Drumnation.org offers an interesting counterpoint in part because it reframes migration not along national lines but along those of similar histories and life trajectories. In defining "Desi" on the homepage, the organizers state especially that while South Asian ancestry is one definition of the term, it includes "people who share a common history of colonization" and "people who have origins in the Indian Subcontinent" as well as "Guyana, Trinidad, and the diaspora."[29] The special mention of Guyana and Trinidad is especially significant in light of the fact that the Indian state's promise of dual citizenship to the diaspora conspicuously excludes PIOs in Guyana and Trinidad. The history of Indian immigration to Guyana and Trinidad is marked predominantly by the voluntary and involuntary relocation of working-class and poor Indians, many of whom served as indentured labor for the British Empire.[30] In making a deliberate mention of the history of oppression, working-class conditions, and migrant struggles shaping one of the historically first diasporic communities of India and South Asia, Drumnation.org articulates the commonalities of an immigrant experience around issues of class oppression and racial discrimination; equally important, it articulates the commonality around the sense of being outside the national narratives of the United States as well as those of the South Asian countries. By ignoring its PIO citizens in Guyana and Trinidad, for example, the Indian nation is doing precisely that—ignoring the complicated, often grim, histories of Indian emigration and extending a homecoming welcome only to the contemporary elites of the diaspora.

Drumnation.org foregrounds some of the class and racial struggles of NRIs and PIOs and in the process calls attention to a growing trend in the diaspora where the NRI and PIO are stereotyped as affluent, highly educated, skilled professionals and where the conservative politics of the few are being used increasingly to shut out any discussion of the workings of race, class, and gender, for example, in everyday living contexts. The site also makes the crucial point that the idea of India is not as central as conservative voices in the community would have us believe; for those routinely marginalized by the nation, it is a critical political stance toward the nation, rather than an uncritical celebration, that is a potential outcome.

It is a similar outlook that frames SAWNET's engagement with women's issues. By addressing the issue of domestic violence—for example, in middle-class NRI and PIO households—SAWNET contaminates the idealized images of Indian sexualized femininity and the caring, responsible "family" man represented on sites such as Namaste.com and Rediff.com respectively. Seen in relation to each other, these representations together bring to the fore repression from the harsh enactment of patriarchal power, as well as the violence and pain inscribed on the minds and bodies of the women within the idealized NRI and PIO families.

The significance of disrupting the ideal by offering alternative representations is better understood when located in relation to conservative trends within the community. An example of such a trend is the concern expressed by Kanwal Rekhi, a prominent member of the PIO community, over current U.S. immigration policy. Rekhi, described by one journalist as "the unofficial but quite undisputed godfather of Silicon Valley's Indian mafia"[31] is known for using his financial and professional clout to gain greater visibility with the elite political circles of India and the United States. Rekhi, who emigrated from India to the United States in the 1970s, recently noted that the entry of "poor quality" immigrants such as taxi drivers and "nonprofessionals" posed a serious threat to the political advancement of American citizens of Indian descent (PIOs) such as himself within mainstream America.[32] In particular, he denounced the 1965 family reunification clause, the cornerstone of immigration policy in the United States, which permitted family members of working immigrants to be reunited in the host country. In Rekhi's view, the clause enabled the entry of poor-quality immigrants who, he fears, might trigger a mainstream American backlash against presumably good-quality immigrants such as himself.

Rekhi's problematic views on labor, transnational mobility, and citizenship are complicit with the elitist biases of the Indian and American states. While the Indian state's recent turn to the diaspora has been primarily an

acknowledgment of the latter's economic and cultural elites, the visa clas-
sifications under current U.S. immigration policy imply a qualitative divide
between the high and low skills of foreign labor. Furthermore, by implying
that working-class elements within the community are the real obstacles
to greater participation within mainstream America, Rekhi, like many of
his peers, continues to ignore the crucial ways in which issues of race and
ethnicity shape such participation, or lack thereof.

Conclusion

This chapter has examined four key representations of "home" on what
has been called the Indian-American Web. The latter refers to the network
of corporations, nonprofit organizations, and individuals in India and the
United States since the 1990s, which have been forging a set of transnational
alliances across the traditional boundaries of the Indian and the American
nation-state, engendering in the process the dynamic Indian-American Web.
It also contends that this Web emerged in the 1990s to target two key constituencies of the broadly defined "Indian diaspora" in the United States—
namely, the NRI and PIO. Both categories emerged within a financially
motivated discourse of the Indian state but have a popular appeal within
sections of the diaspora.

By examining the representations of home on Namaste.com, Rediff
.com, Drumnation.org, and SAWNET, it has been argued that the Web
participates in the construction as well as the disruption of the hegemonic
notions of NRI and PIO identities by articulating diverse imaginations of
home—such as household, homeland, and homepage—to the cultural, economic, and political discourses of nation, family, and community. The examples from Namaste.com and Rediff.com reveal a nexus between a Hindu,
middle-class, gendered nationalism and idealized narratives about the NRI
and the PIO.

In this context, the intersections between the politics of old media such
as television and new media such as the Web are worth noting. In a sophisticated analysis of media, Hindu nationalism, and public culture in contemporary India, Arvind Rajagopal argues that the BJP skillfully used the
televised Hindu epic *Ramayan* (1987–89) to mobilize support for its Hindu
nationalist agenda, which included the controversial Ram Janmabhumi
temple-restoration project. In an influential study of Doordarshan, India's
state-run television, Purnima Mankekar argues that the televised Hindu

religious epic *Mahabharat* (1988–90) became the site for the construction and contestation of narratives about the nation, women, citizenship, and identity at a time of social and cultural upheaval.[33]

Locating Rajagopal's and Mankekar's insightful analyses of television in India within the present discussion about the politics of nation, family, and community on the Indian-American Web reveals that new media technologies often act in tandem with old media technologies. On the one hand, the Indian-American Web's participation in the construction of a gendered nationalism and a Hindu-centric, middle-class "Indian" immigrant identity during a period of increasing transnational mobility of capital, people, and ideas keenly echoes the politics of television in India during a period of economic liberalization, growing consumerism, and greater participation of women in the workplace. On the other hand, sites such as Drumnation .org and SAWNET contribute to a disruption of idealized images of "the immigrant" by foregrounding alternative ways of imagining identity, belonging, and community in their current location in the United States.

In the past decade, the Web has emerged as a crucial space for the enactment of the desires and struggles of a diverse community loosely defined as the Indian diaspora in the United States. Studying the Indian-American Web is not only essential to understand better the contemporary politics and practices of such a community but is eminently relevant to discussions about cyberspace, community, and transnational mobility in our world today.

Notes

1. Indolink NRI Services "Persons of Indian origin-card scheme," http://www .indolink.com/consulate/pio.html (accessed January 2003); D. Nayyar, *Migration, Remittances and Capital Flows: The Indian Experience* (New Delhi: Oxford University Press, 1994).

2. Nayyar, *Migration, Remittances*.

3. Mihir Desai, Devesh Kapur, and John McHale "The fiscal impact of high-skilled emigration flows of Indians to the U.S.," November 2002 http:// www.people.hbs .edu/mdesai/fiscalimpact.pdf (accessed March 2003); K. Murali, "The IIT story: Issues and concerns," *Frontline* 20, no. 3 (2003), http://www.flonnet.com/fl2003/ stories/20030214007506500.htm (accessed March 2003).

4. Desai, Kapur, and McHale, "The fiscal impact"; A. Saxenian, *Silicon Valley's New Immigrant Entrepreneurs* (Berkeley: University of California Press, 2001).

5. V. Anand, "Do not abolish the H1–B visa," http://www.sulekha.com/petitions/ petition.asp?cid=34 July 2003 (accessed July 2003), discussed in http://www.sulekha .com/COLLATERAL/press/prel_cnn.aspx; A. Bora, "Online outrage: American

citizens use the Web to protest against outsourcing and non-immigrant visas," http://www.rediff.com/netguide/2003/jun/23bpo.htm (accessed July 2003).

6. V. Arora, "India sends highest number of students to US universities," IANS, 18 November 2002, http://www.siliconindia.com/shownews/India_sends_highest_number_of_students_to_US_universities-nid-17624.html (accessed January 2003).

7. Karen Leonard, *The South Asian Americans* (Westport, CT: Greenwood Press, 1997); D. Reimers, *Still the Golden Door: The Third World Comes to America* (New York: Columbia University Press, 1985).

8. David Morley, *Home Territories: Media, Mobility and Identity* (London: Routledge, 2000), 2–3.

9. Doreen Massey, "A place called home," *New Formations* 17, no. 9 (1992): 9.

10. Massey, "A place called home," 13.

11. "Namaste.com: Bring India home," *Siliconindia* 4, no. 7 (2000): 69.

12. Rediff NRI Finance Channel, "Know more about ICICI Bank," http://nrifinance.rediff.com/knowmore.asp (accessed January 2002).

13. Rediff NRI Finance Channel, "Know more."

14. Rediff NRI Finance Channel, "Money2India," http://nrifinance.Rediff.com/money2india.asp (accessed February 2003).

15. Rediff NRI Finance Channel, "Home loans and home search," http://nrifinance.rediff.com/homeloans.asp (accessed January 2002).

16. Rediff NRI Finance Channel, "Home loans."

17. Rediff NRI Finance Channel, "NRI services," http://nrifinance.rediff.com/ (accessed January 2002).

18. DRUM, "Desis Rising Up and Moving," http:// www.drumnation.org/drum.html (accessed January 2003).

19. DRUM, "Vision and history," http://www.drumnation.org/drum/vision.html (accessed January 2003).

20. SAWNET, "Domestic violence," http://www.sawnet.org/orgns/violence.php (accessed March 2002).

21. Morley, *Home Territories*.

22. "Namaste.com: Bring India home," *Siliconindia*.

23. Partha Chatterjee, *The Nation and Its Fragments: Colonial and Postcolonial Histories* (Princeton, NJ: Princeton University Press, 2003).

24. Nayyar, *Migration, Remittances*; N. Lakshman, "The money movers: With a growing Indian diaspora, banks and new-age players are pulling out all stops to bag the remittance business," *India Abroad*, April 11, 2003, B3.

25. R. Lakshmi, "India reaches out to emigrants: Millions living abroad encouraged to invest in homeland," *Washington Post*, January 12, 2003, A21, http://www.indianembassy.org/US_Media/2003/jan/washingtonpost_com%20India%20Reaches%20Out%20oto%20Emigrants.htm (accessed March 2003).

26. Lakshmi, "India reaches out."

27. J. Joseph, "Dual citizenship likely for people of Indian origin," *India Abroad*, January 10, 2003, A1.

28. A. Ali, *From Plantation to Politics: Studies on Fiji Indians* (Suva: University of the South Pacific/Fiji Times & Herald, 1980).

29. DRUM, "Desis Rising Up and Moving."

30. Ali, *From Plantation to Politics*.

31. M. Warner, "The Indians of Silicon Valley," *Business 2.0*, http://www.business2 .com/articles/mag/0,1640,7764,00.html (accessed April 2003).

32. S. Din, "Kanwal Rekhi takes up Immigration issue," http://www.rediff.com/ news/2001/apr/28us1.htm (accessed November 2002).

33. Arvind Rajagopal, *Politics after Television: Hindu Nationalism and the Reshaping of the Public in India* (Cambridge: Cambridge University Press, 2001); Purnima Mankekar, *Screening Culture, Viewing Politics: An Ethnography of Television, Womanhood, and Nation in Postcolonial India* (Durham, NC: Duke University Press, 1999).

FOUR

Transnational Brides: Wedding Magazines and the Invention of a Cosmopolitan Indian Tradition

Sujata Moorti

After Bollywood films and cricket, notes Sujata Moorti, weddings are the third passion of India. Given the globalization of Bollywood and the millions of Indians living overseas, it is no surprise that Indian weddings have gone transnational as well. Using multimedia platforms, including glossy magazines and the Internet, wedding planners and consultants have helped families inside and outside India realize their dreams for lavish weddings that look and feel like those depicted in many Bollywood blockbusters. Despite modern forms of communication, sophisticated marketing practices, and the highly commodified matrimonial events, Moorti shows that the wedding industry ultimately uses the female body—as media representation and as an actual laborer in the wedding industry—to construct Indian values that are quite traditional.

Indian weddings appear to have become a recurring concern of diasporic filmmakers in the new century. Whether it is Mira Nair's blockbuster hit *Monsoon Wedding* (2001) or Gurinder Chadha's crossover failure *Bride and Prejudice* (2004), these cinematic representations focus on opulent, colorful, "exotic," spectacular weddings and appear to be replicating a trend that has predominated the Indian movie industry for the past fifteen years. There is one significant difference marking the movies from the West: They depict weddings as a primary vector connecting India with the immigrant communities residing in the United States and the United Kingdom. This chapter highlights diasporic media representations of wedding practices. However, such an examination of Indian diasporic media is impossible without examining Indian media and wedding practices in the homeland. In addition, this is a multimedia analysis of wedding representational practices and is not limited to either print or cinematic depictions. These two aspects, which allow my chapter to straddle continents and media sites, are constitutive of diasporic media practices.

Both *Monsoon Wedding* and *Bride and Prejudice* highlight the lives of transnationally mobile Indian families and the glamorous weddings they plan; any critiques they offer of the institution of weddings are muted by the glossy spectacles they offer.[1] Ali Kazimi's documentary *Runaway Grooms* (2005) offers a new vantage point from which to examine diasporic wedding practices, particularly the exploitative and ugly aspects of such transnational traffic. The film documents an innovative and lucrative money-making scheme deployed by Indian Canadians who tap into some of the structural and institutional fault lines of South Asian marriages. The men go to India, often on a holiday, to marry "authentic" Indian women, staging a clichéd diasporic narrative of the female as the bearer of tradition.[2] Once married, the men return alone to Canada with sizeable sums of money provided by the bride's family to ensure their daughters could obtain the necessary immigration documents. However, once the ugly narrative of dowry extortion has run its course, the men file for divorce in Canadian courts. Since the women lack visas, they cannot be present in court to contest the hearings and the marriages end. The men are then free to get remarried and extract resources, human and material, from India once again. This movie captures many of the aspects that continue to structure Indian ideas of marriage and conjugality, issues that I address in this chapter. In the diaspora, notions of authenticity and cultural purity become associated with women and the homeland, and men are thus compelled to return to India to find their brides. Marriage continues to be a defining feature of Indian women's lives, and divorce is considered ruinous for their reputations. Although family structures in the diaspora are significantly different from those in India, parents continue to play a pivotal role in organizing marriages.[3]

The forms of tradition enabled by transnational weddings as represented by the three films I have described (and there are numerous others) capture the centrality of weddings in the South Asian diasporic experience. Examining the representational practices of wedding media outlets, those geared toward an Indian audience and those toward a diasporic audience in the United States and the United Kingdom—what Vijay Mishra has termed the second diaspora[4]—the media have become primary conduits through which a cosmopolitan Indian tradition is constituted. My analysis works against the background of globalization processes and explores how Indian and diasporic media traffic in tradition and how they have helped, to borrow a phrase from Eric Hobsbawm, "invent" a cosmopolitan Indian tradition, one that gains its traction and saliency from marriages.[5] Through this invented tradition, which is inherently quite malleable, India and things Indian are cathected onto the global. The seemingly oxymoronic term *cosmopolitan Indian tradition* is used to capture the manner in which weddings, a central site of community regeneration, are now being conceptualized simultaneously as Indian and global. In these representational practices, "Indian" weddings become anchored in the transnational. Weddings, whether located in the diaspora or in the subcontinent, become nodes for the transnational traffic in signs and symbols. The cosmopolitan Indian tradition they invent is neither Indian nor Western but is a new brand that borrows promiscuously from the United States, United Kingdom, and India.[6]

This analysis is primarily about media representations of weddings but these practices have also altered lived practices in the diaspora as well as in the subcontinent. Indian journalists have argued that "the big fat Indian wedding" has migrated from screen to everyday life and has altered the wedding landscape in India.[7] Through reiteration and global dispersal, the cosmopolitan Indian tradition has acquired the status of the normative. In particular, relying on Foucault's theories of the power of discursive formations, I illustrate that the cosmopolitan "traditional" wedding is no longer simply commonplace but has become normative. Despite the veneer of change signaled by the cosmopolitan tradition, women continue to be the central focus of weddings. In the first section of the chapter, the commodification processes that characterize contemporary Indian weddings are explored. In the second section, by focusing on media practices, the modalities through which "global" elements enter in the staging of the wedding are highlighted. In the third section, by focusing on women's roles in enabling this cosmopolitan Indian tradition, I re-inscribe gender in globalization processes. Women figure centrally in media representations of weddings in their dual capacity as brides and as laborers whose work is often marginalized. In the final section of the chapter, the cultural work conducted by women's invisible labor and the material significance of this cosmopolitan Indian tradition is examined.

The Big Fat Desi Wedding

In recent years, some Desi weddings have captured world headlines because of their opulence.[8] For instance, the steel magnate Lakshmi Mittal, a Non-Resident Indian (NRI) from London, is estimated to have spent over US$55 million on his daughter's wedding in 2004. Another Indian businessman, Subroto Roy, spent $128 million on his two sons' weddings the same year.[9] For their extravagance, these and other weddings became part of the news cycle. The weddings themselves stretched out over several days; guests were ferried to different sites in private jets, and the monies expended on different aspects of the weddings were closely scrutinized by journalists. These and other opulent weddings have become the focus of Discovery India's 13-part series *The Great Indian Wedding* as well as a six-week series on BBC World entitled *The Wedding Business*.[10] Weddings offer a useful entry point from which one can observe India's participation in the global economy. They also render visible the rugged capitalism that has taken hold of the Indian economy. Scholars such as Leela Fernandes and Arvind Rajagopal have pointed out that commodity culture and consumption have become key signifiers of India's participation in the global economy.[11] They contend that media images present extravagant consumption as a condensation symbol for India's relationship with the world economy. I expand on these insights to encompass diasporic media and argue that the symbiotic relationship between the diaspora and the homeland results in a media feedback loop. Thus, Indian media practices for signaling an engagement with the world economy are reproduced in diasporic media, but in the context of the second diaspora these signification practices take on a different salience. Weddings in India and in diasporic communities help us uncover powerful models of circuits of movement and the socioeconomic changes encompassing contemporary conditions of globality.

Indian magazines boast that weddings are the third passion of the country, preceded only by Bollywood and cricket.[12] Economists and market researchers proclaim that the annual growth rate of the wedding industry exceeds 25 percent. In 2005, revenues of the wedding industry were estimated to be $11 billion; this figure does not include the money families spend on jewelry, which is also increasing at over 7 percent annually. These statistics underscore that weddings are not an ancillary but rather a primary industry, driving a significant portion of the Indian economy. According to wedding planners, the minimum budget for a well-to-do wedding is $34,000 while the wealthy have been known to spend over $2 million.[13] Once again, these figures do not include cash and valuables given as part of a dowry. Since the average Indian middle-class income ranges between $4,500 and $23,000 per year, banks have started to offer wedding loans and some credit card companies have established separate "auspicious" lines exclusively for weddings.[14]

Some other trends that signal the growing significance of weddings can be seen in the emergence of a wedding-planning industry. This includes a rapidly spiraling number of consultants for every stage of the wedding. In addition, wedding malls have emerged in metropolitan centers that are often also the hub of multinational corporations.[15] For instance, Gurgaon, a city built on new-economy money near New Delhi, is the site of the country's first wedding mall. The $16 million construction houses more than 400 stores that cater to different aspects of the wedding.[16] Eight more wedding malls are under construction around the country. In addition, a growing wedding tourism industry caters to the shopping needs of NRIs and others who want to incorporate "authentic Indian" elements in their weddings. The explosion of highly specialized outlets attending to the different aspects of an Indian wedding testifies to the mode in which the market logic has helped commodify this ritual. The components of the wedding have been fragmented and relegated to highly specialized fields, twin processes that have facilitated commodification processes. Significantly, media representations echo these processes of specialization and fragmentation.

It is noteworthy that the majority of these extravagant weddings are hosted not by royal families or the traditionally rich business communities but rather by "the first-generation rich," comprising industrialists, politicians, real estate moguls, and retail chain owners. The lavish wedding is part of a new economy that attends to the desires and disposable incomes of the postliberalization rich. Consequently, the opulent wedding is an uneven phenomenon, most evident in urban North India, followed by Mumbai and then Kolkata. Although people in the diaspora are shaped by these trends in the subcontinent, the effects are muffled. For instance, in North America, South Asians are estimated to spend between $20,000 and $150,000 on their weddings. In the diaspora, the focus remains on a mix-n-match style with authentic "Indian" signs residing comfortably alongside "Western" traditions, such as the bride clad in a designer sari while cutting a tiered wedding cake. Different elements of the wedding—such as the mode of packing the gift bags for guests or the "heirloom" handmade quilt for the trousseau—are painstakingly planned. In each of these instances, diasporic weddings rework forms and traditions that have already been popularized in the homeland, an East-to-West flow that complicates our understanding of globalization processes.

Within the diaspora, one can trace the practices of the lavish wedding to trends within South Asia as well as within the United States.[17] Sociologists who have studied different aspects of what Chrys Ingraham calls the wedding industry complex offer multiple reasons for the growing popularity of lavish weddings.[18] Some contend that weddings are a visible means by which individuals demonstrate and enhance the quality of their social connections. Extravagant weddings enhance social visibility and help communicate social prestige. Others argue that because a woman's status changes more than a man's following a marriage, she has more need of ritual recognition of the event. More recently scholars have pointed out that in the West, especially in the United States, as the social institution of marriage has become fragile and tenuous, the rituals associated with it have become more elaborate. In the Indian and diasporic contexts, it is this complex of explanations along with the growing participation of South Asians in the global marketplace that account for the phenomenal rise of lavish weddings. Although none of the magazines I examined reveal the reasons for this trend, they do reveal the commodification and fetishization of the wedding.

In the Indian context, elaborate weddings are not new, especially in a country where these ceremonies tend to span several days. Thus, the emergence of lavish weddings among Indians cannot be read simplistically as an indicator of Westernization.[19] Since weddings have always been a key site for the formation of *communitas*, the emergence of the lavish transnational wedding perhaps indicates a longing for the formation of a particular kind of community. In postliberalization India, it is the tenor of the weddings that has changed; every facet of the wedding has been thoroughly commodified. This commodification process reveals the hold capitalism and consumer culture have on Indian public culture.

These processes are most evident in the range of "wedding" media outlets such as wedding magazines, wedding websites, and wedding guides that have emerged over the past decade. *Vivaha*, a quarterly glossy magazine, was founded in 2000 by a former advertising executive. In addition to an Indian readership, *Vivaha* explicitly solicits a readership in the United States, United Kingdom, South Africa, and the Persian Gulf Coast countries. Other wedding magazines that are published in India include *Marwar* (2002), *Shaadi* (2004), and the *Mega Wedding Magazine* (2004). In addition, other women's magazines such as *Femina* now publish separate special wedding issues. In the second diaspora, wedding magazines emerged concurrently. The Houston-based *Bibi* magazine was launched in 2002 to provide "inspiration and guidance for . . . [South Asians] who are settled in countries other than their own." Its contents are designed to "make you and your wedding as spectacular as you had envisioned." Other U.K.–based magazines include *Asian Bride* (2001), *Memsahib* (2003), and *Asiana Wedding Magazine* (2003).[20] In addition, a number of Web portals have been set up to deal exclusively with wedding-related tasks. This includes ABCDlady.com and Indianwedding .com in the United States and Shaadi.ca in Canada. Apart from examining the minutiae of wedding planning, these websites offer visitors some insights into legal concerns.

The majority of wedding magazines and Web portals have established so-called bridal expos that work in conjunction with their materials. The bridal expos, or wedding exhibitions as they are termed in India, highlight the commodification process that engulfs contemporary weddings. These shows and exhibitions are a one-stop wedding shop and cater to all of the features that precede and follow the ritual. They host vendors from all over the world who display wares associated with every aspect of a wedding, including luxury items such as designer watches. Bridal Asia was started in 1995 and is the oldest exhibition space; it is noteworthy because it travels to the major metropolitan centers within the South Asian subcontinent. *Vivaha* magazine launched its own version of the wedding exhibition, Vivaha Expo, in 2003; although it started in Mumbai, it now travels to the metropolitan centers as well as some cities in North India, a region where affluent weddings prevail. The expo Brides & Grooms was established by *Marwar* magazine in 2003 and it follows a trajectory similar to the other two. In recent years, the focus of the exhibitions has shifted quite sharply. Earlier, most of the vendors catered to the jewelry and clothing needs; contemporary expos now offer services such as legal help with prenuptial agreements as well as furniture retailers. Significantly these and other exhibitions have now become global, traveling to major cities in the second diaspora as well. For instance, the organizer of Vivaha Expo explains that the NRI population is a "segment that sets a great store by traditions and takes pride in following all rituals that they have left behind in their mother-country."[21]

Masala Wedding reverses this trajectory. A New Jersey–based bridal expo that was established in 2000, Masala Wedding hosts shows in various North American cities and has since 2005 started to travel to major cities in the subcontinent as well. Asian Wedding Expo is a U.S.–based exhibition with a broader purview that includes the other nations in the South Asian subcontinent. Kismet Wedding Show, Dulhan Expo, Suhaag Show, Bollywood Mandap and Décor Solutions, and Rose Events South Asian Bridal Show are Canada-based expos with a range of different vendors. These expos offer seminars on different aspects of the wedding, host fashion shows, and allow visitors to sample food. Increasingly, all of these exhibitions have become transnational in scope; they travel between different sites in the subcontinent, the second diaspora, and Dubai.[22] I elaborate later on the nature of goods that are exhibited in these expos but want to emphasize here how these sites help fragment and thus commodify the different components that comprise an "Indian" wedding. In press releases, each of these expos noted the increased participation of vendors and the corresponding increase in audience size. While it is impossible to verify these claims, the longevity of these exhibitions and their widening reach testify to their popularity. They also signal the manner in which these commodification processes have become commonplace and central to the wedding ritual.

It is important to note that the lavish Indian wedding and its accompanying commodifying processes are different in tenor from the Western wedding industry, which scholars argue has evolved primarily as a mechanism to shore up the fragility of the heterosexual marriage. The wedding industry instead serves to showcase Indians' ability to skillfully reconcile Indian practices with Western practices; the commodities and consumption practices are signifiers of negotiation and reconciliation processes. I have elaborated on wedding magazines and expos at some length to underscore the point that there are feedback and feed-forward loops between diasporic and Indian media practices. The symbiotic nature of this relationship is heightened by the accelerated transnational circuits that characterize contemporary conditions of globality. A close reading of the contents of wedding magazines demonstrates the Indian and non-Indian elements that have come to characterize weddings. I also highlight the feedback loop that exists between Indian and diasporic wedding media.

The Transnationally Anchored Wedding

All of the magazines I examine in this chapter are published in English and are targeted specifically at an upper-class and upper-middle-class elite audience. As Rachel Dwyer points out, even as the metropolitan middle class is fueling India's economic growth, it is also the group that is least examined by scholars.[23] This chapter functions partially to correct this bias in South Asian scholarship. The magazines emerge from and are consumed by the new metropolitan middle class that Dwyer identifies. Within the diaspora too, wedding magazines are directed at middle-class NRIs rather than laborers. The forms of consumption the magazines privilege as well as the commodities they display are geared specifically toward this elite, transnationally mobile readership. The cosmopolitan Indian tradition these magazines invent is partly a product of this specific readership, but it is also produced through a battery of devices that help reconstitute the weddings themselves. In particular, diasporic and subcontinental representational grammars are analogous; these similarities are structural, grounded in media practices, and the product of a set of conjunctures that are made possible by technologies of globalization. The similarities are neither coincidental nor can they be explained as forms of mimicry.[24] Elsewhere I have argued that diasporic media are characterized by a sideways glance that looks simultaneously at two or more places, India and the home(s) in the West; I have designated this representational grammar of inhabiting several places as a diasporic optic.[25] This mode of looking simultaneously at two or more places is a signature feature of wedding magazines, irrespective of their production site. This optic is produced by the nature of the weddings that the magazines represent and does not pertain to the location in which the magazines are produced, whether in India or the diaspora. Since the constitutive nature of diasporic subjectivity requires an engagement with the Indian homeland, one can expect diasporic magazines to reflect some of the trends exhibited in Indian weddings. However, the nature of transnational commodity culture in India also propels Indian magazines to reflect and amplify trends exhibited in diasporic weddings (and wedding magazines). Diasporic and Indian magazines are caught up in a feedback loop where each offers the other images and a particular visual grammar within which to produce Indian culture.[26]

Some facets of wedding magazine representational practices are isolated in order to underscore the transnational elements that go into the constitution of contemporary weddings. I explore how the space of the wedding is depicted, and how the clothing, food, and marriage rituals combine Indian and Western elements to produce a transnationally anchored wedding.

The location of the wedding and the appearance of that setting have acquired a special significance in wedding magazines. Indian wedding magazines elaborate on "romantic" sites such as refurbished palaces of the erstwhile Indian royalty or exotic locales such as Bali, Sri Lanka, or a chateau in Bordeaux. If readers cannot afford to travel to these sites, the magazines suggest constructing a replica of an Indian palace or a Moroccan street. It is important to note that Indian wedding magazines poach from all sites and all non-Indian elements enter the arena marked as "Western." Often, Indian and non-Indian elements are integrated seamlessly with each other to produce what anthropologist Marc Augé has termed a *nonplace*: "If a place can be defined as relational, historical and concerned with identity, then a space which cannot be defined as relational, or historical, or concerned with identity will be a nonplace."[27] Indian wedding magazines offer locales that are dehistoricized and extracted from local cultures and traditions. Instead, the sites they offer readers are highlighted for their spectacular qualities. Thus, tulips from Holland and orchids from Thailand vie for attention within the same nonplace. For the transnationally mobile elite readership of these magazines, wedding sites—which are simultaneously Indian and non-Indian—are emblematic of the readers' economic access under contemporary conditions of globality.

Diasporic magazines undertake a slightly different maneuver in their presentation of wedding sites. In this instance, the longing for the homeland from within the diaspora helps articulate a spatial location that integrates elements of both the home and India. For instance, *Bibi* featured a North American wedding whose topography is equal parts Western pedestrian— the Hilton Hotel—and Indian exotic—a romanticized homeland of maharajas and maharanis. The nondescript locale of the Hilton is carefully reconfigured as the Mysore Palace, a palace belonging to the ruler of the erstwhile rich, princely state in southern India. Significantly, the location of the Hilton Hotel is not covered up but rather is emphasized. Through imaging practices, these magazines indicate how easily new technologies enable the reproduction of India in the West. Thus, diasporic magazines highlight the presence of "Indian" flowers such as marigolds and jasmine that have been shipped in expressly for the weddings. The diasporic wedding magazines participate in an "autoexoticization" process, as Marta Savigliano has described it. Autoexoticization refers to a process whereby colonial exotic symbols, such as palaces, are recast as contemporary national symbols.[28] As numerous postcolonial scholars have shown, dominant representations of Indian culture—whether in art, history, or sociology—replicate to some extent the presuppositions of Orientalism. Through their emphasis on symbols of the Raj,[29] diasporic wedding magazines are not just re-Orientalizing India but they also help transform objects exoticized in the West into national symbols.

Just as the site of the wedding emanates from two or more places, we find a similar anxious inscription of multiplicity in the realms of dress, food, and entertainment. Since weddings tend to be primarily about the display of the bride, the majority of the pages of these magazines are devoted to a discussion of clothes. Here, the transnational accents, or the juxtaposition of Indian and non-Indian elements, is less pronounced. Indian magazines highlight haute couture "traditional" ensembles. Increasingly, however, the ensembles have moved away from the red color associated with weddings to a broader palate of colors that includes white, which is rarely featured as it is considered inauspicious for weddings. In diasporic magazines, the clothes are very carefully scripted as traditional. Articles highlight the efforts individual brides have undertaken to track down a specific "ethnic" style in India. *Bibi* showcased a wedding where a Punjabi bride traveled to rural Rajasthan to replicate a specific "folk" style for the wedding party's coordinated attire. The non-Indian elements enter into this sartorial process with the decision to have a wedding party as well as selecting coordinated attire for them.

Similarly, both sets of magazines foreground henna ceremonies and other "folk" traditions glamorized in Bollywood, trends that have come to occupy center stage in weddings and have now been recast as essentially Indian. In this instance, as in others where the magazines explicitly invoke tradition, the representational practices cite other media images. In subcontinental and diasporic magazines, Indian elements in the attire and style are produced by tapping into a global warehouse of images characteristic of heritage cinema and tourism advertisements. The India that is created and imagined is aesthetically derived from commodity culture; the Indian "tradition" that is produced is routed through "ethnic" or "folk" cultures. Significantly all of the elements that are endorsed in these magazines can be read narrowly as rituals grounded in Hindu religion.

The mix-n-match, pastiche styles that are prevalent in the wedding site are also on display in discussions of the food to be served. Indian wedding magazines prescribe a multicuisine meal. Thus, Punjabi food is served along with sushi, pad thai, French cuisine, Belgian chocolates, and more recently, multitiered wedding cakes (elements that prevail in diasporic weddings). In diasporic magazines, a pan-Indian identity is produced by offering elements of various regional cuisines haphazardly. The West enters the culinary realm through the mandatory multitiered wedding cake. In this instance, a fictional sense of Indianness is manufactured as a pan-Indian identity and not as a regional identity, which may not be legible in the diaspora.

Although the diasporic magazines invoke a culinary style that is atten-tive to the local and the multiply located subjectivities of NRIs, the Indian wedding magazines display a sensibility that replicates the postliberalization consumer culture prevalent in the subcontinent. Similarly, in the realm of entertainment, Indian wedding magazines often follow the advice offered in *Femina Bride*: "Want a wedding with a difference? Pick some of the must-do trends from Western dos and incorporate them into your Desi ones."[30] Thus Bollywood-style musical performances are presented along with flamenco dancers or "classical" South Indian dancers and Ricky Martin look-alike singers perform at the same wedding. This dizzying mix of elements helps produce a pan-Indian tradition that elicits what Arjun Appadurai has called "nostalgia without memory."[31] Diasporic wedding magazines advocate a similar strategy of pastiche.

These different modalities of incorporating elements from India with non-Indian aspects help forge the cosmopolitan Indian tradition of contem-porary weddings. This newly minted tradition seamlessly sutures a series of romantic, idealized traditional practices with Western idioms. Eric Hobs-bawm has pointed out that invented tradition includes both constructed and formally instituted practices and those emerging in a less easily trace-able manner within a brief and dateable period—a matter of a few years perhaps—that establish themselves with great rapidity. These "invented traditions" are "a set of practices, normally governed by overtly or tacitly accepted rules and of a ritual or symbolic nature, which seek to inculcate certain values and norms of behavior by repetition, which automatically implies continuity with the past."[32] Usually, they try to establish links with a suitable historic past, but their connection with this past is tenuous at best. Invented traditions "are responses to novel situations which take the form of reference to old situations, or which establish their own past by quasi-obligatory repetition."[33] All of these practices reveal the overt and covert processes through which wedding magazines invent a cosmopolitan Indian tradition. This is possible only by making tradition itself into a commodity. The invention of the cosmopolitan tradition also signals the tumultuous social changes enacted by forces of globalization.

In both sets of magazines, the West and Western idioms introduce contemporaneity to an invented Indian tradition, thus providing a cosmopolitan, worldly flavor. India and the West are not positioned as binaries or oppositional categories. In Indian wedding magazines, the West—indeed, the global—becomes a great supermarket full of empty malleable signs. The encounter with the rest of the world is in no sense dialogic but instead is cannibalistic. These representational practices make certain forms of urban consumption normative and utopian, "affirming the values of capitalism yet inverting them into symbols of primitive simplicity and pure emotionality," as Eva Illouz puts it.[34]

In both sets of magazines, the Indian tradition that is invoked is not only an invented commodity but significantly also one that results from a fluidity of global and local idioms. They posit a flexible tradition that can incorporate pliable empty signs from the West that, once routed through the folk and the rural, become varnished with a patina of ethnicity. In Indian weddings, cultural identities or a sense of tradition are increasingly defined and sharpened through new modes of production, consumption, and travel. There is seemingly a repossession of culture, but it is achieved through consumer culture and is mobilized in the interests of the global marketplace.

Unlike in the West, where romance is commodified in weddings, tradition is commodified in South Asian weddings. It is important to note that none of the wedding magazines spend time addressing whether the marriages are nonconsultative and arranged or are based on love. An underlying principle of the wedding magazines is that this is a domain that still belongs to the family. It is a family-centered event and is not about individuals.

The magazines evoke ideals of Indian culture and tradition, subtly Hinduized. Plenitude is naturalized and the pleasures of consumption are linked with the valorization of the family. Wealth is linked with Indian culture and tradition, reflecting "the ease with which the market has been embraced within a matrix of upper-class, traditional, Hindu cultural values, with an appropriate dose of religiosity."[35] Weddings are oriented to an outside, a realm beyond the familiar. Although the familiar is all around, it is recoded in the glamorous language of the outside. The cosmopolitan Indian tradition mobilizes an accessible and fluid repertoire of signs that include dress and food, and that then reverberates with other representational practices.

Women's Labor and Techno-Muscular Capitalism

Although my arguments center on representational practices, I pause here to underline the feminized labor that helps produce this cosmopolitan Indian tradition. The wedding per se and the elaborate rituals highlighted earlier in the chapter are the locus of a different set of transnational flows: women's labor in the unpaid and paid arenas, in the formal and informal sectors. Here, I examine briefly how women's work in this growing industry facilitates this eccentric response to global commodity capitalism. Women play a central role as participants and producers in the phenomenon of the cosmopolitan Indian tradition. In particular, I want to highlight the central role media representational practices play in rendering women's labor invisible and how this invisibility is constitutive of the glamorous, romantic weddings.

Casting these transnational weddings as a site of labor helps clarify the two different transnational circuits in which women participate. First, women in third-world economies produce most of the goods consumed during the wedding festivities.[36] These women participate in what has become a familiar and clichéd trajectory: a flow of objects from the third world to the first world. "Third-world women" working in the global assembly line produce the detailed, labor-intensive objects now deemed essential to an Indian wedding. On the second level, women participate in circuits of techno-muscular capitalism (TMC), which are equally transnational in their scope and effects. Scholarship examining women's participation in economic processes of globalization have coined the term *techno-muscular capitalism* to refer to those public expressions of globalization "in which the integrated world of global finance, production, trade and telecommunications valorizes all those norms and practices usually associated with Western capitalist masculinity—deregulation, privatization, strategic alliances—but masked as global or universal."[37]

It is in the bridal expos and other cultural arenas immediately associated with weddings that one sees most clearly the labor associated with techno-muscular capitalism. For the most part, it is women who set up the websites, expos, magazines, and advice columns and rely on the basic elements of the transnational flows of capital and goods as well as technologies that enable these transnational connections. The advice columns and the panoply of practices that have come to be associated with weddings have the imprimatur of women. Examining this aspect of wedding magazines from a Foucauldian perspective, it becomes apparent that women as media practitioners and entrepreneurs have become part of a disciplinary apparatus. They ensure that other women adhere to the various elements that comprise the cosmopolitan Indian tradition. For instance, former brides have established most of the Web portals and the magazines I examined. Their participation in these industries is shaped by a formulaic narrative of discovery. Women realize their hellish experiences with wedding planning and decide to help others by setting up wedding portals or organizing bridal expos. However, women erase their participation in this world of high tech–high finance by producing a self-help discourse, so the commodification of tradition takes on overtones of service work being conducted in the interests of other women. The language that predominates these media sites urges other women to participate in the vigorously regimented and highly fragmented practices they advocate. Women's endorsement of these regimes of labor naturalizes the commodification and fetishization of weddings. Women urge brides to tap into the global marketplace and the technologies of contemporary capitalism to produce a traditional wedding because otherwise the brides would be perceived as failing in an element that is central to their identity.

Similarly, the magazines urge the brides to participate in a mode of laborious, invisible work as well. They exhort brides to participate in a tumultuous and dizzying array of tasks: order jewelry and haute couture clothes for the wedding day as well as the various accompanying rituals; choose and select stationary items, preferably using handmade paper with organic vegetable dyes; coordinate the entertainment and hire performers who combine elements of classical and Bollywood music; choose a choreographer for the hired dancers; arrange the henna ceremony; practice a yearlong beauty regimen, including makeup for the wedding day; select the chefs and cuisines for the reception (sometime as many as seven cuisines); organize gift packets for wedding guests; coordinate wedding planners, caterers, and decorators; plan the honeymoon; and so on. Wedding media offer the same advice for all of the activities associated with diverse events, which may only be peripheral to the ceremony: advance planning. They offer charts of military precision and strategies to cope with crises, counting down from at least month five. One North American Web portal advises, "The minute you know the ring is coming, start researching! It doesn't hurt to look around and bookmark some web sites before you officially start planning. It will really help once the ring is on your finger."[38] The regimentation of activities is strict and attends to all aspects of the wedding. The work brides invest in maintenance of family ties and the production of tradition is hidden and designed to go unnoticed.

In both levels of women's labor, brides' participation in the global marketplace is invoked in the language of choice. Women are urged to make a series of choices and this is recast as empowering and providing agency. This is not simply a rhetorical strategy. Instead, families are evacuated from the wedding organizing so that for the transnationally mobile Indians the wedding becomes a key site for women's agency. Thus, women's participation in the commodification process is now routed through the language of empowerment and liberation.

Figures of Globalization

Through this analysis of wedding magazines and their invention of a cosmopolitan Indian tradition, I seek to re-inscribe the category of gender to globalization practices and circuits of movement. Unlike in traditional theories of globalization that tend to posit the global as masculine and the local as feminine, wedding magazines position the female body as bridging the local and the global (or the nation and the diaspora), and the wedding itself becomes the site where such bridging practices are staged. The contemporary wedding does not locate tradition or culture in a different chronotope. Rather, tradition is produced in a cosmopolitan grammar, one that is attentive to the here and now, the material conditions of contemporary reality.

Weddings have reoccupied the position as the central node for community regeneration in the subcontinent and in the diaspora,[39] but the community they enable and the politics underpinning these practices are deeply problematic. The invention of cosmopolitan tradition allows the Indian cultural imaginary to become elastic, expanding beyond the bounds of the nation-state. The visual of inclusivity—one that envelops the home, the diaspora, and the global in a seamless whole—masks a number of economic and cultural exclusions. With their exclusive focus on Hindu rituals and practices, representational practices of the cosmopolitan Indian tradition naturalize a Hinduized version of tradition, erase the practices of the majority (of those who cannot afford lavish weddings), and produce a minority tradition as the dominant, thereby re-inscribing heteronormativity. Indian and diasporic media are mutually constitutive and together they help produce this new tradition. To understand the contemporary media ecology, we have to look at both India and the diaspora simultaneously. Although I have isolated print media, it is important to remember that these magazines tap into an image bank that is produced in films, the Internet, fashion, and advertisements. Together they help reconfigure India's relation to the world. No longer bounded by colonial histories, through these magazines, India and the Indian imaginary inscribe themselves into a timeless space, eliding a number of crucial issues. This phenomenon of plastic tradition reveals the manner in which the imperatives of the global marketplace shape local processes, remarginalizing the majority of Indians outside the realm of representation. What is significantly absent in the glossy pages of these wedding magazines is the material reality of transnational weddings that Ali Kazimi's *Runaway Grooms* poignantly captures.

Notes

1. Nair's *Monsoon Wedding* helps highlight the transnational mobility of upper-class Indian families as well as the global spread of the Indian diaspora. The movie focuses on the wedding of Aditi, a resident of New Delhi, with an engineer from Houston, and brings together the extended family that now resides in Australia, Dubai, the United Kingdom, and other parts of the globe. See Jenny Sharpe, "Gender, nation and globalization in *Monsoon Wedding* and *Dilwale Dulhania Le Jayenge*," *Meridians* 6, no. 1 (2005): 58–81. Gurinder Chadha's adaptation of Jane Austen's *Pride and Prejudice*, *Bride and Prejudice*, on the other hand, illuminates the devious strategies mothers would adopt to secure an eligible bachelor for their daughters. Both movies normalize glamorous transnational wedding practices.

2. Annanya Bhattacharjee, "The habit of ex-nomination: Nation, woman, and the Indian immigrant bourgeoisie," *Public Culture* 5, no. 1 (1992): 19–44.

3. Journalistic accounts suggest that South Asian men from the diaspora often return to the subcontinent for a holiday, get married, extort dowry, and then disappear—a phenomenon euphemistically termed "holiday brides." Responding to this trend, in late 2006, the Indian government decided to offer legal and financial aid equivalent to US$1,000 to women divorced or deserted within two years of marriage. The Ministry of Overseas Indian Affairs estimates that up to 20,000 women have been abandoned by NRI husbands. Ministry officials believe that most runaway grooms reside in the United States, the United Kingdom, Canada, Australia, and New Zealand, while the brides are from the states of Punjab, Gujarat, and Kerala. See Geeta Pandey, "Scheme to aid duped Indian brides," *BBC News*, 23 February 2007, http://news.bbc.co.uk/2/hi/south_asia/6389365.stm (accessed 8 April 2009).

4. Vijay Mishra offers a useful categorization of the Indian diaspora, focusing on the economic forces propelling the migration of people. The first diaspora comprises the indentured workers from India who were shipped to serve in British plantations in places such as Fiji, Guyana, and the West Indies, and Mishra characterizes this population as the diaspora of classic capitalism. The second diaspora refers to the post-1965 migration of Indians to the United Kingdom, United States, Australia,

and other metropolitan centers of former empires. Members of this diaspora of late capitalism are often referred to as Non-Resident Indians (NRIs). For more, see Vijay Mishra, "Diasporas and the art of impossible mourning," in *In Diaspora: Theories, Histories, Texts*, ed. Makarand Parnjape (New Delhi: Indialog, 2001), 24–51.

5. Eric Hobsbawm, "Introduction: Inventing traditions," in *The Invention of Tradition*, ed. Eric Hobsbawm and Terrence Ranger (New York: Cambridge University Press, 1992), 1–14.

6. There are multiple definitions of cosmopolitanism, highlighting the moral, political, economic, and cultural aspects of this phenomenon. Hannerz characterizes cosmopolitanism as an intellectual and aesthetic stance of openness toward divergent cultural experiences, a search for contrasts rather than uniformity. See Ulf Hannerz, *Transnational Connections: Culture, People, Places* (London: Routledge, 1996). Other scholars contend that cosmopolitanism operates as a "global historic bloc" forming cross-national, cross-cultural global classes that uphold mutual interests and ideological perspectives that institutionalize a common criteria of interpretation and common goals anchored in the idea of an open world economy. See Bruce Robbins and Pheng Cheah, eds., *Cosmopolitics: Thinking and Feeling beyond the Nation* (Minneapolis: University of Minnesota Press, 1998) and Mike Featherstone, *Global Modernities* (Thousand Oaks: Sage, 1996). I use the term to signify a worldly, sophisticated cultural posture that glosses over economic and political considerations.

7. See Anupreeta Das, "Middle-class India plows new wealth into big weddings," *Christian Science Monitor*, 29 September 2005, http://www.csmonitor.com/2005/0929/p01s04-wosc.html (accessed 8 April 2009); Meenakshi Madhavan, "Bunty weds Babli in Bali," *Outlook India*, 26 February 2007, http://outlookindia.com/full.asp?fname=Cover%20Story%20(F)&fodname=20070226&sid=1 (accessed 23 April 2009); Ira Pande, "Fancy and fandangle," *Outlook India*, 26 February 2007, http://outlookindia.com/full.asp?fname=Cover%20Story%20(F)&fodname=20070226&sid=3 (accessed 23 April 2009); and Alex Perry, "Letter from India: Land of the wedding planners," *Time*, 13 February 2006, http://www.time.com/time/magazine/article/0,9171,1159009,00.html (accessed 8 April 2009).

8. *Desi* is a Hindi word meaning "of the nation." Outside India, the term is used to refer to things and people of South Asian origin. Within the diaspora, South Asians often use Desi as a derogatory term to signify a second- or third-generation person's ignorance about things Indian, such as in American-Born Confused Desi (ABCD). In the commercial culture of the West, Desi is often used to refer to the niche market of South Asian consumers. See Vijay Prashad, "The Desi diaspora: Indian migration and nationalism in the 19th and 20th centuries," *AskAsia.org*, 2005, http://www.askasia.org/teachers/essays/essay.php?no=126 (accessed 8 April 2009).

9. Meenakshi Madhavan, "Bunty weds Babli in Bali."

10. The BBC World series ran over six weeks and was designed to explore the "business aspects of the multimillion dollar industry." Tracking a young Indian couple making arrangements for the trousseau and their meetings with the wedding planner, the series "captures the fascinating while at the same time accessing the financial intricacies of modern-day marriage in India." http://www.bbcworld.com/

Pages/ProgrammeMultiFeature.aspx?id=113 (accessed on 23 April 2009). Similarly, television channels in the diaspora have also started to focus on Desi weddings. See Usha Thomas, "Discovery travel and living India unveils first local production," *Indiatelevision.com*, 21 August 2006, http://www.indiantelevision.com/headlines/y2k6/aug/aug117.htm (accessed 8 April 2009).

11. The Indian economy entered the global marketplace falteringly in the mid-1980s. In 1991, however, the Indian government abandoned its socialist principles and started to engage wholeheartedly in the free-market, capitalist global marketplace. Over the past fifteen years, this has transformed the Indian economy and expanded the disposable incomes available to a growing middle class; simultaneously, the gap between the rich and poor has continued to widen. For more on how this liberalization process has affected Indian commodity culture, see Leela Fernandes, "Nationalizing the 'global': Media images, cultural politics and the middle class in India," *Media, Culture and Society* 22 (2000): 611–28; and Arvind Rajagopal, "Thinking through emerging markets: Brand logics and the cultural forms of political society in India," *Social Text* 17, no. 3 (1999): 131–49.

12. Meenakshi Madhavan, "Bunty weds Babli in Bali"; Ira Pande, "Fancy and fandangle."

13. Alex Perry, "Letter from India"; Usha Thomas, "Discovery travel."

14. Anupreeta Das, "Middle-class India."

15. Saskia Sassen uses the term *global city* to refer to cities such as Bangalore, Mumbai, and Chennai, which have been transformed by becoming embedded in the global information economy. She contends that while processes of economic globalization have engendered the formation of global cities, cultural and political processes of these societies are also altered. See Saskia Sassen, "The global city: Strategic site/new frontier," *Seminar*, 2001, http://www.india-seminar.com/2001/503/503%20saskia%20sassen.htm (accessed 8 April 2009). The growth of the "big fat Indian wedding" is symptomatic of these global economic processes.

16. Arundhati Basu, "The bigger bridal bazaar," *The Telegraph*, 27 August 2005, http://www.telegraphindia.com/1050827/asp/weekend/story_5144324.asp# (accessed 8 April 2009).

17. Economists contend that the average wedding in the United States costs $28,000, a figure that has doubled over the past decade. See Hannah Wallace, "The marriage industrial complex," *Salon*, 21 May 2007, http://www.salon.com/mwt/feature/2007/05/21/mead_weddings/ (accessed 8 April 2009).

18. See Chrys Ingraham, *White Weddings: Romancing Heterosexuality in Popular Culture* (London: Taylor & Francis, 1999); Wendy Leeds-Hurwitz, *Wedding as Text: Communicating Cultural Identities through Ritual* (Mahwah, NJ: Lawrence Erlbaum, 2002); Elizabeth Freeman, *The Wedding Complex: Forms of Belonging in Modern American Culture* (Durham, NC: Duke University Press, 2002); Cele Otnes and Elizabeth Pleck, *Cinderella Dreams: The Allure of the Lavish Wedding* (Berkeley: University of California Press, 2003); Vicki Howard, *Brides, Inc.: American Weddings and the Business of Tradition* (Philadelphia: University of Pennsylvania Press, 2006).

19. Sociologists such as Patricia Uberoi have pointed out that "Historically mar-

riage has always been the occasion for making status claims in terms of the relative social status of the intermarrying families, the lavishness of the hospitality and entertainment offered, and the number and importance of the guests in attendance, as well as the value of the gifts given to the daughter and transferred through her marriage to her husband's family. Writing in the 1920s, the colonial administrator, Malcolm Darling (1925), deplored the condition of the Punjabi peasantry who repeatedly drove themselves into debt with extravagant weddings. "The burden of feasting and entertainment, which falls most heavily on the bride's family, is an occasion for conspicuous consumption and the affirmation of social, political and economic standing." See Patricia Uberoi, *Freedom and Destiny: Gender, Popular Culture and Family in India* (New York: Oxford University Press, 2006), 26–27.

20. Mary Hancock. "Glossy title targets Asian women." *BBC News,* 22 October 2002, http://news.bbc.co.uk/2/low/business/2330469.stm (accessed 8 April 2009).

21. http://www.vivaha.indiatimes.com (accessed 8 April 2009).

22. Basu, "The bigger bridal bazaar."

23. Rachel Dwyer, "Shooting stars: The Indian film magazine, *Stardust,*" in *Pleasure and the Nation: History, Politics, and the Consumption of Public Culture in India,* ed. Christopher Pinney and Rachel Dwyer (New York: Oxford University Press, 2005), 247–85.

24. Homi Bhabha has theorized mimicry as (post)colonial representational practice. He characterizes it as a double articulation: "a complex strategy of reform, regulation and discipline, which 'appropriates' the Other as it visualizes power" and it is also the sign of the inappropriate, "a difference or recalcitrance which coheres the dominant strategic function of colonial power, intensifies surveillance, and poses an immanent threat to both 'normalized' knowledges and disciplinary powers." Homi Bhabha, *The Location of Culture* (New York: Routledge, 1995), 90.

25. Sujata Moorti, "Desperately seeking an identity: Diasporic cinema and the articulation of transnational kinship." *International Journal of Cultural Studies* 6, no. 3 (2003): 355–76.

26. Patricia Uberoi elaborates on the mutually constitutive nature of this phenomenon. Similarly, by highlighting cultural practices emanating from within the economic realm, Aiwha Ong has explored how the Chinese diaspora shapes and is shaped by the homeland. See Uberoi, *Freedom and Destiny*; Aiwha Ong, *Flexible Citizenship: The Cultural Logic of Transnationality* (Durham, NC: Duke University Press, 1998).

27. Marc Augé, *Nonplaces: Introduction to an Anthropology of Supermodernity* (New York: Verso, 1995), 77–78.

28. Marta Savigliano, *Tango and the Political Economy of Passion* (Boulder, CO: Westview Press, 1995).

29. The term *Raj* is derived from the Hindi word for rule. The British Raj was used to refer to the British colonization of the Indian subcontinent but increasingly the word *Raj* has become synonymous with all of the cultural and political processes associated with British imperialism. In the 1980s, British popular culture such as the television series *The Jewel in the Crown* returned to the colonial era and fostered a

romantic nostalgia for practices and products associated with British imperialism. In contemporary weddings, Raj symbols such as palaces, ostentatious jewelry, folk styles, and elephants predominate.

30. *Femina Bride* (December 2004): 5.

31. Arjun Appadurai developed the concept to describe Filipino youths' love for American popular music in the 1980s, especially Motown music originally released in the 1960s. The appeal of this music coupled with an absence of any historical or cultural connection to their own nation, created a phantom nostalgia—the youths looked "back to a world they had never lost." Arjun Appadurai, *Modernity at Large: Cultural Dimensions of Globalization* (Minneapolis: University of Minnesota Press, 1996), 30.

32. Hobsbawm, "Introduction: Inventing traditions," 1.

33. Hobsbawm, "Introduction: Inventing traditions," 2.

34. Eva Illouz, *Consuming the Romantic Utopia: Love and the Cultural Contradictions of Capitalism* (Berkeley: University of California Press, 1997), 86.

35. Rustom Bharucha. "Cultural transitions in India today: From Himalayas to Dharavi," in *Contemporary India: Transitions*, ed. Peter Desouza (New Delhi: Sage, 2000), 49–58.

36. I use the contested terms *third world* and *first world* not to refer to geographical spaces but to signify an economic geography where socioeconomic location binds people together across national borders. Thus, the affluent, transnationally mobile upper-class Indians I designate as occupying the first world, whereas the women who work in low-wage occupations around the world I designate as third world. See Kum Kum Sangari, "The politics of the possible," in *The Nature and Context of Minority Discourse*, ed. Abdul JanMohamed and David Lloyd (New York: Oxford University Press, 1990), and Chandra Talpade Mohanty, "Cartographies of struggle: Third world women and the politics of feminism," in *Third World Women and the Politics of Feminism*, ed. Chandra Mohanty, Ann Russo, and Lourdes Torres (Bloomington: Indiana University Press, 1991), 1–50.

37. In their sophisticated analysis of overseas contract workers in Hong Kong, Chang and Ling posit two modes through which women participate in the economic structures characteristic of globalization—techno-muscular capitalism and the regimes of labor intimacy—when referring to many of the invisible sites of women's participation in the "low-skilled" arenas of care work. See Kimberly Chang and L. Ling. "Globalization and its intimate Other: Filipina domestic workers in Hong Kong," in *Gender and Global Restructuring: Sightings, Sites and Resistances*, ed. Marianne Richardson and Anne Runyon (New York: Routledge, 2000), 27–42.

38. IndianWeddingSite.com, http://www.indianweddingsite.com/planning/planning_article.php?articleID=10_First_Steps (accessed 24 April 2009).

39. Bonnie Adrian, *Framing the Bride: Globalizing Beauty and Romance in Taiwan's Bridal Industry* (Berkeley: University of California Press, 2003), and Jiemin Bao, *Marital Acts: Gender, Sexuality and Identity among the Chinese Thai Diaspora* (Honolulu: University of Hawaii Press, 2005).

FIVE

Mapping Tollywood: The Cultural Geography of "Ramoji Film City" in Hyderabad

Shanti Kumar

As earlier chapters in the India section have made eminently clear, Indian cinema has gone global. While Bollywood is the focus of much of this discussion, in this chapter Shanti Kumar points to a fascinating development in another part of India. Tollywood, the nickname for the Telegu-language film industry, has also become an increasingly prominent player in global cinema. Tollywood is centered today in Ramoji Film City, a high-tech movie production center and theme park that is also a transnational media company, a "center for profit and pleasure."

Given the dominance of Hollywood productions in the global media industry, academic and journalistic debates over the rapid increase in transnational flows of television and film have emphasized the potential for either homogenization or fragmentation of national cinemas and television cultures around the world.[1] However, little attention has been focused on the ways in which the transnationalization of production practices outside Hollywood has significantly transformed the circulation of films and television programs around the world.

In terms of Hollywood's role in film and television production, some have argued that "fantasy cities" (such as Universal Studios) and "theme park cities" (such as the Disney kingdoms) in the United States contribute to the globalization of a postmodern culture that is primarily based in a capitalist system of profit and pleasure.[2] However, such Hollywood-centered approaches do not adequately attend to the significant role that cultural location plays in our understanding of capitalist profit and pleasure in the transnational media industries. In this chapter, I redress this gap in the dialogue by exploring the transnational characteristics of global television and film production in one specific cultural context outside Hollywood—Ramoji Film City (RFC) in Hyderabad, India. The emergence of RFC represents a new kind of entertainment-based culture in India that is partly invested in claiming a share in the transnational enterprise of film and television production, and partly interested in creating a postcolonial alternative to the Hollywood-centered world of capitalist profit and pleasure.

A city within a city, Ramoji Film City is the largest, most comprehensive, and professionally planned film production center in the world. Spread over an area of 1,000 acres, the 10,000-million-rupee Film City comprises forty studio floors, a fully equipped prop shop, a set design and construction division, state-of-the-art equipment, experienced production staff, and high-tech digital editing, dubbing, and sound-recording facilities. It is considered by many industry experts to have surpassed the size and facilities offered at Universal Studios and other major film studios in Hollywood.

Located at an hour's drive from the twin cities of Hyderabad and Secunderabad, RFC is also a tourist site with over 2,500 visitors coming to the city every day. In order to reach the Film City, visitors have to either take a city bus or arrange a private mode of transport. The day tour begins at 9:00 A.M. and ends at 6:00 P.M. Once at the imposing black gates of the RFC, visitors are greeted by security and reminded to purchase tickets for the package tour. The visiting charges are Rs. 200 per head on Sunday and Rs. 150 per head on weekdays (when this chapter went to press, the exchange rate was US$1.00 = Rs. 43.62 [Indian rupees]). For children older than three, the ticket costs Rs. 150 on a Sunday and Rs. 100 on a weekday. For visitors who want to take their own cars, the ticket cost is Rs. 700 per person. After a brisk security check, visitors are allowed to get into one of the many waiting RFC buses, and after a short ride on a winding road around rolling hills, the sprawling RFC comes into full view. Promoting RFC as "the Land of

Movies," publicity brochures promise visitors "a truly out-of-this-world experience": "Ramoji Film City, the land of films & fantasy, where dreams turn to reality. A strong favorite of the film fraternity, the world's largest Film City is enchanting, enthralling and spellbinding at the same time. Amidst the rocky Deccan Landscape, in the heart of Andhra Pradesh, the magic of make believe is a heady and engulfing surprise, as you are confronted with the Film City's splash of color and charm. Glamorous, surreal, and breathtakingly beautiful, its mind-boggling mammoth proportions, scores of unbelievable sets and fantastic landscapes offer more than just a glimpse into the thrilling and exciting world of film and television. Grandeur, glamour and professionalism combine to present a truly out-of-this-world experience."

To begin this out-of-world experience, visitors are dropped off at Eureka Point, the Fun Place. Eureka, which is the starting and ending point of the package tour, is a massive mall for food and shopping. Since visitors are not allowed to take food or beverages into the Film City, no fewer than four restaurants are located at Eureka. Alampana restaurant claims to bring its guests authentic Mughalai cuisine all the way from the Royal House of Awadh. For those who like vegetarian cuisine served in Indian "thali" style, Chanakya is the place to go. While Ganga Jamuma serves South Indian cuisine, Gunsmoke provides a taste of fast food from the Wild Wild West.

Architecturally designed to resemble a fort from the Mauryan period in Indian history, Eureka can be accessed via a drawbridge. From here begins the package tour, as well-trained guides escort visitors into jumbo-sized red buses. The first stop is the Sun Fountain adorned by a huge statue of the mythological character Surya holding the reigns of three horses. Tour guides tell curious visitors that the three horses signify Ramoji Film City, Eenadu newspaper, and Eenadu television network—the three major interests in the sprawling media empire of the South Indian business tycoon Cherukuri Ramoji Rao.

Some of the other stops on the way include a mud village, a railway station, a central jail, a temple, an airport, a court, and a palace named "Hawa Mahal." The bus drops the tourists off at the highest point close to Hawa Mahal. From there, visitors can walk around the various gardens by foot. Throughout the Film City, tourists can visit merchandise stores located in the theme parks of Maurya, Maghadha, Black Cat Warehouse, Frontierland, and Meena Bazaar. Meandering through the gardens, parks, and stores, visitors can slowly find their way back. Those tired of walking can take the returning bus to Eureka. From Eureka Point, all visitors are asked to board the RFC bus, which drops them off at the security gate of the main entrance.

For visitors who desire more than a day trip, RFC also offers packages for holidays, honeymoon couples, and state-of-the-art conferencing facilities for corporations. For the newlyweds, RFC has a honeymoon package that, as travel-india.com describes it, is for "those who don't want the run-of-the-mill tourist destination." The travel-india.com website goes on: "Besides a comfortable stay in Sitara, a five-star hotel within the RFC complex with the normal complimentary freebies thrown in, a minifilm unit complete with make-up artist, director, cameraman and the equipment to help you capture unforgettable moments of your honeymoon. Sitara has one of Asia's best health clubs, where guides identify the workstation that Shah Rukh Khan used during the shooting of one of his films. And you could take your pick of some of the more exotically named suites: Cleopatra, Zorba the Greek, and mughal-e-Azam with decor to match."

But what travel-india.com neglects to mention is that all this comes with a steep price tag. A one-day stay at five-star Hotel Sitara for a couple costs Rs. 4800 with (food allowance up to Rs. 1000). For the more economically minded, there is the three-star Hotel Tara where a one-day stay costs Rs. 1890 (with food allowance up to Rs. 600). For its corporate clients, RFC has special package deals that include accommodation at the five-star Hotel Sitara, use of conference facilities, a well-equipped business center, and a health club. The RFC has its own travel agency, transport and telecommunication network to look after ticketing, airport pickups, car rentals, and other requirements.

As the website www.ramojifilmcity.com promises, Ramoji Film City is a one-stop facility that "can offer the best of pre-production, production and post-production facilities for any kind of film or television show."[3] "A producer can walk in with a script and walk out with the canned film," claims Ramoji Rao. "The idea is to save time, energy and resources and focus on creative excellence, executional quality, economical schedules and meticulous planning."[4] The unique selling point of Ramoji Film City is that it is a self-contained world of flexible authenticity. Although located in one place at the outskirts of Hyderabad, RFC provides film and television producers with a vast variety of flexible locales, some clearly identifiable by name (such as the Hawa Mahal) and others more spontaneous (such as the twenty or so gardens on premises). Total control over all aspects of production gives RFC an enviable ability to rebuild any location for a shoot with short notice. On any given day, the city can cater to as many as a hundred film and television productions simultaneously.

A producer can choreograph song sequences in any or all of the gardens and later change the look of the fountain, the layout of the street, the facades of the buildings in the streets, or the shape of the multidimensional pond to create a totally different locale. The sets (a street corner at night, for example) can be remodeled to resemble something else at short notice. This ensures that no location will become jaded from repeated exposure. However, paradoxically enough, it is precisely this flexibility to change the identity of a location that produces a greater sense of "authenticity" in the Film City, and by extension gives Hyderabad a more unique sense of its global identity.

In this sense, Ramoji Rao's ambitious vision of the Film City as a major media facility, a conference site, and a tourist attraction is in line with Chief Minister Chandrababu Naidu's plans to make Hyderabad a unique yet flexible location in the increasingly globalized South India. Moreover, as Sunil Rajanala points out, information technology is not the only commercial sector that Naidu is banking on in his attempts to redefine Hyderabad as a global city. The software industry is already a booming business in India, and Naidu's dream project of establishing a Hi-Tech City in Hyderabad has run into serious competition from other equally capable contenders like Bangalore—often called the Silicon Valley of India. Although there is a healthy rivalry between these two South Indian cities in the information technology sector, there has been hardly any discussion of their role in the global entertainment industry. The entertainment industry is a multimillion-dollar enterprise worldwide, but the Indian share in the business is minimal, to say the least. Rajanala argues that the studios of Hyderabad, led by Ramoji Film City, "have done well to gain a toehold in that market."[5]

Hollywood has already made an early entry—*Nightfall*; and *Dollar Dreams* and *The Return of the Thief of Baghdad* are two English-language films shot in RFC. An Italian film in English, *Gills*, was also shot there. The reasons are obvious. On an average, its costs anything between Rs. 15,000 and Rs. 25,000 a second to produce special effects (SFX) at other film locations in India. However, in Hyderabad, it averages between Rs. 7,500 to Rs. 12,000 per second for films, while it costs anything up to Rs. 250 per second of crude SFX for TV. For instance, the 18.5 minutes of SFX in Kamal Hasan's film *Hey Ram*, done at the Ramoji Film City over a seven-month period, would have cost at least ten times more if done in a studio in the United States. Though RFC is reluctant to divulge the figures, industry sources estimate the same would cost just under Rs. 1 million. In addition, since production is cheaper in Hyderabad than Mumbai by about 30 to 40 percent, filmmakers from Bollywood and other regional languages such as Tamil, Kannada, and Bengali are also lining up at the Film City. Finally, with the Telugu film industry as a captive market in its backyard, the potential is immense.[6]

Telugu cinema—or Tollywood, as some call it—has always provided a rich source of cultural imagination for audiences in Andhra Pradesh. Historically, South Indian audiences have imaginatively drawn upon movies for an understanding of the modern world. More recently, diasporic communities are increasingly looking to the celluloid world for their understanding of global, national, and local flows in the "real" world. It is, then, hardly surprising that Telugu cinema has come to be a creative resource for a variety of political, economic, and cultural practices of everyday life. One significant manifestation of this phenomenon was the mercurial rise of the charismatic celluloid figure of N. T. Rama Rao—or NTR—as the chief minister of Andhra Pradesh in the 1980s. In attaining such political heights, NTR had Tamil cinema's superstar M. G. Ramachandran—or MGR—as an illustrious precedent to draw inspiration from in the neighboring state of Tamil Nadu. In his aptly titled book *The Image Trap*, M. S. S. Pandian documents how MGR rose to power in Tamil Nadu and strode the state's political landscape like a colossus until his death.[7]

Undeniably, there are remarkable similarities between the MGR phenomenon in Tamil Nadu and the NTR phenomenon in Andhra Pradesh. However, the differences between the two are just as remarkable to note. For instance, MGR emerged as a leader in Tamil Nadu in the historical legacy of Dravid identity, its contentious struggles of electoral politics, and the long-established traditions of Tamil cultural pride. On the other hand, NTR and the Telugu Desam Party (TDP) emerged in a historical, political, and cultural vacuum in Andhra Pradesh. For decades, until the emergence of the NTR phenomenon in 1982, Andhra Pradhesh was dominated by the Congress Party, which—in deference to nationalist politics—rarely addressed issues of Andhra history, Telugu identity, or cultural pride in the state's electoral discourse. In this context, much can be said about how NTR drew upon his enormous cinematic appeal among the Telugu-speaking audiences to create his Telugu Desam Party, quite literally from dust.

Shrewdly manipulating his screen personas of Hindu gods like Rama and Krishna, historical figures like Krishnadevaraya, and the common man's heroes like Rikshaw Ramudu, NTR campaigned across the state in a large van that he renamed "Chaitanya Ratham" to stir emotions of Telugu pride among the state's electorate. Sometimes in the conciliatory garb of nation-alism and sometimes in the confrontational voice of regionalism, NTR—always a star-politician—worked the cameras and the microphones to cre-ate and sustain an imagined community of what he called "Telugu Nadu." (Telugu Nadu is a polysemous term that variously translates as the Telugu nation, the land of Telugus, or even the day of the Telugus.) Needless to say, NTR's Telugu Nadu was more a linguistic trope of imagination and less a community of lived experiences, given the significant regional and subregional distinctions in the four major districts of Andhra, Telangana, Rayalaseema, and Godavari. Moreover, to mobilize support for his Telugu Desam Party, NTR shrewdly highlighted these regional distinctions in his whirlwind campaigns across the state.

At times, NTR manipulated the caste sentiments of his wealthy Kamma community to fight political leaders from the powerful Reddy caste and their Brahmin allies who had come to dominate the Congress Party. At other times, he exploited his cinematic identity of the working-class underdog to distance himself from the vested interests of his upper-caste community and ally him-self with the marginalized voices of the lower-caste and religious minorities like Muslims and Christians. However, when necessary, NTR was not averse to blurring distinctions of caste, region, and religion in order to promote his idealized myth of an imagined community called Telugu Nadu.

As Benedict Anderson reminds us, the work of cultural imagination in any community is fraught with many such contradictions of identity and difference. In his highly acclaimed work *Imagined Communities*,[8] Anderson maps the interactions in colonial discourse between the political-economic institutions of industrial capitalism and the cultural imaginations in liter-ary texts such as the modern novel and the newspaper. Anderson creatively coins the term *print-capitalism* to articulate the complex cultural processes by which nations are imagined into existence. Print-capitalism for Ander-son thus describes a mediated set of cultural, political, economic, historical, and geographic conditions that are necessary for the process of imagining a community into existence.

In the process of imagining a new community of Telugu Nadu, NTR found an admirable print-capitalist ally in Ch. Ramoji Rao, whose *Eenadu* newspaper was—and continues to be—the largest circulated daily in Andhra Pradesh. As Robin Jeffrey points out, Ramoji Rao and *Eenadu* worked hand in hand with NTR and the TDP in the elections of 1982–83: "The newspa-per's offices and teleprinters provided the headquarters and communication system for the new party. . . . *Eenadu* correspondents were told to lend all support to the party and even helped to 'select candidates.' Support for the TDP was company policy."[9]

In justifying the close liaison between his Eenadu conglomerate and the Telugu Desam Party during the early 1980s, Ramoji Rao argued that the Congress Party had destroyed the state's political system, and that he and his newspaper threw their weight around NTR to "build up an alternative system which catered to reality." Ramoji Rao's vision of an alternative system that would cater to the lived reality of the Telugu people was driven by a peculiar combination of idealism, political savvy, and economic self-interest. However, this alternative vision of Telugu culture and self-identity was already in evidence in the way in which Ramoji Rao ran his newspaper business by focusing on the regional, vernacular, and local interests of his audiences.

As a young man, Ramoji Rao lived for a number of years in Delhi and participated in the activities of the Communist Party of India. In the 1960s, he moved back to Andhra Pradesh and started a successful chit fund business.[10] When he launched *Eenadu* in 1974, it had a modest beginning: a single edition, hand-composed newspaper that was printed on a flatbed press in the coastal town of Visakhapatnam, in Andhra Pradesh. From the beginning, Ramoji Rao intensely researched the Telugu newspaper industry and used creative editorial and marketing strategies to sell *Eenadu* to both advertisers and readers alike.

To set itself apart from its competition, *Eenadu* drew upon local dialects and colloquial idioms to present headlines and stories, provided colorful photographs and captions to draw attention, and used sarcasm and wit to analyze news events. By 1989, *Eenadu* had devised a strategy to further localize its coverage by inserting a tabloid devoted to local events in the broadsheet edition of each relevant district every day. To gather local news for the tabloid inserts, *Eenadu* created a network of stringers across the state who were paid a small amount if their news item was published in the daily.

The stringers, based in cities and small towns across the state, corresponded with editors by telephone and made arrangements with bus companies to carry their reports to the district headquarters where *Eenadu* employees collected them. To obtain local classifieds and display advertisements for each of its district tabloid inserts, *Eenadu* hired thousands of salespeople to convince local businesses of the virtues of advertising. By 1998, *Eenadu* had transformed into a major regional conglomerate, with daily editions from ten towns, and had cornered 70 percent of Telugu daily circulation.

In allying with NTR and the TDP, Ramoji Rao argued that he and the newspaper had to "play a role in building up the nation." Claiming that "we wanted change . . . not power for ourselves,"[11] on election day in 1983, *Eenadu* declared that in future it would no longer back the NTR uncritically, and would treat the TDP as any other party. Although the relationship between *Eenadu* and the TDP was ambivalent and even strained in later years, it remains an undisputed fact that Ramoji Rao contributed in no uncertain measure to dethroning the Congress Party and to crowning the NTR as the undisputed leader of Andhra Pradesh for over a decade, until his death in 1995. In the power politics of the Telugu Desam Party and the palace intrigues among family members that followed NTR's death, Ramoji Rao and Eenadu once again played a key role in picking winners and losers. Going against conventional wisdom, Ramoji Rao and *Eenadu* threw their weight around Chandrababu Naidu, the rather uncharismatic son-in-law who had challenged NTR's widow for the mantle of the TDP *supremo*.

A clever politician and an efficient technocrat, Naidu quickly consolidated his power in the party and the state, and went on to gain recognition at national and international levels as the cyber-savvy chief minister of Andhra Pradesh. To rapidly develop the capital city of Hyderabad as India's premier high-tech center, Naidu assiduously cultivated the Telugu diaspora in the United States, whose members have played an influential role in the global information technology industry. Taking a leaf out of his charismatic father-in-law's playbook, Naidu appealed not only to the purses but also to the cultural pride of the Telugu diasporic community.

However, in doing so, he went a step beyond NTR's vision of Telugu Nadu as a regional and vernacular identity. Naidu invited some of the world's biggest transnational corporations such as Microsoft, Sun Microsystems, and GE to invest in his more cosmopolitan reimagination of Hyderabad as high-tech global city. The emergence of Ramoji Film City as a transnational media hub on the outskirts of Hyderabad is a concrete embodiment of this phenomenon.

Highlighting the growing transnational appeal of the Indian cinema industry, Carla Power and Sudip Mazumdar tell readers of *Newsweek* that "America isn't the only country that knows how to spin and export fantasies." Arguing that Bollywood is going global, they write:

> The West may have the biggest stalls in the world's media bazaar, but it's not the only player. Globalization isn't merely another word for

Americanization—and the recent expansion of the Indian entertainment industry proves it. For hundreds of millions of fans around the world, it is Bollywood—India's film industry—not Hollywood that spins their screen fantasies. Bollywood, based in Mumbai, has become a global industry. India's entertainment moguls don't merely target the billion South Asians, or *desis*, at home; they make slick movies, songs and TV shows for export. Attracted by a growing Indian middle class and a more welcoming investor environment, foreign companies are flocking to Bollywood, funding films and musicians. The foreign money is already helping India's pop culture to reach even greater audiences. And it may have a benign side effect—cleaning up an Indian movie business long haunted by links to the underworld.[12]

Even the government of India seems to have also taken note of this trend, and the Press Information Bureau (PIB) led the charge with an announcement that "Indian cinema has become global." The inducement for the government of India to make what the PIB called "an unambiguous proclamation that Indian cinema has arrived on the international stage" was the first International Film Festival Awards held in London 2000. According to the PIB news release, "The global reach of the function was symbolized by the presence of Hollywood and European film makers and stars, along with the Indian veterans like Dilip Kumar and Amitabh Bachan [*sic*] at the function."[13] Countless e-zines on the Web, dedicated to Bollywood cinema, have also joined the chorus. Shyam Barooah of Apunkachoice.com, who finds "Indian spice sprinkling the world of cinema," writes, "Indian films are well and truly going global, that's for sure. Until recently, the products of the *desi* film industry were confined to the sub-continental market, except for a few offbeat art films, which made it to the international film festival circuit. The situation has undergone a sea change of late. In the last two-three years, film exports have been growing at over 80 per cent and the Indian Motion Picture Association predicts exports will more than double in the near future."[14]

India Today, the leading English news magazine in India and in the Indian diaspora, seems to agree with this growing sentiment among Bollywood aficionados, as evidenced by the following headline: "Bollywood has gone global, powered by the diaspora dollar [and] with a little effort it could challenge Hollywood." Arguing that the "global Indian" is engendering a transnational chutney culture, *India Today*'s Shankkar Aiyar and Sandeep Unnithan write,

Globalization has always been confused with Americanization. If India has its way, it won't. The technological advances of the past decades have seen Indian movies make money in places like Japan (witness Muthu's conquest in 2001) and *desi* music emanating from the unlikeliest of sources (think Nicole Kidman singing in *Moulin Rouge*). Despite much clamor, India hasn't quite become a power to reckon with on the world stage. No Bollywood film crossed over into mainstream Western theatres, though *Monsoon Wedding* reached the all-time Top 10 foreign box-office hit list in the US and *Bend It Like Beckham* was a hit in the UK. Bhangra pop and Bollywood remixes got clubbers dancing but didn't break out of the world music ghetto. But as India-inspired fiction discovered ever-new stars, some homegrown, some diasporic, Salman Rushdie's voice found many echoes across the globe and proved that cultural imperialism didn't necessarily speak with an American accent.[15]

As is evident from this sprinkling of news reports from a variety of sources, there is a buzz about Indian cinema going global in recent years, even as there is a clear recognition that Bollywood is still a very minor presence in the transnational entertainment industry. The entertainment business is a multibillion-dollar enterprise worldwide, but in terms of sheer dollar values, the Indian share in the business has been minimal. India's movie exports grew from a paltry $10 million at the end of the 1980s to $100 million by the end of the 1990s, and were estimated to be over $250 million in 2000. However, when compared with Hollywood's $6.7 billion profits from foreign markets in the year 2000, some interesting contrasts begin to emerge between the world's largest film industry in Bollywood and the world's richest film industry in Hollywood.

For instance, while the total revenues in Indian cinema were an impressive $500 million in 2000, these numbers pale in comparison to Hollywood's $9.2 billion in ticket sales. Global merchandising and DVD sales rake up another $4 billion, which puts Hollywood's total revenue at over $13 billion in 2002.[16] However, one of the reasons that is often given to account for Bollywood going global is that the Indian entertainment industry is now recognizing the economic incentives of catering to its relatively affluent and culturally passionate diaspora, which is estimated to be 25 million around the world.

The Indian diaspora in the United States and Britain have counted for about 55 percent of international ticket sales for the Bollywood blockbusters *Taal* and *Kuch Kuch Hota Hai*, which grossed US$8 million in foreign markets. But as Power and Mazumdar remind us, Bollywood films have always had millions of Indian and non-Indian fans in the Middle East, Africa, Southeast Asia, and Eastern Europe: "Romany Gypsies in Eastern Europe tune in to India's Sony Entertainment Television, as do Hindi film fans in Fiji and the Philippines. In Israel . . . *Dil to Pagal Hai* is playing to packed houses in Tel Aviv as 'Halev Mistagya'—'Crazy Heart.' In Arab countries, fans opt for Hindi movies over Hollywood ones. . . . In Tanzania's capital, open-air theaters screen the latest Indian romances, with interpreters standing in front of screens translating story lines. In Zanzibar, Swahili-speaking schoolgirls skip down the streets singing Hindi love songs—despite not speaking a word of Hindi."[17]

The noted Hindi film director-producer Subhash Ghai expresses confidence that "Indian entertainment products have been globally accepted." He argues that in terms of international appeal, "No other cultural product—except Hollywood's—has such a sweep."[18] Shekar Kapur, the Indian-born, London-based director of *Elizabeth*, goes one step further and predicts that the "Western dominance of the cinema will be over in 10 years." Kapur writes: "Here is a prediction: in its first week, *Spider-Man* made $150 million and everybody was zonked out. Ten years from now, *Spider-Man* will make $1 billion in its first week. But when Spider-Man takes off his mask, he'll probably be Chinese. And the city in which he operates will not be New York, it will be Shanghai. And yet it will be an international film, it will still be *Spider-Man*."[19]

The reason for this radical shift within a decade, Kapur argues, is that the American entertainment industry is becoming heavily dependent on foreign markets as fewer and fewer films are being funded within the United States. In 2001, one-third of all Hollywood productions were funded by German banks, and by the end of the decade, Kapur believes, "most of the funding will be Asian [and] the next big studio will be Asian." His argument goes somewhat like this: The main Asian markets led by Japan, China, and India constitute 80 percent of the world population. In India alone, almost 60 percent of the country's one-billion-strong population is under the age of thirty years. Since the global entertainment industries mostly desire consumers in the fifteen-to-thirty demographics, Kapur feels that the Asian markets will be the preferred targets for films and television programs produced in the next decade. Gazing through the crystal ball even further into the future, Kapur predicts: "In 15 years from now, we won't be discussing the domination of the Western media but the domination of the Chinese media or the Asian media. Soon we will find that to make a hugely successful film, you have to match Tom Cruise with an Indian or a Chinese actor. What you are seeing with films such as *The Guru* is just the tip of the iceberg."[20]

The Guru—produced by Hugh Grant's London-based company, Working Title—is one of the very few Hollywood films featuring an Indian actor (Jimi Mistry) in the lead role opposite Hollywood stars like Heather Graham and Marisa Tomei. However, it would be far-fetched to suggest that transnational films like *The Guru, Monsoon Wedding, Bend It Like Beckham*, or even Bollywood blockbusters like *Lagaan* and *Devdas* would even make a dent into Tom Cruise's profit margins around the world with films like *Mission Impossible* (1996), *Mission Impossible 2* (2000), and *Mission Impossible 3* (2006)—and maybe *MI 4*—that will surely be produced within the decade. Therefore, some of Kapur's predictions about the coming Asian dominance in the entertainment industry in the next ten to fifteen years may be wishful thinking, and it will take more than a Chinese Spider-Man weaving his magical web over the streets of Shanghai to disrupt Hollywood's hegemony over production, distribution, and exhibition in the transnational entertainment industry in the next ten years.

Although half-a-billion-strong audiences in the fifteen-to-thirty demographics in India may have the numerical strength to attract the attention of many transnational media corporations, it is rather unlikely that Hollywood will revamp its scheduling and promotional strategies aimed at the big Oscars ceremony in March every year to accommodate the Hindu festivals of Dusserah and Divali in October and November. However, one of Kapur's predictions has already come true: the world's biggest film studio—Ramoji Film City—is indeed now in India, and that may induce us to pause and consider some of the other things about the Asian future of the transnational entertainment industry in the next ten to fifteen years.

Notes

1. Chris Barker, *Television, Globalization and Cultural Identities* (Buckingham: Open University Press, 1999); V. S. Gupta and Rajeshwar Dayal, *Media and Market Forces: Challenges and Opportunities* (Delhi: Concept, 1996); Edward S. Herman and Robert W. McChesney, *The Global Media: Missionaries of Corporate Capitalism* (London: Cassel, 1997); Daya Kishan Thussu, ed., *Electronic Empires: Global Media and Local Resistance* (New York: Arnold Publishers, 1998).

2. John Hannigan, *Fantasy City: Pleasure and Profit in the Postmodern Metropolis* (New York: Routledge, 1998); Michael Sorkin, ed., *Variations on a Theme Park: The New American City and the End of Public Space* (New York: Hill and Wang, 1992); Eric

Smoodin, ed., *Disney Discourse: Producing the Magic Kingdom* (New York: Routledge, 1994).

3. As quoted on the RFC website, www.ramojifilmcity.com

4. Renji Kuriakose, "Down in the clouds," *The Week* (India), October 19, 1997, http://www.theweek. com/97cot19/enter.htm (accessed April 6, 2004).

5. Sunil Rajanala, "IT effects: Cyberabad emerging specialist in 3D animation," *Financial Express* May 13, 2000, web.lexis-nexis.com (accessed April 6, 2004).

6. C. Chitti Pantulu, "IT effects—Cyberabad emerging specialist in 3–D animation," May 13, 2000, http://www.expressindia.com/news/fe/daily/20000513/fco13006.html (accessed April 6, 2004).

7. M. S. S. Pandian, *The Image Trap: M. G. Ramachandran in Film and Politics* (Newbury Park: Sage, 1992).

8. Benedict Anderson, *Imagined Communities* (New York: Verso, 1991).

9. Robin Jeffrey, *India's Newspaper Revolution: Capitalism, Politics and the Indian-Language Press 1977–99* (New York: Oxford University Press, 2000), 133.

10. The Chit Fund Department, Government of Delhi, defines a chit fund as "a transaction (whether called chit fund, chit, kuri or by any other name), by which the foreman enters into an agreement with a number of subscribers that everyone of them shall subscribe a certain sum for a certain period and each subscriber in his turn as determined by lot or by auction, shall be entitled to a prized amount." http://chitfund.delhigovt.nic.in/faq_frame.htm (accessed 27 May 2009).

11. Quoted in Jeffery, *India's Newspaper Revolution*, 133.

12. Carla Power and Sudip Mazumdar, "America isn't the only country that knows how to spin and export fantasies: Indian pop culture is huge; Bollywood goes global," *Newsweek*, international edition (February 28, 2000): 52.

13. Raghunath Raina, "Indian cinema goes global," *Press Information Bureau, Government of India*, http://pib.nic.in/feature/feyr2000/faug2000/f29082001 (accessed April 6, 2004).

14. Shyamanga Barooah, "Indian spice sprinkling in the world of cinema," November 26, 2000, http://www.apunkachoice.com/scoop/bollywood/20001126–1.html (accessed April 6, 2004).

15. Shankkar Aiyar and Sandeep Unnithan, "Bollywood's flight: The world a stage," *India Today*, January 13, 2003, The Global Indian: Chutney Culture Section, web.lexis-nexis.com (accessed April 6, 2004).

16. Aiyar and Unnithan, "Bollywood's flight."

17. Power and Mazumdar, "America isn't the only country."

18. Power and Mazumdar, "America isn't the only country."

19. Shekar Kapur, "The Asians are coming," *The Guardian* (London), August 23, 2002, web.lexis-nexis.com (accessed April 6, 2004).

20. Kapur, "The Asians are coming."

SIX

The Global Face of Indian Television

Divya C. McMillin

One of the important consequences of liberalizing Indian broadcasting in the 1990s was the establishment and growth of domestic broadcasters who competed with the state-controlled Doordarshan network. Inevitably, by the mid-1990s, these networks were tapping into the global market of Indians living overseas. The Hindi-language Zee TV was the first of the India-based global television networks, and private networks such as Sahara, Sony, and Sun TV, which broadcast in other Indian languages, quickly followed it. Drawing on interviews and archival materials, Divya McMillin traces the growth of these global television networks, showing how a specific business model emerged that took into account the ethnically ambivalent position of NRIs. In terms of television content, McMillin shows that the success of global Indian television is dependent on formulas developed to emphasize a handful of formats—game shows, music countdown shows, and family dramas—that work to valorize patriarchy and conservative constructions of the nation.

Subrata Ray Sahara, owner of the parent company of the Sahara One television network in India, said, "We may practice our religions in the confines of our homes, but outside, we should be Indians and only Indians. *Bharatiyata* or Nationalism thus becomes our supreme religion." In this emotional call to arms to his *kartavyogis*, as he terms his employees, Sahara strikes at the heart of identity politics.[1] Washing away workers' unique religious identities and anointing them in a supreme national religion is a masterful strategy to channel diverse segments into a collective unit. Conflation of the conglomerate with the national family itself as evident in its self-reference, *Sahara India Pariwar* (or Sahara India Family) makes synonymous the progress of business and nation.

Brand building and brand value management are important strategies to attract and maintain advertisers and subscribers[2]—a particularly challenging task in the transnational arena. While Sahara's plea for national unity may be interpreted as the philosophical longings of a patriotic businessman, it should also be seen as an extremely relevant business plan for a rapidly globalizing Indian television environment. The messiness of diversity may be accommodated within national boundaries; expatriate audiences must default to a unified identity. Non-Resident Indian (NRI) audiences across the world are generally reduced to the urban, middle-class prototype; such a reduction is in harmony with the logics of media globalization, which dictates that standardized products are low risk; copycat television is the way to go.[3]

Arthritic with over sixty years of postcolonial bureaucracy, India's state-sponsored television network, Doordarshan (DD), has faltered at every opportunity to enter the global television marketplace. Unruly private networks have sped ahead, high-fiving urban audiences across the world with their hefty fare of Indian film–based programming. It was only in April 2007, with a £2 million-over-five-years sponsorship by London-based Rayat Television Enterprises, that DD launched DD India and the 24-hour DD News in London as part of the Sky UK satellite television network. Private networks such as Zee TV, Sahara One, B4U (Bollywood for You), and Sun TV had already branded their transnational presence in the Anglo-American, Middle East, Far East, and South Asian markets, as well as in Australia and New Zealand.

Through archival research, review of industry reports, and interviews with marketing personnel, this chapter examines the "family channel" branding of particularly Zee TV, Sahara One, and Sun TV, and their ideological constructions of the "traditional" Indian family in top-rated prime-time dramas for expatriate audiences. The chapter concludes with an assessment of the reorientation of global television brought about by the Indian conglomerates.

All networks entered the transnational arena in the past fifteen years, and, in the case of Zee TV and Sun TV, had already established their presence in the national Indian market before venturing overseas. Comcast Cable in the United States offers Zee TV at the rate of $15 per month. The Dish Network offers, via its EchoStar satellites, a Mega Pack, Jumbo Packs 1, 2, and 3, or a Super Pack for an average of $55 a month or $660 a year.[4] These packages bundle combinations of B4U with the Zee, Sahara, Sony, and Sun TV networks. The Indian networks are not economies of scale in the sense that CNN, BBC, and Star TV are, yet they are examples of synergistic and interdependent industries. They could be regarded as evidence of India's growing global media presence because they are components of a global rather than international media economy.[5] Private television networks follow a global strategy, seeking "local stickiness" wherever they take root. This local contextualization is an important perspective to maintain as we assess the transnational presence of Indian television.[6]

Salaam, Yorkshire: Expanding the Global Circuit

India's 1991 economic liberalization policy is cited over and over by industry watchers and workers as *the* historic document that spurred the entry of private foreign and indigenous television into the Indian media market.[7] While Zee TV was the first private Hindi-language network in 1992 to compete with DD for the national market and was the first to go international around five years later, other vernacular-language private networks were quick to follow the market leader through mimetic and normative "morphism."[8] Each vying for urban consumers across the country and for Non-Resident Indians across the world, the networks import, license, clone, adapt, and reproduce robust formats such as the game show, talk show, and call-in music show. The networks enjoy competitive advantages of language, cultural context, and a certain degree of transnational currency, over the foreign, English-language contenders such as CNN, BBC, and Star TV. For many, initiation into the global market happened at the imperial center, the United Kingdom, as a significant rite of passage.

For example, Sahara One Television—whose corporate philosophy states, "There is a religion higher than religion itself—it is the Indian nationality"—was ironically christened at the 2004 Sangeet Awards at the Royal Albert Hall in London. B4U launched its digital movie and music channels in the United Kingdom in 1999 and in the Middle East, Canada, and the United States six months later. It was only in 2000 that the network crept into the television environment in India, recognizing that its potential—boosted tremendously through majority ownership by Eros International, the largest distributor of Bollywood films in the world—was better realized in the global rather than the national Indian market. As if needing further we-have-arrived authentication from the imperial center, the 2007 Indian International Film Academy (IIFA) Awards was located in Yorkshire, with grandiose declarations from Indian film superstars and Yorkshire dignitaries alike on the powerful influence of Bollywood on the world. The symbolism in the entry of keynote speaker superstar Amitabh Bachchan was obvious: Bachchan rolled in amid smoke, in a gleaming, silver 1959 Morgan driven by a British chauffeur; the *Coolie* was in the house.[9] Eros as a major sponsor of the program subsequently marketed a heavily edited version of the show on DVD to Indian and expatriate markets through the Eros International distribution network.

India's global media presence no doubt is dominated by its film industry. At the end of 2006, *The Times of India* reported that Bollywood outproduced Hollywood by 274 films per year (1,013 films from Bollywood vs. 739 films from Hollywood). Bollywood tickets sold per year averaged around 3.6 billion while Hollywood ticket sales averaged 2.6 billion. Although Hollywood's profits far outranked Bollywood's at $51 billion over $1.3 billion, its production costs per film at $47.7 million vs. Bollywood's $1.5 million, and average marketing costs per film at $27.3 million vs. the latter's $500,000, temper its profit margin. Film studio giants from South India such as Chennai's AVM churn out blockbusters as well, with tremendous transnational success. A fine example is the July 2007 release of *Sivaji: The Boss* featuring the fifty-eight-year-old Tamil movie star Rajnikant, actually a Kannadiga from Bangalore. With fifteen different hairstyles, playing six different characters, and cavorting with a heroine half his age, Rajnikant's *Sivaji* cost US$1.8 million to produce and was released in twenty-five countries. First-day, first-show tickets in movie theaters such as New Jersey's Cine Plaza ran for as much as $200.[10] In partnership with Bollywood and South Indian studios, private Indian television networks carve out distinct brand identities for their transnational pay-per-view clientele. India has been referred to as a big emerging market or BEM.[11] Networks such as Zee TV, Sahara One, B4U, and Sun TV are successful precisely because they project a very local, pristine, traditional "Indianness."

Transnational vs. Ethnic: The Competitive Disadvantage

The Indian media and entertainment (M&E) industry is estimated around $10 billion, with the television industry at $4.2 billion accounting for the largest share of revenue. Rapid growth (19 percent) from 2006 to 2007 is attributed to new distribution platforms such as digital cable, Direct to Home (DTH), and Internet protocol television (IPTV). During the early 2000s, mergers and fold-ups marked the Indian television environment;[12] in the latter part of the decade, big networks have de-merged to combat regulations, to maintain efficient operations, and to respond to different technological requirements in each sector. For example, Zee TV de-merged into four separate businesses: Content Creation and Broadcast, News Broadcast, Cable, and Direct-to-Home. Three new units emerged from these four businesses: Zee News Ltd. (News); Wire and Wireless India Ltd. (Cable) with ownership of Siticable, India's largest MSO;[13] and Dish TV India Ltd. (DTH).[14]

In India, television households are estimated at 112 million. Color-TV homes are estimated at 64 million, with around 68 million homes having access to cable and satellite television. Target consumers are those in their early twenties who are the most active consumers and have the highest purchasing power. Hindi general entertainment channels snag 34 percent of total television viewership, while regional channels enjoy 23 percent of viewership. English movie channels such as HBO and Star Movies are watched by only 7 percent of Indian audiences, while news channels are watched by 5 percent; sports, 4 percent; kid channels, 9 percent; and Hindi cinema channels, 10 percent.[15] DD lags in just about every genre in the urban market, explaining some of its sluggishness in the transnational arena, given that NRI communities are generally from urban India themselves. The mapping of viewer tastes in India offers important lessons for clientele overseas. Although Zee TV and Sun TV first established their dominance over the urban Indian market before expanding internationally, Sahara One and B4U tapped expatriate and the Indian markets almost simultaneously. Zee TV ramped up its Hindi-drama and film-based programming for its audiences abroad and Sahara One and B4U also offer extensive menus of Hindi films, dramas, and variety shows.

As networks power their way through national and transnational markets, branding becomes an important strategy to differentiate each from its competitors. Mukherjee and Roy's *dynamic brand value management* (DBVM) theory offers a way to understand the success of transnational Indian networks.[16] DBVM theory is derived from brand management and marketing literature. It draws from two premises: "the resource based view of the firm that treats firms as collections of strategic resources, and business dynamics that takes a systemic view of management issues."[17] Such an approach requires an understanding that networks and audiences have to be studied as components of a linked, circular, and feedback system. Obviously such a system is a complex one, with irregularities, inertia, delays, and oscillatory behavior. Although the Indian television networks can control *action variables*, which are management objectives and policies, *state variables*—which include advertising revenue, competition from other channels, and viewer interest—pose the following significant challenges:

First, as transnational networks, they have to fight for advertisers who choose other, more established ethnic networks, which Naficy identifies as those carrying programs "primarily produced in the host country by long-established indigenous minorities."[18] Examples would be BET and Univision in the United States. Unlike ethnic networks, Zee TV, Sahara One, B4U, and Sun TV do not have a large enough consumer base. Consequently, they lose out to advertisers who would rather target African American and Hispanic viewers than a narrow and diverse South Asian diaspora.

Second, although Chinese transnational networks may be more appropriate for comparison, conversations with executives in U.S.–based marketing offices for the Indian networks revealed that advertisers are reluctant to sponsor programming on a channel that targets viewers who can speak English. Sameer Targe, a Zee TV area manager based in New Jersey, explained that companies were reluctant to advertize on Zee TV because its audience, unlike some other ethnic groups like the Chinese, was more likely to understand English. Such a population would be exposed to the same advertisements on mainstream networks. It was more efficient for these corporations to invest in advertisements in language-specific markets for those who did not speak or understand English in the United States. Targe commented, "It is *hard* to convince the Chryslers, Wal-Marts, and Merrill Lynches of the world to advertise with us. They don't really consider us an *ethnic* market. They consider us to be quite Westernized."[19]

Sustaining an advertising base of Indian businesses poses its own complications. Many advertisers lack long-term commitment and do not find it particularly useful to advertise on a channel that costs its viewers around $20 per month via cable or around $16 on a dish platform.

Third, although private channels in India enjoy a competitive advantage over DD for urban audiences because of their innovativeness in programming and sophistication of production, they face stiff competition abroad from other well-established, mainstream, and ethnic channels.

Fourth, with respect to viewer interest, senior NRIs and those who emigrated in the 1990s or 2000s are more likely to subscribe to the channel because they either want Indian programming in general or had developed a loyalty to the channel in India. Second-generation immigrants generally prefer mainstream channels.

Finally, in transnational markets, Indian networks face the challenge of the delay between action and state variables that may temper the durability of their brand value. As Mukherjee and Roy explain, a promotion launched by a program or network may result in increased viewership only after a few weeks.[20] So the Indian networks need to enter into bundle agreements with other channels and pay vital attention to network brand value as they approach new markets.

Branding Ethnicity: The Indian Network-Family

Zee TV, Sun TV, and Sahara One all emerged from family-owned businesses. Except for B4U, which carries only Bollywood-based programming, each network brands its transnational package as a family of channels segregated according to genre—that is, news, music, general entertainment, and sports.

Zee TV is a subsidiary of the Essel group, a family-owned industry started in 1926 by Ram Gopal and his eldest son, Jagan Nath Goenka. It was renamed Subhash Chandra Laxmi Narain (SL; and renamed Essel in 1973) in 1969 after a rift in the family. In 1992, the company launched India's first satellite channel under the name Zee Telefilms Limited, with Siticable as its distributer, India's first MSO (multisystem operator). Zee Telefilms, renamed Zee TV, naturally emerged as the market leader in transnational Indian television, launched from a transponder subleased from Star TV. With a fee of US$8.6 million a year to be part of the Star TV platform, Zee TV uplinked to Asia Sat-1 from Hong Kong. Murdoch's News Corporation acquired 49.9 percent of Asia Today, Zee TV's Hong Kong–based holding company, in December 1993. The rest was held by a coalition of Non-Resident Indians. Zee TV entered the U.K. market in 1995, replacing TV Asia. It made its debut in the United States three years later, providing competition to TV Asia, but was more limited in reach because of its pay-TV status.

According to Targe, the network was the first to exploit the expatriate market in the United States and United Kingdom. Launched within a year of India's 1991 liberalization policy, Zee TV was in a prime position to exploit its rollout. As various other private regional-language networks emerged in the next five years, Zee TV was already the market leader, a recognizable brand name. Targe said that in the United States, as more and more Indian households subscribed to the channel, they fostered brand loyalty within their children as well. This, combined with subscriptions from recent immigrants who had grown up watching Zee TV in India, made the network a leader among expatriate audiences as well.[21]

Zee TV has carved a distinct urban, upper-middle-class identity for itself ever since its inception. Zee's early success in India with prime-time dramas centering on upper-middle-class Gujarati family stories led to its branding as a "family channel." The uniquely Gujarati flavor was developed as an initial response to the Mumbai market in the early 1990s and then continued as it proved successful over the years. Gujarati households dominate the subscriber base in the United States. As Targe (2007) explained, "Even in India, the programs that have Guju story lines are in the top eight shows: *Kyo Ki Saas Bhi Kabhi Bahu Thi, Kahani Ghar Ghar Ki, Betiya*—all our top shows have Gujarati story lines." The language is Hindi, the setup is Gujarati. The highly conservative Gujarati context, although highly popular among audiences in India and older-generation Indians in the United States, was lost on younger audiences outside the country. Despite the latter's preference for mainstream American networks such as ABC, NBC, CBS, and Fox, Zee TV kept to its Gujarati themes since its primary audience were Gujarati housewives.[22]

In addition to the Gujarati dramas, Zee's subsidiary ETC Networks Limited has held exclusive rights for the past eleven years to telecast Gurbani live from the Golden Temple, Amritsar. For Sikh viewers across the globe, live telecasts of Gurbani facilitate the invention of a pure homeland in a distortion of the lived nation that characterizes diasporic communities. ETC's rights to an extensive library of films that propel the Zee Cinema channel and Zee Records promotion through the ETC Music Channel[23] is an example of the synergistic relationships in the Essel dynasty. Zee TV is available in the United States, United Kingdom, Ireland, Malaysia, Singapore, and Israel, to name a few countries.[24] The Zee network claims a consumer base of 500 million subscribers worldwide in 120 countries. Its subscriber base is 532,000 in North and Latin America, 174,000 in Europe, 73,000 in Africa, and 2 million in Asia Pacific.[25]

Sun TV followed the urban market leader, Zee TV, in India on Tamil New Year's Day in 1993, with early programming exclusively in Tamil. "With ties to various Tamil movie studios, Sun TV's airtime was filled with films and film-based programming."[26] Like Zee TV, Sun TV is a family-owned network, controlled by Kalanidhi Maran, the nephew of Industry Minister Murasoli Maran and grandson of the family of Dravida Munetra Kazhagam (DMK) chief Muthuvel Karunanidhi.[27] In the early 1990s, many believed Sun TV was nothing more than an extension of DMK propaganda, exacerbated by the fact that the station headquarters in Chennai is the same as that of the DMK. Even the network's symbol, a rising sun, is synonymous with the party's poll symbol. Kalanidhi immediately aired a current affairs program, *Neru-K-Ner* (Face-to-Face) where political leaders were pitted against each other in debates to convey a sense of network objectivity and neutrality. Sun TV has now branched into four separate networks, the flagship Tamil-language Sun TV, the Telugu-language Gemini TV, the Malayalam-language Surya TV, and the Kannada-language Udaya TV. Each network has its own genre-specific channels for a total of twenty-four channels overall.[28] Kalanidhi signed a contract with Star TV for the latter to carry all Sun TV channels on its DTH platforms. Sun TV was available to the North American market in 2002 on the Dish Network. Average cost of the network is $15 on cable and, when bundled with other channels and marketed through the Dish Network or DirecTV, approximately $55–60 per month. In Australia and the United Kingdom, hardware such as a digital decoder box, an 85/95 cm dish, and a Smart Card (costing around $67 with a quarterly payment of around $120) are required to receive pay channels. Average fees are $45 per month and subscribers have to commit to a minimum of twelve months. In Australia and New Zealand,[29] in particular, demand is high for South Indian programming, making the Sun TV network and its affiliate, KTV, far more popular than their Hindi-language competitors. In the United Kingdom, as well, packages are sold for a minimum of twelve months at the approximate rate of $550.

Shammi, a program executive based in Chennai, India, said that the network did not use any rating system to keep track of viewer interests either within India or abroad. Demand was so great for the channel that the overseas strategy rested on infrastructural availability rather than audience interest (Shammi, personal communication, August 12, 2007). Sun TV reaches audiences in India, China, Malaysia, Singapore, and Russia by uplinking to Singapore Cable. It is available via the Eutelsat Hotbird 4 satellite in such European countries as Denmark, France, Norway, Germany, Holland, Sweden, Switzerland, and the United Kingdom. Audiences in South Africa receive Sun TV via DStv cable.

Perhaps no other network promotes its family image as potently as Sahara One. Sahara One's business model parallels that of Zee TV and Sun TV, and is owned by the Sahara family, which started a rudimentary banking business in 1978 with only $45.[30] The thirty-year-old conglomerate calls itself the "World's Largest Family" and launched Sahara TV in 2000 with the twenty-four-hour encrypted Entertainment channel across sixty-six countries. Its movie channel, Filmy, was launched in February 2006 and is fed by films produced in Sahara-owned production houses such as Rajshri Productions, Creative Eye, and Cinevista Production.

The conglomerate's corporate report is a dramatic representation of its family focus. The opening slide depicts the goddess India, a fair-skinned, slim woman clad in a white sari with tricolor border representing the Indian flag (saffron, white, and green). She is bedecked with a thick gold, breastplate-like necklace and waistband. Her right hand holds the Indian flag, with a twist—the blue chakra or the wheel of truth is missing. The flag waves victoriously behind her head and her heavy gold crown is placed within an upright gold halo that acts as the chakra of the flag. The goddess is in a chariot and holds in her left hand the gold reins to the four roaring lions that pull it. The sinewy and ferocious lions are a stark contrast to her serene expression, reflected in four preteen boys pictured before her ensemble. Each boy is light-skinned, clad in white *kurta* or shirt, with a tricolor scarf around his neck. Each wears a hat to represent a religion or philosophy: the first, communism, the second, Islam, the third, Sikhism, the fourth, Christianity. The words *Vande Mataram* (*Hail to the Motherland*) run midway across the slide, with each word on either side of the goddess.[31] Running across the base of this image is the word *Bharatiyata* in white, a word that has its roots in the fundamentalist Bharatiya Janata Party's *Hindutva* credo where Hindu supremacist principles are conflated with cultural nationalism. It is underlined in red with the following legend beneath it: "Our religion, our honor, our belief: Our beautiful and contented coexistence." Corporate literature emphasizes respect for all religions, castes, and classes.

Chairman Subrata Roy Sahara avows in his opening address that Sahara One operates on the philosophy of "collective materialism" where profits are utilized for national development. Specifically, the philosophy states: "In any human relationship, it becomes imperative to take into consideration the materialistic aspect of life—we do so but by giving it second priority. The first priority is given to emotional aspect and with perfect blending of materialism with emotionalism results in continuous collective growth for collective sharing and caring that gives an impetus to our philosophy— COLLECTIVE MATERIALISM."

Profits are shared among *kartavyogi* (40 percent), the company's net owned fund (35 percent), and social development activities (25 percent). The company disallows unions and considers each employee a member of a closely knit family where unions are not necessary to assert individual rights. The goal is to nurture the "six healths" of human beings: "physical, material, mental, emotional, social, and professional." The corporate report ends with a photo montage of the chairman with a motley group of spiritual and political leaders such as Mother Teresa, the Dalai Lama, and former president and current prime minister of India, A. P. J. Abdul Kalam and Manmohan Singh, respectively; industrialists such as the late DhiruBhai Ambani of the Reliance group and Ratan Tata of the Tata group; and finally, American celebrities Michael Douglas, Goldie Hawn, and Bill Clinton.

As a contrast to the media families of Zee TV, Sun TV, and Sahara One, B4U is quite simply the television distributor of Bollywood films. With major investment from Eros International, the largest worldwide Bollywood distributing network, B4U's channels B4U Music and B4U Movies (the latter began in India in 2001) are filled with top Hindi film song-and-dance sequences, and comedy and fight scene countdowns. The channels debuted in U.K., Middle East, and U.S. markets in 1999 and entered the Indian market in 2000. With its primary clientele the Brit-Asian community in the United Kingdom, B4U provides sponsorship and coverage of Bollywood events overseas, most recently the Regent Street Festival in September 2007 that was the culmination of a three-month celebration of the India–London relationship under the banner of "India Now." Each channel of the network is available to the U.K. audience on the Sky network (through the Astra 2A satellite) or on Virgin Media cable. Average subscription price is around $14 a month per B4U channel and, when bundled with another transnational network such as Sony, approximately US$20 per month. In the United States, B4U is available on the Dish Network (on Echostar III satellite) with rates of $20, $45, and $50 per month for Alacarte, Jumbo Pack One (which consists of four channels including B4U), and Mega Pack-5 (which consists of five channels including B4U), respectively. In Europe, B4U is available through the Hotbird 3 satellite in such countries as Austria, Belgium, Denmark, and Finland.[32] Packages range from US$135–$175 per month where B4U is bundled with one or two other channels. B4U reaches audiences in the

Middle East through the Firstnet and Nilesat satellites. Distributors in each country are invariably South Asian merchants who own other businesses such as textiles, video distribution, general imports and exports, and tourism.

What the description of the histories and reach of these networks tells us is that all were launched from already thriving business enterprises. Television was regarded by each parent family as a key area in which to invest. The Indian film industry provides a majority of program content. In-house productions such as dramas, talk shows, and news shows follow time-tested formats to reduce risk.

Of Bollywood, Jollywood, and Urban Indianhood

The preference among national audiences for domestic, vernacular-language programming over foreign programming because of the significant increase in production and reception quality beginning in the 1990s has been well documented.[33] Locally produced programs are chosen even over subtitled foreign programming.[34] Such a trend has been traced to transnational audiences as well.[35] Cloned, copied, unlicensed, and licensed hybrid programs characterize the Asian television market. The thriving format industry in this part of the world further reduces the demand and popularity of foreign programs.

Although DBVM theory is used to "formulate effective dynamic marketing decisions in the presence of perishable demand,"[36] the emphasis here is on format durability to sustain capricious demand. The action variable of the feedback loop that is essential in the analysis of the brand-building ability of program content is impossible when the program is aired for a transnational audience. Only state variables such as interest level and revenue may be addressed. Through such a complication in standard assessment of the durability of transnational television products, attention rightly should rest with format durability.

An extensive analysis of programs available on Zee TV, Sun TV and its regional affiliates, Sahara One, and B4U networks during fieldwork in Delhi and Bangalore, India, during winter 2006 and summer 2007 and a thorough review of program synopses on all network websites revealed that certain formats emerged that were robust over time. Conversations with marketing executives at particularly Zee TV and Sun TV in the United States and India showed that those formats that had withstood the vagaries of the Indian market were promoted overseas. It is virtually impossible to identify the creator of a format because cloning and copying have been the nature of the Indian media environment. In the television industry, the trend had already been set by Bollywood where producers and directors attend international film festivals for the sole purpose of lifting plots to feed a voracious domestic industry.

As stated earlier, licensed and unlicensed clones of game shows, developed countdown music shows, and copied prime-time family drama and call-in program formats have endured in the Indian television industry. These form the bulk of content on transnational networks. *Cloning* pertains to those programs that copy the original completely.[37] Most popular formats for cloning are quiz shows and game shows that feature exorbitant prizes, celebrity anchors, and guests. A prominent example is the British production company Celador's *Who Wants to Be a Millionaire?* which first aired on Independent Television (ITV) in 1998 and has since become the most cloned program in international markets. In India, it debuted on Star TV as *Kaun Banega Crorepathi* (*KBC*) in 2000 with a grand prize of US$227,000 and megastar Amitabh Bachchan as its anchor. So robust was *KBC* that it raised its advertisement rates by 60 percent and still had sufficient sponsors. Telephone lines were jammed on the first day the show aired because of over 100,000 callers trying to reach the show. Around 3 million callers were recorded trying to qualify for the show during the run of the first twelve episodes alone. Zee TV's unlicensed *Sawal Dus Crore Ka* (*SDCK*) soon followed but folded within weeks despite its prize money being ten times higher than *KBC*, primarily because of the lack of star quality in its dual anchors.[38] Sahara One's *Biggest Loser Jeetega* from NBC's *Biggest Loser* is another example of a cloned program. Red and Blue Teams comprising a total of sixteen obese people are pitted against each other for a grueling and emotional sixteen weeks of challenges. The team that loses the most weight wins. Sunil Shetty, a popular Hindi film actor cast mostly in action-oriented roles, hosts the show. A further example is Sahara One's *Fair & Lovely Menz Active Presents Superstars*, cloned from the Netherlands' production company Endemol's *Stars in Their Eyes*, a competition where participants imitate their favorite film stars, with proven success in the Netherlands, United Kingdom, Belgium, and Spain. Sahara Filmy's *Bathroom Singer* is another unlicensed clone, hosted by television personality Gaurav Gera. Based on Freemantle Media's (owned by Bertelsmann of Germany) *Pop Idol* (cloned most famously in the United States as *American Idol*),[39] callers vote for the best singer and two judges with acting and singing credentials provide encouragement and criticism. The winner receives a grand prize of US$57,000. The sets and music vary from *Idol* even though the premise is essentially the same. Cloned programs, whether licensed or unlicensed, carry tremendous potential because of their established success in first-run arenas.

Developing refers to those programs that extend only part of the original format to create a new format.[40] Examples of such programs are the numerous music shows that have adapted the countdown format, attributed to MTV in the 1990s.[41] Although the basic premise of counting down to the number one film song, fight scene, or dance sequence is maintained, this is coupled with anchors interviewing celebrities or selecting film clips based on a particular theme. Examples are B4U's *Countdown Café* and *India Top 10* (which feature the top ten Indian pop songs), *Bollywood 10 on 10* (showcasing the latest film clips), and *Maha Bees* (featuring songs from the latest Hindi film releases). Filmy's *Rokky's 99* countdown of film clips and Sun TV's *Top 10 Movies* and *Super 10*, which rate the top Tamil movies and film songs of the week based on theater and cassette sales, and Gemini TV's (of the Sun TV network) *Neekosam*, which pairs call-in birthday wishes with a countdown of Tollywood comedy scenes, are other examples in this genre. Sun TV's immensely popular *Jollywood Express* contains elements of *Whose Line Is It Anyway?* It presents an "engine driver" Manivannan with Tollywood stars as passengers who perform impromptu skits in response to various fictional premises.

As feeder networks for Indian films, most programs on Zee TV, Sun TV, Sahara One, and B4U are essentially spliced film vignettes presented by young, attractive anchors, invariably female, resulting in extensive copycat programming. The call-in music show is a transfer from call-in radio request programs. Sun TV's *Ungal Choice*, originally *Pepsi Ungal Choice*, is highly popular for the conversations the anchor has with callers. Diffused colors weave in and out on the background screen while anchors joke with and probe the callers for personal information. Others that have followed suit are *Sun Music Special*, *Traffic Jam*, *Yellam Unnakkaga*, *Anbe Anbe*, and *Hello Hello* on the Sun Music channel. The film news program is another new format popular in the Indian market where anchors deliver news from North and South Indian film industries in the same serious style and tone of a bona fide news show. Examples are Filmy's *Aaj Ki FILMY Khabar* and Sun TV's *Thirai Vimarsanam*.

On B4U, *B4U Starstop* features interviews with Bollywood actors, *B4U Special* spotlights Hindi film playback singers, and *B4U Centre Stage* provides behind-the-scenes coverage of Indian celebrities. Sahara One's *Bollywood Cutting* presents Bollywood trivia and Filmy carries *Mike Testing* and *Meri Bhains Ko Anda Kyon Mara?* which present favorite Hindi film songs and comedy scenes. Sun TV's KTV channel spotlights Tamil cinema with such programs as *Muthal Payanam*, *Sirippu Vedigal*, and *Stunt Show* featuring debuting Tamil actors, favorite comedy scenes, and stunt sequences, respectively. Sun TV itself, needless to say, carries substantive film-based content with such programs as *Super Scenes*, *Ninaivugal*, and *Putham Pudhusu* featuring contemporary and classic Tamil films. Gemini TV, Surya TV, and Udaya TV follow their parent company with programs providing the same breadth and depth of treatment of respective regional-language films. Full-length feature films are standard fare given the synergistic relationship each network shares with a variety of film production houses.

Cutthroat competition in the television industry demands imitations on a massive scale, with the drama scenario among channels as incestuous as that of game shows and music shows. Analyses of soaps on Zee TV, Sahara One, and Sun TV during June–July 2007 showed that women-centered narratives dominated prime-time dramas. The middle-class Indian woman herself has proven to be a robust dramatic element where narratives swirl around her sexuality, fertility, virginity, independence, and so on.

Examples of some recurring themes are sisters in conflict (such as in *Mangalya* and *Kadambari* on the Udaya TV channel of Sun TV), mothers and daughters locked in power struggles (as in *Jhansi* and *Chakravakam* on the Gemini TV channel of the Sun TV network), girlfriends feuding over the same man (as in *Arase* on Sun TV), carefree teenagers transforming into sober women (as in *Solah Singaarr* on Sahara One), daughters-in-law suffering the tribulations of their extended family (as in Zee TV's *Kyo Ki Saas Bhi Kabhi Bahu Thi* and Sahara One's *Kuch Apne Kuch Paraye*), and urban women struggling to balance social expectations with their own need for independence (as in Sahara One's *Mai Aisi Kyun Hoon?* and Zee TV's *Saat Phere Saloni Ka Safar* and *Banoo Main Teri Dulhann*). Like the serene, light-skinned goddess of Sahara One's flagship presentation, the middle-class woman remains the badge of Indian tradition and all-giving nationhood. John and Nair address this construction: "Not only has the middle class, upper class woman been the ground on which questions of modernity and tradition are framed, she is the embodiment of boundaries between licit and illicit forms of sexuality, as well as the guardian of the nation's modernity."[42]

Format adaptation is evidence that in the transnational arena Indian networks are truly meeting the competition from mainstream channels, matching them genre for genre, jackpot for jackpot. As a form of hybridity,

Zee TV's *Saat Phere, Saloni Ka Safer,* one of the growing number of women-centered narrative dramas that dominate Indian prime-time television.

it revives the question of whether economic dominance or cultural imperialism is at play.[43] What, then, can we conclude about the reorientation of global television brought about by the Indian television networks? The concluding commentary takes as its point of entry the opening example of this chapter: the IIFA award ceremony in Yorkshire, which provided a rich display of India's transnational credentials.

India's Global Presence

When the piped smoke at the 2007 IIFA award ceremonies cleared and superstar Amitabh Bachchan stepped out of the gleaming Morgan, the audience went wild, rising to their feet to cheer the tall, stately don of Bollywood. The British chauffeur-driven car glided away and all eyes were on Bachchan as he welcomed the celebrities and patrons in Yorkshire and across the globe before making a passionate plea for a greener world. Staging the IIFA in Yorkshire was no doubt a strong message of transnational success for the Bollywood industry. The emphasis on environmental concerns was a further statement that the Indian glitterati were shoulder to shoulder with global glitterati, affluent enough to be concerned about global warming and not just about underdevelopment, as is the assumed agenda of third-world personalities.

Diasporic communities play a significant role in reorienting frames through which their native lands are comprehended. In colonial, pre-1947 India, encounters between colonizer and native typically resulted in a transfiguration of local texts that resulted in the reinstatement of the positional superiority of the former and the inferiority of the latter. For example, bilingual dictionaries played a crucial role in facilitating administrative functions of the British in India. Creation of these texts was fraught with power struggles where native scholars, working with British intellectuals versed in local languages, found their interpretations of words invariably subsumed under British interpretations of the same.[44] Bollywood and its distribution networks, which essentially classify transnational television, retrain the India watcher to new narratives of nation: India can be affluent, India can be technologically savvy, India can be clean. Yet, as the hotspot of outsourced labor and low-cost extension of Silicon Valley in its high-tech urban intellectual base, India as a text, interestingly enough, resurfaces in contemporary global popular consciousness as a feminized object of capitalist desire. The nation continues to be "seen" in the global press through the tropes of neocolonial capitalist patriarchy, which also characterize hybrid programming on the Indian networks.[45]

Transnational Indian television should then be viewed simultaneously as a venue for the assertion of the arrival of the "coolie in the house" and for the reification of neo-Orientalist and patriarchal constructions of nation. Format adaptation and hybrid programming across networks are often cited as examples of empowering media globalization where even the global South can participate in mandates of modernization, once only the prerogative of industrialized imperial centers. As illustrated in the discussion of particularly women-oriented dramas that receive top billing on Zee TV, Sahara One, and Sun TV, NRIs and foreign audiences who subscribe to such networks are still comfortable with time-worn stereotypes of gender, ethnic, class, and religious minorities. As several critical scholars have pointed out, such dramas continue to set adrift the modern woman, placing upon her the burden of being successful both in private and public, modern and traditional, spheres, absolving the others around her from responsibility for the success or failure of the family unit.[46] Dramas resonate with the diaspora's nostalgia for a golden past where women knew their place so that even their ventures into modernity were contained by their recognition that a family's needs came first. Game shows are compatible with global capitalism in their emphases on individual competition and exorbitant prizes.

It is true that transnational Indian television carries the ideological baggage of sexism and classism that still characterizes national television across the world. It also delivers uncritiqued, similar structures from Bollywood and Tollywood. However, we should acknowledge the potency of what things represent on the surface in addition to their deep structures.[47] We should recognize that the stage of transnational Indian television is set not only in diasporic homes but also against the backdrop of anti-Asian riots in Oldham, Bradford, and Brundley in 2001 and the widely publicized racism of Jade Goody toward Bollywood actress Shilpa Shetty on Channel Four's 2007 run of *Celebrity Big Brother*. In a postcolonial, globalizing world, the IIFA spotlights that bathed Indian and British movie stars alike in the same milky glow not only legitimized the ex-colonized's success but also, and more strategically, sealed the "consciousness of the white colonialist"[48] as well. NRIs and Indians could certainly be proud of Bachchan as their spokesperson; theirs was not the embarrassment felt by nationalist leaders in colonial India when Mahatma Gandhi interacted with international leaders and British royalty in his loincloth nakedness. Gandhi may have used his "always out of place" image to symbolize his civil disobedience to the British Empire and its fetishization of social etiquette.[49] Bachchan, equally powerfully, used his absolutely in-place English speech and black Nehru coat to construct a *stylish hybridity*, demonstrating that where Bollywood and transnational television are concerned, postcolonial India just might have the upper hand.[50]

Notes

1. *Kartavyogi* is a Hindi term that means, quite literally, "doer of duty." Here, duty implies more of a moral obligation or commitment rather than a mere job.

2. Avinandan Mukherjee and Rahul Roy, "A system dynamic model of management of a television game show," *Journal of Modeling in Management* 1, no. 2 (2006): 95–115

3. Amos O. Thomas and Keval J. Kumar, "Copied from without and cloned from within: India in the global television format business," in *Television across Asia: Television Industries, Programme Formats and Globalization*, ed. Albert Moran and Michael Keane (London: Routledge Curzon, 2004), 122–37.

4. The Dish Network was launched in 1996 from the EchoStar Communications Corporation started in 1980 by Charles Ergen.

5. Albert Moran, "Television formats in the world/The world of television formats," in *Television across Asia: Television Industries, Programme Formats and Globalization*, ed. Albert Moran and Michael Keane (London: Routledge Curzon, 2004), 1–8.

6. Koichi Iwabuchi, *Recentering Globalization: Popular Culture and Japanese Transnationalism* (Durham, NC: Duke University Press, 2002).

7. Peter Shields and Sundeep R. Muppidi, *Integration, the Indian State and STAR TV: Policy and Theory Issues*, paper presented to the annual meeting of the International Communication Association, Chicago, 1996.

8. Moran, "Television formats." See Moran also for a definition of terms.

9. The word *coolie* is an Anglicization of *kuli*, which can be traced to Hindi, Urdu, Tamil, Gujarati, and Bengali origins. It means day laborer or daily wages. It was used during colonial times, most notably in Asia, as a racial slur for laborer or porter. *Coolie* is a 1983 film starring Amitabh Bachchan as the head porter Iqbal who helps another character, Sunny, avenge the murder of his father. The movie was famous not just for its plot but also for a serious accident during filming where Bachchan ruptured his spleen when he fell on the edge of a table in a fight scene.

10. Lakshmi Subramanian, "The boss," *India Today* (July 9, 2007).

11. Amos O. Thomas, "Cultural economics of TV programme cloning: Or why India has produced multi-millionaires," *International Journal of Emerging Markets* 1, no. 1 (2006): 35–47.

12. Divya C. McMillin, "Localizing the global: Television and hybrid programming in India," *International Journal of Cultural Studies* 4, no. 1 (2001): 45–68.

13. Multisystem operators, or MSOs, play a vital role in the distribution of cable. In the early years of cable (early 1990s), local cable operators, or LCOs, received feeds from MSOs for a fee, which they in turn recovered through subscriptions from end users. This resulted in limited control of customers by MSOs and underreporting of the customer base by LCOs. Currently, with a direct acquisition of 51 percent interest in LCOs, MSOs have greater control of subscribers and greater transparency in LCO declaration of subscriber base. Zee TV plans to go to broadband in the near future and offer high-speed Internet, video on demand, digital video recorder, voiceover Internet protocol (VOIP), and local and long distance services as part of its subscriber package.

14. Dish TV is owned by ASC Enterprises Limited; plans are underway to rename the company Dish TV India Limited. Revenues of the company were up as a consequence, with consolidated revenues up 18 percent from 2006. In 2007, Zee acquired 50 percent of Ten Sports, a leading sports channel.

15. The Essel Group, Media and Entertainment Segment, 2007.

16. Mukherjee and Roy, "A system dynamic model."

17. Mukherjee and Roy, "A system dynamic model," 99.

18. Hamid Naficy, "Narrowcasting in diaspora: Iranian television in Los Angeles," in *Planet TV: A Global Television Reader*, ed. Lisa Parks and Shanti Kumar (New York: New York University Press, 2003), 377.

19. Sameer Targe, personal communication, August 20, 2007.

20. Mukherjee and Roy, "A system dynamic model."

21. Sameer Targe, personal communication, August 20, 2007.

22. Sameer Targe, personal communication, August 20, 2007.

23. In the Indian market, ETC Music leads with 35 percent of the market, MTV

is next with 27 percent, B4U with 18 percent, and Zee Music with 11 percent. The Essel group now has 44 percent holdings in Zee Entertainment Enterprises Ltd., 54 percent in Zee News Ltd. (started in 2004), 44 percent in Wire and Wireless India Ltd. (started in 2006), and 67 percent in Dish TV India Ltd. (started in 2005).

24. Zee TV is available in India (Tata Sky), Malaysia (Astro), Indonesia (Astro Nusantra), United States (Dish Network and Comcast Cablevision), Sri Lanka (Dialog TV), Philippines (Global Destiny Cable), United Kingdom (Sky Digital and Virgin Media and Tiscali TV cable), Ireland (Sky Digital and UPC Ireland cable), Singapore (Astro and StarHub cable), and Israel (HOT cable).

25. The Essel Group, 2007.

26. Moti K. Gokulsing, *Soft-Soaping India: The World of Indian Televised Soap Operas* (Sterling, VA: Trentham Books, 2004).

27. Other media holdings of the Sun TV network include daily newspapers (for example, *Dinakaran, Tamizh Murasu*), FM radio stations, and magazines (for example, *Vannathirai* and *Kumguma Chimizh*).

28. Sun TV channels may be organized according to language. Tamil-language channels are Sun TV, KTV, Sun News, Sun Music, and Chutti TV. Telugu-language channels are Gemini TV, Teja TV, Teja News, Aditya TV, Gemini News, Gemini Music, and GCV. Malayalam-language channels are Surya TV and Kiran TV. Finally, Kannada-language channels are Udaya TV, Udaya Movies, Udaya News, Udaya 2, and Udaya Varthegalu.

29. Sun TV is telecast in Australia and New Zealand via the Optus B3 satellite.

30. Sahara One's diverse businesses include parabanking, life insurance, mutual funds, and housing and shopping complexes such as the exclusive, gated Sahara Grace Lucknow and Sahara Grace Gurgaon, as well as hospitals (in affiliation with the famous Apollo Hospitals in South India) and cineplexes.

31. *Vande Mataram*, an 1876 composition of freedom fighter Bankimchandra Chattopadhyay, was written in Sanskrit and Bengali as a response to the colonial mandate of singing *God Save the Queen* at public events.

32. Other European countries that B4U is available in are France, Germany, Greece, Italy, Norway, Poland, Portugal, Russia, Spain, Sweden, Switzerland, and the Netherlands.

33. Joseph D. Straubhaar, "Beyond media imperialism: Asymmetrical interdependence and cultural proximity," *Critical Studies in Mass Communication* 8 (1991): 39–59; David Waterman and Everett M. Rogers, "The economics of television program production and trade in Far East Asia," *Journal of Communication* 44, no. 3 (1994): 89–111.

34. Michel Dupagne and David Waterman, "Determinants of US television fiction imports in western Europe," *Journal of Broadcasting and Electronic Media* 42, no. 2 (1999): 208–19; G. Wang, "Satellite television and the future of broadcast television in the Asia-Pacific," *Media Asia* 20, no. 3 (1993): 140–48.

35. Kalyani Chadha and Anandam P. Kavoori. "Media imperialism revisited: Some findings from the Asian case," *Media, Culture & Society* 22, no. 2 (2000): 415—32.

36. Mukherjee and Roy, "A system dynamic model," 99.

37. Dong-Hoo Lee, "A local mode of programme adaptation: South Korea in the global television format business," in *Television across Asia: Television Industries, Programme Formats and Globalization*, ed. Albert Moran and Michael Keane (London: Routledge Curzon. 2003), 36–53.

38. L. Vachini, "Bachan-alias: The many faces of a film icon," in *Image Journeys: Audio-Visual Media and Cultural Change in India*, ed. C. Brosius and M. Butcher (New Delhi: Sage, 1999), 199–232.

39. Sony ET clones the Idol program as *Indian Idol* and unlicensed copies abound across all networks.

40. Lee, "A local mode of programme adaptation."

41. Vamsee Juluri, *Becoming a Global Audience: Longing and Belonging in Indian Music Television* (New York: Peter Lang, 2003).

42. Mary John and Janaki Nair, eds. *A Question of Silence? The Sexual Economies of Modern India* (New Delhi: Kali for Women, 2001), 8.

43. Thomas, "Cultural economics of TV programme cloning."

44. P. Sudhir, "Colonialism and the vocabularies of dominance," in *Interrogating Modernity: Culture and Colonialism in India*, ed. T. Niranjana, P. Sudhir, and V. Dhareshwar (Calcutta/Kolkata: Seagull, 1993).

45. Divya C. McMillin, *International Media Studies* (Oxford: Blackwell, 2007).

46. Leela Fernandes, "Nationalizing 'the global': Media images, cultural politics and the middle class in India," *Media, Culture & Society* 22 (2000): 611—28; R. Sunder Rajan, "The subject of sati," in *Interrogating Modernity: Culture and Colonialism in India*, ed. T. Niranjana, P. Sudhir, and V. Dhareshwar (Calcutta/Kolkata: Seagull, 1993).

47. Ritty Lukose, "The children of liberalization: Youth agency and globalization in India," in *Youth Moves: Identities and Education in Global Perspective*, ed. Nadine Dolby and Fazal Rizvi (New York: Routledge, 2008), 133–149; Michael D. Giardina, "Consuming difference: Stylish hybridity, diasporic identity, and the politics of youth culture," in *Youth Moves: Identities and Education in Global Perspective*, ed. Nadine Dolby and Fazal Rizvi (New York: Routledge, 2008), 69–84.

48. Cameron McCarthy and Jennifer Logue, "Shoot the elephant: Antagonistic identities, neo-Marxist nostalgia and the remorselessly vanishing pasts," in *Youth Moves: Identities and Education in Global Perspective*, ed. Nadine Dolby and Fazal Rizvi (New York: Routledge, 2008), 33–52.

49. Robert J. C. Young, *Postcolonialism: An Historical Introduction* (Oxford: Blackwell, 2001).

50. Giardina, "Consuming difference," 74.

SEVEN

Localizing the Global: Bombay's Sojourn from the Cosmopolitan Urbane to *Aamchi Mumbai*

Sreya Mitra

Bombay, or Mumbai as it was rechristened in 1995, has always enjoyed a unique place in Hindi film lore. In the popular Hindi film tradition, "going to the city" meant going to Bombay. Scenes of urban life were invariably represented through stock shots of Bombay, underlining both the city's cosmopolitan urban ethos and its expanse of space. Devoid of any regional character, Bombay functioned as the urban archetype in early Hindi cinema. However, in recent years there has been a significant change in the city's cinematic image. The city is no longer conceived primarily as a cosmopolitan urban space but is now imagined as a localized milieu inscribed with a regional flavor. In this chapter, Sreya Mitra explores Bombay's resignification from an urbane space to a local milieu by examining the industrial dynamics as well as the sociopolitical and economic events that played a role in reimagining the city.

In *Bunty aur Babli* (2005, Shaad Ali) the protagonists, Rakesh (Abhishek Bachchan) and Vimmi (Rani Mukherji), in their attempt to escape the claustrophobic environs of small-town India, dream of going to Bombay. For them, cities like Lucknow, Patna, Calcutta, or even the allure of the nation's capital, Delhi, the city of powerbrokers and politicians, do not exist as more attractive and viable alternatives, despite their geographical proximity. It is only Bombay—the *sapnon ka shehar* (the city of dreams), the *maya nagari* (the magical city)—that offers them reprieve from the stifling conventionality and monotonous existence of rural and small-town India and, consequently, the only city that promises to fulfill the proverbial "rags to riches" tale of Hindi films.

Bombay, or Mumbai as it was rechristened in 1995, has always enjoyed a unique place in Hindi film lore. In the popular Hindi film tradition, "going to the city" was often equated with going to Bombay. The urban space unequivocally implied *Bambai* (Bombay). Unlike other Indian cities such as Delhi, Madras, or Calcutta, Bombay, adhering to its cosmopolitan demeanor, was devoid of any regional character. In the cinematic imaginary, Bombay was simply "the city"—the *sapnon ka shehar*. As Madhava Prasad commented, "Bombay is Bombay plus the city."[1] Bombay, in its garb of the "generic metropolitan other,"[2] reiterated the city–country dyad, the rural–urban divide that was often the defining leitmotif of postcolonial Hindi cinema. With the village as the locus for virginal innocence and tradition, the city was reconfigured as a site of both moral decline and corruption, and simultaneously as offering endless possibilities. Bombay emerged as the "mythic city," a "constant and overwhelming presence" in the Hindi film narrative.[3] Moreover, following the demise of the film studios in Calcutta in the 1930s and the migration of actors, directors, and scriptwriters from Lahore in the aftermath of the 1947 India–Pakistan partition, Bombay emerged as the Mecca of the Hindi film industry, which further enhanced its larger-than-life role in Hindi cinema.

However, in recent years, popular Hindi cinema has witnessed a crucial shift in the representation of its "mythic city." In contrast to its earlier avatar, Bombay is no longer imagined primarily as the nation's archetypal urban milieu but rather as imbibed with the regional character of Maharashtra, the state where the city, now known as Mumbai, is situated. Moreover, with the rural–urban dyad in Hindi films being increasingly transformed into a national–transnational binary, Bombay's place as the "mythic city" has been usurped by global megacities like London, New York, and Melbourne. In the aftermath of globalization and transnational cultural flows, the Hindi film protagonist no longer remains rooted in his territorial and geographical space but instead effortlessly traverses the "globalscape," reiterating the Indian subject's subscription to a global citizenship. In this new scenario of the "global–national subject," Bombay ceases to function as Hindi cinema's urban archetype and is instead reconfigured as a local and regional milieu. In this chapter, I trace the cinematic transformation of Bombay from the *Bambai shehar* (the Bombay city), a cosmopolitan urban metropolis, to *aamchi Mumbai* (meaning "our Mumbai" in Marathi), which by its very name declares its allegiance to Maharashtra. In mapping the emergence of *aamchi Mumbai* in the Hindi film narrative, I argue that the city's increasing "localization" is motivated by a multitude of factors—changing dynamics of production, distribution, and exhibition in the Hindi film industry as well as recent socioeconomic and political events that have played a crucial role in Bombay's urbanscape. However, before discussing the city's new cinematic avatar, I briefly outline a history of Bombay's inception and its subsequent role as the urban archetype in Hindi cinema.

Bombay: The Gateway to India

From its very inception, Bombay has assumed a Janus-like demeanor, straddling tropes of contradictory natures. This was exemplified by the symbolic value the city held for its British creators and its indigenous populace, the Maharashtrians. While for the British the city was "a home away from home," the replication of the "English way" in an exotic locale and an affirmation of the achievements of the British Raj,[4] for the Maharashtrians, it signified a very different reality. The city was an "alien intrusion upon their soil,"[5] a reminder of the loss of their political hegemony to the British.[6] In the later decades of the nineteenth century, Bombay with its ethnically and communally diverse population was perceived as a threat to the supremacy of the upper-caste Hindu Maharashtrians. Though the Maharashtrians eventually grew to admire and even accept the city, their relationship with Bombay remains problematic to this day. As Meera Kosambi emphasizes, the city "was *in* Maharashtra but not *of* it."[7] Bombay was essentially an extension of the East India Company's trade with Gujarat and subsequently straddled two different realms—its "commercial hinterland," Gujarat, to which it was connected by coastal transportation links, and its "geographical hinterland," Maharashtra, from which it was cut off by both physical and political barriers, the Sahyadrian mountain range and the hostile Maratha regime in Poona. The defeat of the Marathas in 1817–18 and the annexation of their dominions by the British laid the foundation of Bombay's political ascendancy. This was followed by the city's reconfiguration as the commercial capital of British India in the late nineteenth century, eclipsing the supremacy of Calcutta. The city soon became a thriving center of cotton mills, earning the epithet "Manchester of India," and consequently attracting migrant laborers from the neighboring regions of Gujarat and Saurashtra. The opening of the Suez Canal in 1869 and the introduction of the first railway track in India, from the Bombay suburb of Byculla to neighboring Thane, in 1853 further reiterated Bombay's industrial supremacy, defining it as "the gateway to India."

Bombay's newfound industrial dominance also presented a picture of contentious duality. As Sujata Patel notes, though the city functioned as a facilitator in the colonial expansion of western India, it also laid the foundation for a national commerce based on the domestic market.[8] The city's ascendancy was furthermore attributed to its inherent cosmopolitan ethos that ensured both adaptability and a proclivity for new challenges.[9] Bombay became India's cosmopolitan hub, looking outward toward the world: "a constant source of wonder and admiration, as well as proof that a true 'world city' had been fashioned by its British creators."[10] Unlike Madras or Calcutta, it was not defined by its geographical location (Maharashtra) but rather by its diverse population of Europeans, Arabs, and Jews, as well as Gujaratis, Parsis, and Maharashtrians. The city, unlike other Indian towns, was not provincial, but "pan-Indian."[11] It is this lack of provinciality that would later ensure Bombay's nickname as *maya nagari* (the magical city) and its permanence in the Indian cinematic imaginary as the "generic metropolitan other."[12]

Creating the Mythic City

In the cinematic imagination, Bombay has often evoked contradictory images—a city with infinite opportunities that simultaneously reaffirms the image of the urban sphere as one of ruthless narcissism, lacking in any humanistic attributes. In the 1956 crime noir classic *C.I.D.*, comedian Johnny Walker croons, "*Aye dil hai mushkil jeena yahan, zara hatke zara bachke, yeh hai Bombay meri jaan*" (My heart, it is difficult to live in this place; step aside, watch out, this is Bombay, my love). As the proverbial *sapno ka shehar*, Bombay promised both "pleasure and danger . . . thrilling anonymity as well as distressing inequality."[13] For the Hindi film narrative, functioning as a repository of the national ethos, Bombay seemed the obvious site for its protagonist—a modern, global world city, devoid of any parochial provinciality and offering the realization of the impossible dream.

For the newly independent Indian state, nationhood not only comprised the challenges of unyoking a colonial past and integrating diverse linguistic and regional identities within a composite and singular identity but also of reimagining itself as the archetypal modern nation. The Five-Year Plans introduced by Prime Minister Jawaharlal Nehru attempted to usher in a modernization agenda, dominated by dams, bridges, and industries. Modernity, it was emphasized, resided in the urban industrial haven—a notion that not only situated the national subject firmly in the domain of the city but also consequently relegated the village to a mythical symbolism. The village was no longer conceived as an entity in its own right but rather functioned as a counterpoint to the city. Consequently, it was only the city that could accord any articulation of the individual self, an identity that was foreclosed by the communal life of the village. For the Hindi film hero, a journey to the *shehar* (the city) became imperative—not only to lay claim to modernity but also to articulate his individuality, an articulation that would be conceived as impossible within the cloistered environs of the *gaon* (the village). Thus, the Hindi film protagonist of the 1940s–1950s in his journey to *Bambai* (Bombay) embodied not only the journey of the national subject from an archaic colonial past to a modern present but also his adherence to notions of democracy, secularism, and the individual spirit—notions intrinsically linked to modernity.

However, the move to the city also results in the loss of the shared communal identity fostered by the village: "in urban spaces individuals encounter each other as strangers, reified entities, whose position in a social network cannot be known immediately."[14] This sense of loss is further aggravated by the alienation and displacement experienced by the hero in the urban chaos. Bombay, the teeming cosmopolitan hub, is devoid of any humanistic ethos. Sudipta Kaviraj, in his reading of the *C.I.D.* song *"yeh hai Bombay meri jaan,"* underlines Bombay's reality, "What it misses . . . is not a rural, traditional ethic, but a general humanistic sympathy: there is no sign of the general sign of 'man' (*insaan ka nahin naam o nishan*)."[15] While the village with its traditional ethos signified "control over self," Bombay the "mythic city" symbolized "self-indulgence and the absence of self-restraint."[16] Whether it is 1950s icon Raj Kapoor in *Shree 420* (*Mister 420*, 1951, Raj Kapoor) or current Bollywood superstar Shah Rukh Khan in *Raju Ban Gaya Gentleman* (*Raju Has Become a Gentleman*, 1993, Aziz Mirza), the Hindi film hero, in his sojourn to Bombay and consequently in his materialistic avarice, was destined to lose his Nehruvian idealism. Ironically, Bombay, the mythic city, offered both the realization of an individual entity, and simultaneously, the erosion of the very values that were perceived as integral to the postcolonial Indian subject.

The Subaltern Voice

Though Bombay was configured as the "mythic city" and functioned as oppositional to the rural idyll, nevertheless its cinematic counterpart was not a singular entity but rather embodied an assortment of fractured identities. Madhava Prasad, talking about the cinematic representation of Bombay, points out its two very different filmic incarnations—the Bombay of the 1950s, especially the crime noir of Navketan Films and Guru Dutt, where the city is signified as a site of both danger and pleasure, and the Bombay of post-1970s, where its threatening yet alluring image is reimagined in a more gritty ambience, against which Bombay was imagined as a site for the articulation of the subaltern voice.

The centrality of the subaltern subject in the Hindi film narrative is not a recent phenomenon. However, it was only in the seventies that popular Hindi cinema witnessed a distinct shift in the portrayal of the archetypal hero—from the moralistic middle-class protagonist to the plebian rebel crusader. This crucial shift is personified in the star image and iconic films of actor Amitabh Bachchan. Bachchan's "angry young man" image, his angst-ridden roles and marginalized characters, not only embodied the political turbulence of the 1970s but were also indicative of a significant shift in the audience demographic.[17]

With the proliferation of VCRs and neighborhood video-rental shops in the 1980s, the middle-class audience preferred to experience "movie watching" in the privacy of their homes. As the middle-class viewer ceased going to the theaters, cinema halls became populated with the plebian masses—young lower-class and working-class men, much like Bachchan's onscreen avatars. However, as Fareeduddin Kazmi argues, the subalternity of Bachchan's characters is contradicted, and subsequently neutralized, through the "declassification" of his character. Unlike the 1950s social melodrama of filmmakers like Bimal Roy, there is little attempt to anchor Bachchan within the specific context of a socioeconomic milieu. He is instead configured as classless, as the archetypal Angry Young Man, functioning more as a reaffirmation of masculinity than of any particular social or economic class. Thus, in spite of his personification of the subaltern and the oppressed, as

Kazmi points out, "The focus is never on his social role or on the problems arising out of his socio-economic position in society."[18]

However, it is in Bachchan's persona as the bootlegger Anthony Gonzalves (*Amar Akbar Anthony*, 1977, Manmohan Desai) that we first see the emergence of a localized Mumbai-centric figure, the *tapori* (vagabond). As Ranjani Mazumdar discusses in detail, the *tapori*, symbolizing "part small time street hood, and part social conscience of the neighborhood," is a figure "strongly rooted in the hybrid cultures of Bombay's multilingual and regional diversity."[19] Director Aziz Mirza, in conversation with Mazumdar, emphasizes how the *tapori* does not belong to any generic urban space but is particular to the urban milieu of Bombay, underlined by his use of the Bombay-specific Hindi dialect *Bambayya*: "*Tapori* is a character you can only get in Mumbai because the very nature of the city, its cosmopolitanism makes the *tapori* use a language of his own, which is very *Bambayya*."[20] The *tapori* character became a popular and recurrent figure in the Hindi film idiom, often straddling contradictory worlds of morality and vice, dabbling in petty crime while simultaneously exercising moral authority. However, in spite of the popularity of the *tapori* in films like *Rangeela* (*Full of Color*, 1995, Ram Gopal Varma), *Ghulam* (*Slave*, 1998, Vikram Bhatt), and *Ram Jaane* (*God Knows*, 1995, Rajiv Mehra), he remained symbolic of the cosmopolitan, urban space of Bombay and thus only functioned as a reaffirmation of the city as the urban other. The city's recent cinematic resignification as the "localized" Mumbai and the emergence of protagonists proclaiming allegiance to a Marathi ethos has been made possible, to a large extent, by the changing economics of the Hindi film industry. New modes of production, distribution, and exhibition, as well as changing audience demographics, have undoubtedly facilitated narratives and plots that attempt to break away from the conventions of the formulaic Hindi film.

New Economies, New Narratives: The Changing Face of the Bombay Cinema

In recent years, the Hindi film narrative has witnessed a significant shift in its construction of the national imaginary: The protagonist is no longer imagined in the simplistic binaries of foreign–indigenous or rural–urban. Hindi films no longer speak to a generic "Hindi film audience" and consequently, the formulaic Hindi film and its "hero" seem to have disintegrated into multiple images. As scriptwriter Jaideep Sahni asserts, "There is no pan-Indian movie because there is no pan-India."[21] Contemporary Bollywood narratives, much like postglobalization India, have assumed a multifaceted demeanor, speaking a polyglot language to its diverse audience. The "pan-Indian" Hindi film is now conceived in multiple terms—the "multiplex film," the "NRI film," the "Hinglish film"—all catering to diverse audiences. The 1990s was a landmark decade; not only was the industry able to recover from a protracted financial slump and the temporary retirement of Amitabh Bachchan, but the economic liberalization policies introduced by the government and the rediscovery of the diasporic subject also engendered new developments that radically altered the norms of the Hindi film industry.

The introduction of economic liberalization in the early 1990s coupled with the demise of the *license raj*[22] heralded a new Indian middle class that seemed to have become increasingly consumerist and determined to unyoke all remnants of a socialist past. As Pavan Varma observes, though consumerist desires and inclinations had always been present, the economic reforms now bestowed upon them the endorsement and support of official acceptance.[23] Consequently, movie watching became a part of an entire gamut of consumerist excursion. Single-screen movie theaters in most Indian cities were replaced by multiplex theaters situated mostly at shopping malls that already boasted McDonald's, Pizza Hut, and Benetton outlets. As Manmohan Shetty, chairman of Adlab Films, one of the leading film processing companies and multiplex theater chains in the country, remarks, "In metro cities, it has become almost mandatory to visit multiplexes on weekends."[24] The introduction of multiplex theaters in 1997 diametrically changed the cinematic experience for the Indian audience. With some state governments announcing the theaters' exemption from the entertainment tax, a "multiplex boom" ensued. By 2005, India had 73 multiplexes, with 276 screens and 89,470 seats.[25] The following two years witnessed the addition of another 74 multiplex theaters, and the prediction for 2012–13 is 1,800 more screens, a substantial growth from the earlier scenario of only 12,000 single screens.[26] The multiplex penetration is not just limited to urban metropolises. Even small-town India now boasts of multiscreen theaters rapidly replacing single-screen theaters.[27]

Multiplexes have not only become an increasingly visible facet of the Indian cinematic experience but have also been instrumental in engendering new forms of Hindi film narratives such as the "Indie" Hindi film, a low-budget, nonformulaic movie aimed at audiences with "an urbane uniquely Indian sensibility." As film critic Anupama Chopra describes these *hatke* (different) films, "[They] have none of the overt glamour or sunny disposition of the mainstream movies. Emotions are messy, characters have pasts and endings aren't always happy."[28] With mainstream Bollywood actors like Saif Ali Khan willing to work for a lower remuneration, these new multiplex narratives offer filmmakers a flexibility that was hitherto inconceivable. Director Ram Gopal Varma, noted for his gritty Bombay underworld sagas, explains, "The multiplex gives me flexibility and enables me to have a conversation with my intended audience without worrying about small towns and villages."[29] Moreover, multiplexes have also been instrumental in bringing the middle class back to the theaters. Varma and the new breed of Hindi film directors are no longer concerned with a pan-Indian audience or with the urban–rural dyad, catering instead to an exclusively urban, upper-middle-class audience. As distributor Anil Thadani rightly points out, this "shift in storytelling" reflects the shift in economics—although multiplexes constitute less than 0.6 percent of the approximately 12,000 movie theaters in India, they account for nearly 28 to 34 percent of the box-office returns.[30]

In addition to these changes within India, the diasporic subject has also been instrumental in redefining the Hindi film narrative. The export of Hindi films to the diasporic community is not a recent phenomenon; whether it was the immigrant South Indian population in the Gulf countries, the descendants of indentured Indian laborers in Fiji and the West Indies, or the more recent arrivals in the United Kingdom and United States, Indian popular cinema always functioned as a reaffirmation of the umbilical attachment with the homeland. However, it is only recently that the NRI (Non-Resident Indian) audience has been configured as central to both the economics of the film industry and the construction of the national ethos. The overseas audience now constitutes a significant part of the revenue. Australia, for instance, which was earlier estimated to be worth $50,000, has grown tenfold.[31] As Ronnie Screwvala, CEO of United Television (UTV),[32] points out, "The rising financial and social profile of the NRIs is making mainstream theatre chains in the US and UK play Hindi movies."[33]

Consequently, "Indianness"—like the distribution of Hindi films—has become dispersed, requiring minimal reference to the homeland or notions of cultural identity. By virtue of being an Indian, the national subject can now lay claim to Indianness. Notions of citizenship and national identity are no longer circumscribed by geographical or national borders. The geographical and physical proximity is no longer a determinant—a contrast to earlier narratives where cultural identity was intrinsically and inherently linked to the geographical and national space. The national space in Hindi cinema, as Lakshmi Srinivas emphasizes, is now produced "by communicating a sense of place as feeling."[34]

Localizing the Global City: From Bombay to Mumbai

In such a scenario where the notion of place and space in the cinematic text is communicated as "feeling," Bombay ceases to function as the sole repository of the urban ethos. As mentioned earlier, Bombay's role as the "mythic city" has been usurped by global megacities like London and New York, further reaffirming the Hindi film protagonist's claim to a global citizenship. Thus, no longer signified as the "generic metropolitan other" in the cinematic text, Bombay is now "aamchi Mumbai," invested with more specificity and marked as regional and local rather than cosmopolitan. However, this transition from Bombay to Mumbai, the reconfiguration of citizenship from the cosmopolitan "Bombayite" to the local "Mumbaikar," not only signifies the negation of the city as the archetypal urban but is also reflective of certain socioeconomic and political events that have conspired to radically alter its topography. The representation of Mumbai in Hindi film narratives, though adhering to the familiar motif of the city as an alienating, emotionless vacuum, is distinct from the earlier tropes of the city. Bombay is no longer perceived as a montage of stock shots—Juhu Beach, Bandra Bandstand, Marine Drive, Gateway of India—sites that are specific but still define the city as an expanse of space. Instead, the new cinematic images of the city intrude into its suburbs and interiors (Byculla, Ghatkopar, Matunga)—localities defined by their regional and linguistic specificity. Mumbai, unlike Bombay, is not defined as an infinite expanse of space, as the "mythic city." Rather, it exposes the squalor and lack of space, the housing problems, slums and illegal tenements, land sharks—a city plagued with problems and seething with discontent. As film critic Maithali Rao describes, "The dark alleys and seedy *chawls*, the garish bars and smelly buffalo sheds, all reveal a side of the city that has never been shown in our cinema with such a graphic sense of doom and yet, vibrant with life and opportunity."[35]

Bombay's representation in Hindi film narratives had always been contradictory—oscillating between images of the city as a cold, ruthless metropolis and a site of infinite opportunities. However, from the 1980s onward, the city became increasingly imagined as a lack of space rather than as an expanse of space. The continuing popularity of action films and the figure of the *tapori* configured slums and *chawls* (buildings where families often live in congested conditions) as the site of the underdog-protagonist. Though films like *Piya Ka Ghar* (*My Sweetheart's Home*, 1972, Basu Chatterjee), *Gharonda* (*The Nest*, 1977, Gulzar), and *Katha* (*The Tale*, 1983, Sai Paranjpye) had attempted a more realistic portrayal of Bombay, the protagonists in these films were still symbolic of the "common man" rather than the larger-than-life hero of Hindi films. With the advent of young action stars like Sanjay Dutt, Jackie Shroff, Sunny Deol, and Anil Kapoor, the 1980s witnessed a slew of films centered on the *tapori*. In *Rakhwala* (*The Guardian*, 1989, K. Murali Mohan Rao), Anil Kapoor, as the neighborhood *tapori*, sings "Bam Bam Bam Bambai Meri Hai" ("Bam Bam Bam Bambai is mine"), claiming the city as his own; in *Badmaash* (*The Villain*, 1998, Gautam Pawar), Jackie Shroff croons "aamchi Mumbai" ("our Mumbai"), obviously in response to the ongoing rhetoric over the city's renaming. However, though films like *Arjun* (1985, Rahul Rawail), *Hathyaar* (*Weapon*, 1989, J. P. Dutta), and *Angaar* (*Fire*, 1992, Shashilal K. Nair) presented a picture of urban squalor and congestion, the protagonist was still the archetypal Angry Young Man and not imbibed with the local color of a Mumbaikar. Moreover, Hindi films still continued to project Bombay as "the city"—in *Haadsaa* (*The Event*, 1983, Akbar Khan), Bombay is "haadson ka shehar" ("the city of events"); in *Krodh* (*Anger*, 1990, Shashilal K. Nair), Sanjay Dutt and Sunny Deol sing an ode to the city ("Bombay Bombay"). It is only later, especially in the films of Ram Gopal Varma—*Satya* (*The Truth*, 1998), *Company* (2002), and *Sarkar* (2005)—that Bombay's transition from the urban other to a local entity becomes more evident.

Mum"bhai": Claiming the City as Its Own

Ram Gopal Varma, who enjoys a reputation as maverick auteur, has not only immortalized the figure of the *bhai* (underworld kingpin) but has also been credited with portraying Bombay and its criminal underbelly in a more realistic light. Noted director Shyam Benegal credits him for having set "a reference point for any film based in Mumbai."[36] For the Hindi film audience, Varma's films strike a chord with oblique references to mafia dons like Dawood Ibrahim and Chota Rajan, police encounters, and the nexus between the Bombay film industry and the underworld. In 1998 Varma directed *Satya* (*The Truth*), the first film in his quartet on the Bombay underworld. With a relatively unknown cast and its dark melancholy undertone, *Satya* proved to be a surprise hit. The film followed the journey of its protagonist, Satya (Chakravarty), from a nameless anonymous migrant to a key player in the Bombay underworld. Unlike conventional Hindi films, *Satya* did not offer a clear binary of good and evil; the characters were usually blurry and gray, and the audience's sympathies lay with Satya and his friend Bhiku Mhatre (Manoj Bajpai), men who seemed to kill without any remorse or guilt. Varma followed *Satya* with *Company* (2002), another treatise on the *bhais*. Inspired by the real-life saga of friends-turned-foes Dawood Ibrahim and Chota Rajan, Malik (Ajay Devgan) and Chandu (Vivek Oberoi) in *Company* blur the line between good and evil. Unlike Bachchan's Angry Young Man, the protagonists of these new Mumbai narratives are not embroiled in a crusade against the corrupt, bureaucratic system but instead perceive the underworld as simply another means of sustenance and livelihood. In *Company*, the title song proclaims, "sab ganda hai par dhanda hai yeh" (it's all dirty but it's business). Chandu's mother is overjoyed that her son is working with the mafia boss Malik; his girlfriend wants to marry him because he is a *bhai*—a far cry from films like *Deewaar* (*The Wall*, 1975, Yash Chopra) where the mother (Nirupa Roy) disowns her son (Amitabh Bachchan) because of his nefarious activities.

Varma, in his third film, *Sarkar* (2005), legitimizes the moral authority of the underworld further. Reminiscent of Francis Ford Coppola's *Godfather*, *Sarkar* is centered on the enigmatic figure of "Sarkar" Subhash Nagre (Amitabh Bachchan), a character who shares an uncanny resemblance to Shiv Sena leader Bal Thackeray.[37] In the 2008 sequel to *Sarkar*, titled *Sarkar Raj* (*The Rule of the Sarkar*, 2008, Ram Gopal Varma), Sarkar's legacy is now carried on by his son, Shankar (Abhishek Bachchan), who defends his actions with treatises on *adharsh* (values) and *usool* (principle); the mafiosi in Varma's Mumbai underworld sagas seem to exist in a moral universe of their own. Varma's films, with their unrepentant *bhais*, not only position the Hindi film hero in a gray, nebulous zone between morality and immorality, virtue and vice, but also locate the narrative specifically in the localized milieu of contemporary Mumbai. As Varma himself admits, "In *Satya* the situations that I have shown could not have taken place anywhere else except in Mumbai."[38] Satya represents the "millions of atomized and isolated individuals,"[39] migrants who come to the *maya nagari* (the magical city) to realize their dreams, yet unlike earlier narratives, there is no attempt to attribute to him a history or a past. By marking him as "a man without history,"[40] he is inscribed as rootless, devoid of any antecedents that can be traced to the rural idyll, and consequently, he is imagined only within the localized domain of Mumbai. In *Sarkar Raj*, lines like "Maharashtra ke tarakki ke samne koi nahin" (Nothing is more important than Maharashtra's progress) not only privilege the Marathi ethos over the erstwhile cosmopolitan spirit of Bombay but also clearly reiterate Bombay's allegiance to Maharashtra and the state's claim over it.

Varma's films reflect the increasing "localization" of the city but also capture effectively the political and socioeconomic backdrop. As Ranjani Mazumdar emphasizes, "In the gangster films, the banality of everyday life unleashes a torrential force of excess, whose imaginary relationship to Bombay's contemporary social topography is crucial."[41] Thus, in these gangster narratives, "the mythology of the underworld that is reproduced" is a "combination of 'real' events, a contemporary sensibility about Bombay's spatial crisis, and mythmaking."[42] In his discussion of *Satya*, Sandeep Pendse outlines how the film can be seen as representative of the changing face of Bombay—a shift that reflects not only the exclusivist rhetoric of the "sons of the soil" political outfit, Shiv Sena,[43] but also the change in the city's industrial practices.

The recurrent motifs of hotels, restaurants, and dance bars[44] in the film indicate the shift from an industrial character to a service industry–based culture. Following the failure of the drawn-out Bombay textile strike (launched in 1982) and the subsequent decline of the city's once-active trade unions, Bombay's textile mills receded into the background, facilitating the emergence of new leisure and entertainment industries. With industries closing down or relocating to other towns, production became fragmented, decentralized, and dispersed. The decline in organized industrial employment coupled with the diminishing political power of the trade unions adversely affected the "social and political weight" of the workers—resulting in "a dispersal if not decimation of the organized working class."[45] However, in the midst of these changes, the middle class remained unscathed, reaping the benefits of Bombay's increasing commercialization. Sandeep Pendse emphasizes this dichotomy: "Mumbai faced a decline and sickness as an industrial city but continued to prosper as a commercial-financial centre. . . . Consumerism was rampant; consumption was ostentatious and luxurious; disparity vulgarly marked."[46] In marked contrast, the working class became "refugees in their own city as more and more areas and public spaces were denied to them, and they were confined to more or less specific localities."[47]

In Varma's underworld sagas, it is this teeming discontent and frustration of the working class that finds vent. However, unlike the films of Amitabh

Bachchan, where Bachchan's image as the Angry Young Man functioned as a symbolic icon for the Indian lower-middle-class, the protagonists of *Satya* and *Company* are marked distinctly as Mumbaikars; they speak only to the disgruntled subaltern of the city, of the "localized" Bombay, and not to a pan-Indian working class. However, films like *Satya*, *Company*, and *Vaastav* (*The Reality*, 1999, Mahesh Manjrekar) do not simply privilege the hitherto excluded working class of Bombay but also reclaim the city for its indigenous inhabitant, the Maharashtrian. In spite of Bombay being the capital of the Maharashtra state, it was outsiders like South Indians, Gujaratis, and Sindhis who controlled the reins of the city's commercial and industrial ethos. For the Marathis, confined to mostly clerical or menial jobs, it was a rampant mockery of their claims of ownership; relegated to the periphery and marginalized, the indigenous Mumbaikar could only feel alienated and frustrated. The underworld dons in contemporary Bollywood narratives, in their struggle for hegemony, replicate the recent militant endeavors of the Marathi (particularly exemplified by the nativist rhetoric of Shiv Sena) to claim Mumbai. Celebrating the death of his longtime rival, Bhiku Mhatre in *Satya* proclaims, "Mumbai ka raja kaun? Bhiku Mhatre!" (Who is the king of Mumbai? It is Bhiku Mhatre!). Bhiku's joyous shout exemplifies the dream of the Maharashtrian: hegemony over Mumbai, and reclaiming what rightfully belongs to the Marathi ethos. The Marathi resentment toward the outsider cuts across divides of class and caste, and configures the entire religious–linguistic community as a singular entity. However, it is the working class for whom the "outsider" represents not only a loss of territorial and cultural hegemony but also a more quotidian reality of unemployment and displacement. In a scene from *Company*, as Chandu and his friends discuss their plans of ascendancy in the Mumbai underworld milieu, a skirmish breaks out among them, startling the only other passenger in the suburban local train (presumably a white-collar worker and possibly a non-Maharashtrian). Chandu makes no attempt to reassure the passenger but instead uses threats to cower him into submission—a signifier of the changing times where the Marathi refuse to remain the underdog any longer.

Moreover, the Marathi ethos has been internalized even in films that do not include any reference to the *bhai*—most conspicuously in the song-and-dance sequences. Religious festivals have always figured prominently in song sequences, particularly the festival of colors, Holi. However, in recent Bollywood narratives, it is the popular Maharashtrian festival Ganesh Chaturthi[48] that has become a recurrent motif. In *Don—The Chase Begins*

Again (2006, Farhan Akhtar), the narrative differs from its original, the Amitabh Bachchan cult classic *Don* (1978, Chandra Barot), in more ways than one. Not only is the film now situated in the "globalscape" (Malaysia) but the protagonist, Vijay (Shah Rukh Khan), is introduced to the audience not with the original song extolling Bombay—"yeh hai Bambai nagariya, tu dekh babua" (This is the Bombay city, have a look at it)—but with a song dedicated to Ganesh Chaturthi ("moriya re moriya"). Hindi films' privileging of this Maharashtra-centric festival is linked intrinsically to its popularization by the Shiv Sena. Ganesh Chaturthi has been employed by the party not only to facilitate the "production" of locality, since localities "both constitute and require contexts,"[49] but also to reiterate the notion of a Marathi brotherhood, a sense of shared identity that further underlines the claims of "Mumbai for Mumbaikars." Such attempts at community building reaffirm both the Sena as the voice of the Marathi subaltern and also define its politicians as "social workers" and "protectors" (since their political agenda is claimed to be secondary to their communal and regional objectives).

Amitabh Bachchan in *Don* (1978); a stock shot of the Bombay skyline that reiterates its role as the "generic metropolitan other."

Conclusion

Bombay's transformation from the "generic metropolitan other" to the localized "aamchi Mumbai" certainly needs to be perceived in the context of globalization and transnational cultural flows. As John Tomlinson argues, globalization cannot be seen in the sanitized corridors of global travel but rather should be comprehended in the engagement of the "local" with the "global" in the context of the former.[50] Arif Dirlik points out, "In its most recent manifestation, place consciousness is closely linked to, and appears as the radical other of, that other conspicuous phenomenon of the last decade, globalism."[51] Thus, Bombay's increasing localization can be perceived as the city's response to globalism. However, the transition from Bombay to Mumbai cannot be attributed to any singular factor, whether contemporary socioeconomic and political events or changing dynamics of the film industry, but rather should be perceived as a culmination of these various factors. Ram Gopal Varma's Mumbai-centric films have thus been engendered not only by the emergence of the middle-class urbane multiplex audience, which gives him the flexibility to defy the norms of conventional Hindi cinema, but also by the city's displacement as the "generic metropolitan other." In the absence of its earlier label as the "mythic city," Bombay/Mumbai now ascribes itself with a more localized aura. In *Aap Ke Khatir* (*For Your Sake*, 2006, Dharmesh Darshan), though the hero travels to London, he does not cease to be a Mumbaikar. His national identity would not mark him as "different," especially when he is surrounded by NRIs (whose claim to Indianness might be greater since they succeed in retaining their "Indian ethos" in spite of their foreign locale), but his local specificity would. Throughout the film, he identifies himself as "Mr. Lokhandwala" alluding to his Mumbai suburb, Lokhandwala. In order to confront the NRI, in the global context, the Bombayite can no longer afford to be simply the generic metropolitan other but instead has to subscribe to a more specific and local identity, that of the Mumbaikar. This transition from a pan-Indian to a regional identity of both Bombay and the Hindi film hero is evident in Ram Gopal Varma's adaptation of director Ramesh Sippy's classic *Sholay* (*Flames*, 1975). Titled *Ram Gopal Varma ki Aag* (*Ram Gopal Varma's Fire*, 2007), the remake relocates the narrative from a generic pan-Indian village to Bombay, thus not only underlining the demise of the village in the cinematic imagination but also marking the specificity of Bombay.

However, in spite of being inscribed as more local, the city still retains some of its earlier traits, especially in comparison with other Indian cities like Delhi. In *Pyar Ke Side Effects* (*The Side Effects of Love*, 2006, Saket Chaudhary), the protagonist is shocked when he visits Delhi—auto drivers refuse to use the meter, and revelers at a marriage party brandish their guns. Tempered by Bombay's professionalism and cosmopolitanism, it becomes difficult for him to accept the lawlessness and sheer arbitrariness of Delhi. Thus, the Hindi film narrative makes it explicit—Bombay might be transformed into Mumbai, inscribed with a local character, but yet this transition does not affect the city's intrinsic ethos. Moreover, in spite of the attempts to resignify the city as a localized milieu, it still dominates the cinematic imagination as the *sapnon ka shehar*, the *maya nagari* (the magical city). In *Taxi 9211* (2006, Milan Luthria), the title song pays homage to Bombay's magnetism and allure: "Laakh Roz Aake Bas Jaate Hai, Iss Sheher Se Is Dil Laga Ke Phas Jaate Hai . . . Shola Hai Ya Hai Bijuriya Dil Ki Bajariya Bambai Nagariya" ("Millions come here every day to settle, they fall in love with this city and are entrapped . . . a flame or a lightning, a marketplace of hearts, this is Bombay city"). Thus, Bombay might have been replaced as the "mythic city" and imbibed with the localism of Mumbai, but it continues to govern the cinematic imagination of the Hindi film narrative.

Notes

1. M. Madhava Prasad, "Realism and fantasy in representations of metropolitan life in Indian cinema," in *City Flicks: Indian Cinema and the Urban Experience*, ed. Preben Kaarsholm (Kolkata: Seagull Books, 2004), 87.

2. Prasad, "Realism and fantasy," 87.

3. Prasad, "Realism and fantasy," 86.

4. Meera Kosambi, "British Bombay and Marathi Mumbai: Some nineteenth century perceptions," in *Bombay: Mosaic of Modern Culture*, ed. Sujata Patel and Alice Thorner (Bombay: Oxford University Press, 1995), 13.

5. Alice Thorner, "Bombay: Diversity and exchange," in *Bombay: Mosaic of Modern Culture*, ed. Sujata Patel and Alice Thorner (Bombay: Oxford University Press, 1995), xv.

6. After the defeat of the Maratha ruler, the Peshwa of Poona, in 1817–18, the Maratha dominions were included within the Bombay Presidency of the British Raj. Bombay functioned as the capital of the presidency and was the center of the British naval, commercial, and most importantly, political control over western India.

7. Kosambi, "British Bombay and Marathi Mumbai," 4.

8. Sujata Patel, "Bombay and Mumbai: Identities, politics, and populism," in *Bombay and Mumbai: The City in Transition*, ed. Sujata Patel and Jim Masselos (New Delhi: Oxford University Press, 2003), 3–30.

9. Claude Markovits, "Bombay as a business centre in the colonial period: A comparison with Calcutta," in *Bombay: Metaphor for Modern India*, ed. Sujata Patel and Alice Thorner (Bombay: Oxford University Press, 1996), 26–46.

10. Kosambi, "British Bombay and Marathi Mumbai," 15.

11. Thorner, "Bombay: Diversity and exchange," xiv.

12. Prasad, "Realism and fantasy," 87.

13. Prasad, "Realism and fantasy," 87.

14. Prasad, "Realism and fantasy," 85.

15. Sudipta Kaviraj, "Reading a song of the city: Images of the city in literature and films," in *City Flicks: Indian Cinema and the Urban Experience*, ed. Preben Kaarsholm (Kolkata: Seagull Books, 2004), 70.

16. Ashis Nandy, *An Ambiguous Journey to the City: The Village and Other Odd Ruins of the Self in the Indian Imagination* (New Delhi: Oxford University Press, 2001), 13.

17. Vijay Mishra, *Bollywood Cinema: Temples of Desire* (New York: Routledge, 2002), 125–56.

18. Fareeduddin Kazmi, "How angry is the 'Angry Young Man'? 'Rebellion' in conventional Hindi films," in *The Secret Politics of Our Desires: Innocence, Culpability and Popular Indian Cinema*, ed. Ashis Nandy (Delhi; New York: Oxford University Press, 1998), 144.

19. Ranjani Mazumdar, *Bombay Cinema: An Archive of the City* (Minneapolis: University of Minnesota Press, 2007), 41.

20. Cited in Mazumdar, *Bombay Cinema*, 51.

21. Anupama Chopra, "Hindi film gets the indie spirit (no dancing, please)," *New York Times*, 13 November 2005.

22. The economic liberalization package introduced by Prime Minister P. V. Narasimha Rao and Finance Minister Manmohan Singh reduced the red tape that had previously impeded business growth, and introduced foreign direct investment.

23. Pawan Varma, *The Great Indian Middle Class* (New Delhi: Viking, 1998).

24. Namrata Joshi, "Bole To . . . It's Dhoomtime," *Outlook* (New Delhi), 4 December 2006.

25. Chopra, "Hindi film gets the indie spirit."

26. Kaveree Bamzai, "Bollywood extra large: Everything is magnified," *India Today* (New Delhi), 14 April 2008.

27. Gayatri Ramanathan, "Theatres in small cities get facelift; multiplex culture catching on," *Livemint*, 23 November 2007

28. Chopra, "Hindi film gets the indie spirit."

29. Chopra, "Hindi Film gets the indie spirit."

30. Chopra, "Hindi film gets the indie spirit."

31. Joshi, "Bole To . . . It's Dhoomtime."

32. UTV is one of India's largest media organizations, with stakes in television, gaming, Web content, film production, and distribution. One of the key players involved with the Bombay film industry's increasing corporatization, UTV has, in recent years, collaborated with Sony, Fox Searchlight, Walt Disney, and Will Smith's Overbrook Entertainment in an attempt to expand its global reach. UTV official website, http://www.utvnet.com/ (accessed 27 May 2009).

33. Joshi, "Bole To . . . It's Dhoomtime."

34. Lakshmi Srinivas, "Communicating globalization in Bombay cinema: Everyday life, imagination and the persistence of the local," *International Journal of Comparative American Studies* 3, no. 3 (2005): 319.

35. Maithili Rao, "The city as Kurukshetra," *The Hindu* (Chennai), 14 January 2001.

36. Anuradha Sengupta, "Being: Kingpin Ram Gopal Varma," interview of Ram Gopal Varma, CNN IBN (13 August 2006).

37. Raja Sen, "If Thackeray can exist, Sarkar can exist," interview of Ram Gopal Varma, *Rediff* (30 June 2005).

38. Sengupta, "Being: Kingpin Ram Gopal Varma."

39. Sandeep Pendse, "*Satya*'s Mumbai: Mumbai's *Satya*," in *Bombay and Mumbai: The City in Transition*, ed. Sujata Patel and Jim Masselos (New Delhi: Oxford University Press, 2003), 315.

40. Pendse, "*Satya*'s Mumbai," 316.

41. Mazumdar, *Bombay Cinema*, 153.

42. Mazumdar, *Bombay Cinema*, 159.

43. The Shiv Sena was founded in 1966 by cartoonist Bal Thackeray as a nativist "sons of the soil" political outfit. Though Thackeray never held any office, even when the BJP–Shiv Sena combination was in power in Maharashtra, he was perceived as a parallel government, especially in the 1990s. During its initial years (1960s–70s), the Shiv Sena's "outsider" rhetoric was targeted at the non-Marathi communities in Bombay, particularly the South Indians, who, the Sena alleged, had cornered all the white-collar jobs. For a more detailed discussion of the Shiv Sena, see Gerard Hueze, "Cultural populism: The appeal of the Shiv Sena," in *Bombay: Metaphor for Modern India*, ed. Sujata Patel and Alice Thorner (Bombay: Oxford University Press, 1996), 213–47.

44. There are nearly 1,500 dance bars in Maharashtra (mostly in Bombay) employing more than 100,000 women who dance to Bollywood songs for the bar's clientele. Dance bars have figured in some contemporary Bollywood films, most notably Madhur Bhandarkar's *Chandni Bar* (2001) and Sudhir Mishra's *Chameli* (2003).

45. Pendse, "*Satya*'s Mumbai," 308.

46. Pendse, "*Satya*'s Mumbai," 308.

47. Pendse, "*Satya*'s Mumbai," 309.

48. Ganesh Chaturthi is a popular religious festival commemorating the Hindu deity Ganesh. Though popular throughout the country, it is most elaborate in Maharashtra, Gujarat, Karnataka, and Andhra Pradesh.

49. Arjun Appadurai, *Modernity at Large: Cultural Dimensions of Globalization* (Minneapolis: University of Minnesota Press, 1996), 186.

50. John Tomlinson, *Globalization and Culture* (Chicago: University of Chicago Press, 1999), 5.

51. Arif Dirlik, "Place-based imagination: Globalism and the politics of place," in *Places and Politics in an Age of Globalization*, ed. Arif Dirlik and Roxann Prazniak (Lanham, MD: Rowman & Littlefield, 2001), 15.

PART TWO

Global China Media

Whose *Hero?* The "Spirit" and "Structure" of a Made-in-China Global Blockbuster

Yuezhi Zhao

The Chinese movie industry has changed dramatically since the 1980s, when a new generation of directors began to shift attention from the propaganda films of the Maoist era to more personalized accounts of everyday life among Chinese citizens, especially in rural locales. More recently, many movies have redirected their attention to urban themes and characters, but the most commercially successful films have been historical epics featuring legendary characters, such as emperors, warriors, and martial arts heroes. Although set in the past, many of these films comment on contemporary issues and concerns. Yuezhi Zhao shows how one of the most successful feature films, Zhang Yimou's Hero, *can be interpreted as a reflection on China's place in the global political and economic order.*

Hero debuted triumphantly on the Chinese and East Asian movie screens in December 2002, marking the end of what mainland media referred to as "Year One after World Trade Organization (WTO) Entry" (*rushi yuannian*).[1] With domestic box-office revenues that surpassed the record set by *Titanic*,[2] *Hero* was widely celebrated as a quintessential product of a rejuvenated Chinese film industry. When Hollywood finally embraced *Hero* after much

These posters for Zhang Yimou's blockbuster film *Hero* feature Jet Li, who played an assassin called "Nameless." Nameless ultimately gives up his quest to kill the Qin emperor in the interest of peace under heaven.

delay and released it to the North American market in late August 2004, it garnered US$18.0 million in ticket sales during its first weekend, making it the biggest late-August premier ever, and thus a truly global blockbuster.[3] These domestic and global box-office successes made *Hero* an interesting case study of the "spirit" and "structure" of a "created-in-China" cultural product for "global Hollywood."[4]

The chapter is organized into four sections. The first two sections examine the "spirit"—that is, the ideological dimensions of *Hero*—within the Chinese and global contexts respectively. The last two sections analyze the "structure"—that is, the domestic and global political economic dimensions—of the film. Since much has been written on the nature of China's global integration through the lenses of communication in more general terms,[5] my aim is a very modest one of providing a particular political economic and cultural interpretation of a landmark product of China's global media integration at a specific world historical juncture.

The "Spirit" of *Hero* in the Chinese Context

Hero is set in the feudal Warring States period (475 to 222 B.C.) and draws on popular legends about revenge and assassination against the ruthless Qin Shihuang—the legendary emperor who used military power to unify China and maintain political and cultural control by burning books, burying dissenting intellectuals alive, and building the Great Wall. *Hero* is, in essence, a martial arts extravaganza that celebrates absolute imperial power. The film begins with a potential critique of the absolute power of Emperor Qin and revolves around intriguing assassination plots that are portrayed in a *Rashomon*-style narrative[6] and delivered via digitally enhanced, gravity-defying swordplay stunts. Filmmaker Zhang Yimou portrays the professional assassins as heroes, led by "Nameless," the most capable assassin of all. After numerous trials and tribulations, Nameless finally gains access to the emperor but then decides at the last second that his highest calling is to abandon his personal quest for revenge and to let Emperor Qin accomplish his hegemonic mission in the name of "*Tian Xia*," translated as "all under heaven" in the English subtitles but more accurately understood as "the greater common good under heaven." As Chinese film critic Jia Leilei argues convincingly, Nameless subjugates himself to the emperor both visually and spiritually in the closing scene, which has the effect of turning Emperor Qin into the ultimate hero of the movie.[7]

The symbolic resources of *Hero* draw on a famous legend of the period that has been the subject of many forms of cultural representation, but one might note that the arguably fascist "spirit" of *Hero* derives from the positive portrayal of imperial peace achieved through war and self-sacrifice in service of the greater good as defined by the powerful. This interpretation has particular salience in the post-Tiananmen era where it resonates with official state policy and with recent strains of Chinese nationalism. Wang Shan, author of the best-selling, mid-1990s neoauthoritarian text entitled *A Third Eye on China*, endorses a cult of personality, and sanctions the sacrifice of one social class so that a superior social class might fulfill the "great destiny" of the Chinese nation.[8] The antidemocratic thrust of *Hero* can also be seen in hundreds of episodes of "emperor shows" that have been popular on Chinese television screens since the late 1990s. Typically revolving around court politics, these mainstream costume dramas often depict imperial projects and paternalistic benevolence as necessary and socially beneficial.

However, *Hero* departs significantly from previous treatments of the subject matter, both in thematic orientation and narrative strategies. In previous assassination legends, as well as in popular Chinese imagination, the story is always told from the perspective of the weak. As cultural critic Zhang Yiwu puts it, the binary "ruthless ruler/assassin" is equated with the binaries of "oppression/resistance" and "evil/justice." The righteous use of violence by the weak to oppose mighty power is "one of the cornerstones of the cultural imaginaries of Chinese modernity."[9] As Zhang further points out, such a thematic orientation is the dominant ideological theme of modern Chinese culture. It is doubly articulated as a domestic class-based narrative of the weak against the powerful and as an anticolonial narrative of the weaker nation struggling for national independence against imperial power from the outside.[10] For revolutionary playwright Guo Moruo, who wrote a play about Qin Shihuang and his assassin in 1942 during the height of the Communist Party's antinationalist struggles, Emperor Qin was a metaphor for the oppressive nationalist leader Chiang Kai-shek.[11] Contemporary filmmaker Chen Kaige, whose 1998 film *The Emperor and the Assassin* presented a much more nuanced and complicated portrayal of Emperor Qin than has Guo, devised the character of Lady Zhao as the love of Qin's life who functions as his counterpoint and who gives a "voice to the masses," to the "people who want humanity to prevail over bloodletting and power-thirsty dictators," and "who weep over the senseless loss of life, and want a peaceful solution instead."[12]

Hero turns this thematic orientation upside down. The logic of the powerful receives unprecedented expression, explication, and affirmation, while the resistant power and justice of the weak is put in doubt for the first time in modernist representation of this subject matter. This departure can be appreciated by locating *Hero* in the two broader and often overlapping genres that it draws upon: martial arts fiction and the emperor shows on television. In the typical martial arts genre, the good *Gong-fu* master typically assumes the Robin Hood–spirit of standing outside the system and pursuing justice on behalf of the weak. Even the emperor shows, with all their imperial underpinnings, ultimately endorse the justice of the disempowered. As Jia Leilei argues, *Hero* not only subverts the commonsense understanding that eternal peace and the common good can only be achieved with the overthrow of the ruthless ruler and the sharing of a common culture on the basis of a plurality of national cultures, but also endorses the imposition of the culture of one state over all others and the articulation of the dominant state's interest as representing the interest of all others. Thus, in the *Tian Xia* that Emperor Qin finally establishes through violence, conquest, and betrayal, there is no humanity, no morality, and no justice to speak of. In the film, innocent and defenseless scholars practicing calligraphy are slaughtered by the arrows of the Qin army; small, defenseless villages are laid to waste; and in the end, Nameless is killed even though he abandons his quest and subjugates himself to the emperor. Although historically one of the rationales for Emperor Qin's imperial project was to unify the seven warring states for their collective security vis-à-vis external enemies (that is, "barbarian nations" such as the Xiongnu), Jia points out that *Hero* ignores this theme and instead constructs a *Tian Xia* devoid of national identities and territorial boundaries. [13]

Furthermore, *Hero*'s spirit resonates with that of Wang Shan's *A Third Eye on China*, but there is a clear contrast in the mode of expression. Wang Shan published the book as a translation of the work of a nonexistent German Sinologist, hoping to provide a cover for the expression of an uncomfortable neoauthoritarian proposition. By contrast, in *Hero*, Zhang Yimou expresses this theme in the form of what is often referred to in Chinese domestic reviews as "a grand visual banquet" or, in the words of an American review, an "example of visual poetry." [14] There is an endless glorification of technical efficiency and superiority—whether that of the Qin army, the professional assassins, or Zhang's own cinematic skills. There is no blood and copious gore. Ordinary people and their sufferings, vividly and movingly depicted in Chen Kaige's *The Emperor and the Assassin*, are displaced to make room for soldiers in formations on various occasions of warfare. With perhaps the most notable exception of the calligraphy school scene, the backdrop for the heroes is characteristically made up of a spectacular and yet socially empty Chinese landscape.

Not surprisingly, Chinese liberal intellectuals, together with Western reviewers and critics, were quick to interpret the authoritarian thrust of the movie for its contemporary political implications. For example, the February 2003 issue of *Open* (*Kaifang*), the liberal Hong Kong current affairs monthly, included a collection of articles that critiqued the movie's neofascist themes and aesthetics. Cui Weiping, a professor from the Beijing Film Academy, bluntly stated that *Hero* uses fascist aesthetics to legitimate totalitarian rulers. Writing from an anticommunist perspective, Cui called it a "political blockbuster," entitling his article, "A Movie That Is Dedicated to Saddam and Kim Jung-Il."[15] Outside China, the *Economist* noted, "one of the themes in *Hero* echoes the slogan repeated so often by the Communist Party to justify its clampdown on dissent: *wending yadao yiqie*—stability is of paramount importance."[16]

This preferred reading of the movie was furthermore driven home in remarks made by Tony Leung, the Hong Kong actor who plays the character of Broken Sword, an assassin sympathetic to the emperor's imperial mission who persuades his fellow assassins to give up. Leung applauded *Hero*'s message of "peace and human kindness" in an interview and went on to say that what the Chinese government did in 1989 "was right—to maintain stability, which was good for everybody."[17] Leung's subsequent rebuttal of this statement, saying that he was speaking not for himself but from the perspective of his character in the film, only further reaffirmed such a preferred reading of the film. In a way, it can be argued that Leung's character is a metaphor for the post-1989 educated elite who have come to understand the party's 1989 suppression in the name of China's modernization and national power, while rationalizing the suffering of lower social classes as the unavoidable price of reform and progress. In short, as Evans Chan puts it eloquently, "the impulse behind the film can be called fascist—it promotes a personality cult that claims oneness with the progression of the national destiny, and which inspires wilful, bloody sacrifices."[18]

The "Spirit" of *Hero* in the Post–9/11 Global Order

To simply interpret the spirit of *Hero* either as exclusively Chinese or, in an Orientalist reading, as embodying a quintessential form of Chinese authoritarianism, would be to misconstrue the broader ideological intentions of the movie and the specific contemporary world historical context within which it was produced and promoted. Although Evans Chan's contention that the film "resonates with the awakened ambitions of Empire within contemporary China"[19] is highly provocative, it does not quite capture the preferred meanings of *Hero*. Chan arrived at this interpretation exclusively against the backdrop of the nationalistic "China Can Say No" discourse inside the mainland, making his argument unwittingly reflective of the popular American right-wing prophesy of a "coming conflict" between the United States as a reigning superpower and China as a would-be one.

Yet Chan ignores the complexity of popular and official nationalisms in China. Although there has indeed been a strong anti-American sentiment at the popular and official levels, as I have argued elsewhere, influential pro-American liberal elites within the Chinese intellectual and foreign policy establishments have persistently argued for accommodation with the United States, urging China to accept the U.S.–dominated global order. The Chinese state has also on various occasions suppressed popular nationalistic outcries against the United States.[20] In fact, the foreign policy and mainstream intellectual response to the nationalistic bestselling *China Can Say No* is the book *China Will Not Be "Mr. No."*[21] Written by elite foreign policy expert Shen Jiru, it explicitly rejects the nationalistic sentiments of *China Can Say No* and argues instead for a nonconfrontational approach toward the United States. The nonconfrontational position of the Chinese state—be it tactical or strategic—is evident in its endorsement of the U.S.–led "war on terrorism." At the same time, many of China's liberal intellectuals' more blunt pro-American positions were brought into sharp focus by the fact that, following the American invasion of Iraq and in response to a leftist statement against the invasion, they issued a statement in support of the war in an explicit celebration of American imperial power and its benevolent nature. Instead of reading *Hero* through the popular nationalistic text *China Can Say No*, it is at least equally plausible to read it through the more official *China Will Not Be "Mr. No"* given the elite status of Zhang Yimou and the official support the film received. Moreover, there was no textual evidence to support a reading of *Hero* as projecting a conflictual relationship between China and the United States. There is neither an existing superpower to challenge nor an inspiring one to emerge under *Tian Xia*.

In fact, *Hero* pays homage to the United States as the global hegemonic power. As Jia Leilei's above analysis contends, the *Tian Xia* in *Hero* is not a historically, geographically, and ethnoculturally specific Chinese *Tian Xia*, but rather it is the entire world in the post–9/11 era.[22] That is, *Hero* is "a metaphor of the new century," and the "spirit" of *Hero* is the dominant ideology of global capitalism. Within this framework, the logic of the powerful is today's dominant logic of globalization, and Emperor Qin's logic of peace without justice is the ideology of the war on terrorism. As Zhang Yiwu argues, textual and circumstantial evidence supports this interpretation. First, there is the explicitly expressed intention or preferred reading of film revealed by the director and the producer in the film's promotional material. The 9/11 terrorist attacks on the United States occurred exactly one month after the beginning of the film's shooting. Consequently, Zhang Yimou decided to elevate the theme to the level of world peace. In fact, Zhang stated explicitly in the movie's tie-in documentary that *Tian Xia* referred to peace in a global context. Documentary producer Zhang Weiping meanwhile added a personalized dimension, pointing out that lead actress and global film star Zhang Ziyi often visits the United States. "She has a unique perspective on [9/11]," he observes. "She said that *Hero* will rally and uplift the national spirit of the American people and that the American people currently need myths about heroes."[23] Second, although *Hero* seems to draw upon Chinese history, the film consciously suppresses historical and geographical specificity so that *Tian Xia* is universalized to represent the global order. This is made clear in Emperor Qin's vision of *Tian Xia* as a "big, big territory" beyond the sum of the warring nation states, and perhaps more explicitly, in Zhang's unprecedented erasure of the names of the specific assassins, which are as familiar as that of Emperor Qin himself, preferring instead to refer to them abstractly as "Nameless," "Long Sky," "Broken Sword," and "Flying Snow."

As Zhang Yiwu points out, Zhang Yimou gained global notoriety in the 1980s and early 1990s by exploring the sufferings of the disempowered in China, especially women, and he did so with a self-Orientalizing narrative strategy that constructed China as a third-world country,[24] and I would add, a communist country. Movies such as *Raise the Red Lantern*, *To Live: The Story of Qui Ju*, and *Not One Less* express this point of view. In *Hero*, Zhang abandons his identification with the weak and common people, and disposes of a third-world narrative perspective. In short, this is a Zhang Yimou who no longer tells the "national myths of a third-world country," but one who wants to make a statement about the entire global order in a universalizing framework and who does so with all the confidence, self-righteousness, and authority of the powerful. That is, with the deepening of globalization and China's rapid economic growth, parts of the Chinese imaginary have become more and more detached from the original third-world narrative that defined the cultural imaginaries of Chinese modernity. And this global dimension in the spirit of *Hero* is the film's most novel aspect.[25]

True to the new spirit of a commodified and globally integrated Chinese cultural industry, Zhang Yimou foregrounds the theme of imperial peace in the movie's promotional material while disavowing any ideology in the film and dismissing any serious critique of it. Zhang explicitly asked viewers to "look at the visual images" and was cited as saying, "The only test of success for a film, especially a martial arts film, is whether it can keep the audience's attention for 90 minutes, not its metaphysics."[26] From this perspective, then, a film is simply a piece of entertainment. It is not the message but the spectacle—the "grand visual banquet" as *Hero* is often referred to in the Chinese media—and the act of consuming this spectacle that are most important! Finally, it seems that the Chinese film industry has managed to "connect with the world track" of capitalist ideological work: the best strategy is to deny that there is ideology at all!

As Hardt and Negri pointed out, Guy Debord's spectacle, conceptualized as "an integrated and diffuse apparatus of images and ideas that produces and regulates public discourse and opinion," is the prevailing discursive mode and "the glue that holds together the diverse functions and bodies of the hybrid constitution" of empire.[27] The two planks of the movie's self-promotion—the serious political message and the visual spectacle—are not contradictory; they unabashedly express the twin components of the dominant ideology of global capitalism: imperial peace through the war on terrorism on the high political plane and commodity consumption at the popular level.

Thus, *Hero* is not simply a political "sell-out" to Chinese authoritarianism, nor is it simply an expression of the temptations of a Chinese empire. It is also an allegory for the post–9/11 global order and its dominant imperial logic, and a manifestation of an emerging post–WTO Chinese cultural imaginary that identifies with this dominant order and logic. Thus, even if *Hero* is to be seen as a political sell-out, it is "a double political sell-out," a tribute to the authoritarianism of the Chinese state and its newly awakened nationalistic ambition as an emerging global power, and a coordinated effort to bolster the war on terrorism and the imperial project of the United States.[28] Zhang Yimou shrewdly plays into the ambiguities and indeterminate nature of the current historical order.[29]

Yet it would be too easy and Orientalist to simply single out Zhang as commercially opportunistic in the way that Geremie Barmé has character-ized many Chinese cultural producers,[30] or worse, to dismiss Zhang as a quintessential Chinese intellectual who lacks the backbone to stand up to the regime of party censorship.[31] After all, at the same time that Zhang Yimou was reorienting his movie to articulate it with the ideology of the war on terrorism, representatives of Hollywood's major studios, television networks, and creative community met with a White House delegation to discuss how the entertainment industry could help in the war against terrorism. Ideas mentioned during the meeting included "themes" such as "The September 11 attacks were an attack against civilization and require a global response" and "The antiterrorism campaign is a war against evil."[32]

Although Zhang Yimou was not invited to the White House or the Central Propaganda Department in Beijing, *Hero* can nevertheless be un-derstood as an expression of the consciousness of the "transnational capital-ist class" in a neoliberalized global capitalist order.[33] After all, the Chinese state has long been invited to behave as a responsible member of the global capitalist political economic order. In making *Hero*, Zhang and his crew were only acting as "responsible members" of the Chinese segment of the transnational cultural industry elite and an important constituent bloc of the "transnational capitalist class." In fact, although the *New York Times* described Zhang's turn in cinematic direction as "a little like Fellini sud-denly promoting Victorian values,"[34] there is nothing sudden about Zhang Yimou's intellectual reorientation. If Zhang's relation with the Chinese state has always been ambiguous, his embrace of the ideology of neoliberal glo-balization has become unambiguous in *Hero*.[35] In addition to making *Hero*, Zhang has been the chief artistic promoter for China's globalist projects by directing not only promotional films for the 2008 Beijing Olympics and 2010 Shanghai World Expo but also the spectacular Opening Ceremony of the 2008 Beijing Olympics. Moreover, as a delegate to the Chinese People's Political Consultative Conference, he is officially a member of the Chinese political elite. Thus, on the one hand, Zhang supports the Chinese state's globalization project by mobilizing his own cultural capital in the service of the state; on the other hand, the Chinese state not only confers political status to Zhang but also ensures his further accumulation of financial and cultural capital in the global film market.

The Trajectory of the Chinese
Film Industry's Global Integration

The "structure"—that is, the institutional setting behind the production, marketing, distribution, and exhibition—of *Hero* is a combination of Chinese and Hollywood coordination, as well as a dual mobilization of state and market forces. To appreciate the significance of this development, it is necessary to briefly review the historical trajectory of the Chinese film industry and its uneasy reengagement with Hollywood.

Hollywood had a strong influence on the Chinese film market before 1949. The Maoist regime not only ended Hollywood's fortunes in China but also developed a strong indigenous national film industry. In the initial stages of the reform era (that is, the early 1980s), Chinese films enjoyed enormous popularity, but as the "reform and openness" process deepened, a number of factors—political control, underinvestment, competition from commercialized state television and other entertainment forms, and drastic social stratification and audience market fragmentation—combined to undermine the viability of a domestic film industry organized under the planned economy. By the early 1990s, the Chinese film industry was in deep crisis.[36] Annual attendance at theaters dropped from 21 billion in 1982 to just under 4.5 billion in 1991.[37]

Hollywood, meanwhile, tried to reenter the Chinese market as soon as U.S.–China diplomatic relations were restored in 1979. Chinese audiences, isolated from Hollywood for nearly thirty years, had some catching up to do. Hollywood's reentry into China thus began with public screenings, especially on state television, of cheap Hollywood classics, with Rupert Murdoch's 20th Century Fox playing a leading role in supplying them. In 1985, when the Hollywood blockbuster *Rambo: First Blood* was released in China and caused a national sensation, China's reengagement with Hollywood had already intensified significantly.

In the aftermath of Deng Xiaoping's "Southern Tour" in 1992, which unleashed market forces and accelerated China's capitalistic-style reforms, the Chinese film industry, desperate for a solution to the decline of the state-funded film studio system and its concurrent monopolistic state distribution system, started decentralizing and marketizing distribution.[38] As the "the wolf at the door," Hollywood, of course, seized the opportunity.[39] By 1994, under the double pressure of Hollywood and the domestic distribution industry, China decided to accept an annual importation of ten first-run Hollywood films on a revenue-sharing basis. Driven by profit considerations and the sensibilities of young and affluent urban viewers who had come to regard seeing the latest Hollywood blockbuster as part of their global cultural citizenship, the state-controlled film distribution apparatus enthusiastically promoted Hollywood movies while ignoring domestic productions. By 1998, when *Titanic* garnered a quarter of the year's total box-office revenues, domestic Chinese film production—which had ranged between 100 and 130 films annually in the 1980s—had dropped to a record low of 37. The prestigious Xi'an Film Studio had to lay off more than 10 percent of its workforce, while "the larger studios in Beijing and Shanghai were surviving only by turning themselves into service centers for productions financed from Hong Kong or Taiwan."[40] Although I do not imply any monocausal linkage between Hollywood imports and the decline of domestic film production, there is no question that these two developments were intertwined manifestations of a broad transformation of the Chinese film industry with respect to market rationalities, profit motives, and reintegration with Hollywood.

Of course, the more innovative and ambitious Chinese filmmakers, in an attempt to circumvent domestic political control and with a desire to seek international prestige, started to look to a global audience as early as the first half of the 1980s. The success of "Fifth Generation" filmmakers such as Chen Kaige and Zhang Yimou on the major international film awards circuit in the 1980s and early 1990s, and the inclusion of their films in the "foreign" section of major video-rental chains in North America, signalled the beginning of the selective incorporation of a Chinese filmmaking elite into an American-dominated global film industry that was becoming increasingly multicultural. To be sure, these Fifth Generation filmmakers did not launch themselves directly into the global film scene by seeking investments from Hollywood majors and producing films for the global mass market. Rather, they started with international film festivals and global art-house cinema niche markets. Thus, if Hollywood's reentry into China started with the mass screening of cheap Hollywood classics, China's incorporation into "global Hollywood" was facilitated by the international film elite's enchantment with China's Fifth Generation filmmakers who were eager to tell their Chinese stories to an elite Western audience. Reduced state funding and inflation in the post-1992 period further compelled domestic filmmakers to adopt new strategies to survive by looking abroad for finance and attracting coproductions financed through Hong Kong.[41] With the further commercialization of the Chinese film industry, and as the Chinese state started to push the Chinese culture industry to "go global," the internationally most successful members of the Fifth Generation filmmakers, as the pioneers of the Chinese culture industry's globalization, started to leverage their global fame and transnational linkages and reoriented themselves toward the adoption of Hollywood aesthetics and business models, thus establishing themselves as part "global Hollywood."

China's WTO entry provisions with regard to the film industry have further extended and consolidated the Chinese film industry's global reintegration. Under the agreement, China committed to quadruple film imports to forty films per year upon accession in 2001. The number increased to fifty in 2005, of which twenty are first-run Hollywood blockbuster movies. The agreement committed China to reduce tariffs on audiovisual imports, open up its market for audiovisual products to foreign distributors, and most importantly, allow foreign investors to own up to a 49 percent share in companies that build, own, and operate cinemas in China. A full-scale restructuring of the film industry in China—from production to distribution, exhibition, and consumption—has been underway. Major transnational entertainment conglomerates such as Time-Warner have teamed up with domestic Chinese partners to establish production facilities and revamp the Chinese cinema infrastructure. Moreover, they have managed to secure new terms of market openness far beyond the original terms set in China's WTO accession agreements. In December 2003, the Chinese state issued new rules allowing foreign investors to hold up to a 75 percent stake in joint-venture cinemas in seven of China's largest cities, effective January 1, 2004. In reporting this new rule, the *People's Daily* cited a Chinese film official as saying that "the new regulation makes China a more attractive place for foreign cinema giants."[42] As I have argued elsewhere, the interests of the Chinese film industry are now increasingly linked to transnational capital.[43]

The "Structure" of *Hero* in the New International Division of Cultural Labor

The above, then, is the domestic and global context for the production and consumption of *Hero*, a tribute to both the globalizing strategies of Hollywood majors and the global ambitions of Chinese cultural entrepreneurs. To begin with, this US$31 million project was backed by Walt Disney's Miramax Films, which purchased its distribution rights in North America, Australia, New Zealand, United Kingdom, Italy, Latin America, and Africa in advance for $22 million. The film was coproduced by the Beijing New Picture Film Co., a private Chinese film company, and a Hong Kong–based company led by Bill Kong, who gained global commercial success by producing *Crouching Tiger, Hidden Dragon* for Sony Pictures. The marketing machine for the film, which drew its inspiration from Hollywood studios, was unprecedented in the history of the Chinese movie industry both in scope and depth. It included a commissioned book, picture albums, and commemorative stamps, all serving as advance advertising. Prerelease advertising totalled US$2.4 million, which included such firms as China Mobile and Toyota. A documentary entitled *Hero—The Cause* (*Yuanqi*) and a videogame of the same name added to the film's postproduction merchandising revenues. A mobile phone promotional tie-in flatters the targeted upscale urban filmgoers with ads for the super expensive Dopod 688, "the hero of mobile phones."[44] This campaign overlapped nicely with the party's promotion of the newly enfranchised digital elite as "net heroes" and "knowledge heroes." Like the movie, which was framed as a national champion of the global market, these information elite members, many of them with transnational backgrounds, have received extensive state support and have been entrusted with a techno-nationalist agenda of developing Chinese informational capitalism.

In addition to its speedy approval of *Hero* during the censorship process and its nomination as the official Chinese entry for the Golden Bear and Oscar contests, the involvement of state apparatuses in this collaboration was considerable: The Peoples' Liberation Army was hired to play the emperor's army in the film, and the Great Hall of the People was used for the film's premiere to an audience of Chinese officials, cultural elites, and journalists from more than 600 domestic and foreign media outlets. As well, the state's antipiracy forces joined with private security guards hired by cinema chains to mount an unprecedented operation to protect the movie, using draconian measures that may indeed be called fascistic: "Viewers had identity card numbers inscribed in their tickets. They were videotaped as they entered the theater's foyer. They handed over all cell phones, watches, lighters, car keys, necklaces and pens and put them in storage. Before taking their seats, they passed through a metal detector. . . . Security guards heightened the drama at the theater. They ordered people to leave behind jewelry and pens to protect against 'needlepoint' digital camcorders. . . . Uniformed policemen roamed the aisles during the film. A few sat in front of the screen and watched the audience with what appeared to be night-vision binoculars."[45]

The financial benefit for the film's private producers, of course, made all the authoritarian measures worthwhile: Home-video and DVD rights sold for 17.8 million yuan (US$2.15 million),[46] an unprecedented triumph of the official film industry over the piracy industry. Antipiracy is no longer just an issue for "trade dispute" between China and the United States. It is now a common cause of Chinese and transnational cultural industrialists.

Though there were domestic criticisms of the film's artistic merits and its glorification of a controversial emperor, the Chinese media, from official party organs to commercial websites, were fully mobilized in an unprecedented marketing effort for *Hero*, including prime-time advertising on CCTV-1, unprecedented in Chinese media, with an overwhelming nationalistic frame celebrating a homegrown hero for the Chinese film industry. Articulating the official take on *Hero*, a commentary written by a reporter for the *People's Net* focused exclusively on the film's business side, pronouncing it as "embodying the highest quality of domestic filmmaking," and reflective of the Chinese film industry in "Year One of WTO Entry."[47] While noting that competition between Hollywood and the Chinese film industry is still one of "the Elephant versus the Ant," the article framed the market success of *Hero* as a nationalist achievement. Similarly, the *Beijing Youth Daily* exclaimed, "China's *Hero* is telling the world that Chinese culture is fighting back!"[48] As *Hero* premiered in China in December 2002 to a stunning market success, earning 200 million yuan (US $24.2 million) in the first twenty-one days of release, Miramax screened the movie for U.S. critics, making the emergence of *Hero* a global media event. Echoing the Chinese media, global reports heralded *Hero* as a Chinese response to Hollywood and as the hope of "Chinese" or "Asian" film in the global market.

It is important to underscore once again, this time in terms of its production and marketing structure, the transnational dimensions of *Hero*. After all, it drew upon Hollywood (and Hong Kong) capital and business practices, as well as managerial and star power (from martial arts superstar Jet Li to violinist Itzhak Perlman to cinematographer Christopher Doyle), and was created with the global market in mind. Within this context, the question "Whose hero?" is indeed an important one to posit.[49] As Stanley Rosen observed, since the international success of *Crouching Tiger, Hidden Dragon*,

"Hollywood has accelerated its efforts to co-opt Chinese filmmakers who demonstrate commercial potential"; consequently, "China's national film industry is becoming increasingly transnational."[50]

Thus, as "China goes Hollywood" by trying to revitalize and restructure its film industry, and reshapes its business practices and narrative styles with Hollywood financial and cultural capital, Hollywood incorporates China into "global Hollywood" and its "new international division of cultural labour,"[51] seeking its cultural resources, cheap production costs, and vast movie audience. Although *Hero* appears triumphant in China, it says little about the independence of the Chinese film industry on the global stage. Instead, *Hero* testifies to the triumph of the Hollywood-style commercial mode of film production in China.

Thus, if one takes a commercial and national logic for granted, then *Hero*'s triumphant rise is significant for Chinese cinema. But if one takes issue with the spread of a capitalist logic in cultural production, then *Hero*'s "Chineseness" is a sign of the success of global capitalism. Similarly, while *Hero* does embody one particular interpretation of Chinese history and culture, it is one viewed from the perspective of the rulers and the co-opted, and one that erases the very appearance, not to mention the perspective, of the ruled.

Conclusion

It is no longer adequate to merely understand *Hero* as a politically correct "Chinese" film. Rather, it is a globally "integrated spectacle"[52] in every sense. Of course, it would be overtly deterministic to accept the conclusion that the biggest Chinese blockbuster can only be a "politically correct" film[53] or that a globally integrated Chinese film industry will necessarily produce profoundly antidemocratic movies. Moreover, there is still the possibility that independent and politically challenging movies may find a place at the margins of China's global film industry. Nevertheless, to the extent that Zhang Yimou and his fellow Chinese cultural entrepreneurs and their foreign investors have to get Chinese official approval to launch their global productions and rely on the state to combat piracy and ensure the smooth realization of the accumulation process within China, and to the extent that a blockbuster movie is no small investment, political and social conservatism will likely be the norm, rather than the exception, for "created-in-China" blockbusters with global ambitions.

Moreover, just as the Hollywood–China relationship must be understood as an important component of a much broader and more complex U.S.–China relationship, and *Hero's* market success in the United States as one manifestation of what Dan Schiller has described as a "sweeping process of cultural emergence" of China in the United States,[54] the significance of *Hero* also needs to be understood in the broader patterns of domestic Chinese social communication. In early 2003, just as the Chinese media were mobilized in the service of the *Hero* marketing machine, foreign media reported that Yao Fuxin and Xiao Yunling, leaders of the large-scale March 2002 labor strike in Liaoyang City, were put on trial for subverting state power.[55] When I searched for information on these two accused criminals of the Chinese people on the Chinese Internet, the result was predictable—no mention whatsoever. Sina.com, the most popular commercial website, tried to help me by giving a tip: "Use only the full name of a person you are searching for, for example, Zhang Ziyi, and do not add any modifiers, such as actress Zhang Ziyi." Of course, the bare name, "Yao Fuxin," was exactly what I had entered. I failed to find anything about Yao Fuxin not because I had added any label to his name, but because he *is* a labor activist and perhaps the "hero" of his fellow striking workers. I then logged on to the *People's Net* to search for news on Yao's hometown, Liaoyang, one of China's most economically depressed industrial rust-belt towns in the northeast. Of the 120 stories between December 17, 2001, and March 17, 2003, not a single story was on the conditions of Liaoyang workers, except for several positive stories about how local authorities were perfecting the welfare system and providing comprehensive job training for laid-off workers. Meanwhile, by March 17, 2003, the number of articles and photo reports on the *People's Net* about *Hero*, which had been officially submitted by the government as China's nominee for the Oscar Award as best foreign film, had increased to 196.

As I have described in great detail elsewhere, China's global reintegration process is profoundly contradictory both internally and externally.[56] Uneven development has not only exposed the limits of consumerism as an integrative economic and cultural force but also nurtured, in the words of Leslie Sklair, "an arrogant overconfidence in the overprivileged and sometimes violent and sometimes fatalistic reactions in the underprivileged."[57] Furthermore, sentiments and forces of imperialism, protectionism, as well as the hegemony of the liberal human rights discourse in the United States continue to feed Chinese sentiments and forces of nationalism and anti-Americanism, if not always anti-imperialism. Hollywood, because of its prominent role in global cultural politics, has inevitably found itself at the center of discursive contestations over "China's rising." Director Steven Spielberg compelled many Chinese to think about the politics of Hollywood beyond the supposedly "pure" pleasure of entertainment when he withdrew from his role as an artistic adviser to the opening ceremony of the 2008 Beijing Olympics, protesting against China's foreign policy toward Sudan. Actress Sharon Stone infuriated still many more Chinese citizens with her remarks about the devastating May 12, 2008, earthquake in Sichuan as karma for China's mistreatment of Tibetans. Although Zhang Yimou had tried to integrate with "global Hollywood" by articulating *Hero* with the spirit of neoliberal globalization and the war on terrorism, the words and deeds of Hollywood icons such as Spielberg and Stone have reminded Chinese audiences that China's reintegration with an American-dominated global capitalistic order will not be a smooth ride.

Within the domestic realm, discursive contestations of nationalism and globalism, left and right, as well as elite and popular social forces, are fierce in Chinese communication politics. Despite the discrediting of the Maoist state socialist legacy among elite liberal intellectuals and the party-state's deeply entrenched market reform agenda, China's disenfranchised social classes, who hardly can afford a movie ticket in the increasingly fancy and foreign-invested cinema complexes, continue to wage daily struggles in pursuit of social justice and equality in an increasingly globalized economy. Unlike Zhang Yimou in *Hero*, the architects of China's capitalistic reintegration project cannot simply erase these social forces from the picture. Zhang Yimou's *Tian Xia* is not the only vision of the current social order inside China. Nor is spectacle the only language of Chinese political communication. As *Hero* and its successors such as *House of Flying Daggers*, *The Promise*, and *Forbidden Kingdom* launched themselves one after another onto the "global Hollywood" stage, the disenfranchised of China were asserting their media presence as well—be they grandmothers protesting environmental degradation in coastal Zhejiang Province, workers resisting the privatization of their factories in China's industrial heartlands, or outraged parents demanding an official explanation for the needless slaughter of children that were crushed to death in shoddily constructed school buildings during the devastating Sichuan earthquake.[58]

Notes

1. The title of this chapter alludes to the title of Robert A. Brady's book, *The Spirit and Structure of German Fascism* (London: V. Gollancz, 1937). In the book, Brady discusses the ideological and structural coordination of fascism in Germany and elsewhere in the industrialized countries. While I am mindful of the differences between an entire historical formation and a single film, Brady's analytical grid of the cultural and institutional dimension of monopoly capitalism in the early twentieth century serves as a useful point of reference for grasping the unprecedented collaboration between transnational capital, the Chinese state, and transnationally located cultural entrepreneurs.

2. Yuezhi Zhao and Dan Schiller, "Dances with wolves? China's integration with digital capitalism," *Info* 3, no. 2 (2001): 142–43.

3. Brandon Gray, "*Hero* soars to Late August record," August 29, 2004, http://www.boxofficemojo.com/news/?id=1445&p=.htm (accessed November 9, 2005).

4. Toby Miller, Nathan Govil, J. McMurria, and Richard Maxwell, *Global Hollywood* (London: British Film Institute, 2001).

5. For a sample of this literature, see Zhao and Schiller, "Dances with wolves?"; Yuezhi Zhao, "Transnational capital, the state, and China's communication industries in a fractured society," *Javnost* 10, no. 4 (2003): 58–74; Yuezhi Zhao, "The media matrix: China's integration into global capitalism," *Socialist Register 2005* (London: Merlin Press, 2004), 197–217; Yuezhi Zhao, *Communication in China: Political Economy, Power, and Conflict* (Lanham, MD: Rowman & Littlefield, 2008), chap. 3; Chin-Chuan Lee, ed., *Chinese Media, Global Contexts* (London: Routledge/Curzon, 2003); Dan Schiller, "Poles of market growth: Open questions about China, information and the world economy," *Global Media and Communication* 1, no. 1 (2005): 79–103; Anthony Fung, "Think globally, act locally: China's rendezvous with MTV," *Global Media and Communication* 2, no. 1 (2006): 71–88; Michael Keane, "Once were peripheral: Creating media capacity in East Asia," *Media, Culture & Society* 28, no. 6 (2006): 835–55.

6. *Rashomon* is a 1950 Japanese film directed by Akira Kurosawa. In the film, a heinous crime and its aftermath are recollected from different points of view.

7. Jia Leilei, "*Heise wuxia*" (Black martial arts), in *Chongtu, hexie: quanqiuhua he Yazhou dianying* (Conflict/Harmony: Globalization and Asian Cinema), ed. Meng Jian, Li Yizhong, and Stefan Friedrich (Shanghai: Fudan University Press, 2003), 192–203, 197.

8. For different discussions of this book in the English literature, see Joseph Fewsmith, *China since Tiananmen: The Logics of Transition* (Cambridge: Cambridge University Press, 2001), 146–51; Liu Kang, *Globalization and Cultural Trends in China* (Honolulu: University of Hawai'i Press, 2004), 42–44.

9. Zhang Yiwu, "*Yingxiong*: Xinshiji de yingyu" (*Hero*: A Metaphor of the New Century), *Cultural Studies* (*Wenhua Yanju*) 4 (2003): 135.

10. Zhang, "*Yingxiong*," 135.

11. Zhang, "*Yingxiong*," 135.

12. LunaSea, Review of "The Emperor and the Assassin," http://www.lovehkfilm
.com/panasia/emperor_and_assassin_final.htm (accessed November 9, 2005).

13. Jia, "*Heise wuxia,*" 197.

14. James Berardinelli, Review of *Hero*, http://movie-reviews.colossus.net/
movies/h/hero.html (accessed November 9, 2005).

15. Cui Weiping, "A movie dedicated to Saddam and Kim Jung-Il," *Open* (*Kaifang*)
(February 2003): 30.

16. "My emperor, right or wrong," *Economist* (March 15, 2003): 100.

17. Joseph Khan, "Film on ruthless dynasty delights China's leaders," *New York
Times,* January 2, 2003.

18. Evans Chan, "Zhang Yimou's *Hero*—The temptations of fascism," http://www
.filmint.nu/netonly/eng/heroevanschan.htm (accessed December 7, 2005).

19. Evans, "Zhang Yimou's *Hero.*"

20. Zhao, *Communication in China*, 137–93.

21. Song Qiang, Zhang Zangzang, and Qiao Bian, *Zhongguo keyi shuo bu: Hou
lengzhan shidai de zhengzhi yu qinggan jueze* (China Can Say No: A Choice of Politics and Attitude in the Post–Cold War Era) (Beijing: Zhongguo gongshang lianhe
chubanshe, 1996); Shen Jiruo, *Zhongguo budang "bu xiansheng": Dangdai Zhongguo de
guoji zhanlue wenti* (China Does Not Want to Be "Mr. No": Contemporary Strategic
Chinese Issues) (Beijing: Jingri Zhongguo chubanshe, 1998).

22. I had independently reached the same reading of the text before I came across
Zhang's article in April 2005, and I had presented a reading of my paper at the Inter-
national Communication Association Conference in 2003, and at the Transnational
Media Corporation and National Media Systems Conference, May 2003, Rockefeller
Study and Conference Centre, Bellagio, Italy.

23. Yahoo China (November 4, 2002), cited in Zhang, "*Yingxiong,*" 133.

24. Zhang, "*Yingxiong,*" 143.

25. Zhang, "*Yingxiong,*" 135.

26. Joseph Kahn, "Film on ruthless dynasty."

27. Michael Hardt and Antonio Negri, *Empire* (Cambridge, MA: Harvard University Press, 2000), 321.

28. Zhu Jianguo, "*Zigu yingxiong liangtiaolu*" (Two choices for heroes in history),
Open (*Kaifang*) (February 2003): 37.

29. The understanding of the film by Matt Brodlie, senior vice president of acquisition at Miramax, is noteworthy within this context. According to Mr. Brodlie,
what really sold *Hero* to him was the script, because it "has a deep message about
peace and war and what violence means." Karen Mazurkewich, "Gunning for another
'Tiger'—China's movie makers aspire to make blockbuster rivaling global crowd
pleaser of 2000," *Wall Street Journal*, December 31, 2002, A9.

30. Geremie Barmé, *In the Red: Contemporary Chinese Culture* (New York: Columbia
University Press, 1999).

31. Chan, "Zhang Yimou's *Hero.*"

32. "Hollywood Considers Role in War Effort," CNN News, November 12, 2001,

http://archives.cnn.com/2001/US/11/11/rec.hollywood.terror/ (accessed November 9, 2005).

33. For an elaboration of the concept of "transnational capitalist class," see Leslie Sklair, *The Transnational Capitalist Class* (Oxford: Blackwell, 2001); for further discussion of the ideological and cultural role of globally integrated Chinese media and cultural production, see Zhao, *Communication in China*.

34. Kahn, "Film on ruthless dynasty."

35. Chan, "Zhang Yimou's *Hero*."

36. For a detailed account of the evolution of the Chinese film industry during the reform era, see Zhu Ying, *Chinese Cinema during the Era of Reform: The Ingenuity of the System* (Westport, CT: Praeger, 2003).

37. Stanley Rosen, "China goes Hollywood," *Foreign Policy* (January/February 2003): 94–98. For a more elaborated discussion, see Stanley Rosen, "The wolf at the door: Hollywood and the film market in China," in *Southern California and the World*, ed. Eric J. Heikkila and Rafael Pizarra (Westport, CT: Praeger, 2002), 49–50.

38. Rosen, "The wolf at the door," 50.

39. Rosen, "The wolf at the door," 68.

40. Liu Xitao, "China's film industry suffers a major blow with WTO entry," *Chinese Press* (Qiaobao) (November 24, 1999): B1; Rosen, "The wolf at the door," 50.

41. Rosen, "The wolf at the door," 50.

42. "Warner Brothers marches into China's cinema market," *People's Daily*, January 18, 2004, http://english.peopledaily.com.cn/200401/18/print20040118_132895.html (accessed April 26, 2009).

43. Yuezhi Zhao, "The media Matrix," 204.

44. "*Nengkan dianying de shouji duopuda yanyi Yingxiong dapian*" (The Dopod cell phone that can show a movie shows blockbuster *Hero*), December 17, 2002, http://tech.sina.com.cn/it2/2002-12-17/1619156346.shtml (accessed December 5, 2005).

45. Joseph Kahn, "The pinch of piracy wakes China up on copyright issue: It's more than a trade dispute when the victims are Chinese," *New York Times*, November 1, 2002, A1.

46. Karen Mazurkewich, "China's martial arts epic 'Hero' sets mainland box-office record," *Wall Street Journal*, January 14, 2003.

47. Wang Xiaodong, "*Yingxiong: Zhongguo dianying de 'rushixiaojie'?*" (Hero: A Mini Post-WTO Summation of Chinese Cinema?), December 20, 2002, http://www.people.com.cn/GB/wenyu/223/9307/9301/20021220/891985.html (accessed January 5, 2003).

48. Bingchun Meng, "A hero of whom? A case of global-local alliance in the Chinese film industry." Paper presented at the Union for Democratic Communication conference, St. Louis (April 22–24, 2004), 1.

49. Meng, "A hero of whom?"

50. Rosen, "China goes Hollywood."

51. Miller et al., *Global Hollywood*.

52. I borrowed this phrase from the title of James Compton's book, *The Integrated News Spectacle: A Political Economy of Cultural Performance* (New York: Peter Lang, 2004).

53. Cui, "A movie," 30.

54. Dan Schiller, "China in the United States," *Communication and Critical/Cultural Studies* 5, no. 4 (2008): 411.

55. "Trials quash hopes that the new regime would ease repression," *Los Angeles Times*, January 17, 2003; "China's relentless repression," *New York Times*, January 20, 2003.

56. Zhao and Schiller, "Dances with wolves"; Zhao, "Transnational capital"; Zhao, "The media matrix"; Schiller, "Poles of market growth?" For a book-length discussion, see Zhao, *Communication in China*.

57. Sklair, *The Transnational Capitalist Class*, 29.

58. For more discussions of the communication politics of resistance, see Yuezhi Zhao, "After mobile phones, what? Re-embedding the social in China's 'digital revolution,'" *International Journal of Communication* 1, no. 1 (January 2007): 92–102; Zhao, *Communication in China*, chapters 5 and 6, and conclusion; and Geoffrey York, "Beijing can't muzzle outrage over deadly collapsed schools," *Global and Mail*, June 16, 2008, A1, A11.

NINE

The Deferral of Pan-Asian: A Critical Appraisal of Film Marketization in China

Emilie Yueh-yu Yeh

The easing of trade restrictions and the liberalization of national media regulations since the 1980s has encouraged companies around the world to explore the prospect of transnational production and distribution of media products. Many movie producers have expressed excitement about the prospect of a pan-Asian film market that would make it possible for companies to draw talent and resources from across the region in order to fashion projects aimed at audiences throughout East Asia. Yet, as Emilie Yeh demonstrates in this chapter, the Mainland China market exerts a growing influence on pan-Asian media products. This is partly due to the vast scale and purchasing power of its audience but is also due to the distinctive ways in which political connections and priorities influence the movie business. This has in turn affected the types of film projects that pan-Asian producers undertake.

Pan-Asian movie projects have become increasingly common over the past decade, transforming the creative strategies of producers and talent, as well as the practices of audiences, distributors, and movie promoters. This chapter argues that despite the transnational qualities of pan-Asian movies, they are nevertheless influenced by "marketization" (a market-oriented managerial approach) of the most populous nation in the region, the People's Republic of China. By linking pan-Asian cinema with the China market,

I examine the increasing dominance of the PRC and its hegemonic film culture. The chapter has three parts. It begins with a recent controversy in China, starkly illustrating the contradictions inherent in China's film distribution market. Interestingly, these irregularities engender opportunities for outside players, including pan-Asian filmmakers who have been quick to reconstitute their work in ways that ensure them access to the vast and growing mainland market.

The second part documents the refashioning of several independent producers from Hong Kong, Taiwan, and Japan. The new pan-Asian cinema not only allows creative intervention by high-concept Hollywood projects but also generates synergies and cooperation among talent throughout the region. The final section traces the evolution of a leading pan-Asian company, Applause Pictures, within the context of a rising China market to arrive at a critique of the deferral of the pan-Asian mode of film production and distribution.

China Market and Marketization: What Is It?

In December 2006, there was a public outcry against unfair practices in China's screen industry. PolyBona Film Distribution alleged that a one-month blackout of foreign films was secretly prearranged with government officials in order to benefit Zhang Yimou's *Curse of the Golden Flower*. The measure denied access to more than two hundred digital screens at one of the peaks of the movie season. From December 14 to January 14, *Curse of the Golden Flower* would be the only film shown on digital screens in Beijing, Shanghai, and Guangzhou. "*Curse* has broken the principle of fair competition and has monopolized the market," wrote PolyBona CEO Yu Dong in the open letter.[1] Squeezed out of the lucrative digital market, Yu's company quickly struck hundreds of expensive celluloid prints of its new film, *Confession of Pain*, hoping to compensate for the digital ban with an expanded release to traditional screens. *Curse*'s digital monopoly was a devastating blow to the independently produced *Confession*, which was a coproduction that brought together partners from China, Hong Kong, and Japan. Other films suffered as well. The Venice award winner *Still Life*, directed by China's leading independent, Jia Zhangke, was also excluded by the blackout.[2] *Curse* was an all-too-familiar blow in the fortunes of independent cinema in China, but it also tainted the prospects of powerful imports as well. As if echoing Yu's accusation, Hollywood distributors chose not open a single picture during the blackout with the exception of *Painted Veil*. As a result, eleven hundred prints of *Curse*[3] headed for China's three thousand screens[4] over four weeks in the prime moviegoing season. Imagine a one-month period where over one third of the 38,000 screens in the United States showed exactly the same picture and nothing else. Questions would be raised, loudly, about the corporate maneuvering in such a drastic scenario.

In response to the complaint, *Curse*'s distributors at Beijing New Picture Films proclaimed, "If digital cinemas choose to screen only *Curse*, it is the choice of the market."[5] In the first three weeks of the blackout, *Curse* sold a record US$35 million worth of tickets.[6] Despite its apparent success, "the market" emerges as a contested keyword in the eye of an emerging storm. As companies around the world now covet China's 1.3 billion potential consumers, the market and marketization have become an obsession of all who wish to benefit from China's economic transformation.

Ever since reforms in the early 1990s, the film market in China has been closely guarded and regulated by the state authorities.[7] Before the 1990s, government officials managed the vertically integrated film industry, but the state monopoly system was not only ineffective but ultimately ruinous to the industry as a whole. With the introduction of market reforms, the old monopoly practices were replaced with a new logic that promised prosperity for those allowed into the game. But the market's opening was painstakingly monitored to ensure that the government kept full control over lucrative opportunities. Only in 2003 did China allow domestic private distributors, including PolyBona, access to the nationwide market, which was until then controlled by five state conglomerates. PolyBona and a few other private distributors proved formidable competitors in the new environment. In 2003, PolyBona handled thirteen Chinese films, taking up 17 percent of total market share.[8] By 2007, it had established itself as a mini-major, "the Chinese Miramax," with a track record of 100 releases and more than 20 percent of the overall market for four years running.[9] For PolyBona, whose major challenge in the new market has been to find a niche among the distribution majors such as state-owned China Film Corporation and semiprivate affiliate Huaxia, the ripening domestic market is too tempting not to fight domination by rival companies of its own scale. One such competitor is Beijing New Picture Films, a private firm that produces Zhang Yimou's pictures. PolyBona's Yu Dong wanted to ensure that fair competition was in place to prevent monopoly and monopsony, a major cause of the industry's former woes. Interestingly, it was this very logic of market access that Beijing New Picture Films used to defend the exclusive screening of *Curse of the Golden Flower*. Everyone in China wanted to see the latest Zhang Yimou blockbuster, it argued. Therefore, cinemas were simply following the will of the people's market. And to back up its claim, the distributor pointed out that *Curse of the Golden Flower* opened as the top grossing picture not just in China but in other territories as well, including Hong Kong, Taiwan, Singapore, and Malaysia.[10]

This was not the first time Beijing New Pictures was granted an exclusive product slot. Two previous New Pictures' blockbusters helmed by Zhang Yimou—*Hero* (2002) and *House of Flying Daggers* (2004)—enjoyed monopoly exposure authorized by the State Administration of Film, Radio, and Television (SARFT) in the New Year and summer holidays. During these periods, Hollywood imports were suspended and domestic releases were postponed.[11] *Hero*, being the first Hollywood-style blockbuster ever released by a Chinese studio, got no complaints for hogging the screens, but *House of Flying Daggers'* exclusive position from June 15 to August 5, 2004, generated questions and concerns. This was because another PolyBona film was affected—Johnnie To's *Breaking News*, a police thriller coproduced with Hong Kong studio Media Asia. Because of *Flying Daggers'* monopoly, *Breaking News* opened earlier and was therefore forced to compete with Hollywood blockbusters *The Day after Tomorrow* and *Troy*. *Breaking News* grossed $900,000 in China[12] and retrieved only one third of its production budget. Media Asia blamed *Flying Daggers* for preventing it from making more money in the mainland.[13] Complaints circulated, but they were informal and restrained, expressed only as journalists' notes and academic discussion. But in 2006, PolyBona publicly questioned the effects of government regulations on the mainland market.

The deployment of the term *market* by Chinese distributors is loaded with a range of connotations. With external pressure to deregulate the movie business and the rapid rise of domestic consumption, "the market" has become a key figure in the new ideology of China's screen industry. But disputing parties raise conflicting interpretations, suggesting a guarantee of fair trade practices on the one hand and a popularity contest on the other ("the choice of the market," to New Pictures). One requires firm controls and regulation, such as ordinances, monitoring, and enforcement, while the other involves cutthroat competition, branding power, and marketing spin. With the row over *Curse of the Golden Flower*, the latter prevailed, as the horserace image of market dominated over questions about rules or due process. The question then is: What kind of market is the China market? Is it a capitalist economy with Chinese characteristics? Or must we employ a thoroughly different idea to understand marketization in China? Does marketization lead to an open, diverse, perhaps even democratic film industry? How does globalization affect marketization in China?

The existing literature on marketization in China exhibits at least six important features:

1. In order to remain a socialist state, the Chinese communist government opted for market-oriented practices—market economy, rather than capitalism—in the country's economic reform. In light of this, Western notions such as deregulation and privatization of industries have only been partially adopted.

2. Marketization (a market-oriented managerial approach) and corporatization (the transformation of state-owned enterprises into shareholding corporations) are the two concepts used within the new market economy to distinguish it from a capitalist economy.[14]

3. Based on the first and the second points, it is generally recognized that the China market might be the world's largest but is also among the most restricted. China is "too frustrating to deal with but too lucrative to ignore" says one corporate insider.[15]

4. To set up business in China, foreign companies must acquire local partners and are limited to partial ownership. Localization enables non-Chinese companies or products to access institutional, logistical, and cultural support.

5. Marketization is not a self-governing process but an enhancement of state power that harnesses the forms and appearance of liberalization (choice, quality, price, competition) to promote both the ideology and apparatus of the repressive state, according to China's neoleftist intellectuals.[16]

6. Marketization has resulted in an uneven distribution in wealth and resources. Political and cultural capital have been reshuffled to favor a minority of entrepreneurs with visible or invisible connections to government and party officials.

We can apply these features to China's media economy. For example, we see that new forms of corporate elitism and cartelization are replacing the old cadres that guarded the portals of centralized planning. Corporate elites have become the most influential players, and the CEOs of big media corporations, private and state-owned, are packaged as media moguls and visionaries of China's future screen development. Their images and personae are seen as representations of media liberalization. Working directly with cultural bureaucrats and state watchdogs, these CEOs cultivate, expand, and exploit varieties of marketization. One by one, they have formed strategic alliances with their domestic and overseas partners and investors to increase their influence and dominance; one after another, they produced China's blockbusters, monopolizing the market by fending off Hollywood and other competitors.

We also can see marketization in a regional and transnational framework with China's push to market as part of its political consolidation within the Asia-Pacific sphere. As domestic control stabilized—not without quarrels and disputes—Chinese officials began to reach out for regional cooperation, especially in those territories with political, cultural, and linguistic affinities, such as Hong Kong, Taiwan, South Korea, and Japan. This not only changed the direction of flows from one way (from Asia-Pacific to China) to two-way (between China and Asia-Pacific), it also encouraged contacts and possible diversification of Chinese and other Asian cinemas. But as the case study below shows, these contacts have failed to expand or diversify East Asian cinemas. Rather, coproductions between China and East Asia appropriate "foreign" elements into a pan-Chinese repertoire and further enhance the standardization of commercial Chinese cinema.

Pan-Asian Cinema and Applause Pictures

Pan-Asian cinema takes various forms: talent sharing, cross-border investment, coproductions, and market consolidation through distribution and investment in foreign infrastructure. Although the pan-Asian concept was initiated in the late nineteenth century by Japanese writers and politicians,[17] and pan-Chinese networks date back to the 1920s,[18] it was nevertheless limited by protectionism and culturally insular markets. A key factor in the resurgence of pan-Asian operations was the decline of individual national cinemas in Taiwan, Hong Kong, China, Singapore, South Korea, and Japan, which necessitated investment schemes to amplify markets and spread risk. Meanwhile, increasing media flows among these territories[19] and the rise of a transnational popular youth culture prompted opportunities to consolidate separate markets and to create regional blockbusters across linguistic and cultural borders.

With the exception of Japan and China, movie markets in East Asian countries are relatively small. But taken together, East Asian countries have more moviegoers than North America. The population of Thailand is 62 million; South Korea, 50 million; Taiwan, 23 million; Hong Kong, 7 million; Singapore 4.5 million; and Japan, over 127 million. Taken together, this is 270 million people to which one must now add the massive population of the People's Republic of China. If Asian pictures consistently satisfied these audiences, intra-Asian box offices would not only cover production costs but also create handsome profits. In its various forms, pan-Asian cinema seeks to promote regional films to a regional market, taking advantage of the "home-field advantage" by uniting its audiences. For Hong Kong–based Peter Chan Ho-sun, pan-Asian film is really "a collaboration that tries to break through market barriers, the culture barriers, and language barriers so [that] we have enough population to sustain a healthy industry."[20]

With this background, a network of regional and transnational production and distribution processes emerged, connecting East Asian, Southeast Asian, Australasian, and European agents. Although many strands of pan-Asian coproduction are based primarily in one country, others have dual or multiple bases. They may be independents, large studios, or specialty arms of multimedia firms and government-backed initiatives. They play key roles at trade fairs, film markets, and international festivals—essential institutions for coproduction activities. There are at least five kinds of pan-Asian activities: Euro-Asian cultural connections; intra-Asian coproductions; pan-Chinese coproductions; pan-Asian program packages or series; and lastly, Hollywood-Asia cooperation.[21]

In practice, the same firm may engage in more than one type of pan-Asian activity. For instance, intra-Asian and pan-Chinese coproductions often overlap. Pan-Asian collaborations may also aim at market potential outside the region. Backed by European distributors, Taiwan-based Arc Light produced *Blue Gate Crossing* (2002, Yi Chih-yen) as part of a city series that did well in Europe, Japan, Taiwan, and Hong Kong. Similarly, a "combined Asian" trilogy that included *The Island Tale* (2000, Stanley Kwan, Japan/Hong Kong), *YiYi, a One and a Two* (2000, Edward Yang, Japan/Taiwan), and *All about Lily Chou-Chou* (2001, Iwai Shinji, Japan) was produced by Japan's major foreign film distributor Pony Canyon.[22] These films were intended to represent "Asia" to the West as well as to Asian viewers in different countries. Edward Yang's *YiYi* was awarded Best Director prize at Cannes in 2000, along with several major awards in the United States, and then became Yang's first work to receive theatrical release in the United States. The variety, quality, and achievements of these early pan-Asian movies suggest a diverse, expandable media environment in the making. These modes of operation and market orientations produced a prosperous film culture and economy between 2000 and 2005. According to Seoul-based producer Lee Joo-ick of Boram Entertainment, who was involved in the 2007 pan-Asian hit *A Battle of Wits* (directed by Jacob Cheung), the benefits of pan-Asian strategies include a larger budget, a wider pool of talent, and the ability to spread the risk among various markets. "Eventually," says Lee, "Asia is going to emerge as one big market, or at least as a region where interdependency is much greater."[23]

That the pan-Asian strategy became well recognized was due to its promotion by a Hong Kong–based production house, Applause Pictures. Before Applause, Taiwan's Arc Light and Japan's Pony Canyon had some pan-Asian success, but neither continued to pursue pan-Asian sources as a key to financing, distribution, and marketing. Other major companies such as Media Asia (Hong Kong) or MediaCorp (Singapore) were interested in high-budget pan-Chinese pictures for major releases, but Applause took pan-Asian strategies to a level beyond just commercial reward and flexible packaging. Under Applause, pan-Asian concepts became an explicit and pronounced strategy that was materially elaborated. This was partly because of Peter Chan's diagnosis of Asian screen prospects and his articulation of a pan-Asian course of action.

Applause Pictures was cofounded by Peter Chan Ho-sun, a Thai-Chinese director-producer and entrepreneur behind the UFO film group in Hong Kong. With former UFO associates Teddy Chen and Allen Fung, Chan launched Applause Pictures in 2000. From the start, Applause was set up to promote the transnational drive to reconnect Asia-Pacific markets. Applause initiated midsize coproductions to cultivate audience interest in regional cinema. It utilized distinctive locales, reputable directors, and popular genres to create new, artful commercial pictures. *One Fine Spring Day, Jan Dara*, and *The Eye* all demonstrate transborder coproductions with local talent, location shooting, and a new twist on genre. The Korean melodrama *One Fine Spring Day* (2001) had a modest budget of US$1.5 million, cofinanced by South Korea's Sidus Pictures, Applause Pictures, and Japan's major studio Shochiku.[24] Directed by Hur Jin-ho, who had a reputation with his romantic hit *Christmas in August* (1998), the film was able to reach the Korean, Japanese, Hong Kong, and Taiwanese markets. In the Thai-language erotic melodrama *Jan Dara* (2001, Nonzee Nimibutr), Applause adapted an autobiography banned in Thailand for its explicit sexuality and illicit relationships. These became key elements of the film's publicity campaign.

Besides romance and eroticism, Applause produced several successful horror films, such as *The Eye* (2002, Oxide and Danny Pang, Hong Kong/Singapore/Thai coproduction). As such, it participated in a wave of horror films that were sparked by the regional popularity of low-budget J-horror hits, such as *The Ring* (*Ringu*, 1998, Hideo Nakata) and its many sequels. Horror is an adaptable and translatable genre, given its widespread use in Asian mythologies and cinema. Applause seized the opportunity to rework traditional materials into a new type of "C-horror" for Chinese-speaking audiences, thereby localizing a broad popular formula. Invoking folktales of gifted seers, *The Eye* tells a story of a woman with supernatural vision. She sees lingering spirits that refuse to relinquish their attachment to the human world, but she helps them reconcile their grievances. *The Eye* did well in East Asia and was surprisingly profitable in several European countries (see table 9.1). It remains Applause's most commercially successful film.

With *The Eye*'s handsome box-office returns, Applause set about producing two omnibus horror pictures: *Three* (2003, Nonzee Nimibutr, Kim Ji-woon, Peter Chan) and *Three . . . Extremes* (2004, Miike Takashi, Park Chan-wook, Fruit Chan). Here, its business model is clearest. Both are portmanteau films that include contributions from three different countries, styles, and directors. The material and the market is tripled: three directors, three territories, three scary stories. In the sequel, *Extremes*, Miike Takashi, the Japanese cult director known for shocking genre experimentation, contributed his short, *Box*. Each of the films has regional and genre variations, comprised of supernatural visitations, nocturnal chills, and psychological thrills. Two of the shorts in the portmanteau films were furthermore spun off into feature-length horror films, *Going Home* (Peter Chan) and *Dumplings* (Fruit Chan). Both films

Table 9.1. Box-office Revenue of Pan-Asian Coproductions by Applause Pictures (2001–2004)

Year	Title	Hong Kong	Regional	Europe	United States	Worldwide
2001	*One Fine Spring Day*	53,954	3,574,626	N/A	N/A	3,628,580
2001	*Jan Dara*	968,558	114,847	N/A	N/A	1,083,405
2002	*The Eye*	1,760,751	9,220,973	1,094,266	512,049	12,588,039
2002	*Three*	949,471	682,496	N/A	N/A	1,631,967
2004	*Three ... Extremes*	757,940	329,359	N/A	77,532	1,164,831

All box-office figures in U.S. dollars
Sources: *City Entertainment*; Box Office Mojo; Taipei Box Office; *KR Films*; Singapore Film Commission.

won awards in Hong Kong and Taiwan for their distinctive treatments of the horror genre. This recognition showed that Applause's pan-Asian strategy of repackaging genre films can even pay off in prestige, an important value added to the company's branding and visibility.

Applause employs folklore together with Asian genre conventions, regional marketing, creative collaboration, and industrial alliances to create multiple trajectories of production, consumption, and distribution. Here the local is redefined in regional, transnational terms: Hong Kong–initiated projects get spun out into films aimed at East Asian audiences. By capitalizing on moviegoers' familiarity with neighboring cinemas, Chan hopes to "build a unified Asian marketplace."[25] But this vision, before reaching full maturity, shifted focus when China, Asia's biggest territory, accelerated its media marketization and opened up. Like most Hong Kong producers, Applause Pictures quickly shifted direction and traded pan-Asian for pan-Chinese production. Horror, Applause's major strength, was taboo to Chinese censors, so it was exchanged for more suitable genres such as crime, costume, and martial arts films.

To China! Displacing Pan-Asian with Pan-Chinese Markets

At the beginning of this chapter, I sketched a dispute over Chinese New Year releases in 2007. That quarrel exemplifies the contradictions of media marketization and the tension between the state and industry practice in China today. Although centralized planning has relaxed, new administrative measures prop up state control and maintain a level of protectionism for domestic production and a few carefully chosen players. Market entry remains closely guarded, with preferential treatment to high-budget Chinese blockbusters such as *Curse of the Golden Flower*. For Hong Kong producers, a window of opportunity opened with the introduction of CEPA, the Closer Economic Partnership Arrangement, a scheme designed to allow Hong Kong access to the fruits of China's marketization.

CEPA lowers trade barriers and reduces obstacles to Hong Kong imports, such as films, video, television programming, and cinema infrastructure. When key conditions are met, Hong Kong movies receive exemption from the annual quota of twenty foreign film imports now allowed into China. Under CEPA, Hong Kong films count as domestic Chinese releases and are not subject to limitations prescribed by China Film Corporation, the country's main importer of foreign films.[26] CEPA provisions not only relaxed import restrictions, they also allowed greater flexibility for coproductions between Hong Kong and mainland partners:

* Coproductions are exempt from the foreign film quota.
* Coproduction may draw up to 70 percent of creative talent and staff from Hong Kong.
* Coproductions no longer needed to be filmed completely in China and stories need not be China related (although one third of the cast must be Chinese, in effect stipulating material appropriate to the PRC).
* Hong Kong investors may own up to 90 percent interest in PRC theaters.
* Hong Kong investors may own up to 70 percent of PRC audiovisual companies.[27]

To take advantage of these new opportunities, Hong Kong producers needed to make content adjustments in order to cater to the mainland audience's taste and satisfy censors. They also had to cultivate mainland talent and story angles in order to succeed. In some cases, Hong Kong directors such as Stanley Kwan and Stephen Chow moved their productions across the border so they could directly tap into the mainland market.

Changes occurred on the other side of the border as well. PRC film projects began absorbing resources from the region to support the Chinese blockbuster film, *dapian* (big pictures). *Dapian* means costume pictures with martial arts, big budget, big stars, big directors, big special effects, and backing from the authorities. Zhang Yimou's *Hero* (2002) and *Curse of the Golden Flower* (2006), Chen Kaige's *The Promise* (2005), and John Woo's *Red Cliff* (2008) are representative examples, receiving transnational investment as well as acting and technical talent from the region.

For an independent like Applause, this meant a shift from small-budget genre films to high-profile media events tailored for Chinese audiences, from pan-Asian branding to pan-Chinese *dapian*. Here, Chan chose to make a Chinese musical, *Perhaps Love*. Set in Shanghai, the production was assisted by Shanghai Film Corp, the second-largest media conglomerate in China. Making a media-event film means large capital, maximum PR, and alliances with the biggest possible players. For this, Applause restructured and enlarged the scale of its productions. Peter Chan teamed with Andre Morgan, former U.S. partner of Golden Harvest, to form Morgan and Chan Films Ltd. The new company sought investment from Hong Kong's broadcaster

TVB and Malaysian television platform Astro, whose subsidiary Celestial Pictures handled international sales. China's exhibitor Stellar Media Group partnered with China Film Corp. in multiplexes for the mainland release.

Peter Chan knew that it would be folly to abandon the profile and company brand that Applause had built up, so he mixed and matched pan-Asian ingredients with Chinese elements with respect to talent, locale, and narrative, creating a film that would interlock market segments and territories. *Perhaps Love* stars Takeshi Kaneshiro, a half-Japanese, half-Taiwanese actor with art-house credentials and strong commercial appeal in East Asia. Next, Chan cast singer-actor Jacky Cheung, known for his music, movie, and theatrical successes. Cheung's fan base is no less than that of Kaneshiro, appealing to all ages in China, Taiwan, and Southeast Asia. *Perhaps Love*'s femme fatale is mainlander Zhou Xun, who began her career in a Taiwan–PRC coproduced television series and then crossed over to art-film acclaim with *Suzhou River* (1999, Lou Ye, China/Germany), *Balzac and the Little Chinese Seamstress* (2004, Dai Sijie, France), *Hollywood Hong Kong* (2002, Fruit Chan, Hong Kong), and *Bao'ber in Love* (2004, Li Shaohong, China). Finally, Korean TV star Ji Jin-hee was cast as the narrator-ringmaster of the film. He provides an overture, linking the show-business story with lives of ordinary, anonymous people. Ji Jin-hee's casting capitalizes on his own following among K-drama fans—particularly followers of 2003's pan-Asian superhit *Jewel in the Crown*.

Perhaps Love presents itself as a "Shanghai film," with glamour, nostalgia, and a touch of decadence. Dance numbers were arranged by Farah Khan (*Om Shanti Om*, 2007), a famous Bollywood choreographer, and peopled by African and South Asian dancers, bringing a borderless, cosmopolitan flavor, much like *Moulin Rouge* and *Chicago*. Postproduction complete, the movie opened in Shanghai in mid-November 2005, followed by premieres in Beijing, Kuala Lumpur, Singapore, and Hong Kong. In the end, however, *Perhaps Love* grossed a disappointing $7 million worldwide, barely more than half of Applause's previous hit, *The Eye*.

Perhaps Love shows pan-Asian cinema has evolved from regional consolidation to a mainland orientation in hopes of exploiting the China market. No longer just a stylistic device or a cost-efficiency strategy, pan-Asian cinema has turned to China in hopes of amplifying production scale and market prospects of big-budget movies. But during this process, the pan-Asian elements receded. Diversity gave way to martial arts and costume pictures aimed at the China market, which currently remains a terrain dominated by capricious rules. Despite Applause's strategy, *Perhaps Love*'s $3.7 million box-office take in China was unsatisfactory. It fell far behind another *dapian*, *The Promise*, a martial arts fantasy with Korean and Japanese actors dubbed in Chinese (see table 9.2). It shows that the pan-Asian concept is less marketable than that of a grand China vision containing Asia within its imagination. Musicals, Bollywood, and Shanghai glamour are perhaps incompatible with the standard *dapian* ingredients of marital arts, costume dramas, and mythical Chinese settings. Moreover, the transnational, diasporic identity of the man behind *Perhaps Love*, Peter Chan, signals the instability and confusion of the film's nationality. Chinese audiences and the political establishment would probably feel more comfortable with Chen Kaige, China's blue blood, rather than Peter Chan, a UCLA-educated Chinese from Southeast Asia (Chen and Chan share the same Chinese character but different dialect pronunciations). Transnationality might in this case be more acceptable if it were subsumed to nationality.

Immediately after *Perhaps Love*, Peter Chan teamed up with award-winning Hong Kong director Derek Yee. The result was a pan-Chinese hit, *Protégé*. This 2007 Hong Kong–China coproduction was financed by capital from Hong Kong, China, Singapore, the United States, and the United Kingdom. It has an all-Chinese cast and centers on Chinese activities in the criminal underworld of the Golden Triangle. Imbued with pan-Asian motifs like border crossings, transnational triad transactions, multiple identities, and networking, not a single non-Chinese character or actor is featured as a principal character. Pan-Asian, at this point, appeared to have dissolved into a field for pan-Chinese intrigue and consumption. The film grossed more than $10 million in only two weeks in China and Hong Kong and was the box-office champion during the lunar New Year holiday period.

Concurrent with the making of *Protégé*, Chan began his new film, *The Warlords*, for Christmas release 2007. Starring three of East Asia's most bankable male stars—Jet Li, Andy Lau, and Takeshi Kaneshiro—the film was backed by the industry's top players, including China Film Corp., Warner-China HG Corp., PolyBona, and Media Asia. A $40 million costume extravaganza, *The Warlords* is Peter Chan's first period picture and represents a significant departure from the scale and repertoire of Applause's earlier films. Evidently packaged to be yet another pan-Chinese *dapian* for mass consumption, *The Warlords* grossed $27 million in the mainland market

Table 9.2. Box-Office Revenue of Pan-China Coproductions (2000–2008)

Year	Title	China	East Asia except China	Europe	United States	Worldwide
2000	Crouching Tiger, Hidden Dragon	1,691,148	6,500,639	17,933,123	128,078,872	213,525,736
2002	Hero	29,227,053	57,317,355	20,531,400	53,710,019	177,394,432
2003	Infernal Affairs III	4,347,826	5,181,537	N/A	N/A	9,529,363
2004	House of Flying Daggers	18,550,725	29,549,735	10,647,679	11,050,094	92,801,097
2004	A World without Thieves	14,492,754	656,957	N/A	N/A	15,149,710
2004	Kung Fu Hustle	20,291,436	44,562,560	7,508,792	17,108,591	100,912,445
2005	Initial D	7,901,235	11,253,951	N/A	N/A	19,155,186
2005	Seven Swords	10,246,914	3,110,436	N/A	N/A	13,357,350
2005	The Myth	11,866,502	6,347,627	N/A	N/A	18,214,129
2005	Perhaps Love	3,717,472	3,148,070	N/A	N/A	6,865,542
2005	The Promise	22,304,833	10,383,730	1,159,735	669,625	34,517,922
2006	The Banquet	17,902,813	5,928,676	N/A	N/A	23,831,489
2006	A Battle of Wits	8,545,918	9,238,843	N/A	N/A	17,784,761
2006	Curse of the Golden Flower	37,500,000	15,318,738	15,277,343	6,566,773	78,598,977
2007	Protégé	8,069,097	4,699,327	N/A	N/A	12,768,424
2007	Lust, Caution	17,109,185	31,119,203	12,060,800	4,604,982	66,054,977
2007	The Warlords	27,601,246	13,560,227	N/A	N/A	41,161,473
2007	Assembly	34,089,912	687,965	N/A	N/A	34,777,877
2008	CJ7	26,166,803	20,211,297	N/A	207,378	46,698,785
2008	Kung Fu Dunk	15,883,165	6,032,797	N/A	N/A	21,915,962

All box offices in U.S. dollars

Sources: City Entertainment; Box Office Mojo; Taipei Box Office; *KR Films*; *Variety Asia Online*; *Screendaily*; Singapore Film Commission; *China Film Market*, *China Film Yearbook*, 2002–2006

Andy Lau, Jet Li, and Takeshi Kaneshiro in Peter Chan's costume action film *The Warlords* (2008).

alone, finishing at second place in China's 2007 top-ten chart for Chinese-language releases. It went ahead to gross $41 million worldwide (see table 9.2). For Chan, the shift to China paid off, at least in the box office.

With Applause's architect Peter Chan moving into the PRC market, both he and his company abandoned some pan-Asian strategies to comply with Chinese censorship standards. For example, they abandoned problem genres such as horror and eroticism, both of which had been Applause house specialties. To guarantee success in China, cooperation with local business was necessary, as well as assimilation of Asian ingredients into approved Chinese subject matter. China represents the future of the trade, so in order to exploit this new opportunity, Applause was reinvented to become something else—bigger, safer, and more Chinese. In the closing credits for both *Protégé* and *The Warlords*, Applause Pictures was barely acknowledged; its sole credit was ARM (Applause-Ruddy Morgan), the company in charge of overseas sales.

Conclusion

By examining the history of Applause Pictures, we see the initial promise and the eventual compromise of pan-Asian coproduction. To an extent, these films pioneered a fresh, creative vision for Asian cinema, but before the pan-Asian strategy reached maturity, it was derailed by the allure of the China market. According to the current market logic, pan-Asian coproductions have dim prospects without backing from China's official agencies.[28] And when pan-Asian aligns with pan-Chinese production, it must accede to political censorship and China's state-regulated distribution system. Finally, although the PRC market did help to create Chinese blockbuster films that repelled Hollywood imports, it also engendered distribution bottlenecks that have undermined the prospects of many Asian and Chinese producers that lack political influence and connections.

Seen from a macro perspective, Applause represents the endeavor of independents to get into the China game, already populated by big players from around the world. Hong Kong's Media Asia and Edko Film, as well as News Corp., Warner Bros, and Columbia-Asia, all have joint ventures in the PRC. This list continues to grow with the arrival of big Japanese and South Korean screen players. In a way, pan-Asian cinema is now fulfilled via partnerships with state-sanctioned Chinese companies. But pan-Asian notions of diversity and audience-centered entertainment are compromised by these alliances. Regarding *The Warlords*, Peter Chan Ho-sun comments on the tradeoffs involved in such transactions: "The budget involved is so big and there are so many parties putting money into it. . . . I've never seen so much politics in a production I've been involved in. But will this change how I deal with other people? Maybe not. But the frustration and the pressure generated by this film might eventually resurface in future films."[29]

For pan-Asian cinema, the object is to coproduce films for audiences across the region. It is an inviting option to boost attendance in every East Asian market, producing pan-Asian films that sell "from Bangkok to Tokyo."[30] Nevertheless, in the present China market, pan-Chinese—not pan-Asian—is the dominant order. As long as market entry remains regulated by the Chinese state, pan-Asian cinema will be deferred until there is a better integration between China and the rest of East Asia.

Acknowledgments

Research for this article is supported by Hong Kong Research Grant Council (HKBU2428/05). The author thanks Darrell W. Davis, the editors, and the anonymous reader for their valuable comments.

Notes

1. Sen-lun Yu, "*Golden Flower* triggers dispute in Mainland China," Screendaily.com, 19 December 2006, www.screendaily.com/story.asp?storyid =29994 (accessed 19 December 2006).

2. Jiaqi Liu, "*Curse* dominates digital screens enraged *Pain*," *Dongfang Morning Post*, 13 December 2006, ent.sina.com.cn/m/c/2006–12–13/11131367678.html (accessed 7 February 2006).

3. Liu, "*Curse* dominates."

4. Clifford Coonan, "Period epics continue dynastic Chinese reign," *Variety Asia Daily News*, 15 January 2007.

5. Yu, "*Golden Flower*."

6. Clifford Coonan, "Hong Kong feeds off China's power," *Variety Asia Daily News*, 12 February 2007.

7. Ying Zhu, *Chinese Cinema during the Era of Reform: The Ingenuity of the System* (Westport, CT: Praeger, 2003).

8. Zhaoyang Lu, "An examination of China's current private screen enterprises and their future business strategies," forum on Chinese Cinema, the thirteenth annual Golden Rooster Awards and Hundred Flowers Awards Festival (2004).

9. Clifford Coonan, "East meets West on biz's front line," *Variety Asia Daily News*, 12 February 2007, www.varietyasiaonline.com/index2.php?option=com _content$tast=view&id=768&po (accessed 13 February 2007).

10. Liz Shackleton, "*Curse* continues to be blessed in Asian rollout," Screendaily.com, 2 January 2007, www.screendaily.com/story.asp?storyid=30089 (accessed 3 January 2007).

11. Hong Song, "*House of Flying Daggers* triggers industry outcry," *Sizhuan Business Daily*, 18 June 2004, ent.tom.com/1002/1011/2004618–84404.html (accessed 7 March 2007).

12. Yilan Ting, "2004 box office chart of co-produced Films in Mainland China," *Chinese Film Industry Weekly* 835 (17 March 2005): 10.

13. Song, "*House of Flying Daggers* triggers industry outcry."

14. Elizabeth Freund Larus, *Economic Reform in China, 1979–2003: The Marketization of Labor and State Enterprises* (Lewiston, NY: Edwin Mellen Press, 2005).

15. Patrick Frater, "China and India face off for Hollywood cash," *Variety Asia Daily News*, 12 February 2007, www.varietyasiaonline.com/index2.php?option=com _content$tast=view&id=780&po (accessed 13 February 2007).

16. Hui Wang, *China's New Order: Society, Politics and Economy in Transition*, ed. Theodore Huters (Cambridge, MA: Harvard University Press, 2003), 114.

17. Darrell William Davis and Emilie Yueh-yu Yeh, *East Asian Screen Industries* (London: British Film Institute, 2007).

18. Poshek Fu, *Between Shanghai and Hong Kong: The Politics of Chinese Cinemas* (Stanford, CA: Stanford University Press, 2003).

19. Emilie Yueh-yu Yeh and Darrell William Davis. "Japan Hongscreen: Pan-Asian cinema and flexible accumulation," *Historical Journal of Film, Radio and Television* 22, no. 1 (2002): 61–82.

20. Peter Chan, panel on Pan-Asian Cinema, Asian Cultural Cooperation Forum, Hong Kong Academy of Performing Arts, 11 November 2005.

21. Davis and Yeh, *East Asian Screen Industries*.

22. Naoko Tsukeda, Asian Coproduction Panel, seminar on Asian Convergence, the twenty-first Hong Kong Film Awards, Intercontinental Hotel, 20 April 2002.

23. Darcy Paquet, "Dependency on local market poses danger," *Variety Asia Daily News*, 13 February 2007.

24. Mark Russell, "Sector report: Korea," *Hollywood Reporter*, 24 May 2005.

25. Wendy Kan, "Applause Pics bring Asian talent together," *Variety* (22 April 2002).

26. Liu, "*Curse* dominates."

27. *Hong Kong FILMART*, brochure, 2004.

28. Emilie Yueh-yu Yeh and Darrell William Davis, "Re-nationalizing China's film industry: Case study on the China Film Group and film marketization," *Journal of Chinese Cinemas* 2, no. 1 (2008): 37–51.

29. Clarence Tsui, "Left, right and wrong," *South China Morning Post*, 9 December 2007, 1.

30. Gregory Beals, "The birth of Asiawood," *Asiaweek* (21 May 2001): 57–60, 57.

TEN

Cultural Globalization and Chinese Television: A Case of Hybridization

Joseph M. Chan

Research and commentary regarding media globalization tend to use the term globalization *in a variety of ways. For some, globalization conjures up a vision of Western conglomerates coming to dominate media imagery worldwide. For others, it suggests a dynamic interaction between forces near and far, what John Tomlinson refers to as the push–pull of globalization. In this chapter, Joseph Chan contends television in the People's Republic of China is increasingly influenced by media from other parts of East Asia as well as the West. Chinese television channels commonly acquire programs from Hong Kong, Taiwan, and Korea. They likewise engage in coproductions with regional partners, and they adapt formats, genres, and industrial practices from counterparts throughout East Asia. Chinese TV shows are therefore a hybrid mixture of elements from near and far that have been adapted to suit the interests of viewers within the context of a state-controlled, semicommercial media system.*

In the past two decades, China has transformed its planned economy into a socialist market economy. In tandem with this economic restructuring is the transformation of its media from being the mouthpiece of the party-state to being state-owned enterprises that rely primarily on market opportunities for survival. Although ideological control persists, the unfinished project of media commercialization has redefined the boundaries and configuration of Chinese culture in many important ways. Susceptible to the forces of globalization, it no longer represents an isolated system. The thesis of this chapter is that even a socialist television culture such as China's is hybridized, subject to influences from other social systems. I draw on selected studies of Chinese television and take note of recent media-cultural formations in China and East Asia to explore how the globalization of television culture fares with respect to China.

Hybridization and the Dialectics of Cultural Globalization

In the study of international communication, the theory of cultural imperialism that played a visible role in the 1970s gradually lost its influence in the 1980s. In its place is the rise in popularity of the idea of globalization, which by now has become a key word in professional, academic, political, business, and journalistic discourses around the world. In spite of its popularity, globalization remains an elusive concept.[1] It can be viewed as an extension of modernity, the compression of time and space, an increase in global interconnectedness, the growth of mutual interdependence, and a project for the diffusion of liberal capitalism.[2] Some argue that globalization is a misconception because of the growing gaps between the have and have-not countries. Although globalization can be viewed positively or negatively, depending on one's political orientation, it is often feared that it will result in cultural homogenization.[3] Fueling the belief of global cultural homogenization are academic studies showing how Western culture spreads around the world, as in the case of McDonaldization[4] and Disneyfication.[5] Best-sellers promoting the idea of globalization such as Thomas Friedman's *The World Is Flat* also fuel the assumption of the inevitability of cultural homogenization.[6]

In contrast, the perspective informing this analysis views the global as a matter of dialectics, in which the global is always becoming.[7] This perspective finds the power vector an integral part of globalization that tends to result in domination, be it economic, political, or cultural, in favor of the power center. Yet the dominating culture can be transculturated as the world economy becomes increasingly integrated and cultural exchange rapidly intensifies. Global change here is understood as the transformation of the principles organizing social life and world order, as Held and McGrew put it.[8] This conception allows a place for global media that owe their influence to their capacity to reach a transnational audience, shape international public opinion, and redefine the agenda of local, national, and global politics. However, this global change can hardly be understood without reference to the local.[9] The local—which is tied to soil, blood, and history—is less susceptible to changes and is resistant to the forces of globalization. The local can be so strong that the global becomes localized in the course of cultural production, marketing, and distribution. Despite the capacity of information technologies to transcend national boundaries, what persists is the continual "search for boundary technologies that will allow some continuing control over internal information space."[10] In this sense, national and local interests are expected to continue to play a pivotal role in this age of globalization. This contrasts with some globalists' accounts that reserve little autonomy for the nation-state. In the ever-becoming process of globalization, the global is mediated by the local while there is a strong tendency for the local to reassert itself. The resultant national response is a product of negotiation between the nation-states, governments, multinational organizations, and other global, regional, and local entities.

In tune with this dialectical view of cultural globalization is the notion of hybridization, which, as defined by Kraidy, is "the fusion of two hitherto relatively distinct forms, styles, or identities, a cross-cultural contact, which often occurs across national borders as well as across cultural boundaries."[11] Thanks to the general adoption of market mechanisms around the world and the increased interconnectivity across social systems, hybridity is becoming a cultural norm. In spite of its pervasiveness, I do not think it is productive to stress hybridity so much that it glosses over the power imbalances that were illuminated by the theory of media imperialism.[12] At the same time, critics of media imperialism must make room for hybridity in their analysis of global culture. As Waisbord demonstrated, there are many national variations beneath the surface of apparent content standardization even in the case of global diffusion of television formats.[13] Although globalization has resulted in the circulation of television formats around the world, they are nevertheless tied to national cultures at the same time. It is not a simple case of homogenization.

By Holton's account, hybridization is one of the three major cultural consequences of globalization, in addition to homogenization and polarization.[14] Each of the three characterizations has its elements of truth. Although some evidence shows that the world is becoming standardized around a Western or American pattern, there are significant signs of polarization as evidenced by resistance to Western norms in many parts of the world. But both approaches appear to have neglected hybridization, the borrowing of cultures from one another to create complex syncretic cultural forms. The syncretization perspective is a corrective to the homogenization and polarization approaches because it allows for interaction effects. This observation is in line with Kraidy's contention that hybridization is the "cultural logic of globalization," arguing that all cultures are inherently mixed.[15] The task that remains is to understand the depth, scope, and directions of various levels of hybridity at the social level. Viewing globalization as hybridization, Jan Nederveen Pieterse maintains that hybridization can take place as structural hybridization (the emergence of mixed forms of social cooperation) and cultural hybridization (the development of translocal mélange cultures).[16] Cultural homogenization is not stressed in this perspective because cultural differences are seen to be enduring, with new differences constantly being generated in the process of cultural hybridization.

Hybridity can also be viewed as the result of cultural appropriation, an act broadly defined "as the use of a culture's symbols, artifacts, genres, rituals, or technologies by members of another culture."[17] Again, power relations are a key issue in the politics of cultural appropriation; it helps differentiate different forms of appropriation that range from cultural exchange, cultural dominance, and cultural exploitation to transculturation. Analogous to hybridization, transculturation is the adoption of elements from a foreign culture for self-aggrandizement.[18] While this transculturational perspective finds the essentialized view of culture problematic, it tends to assume that the originating culture is transcultural in the first place.[19] In fact, it is more often the case that the cultural appropriation originates from multiple cultures. Hybridity and transculturation are inevitable when cultures are allowed to interact with one another. Cultural appropriation can be a voluntary act or the result of structural forces posed by market demands, technological changes, and organizational imperatives.

Most studies of hybridity examine cultural forms and styles, but for this study of television culture, I analyze industry structure, program flows, and textual representation. Structure refers to the ways that television institutions are organized. Program flows are cross-cultural contacts via program sales, satellite transmissions, and other means. Representation refers to the form and content of specific programs or genres.

The Chinese television culture is a significant case for the study of media globalization. According to many per capita indicators, China belongs to the developing world, haunted by developmental problems such as rampant corruption, a widening gap between the rich and poor, an inequitable distribution of political power, and the absence of the rule of law. But size matters. China owes its strength to its absolute economic power and the sheer size of its population. By 2008, China had already become the third-largest economic power, ranking behind the United States and Japan. It has surpassed Japan as the world's largest holder of foreign currency reserves. And China's population of 1.3 billion constitutes about one fifth of humanity. Whatever happens to China is therefore destined to be important to the world, if not because of its kind, then because of its sheer size. Anything that happens with China has implications for humanity.

China's status as a significant case study of social science is also attributable to the multiple transformations it is currently undergoing, from a planned economy into a market economy, from a closed society into an open society, and from an authoritarian state into a more pluralistic society. While one may not be certain where China is heading, it is fair to say that China has made significant progress over the past few decades. However, China remains a country that differs from the Western model in terms of ideology, cultural values, economic composition, and sociopolitical structure. It is a case that no student of cultural globalization can ignore.

Media Commercialization with Chinese Characteristics

The globalization and hybridization of Chinese television culture can be observed at three levels: industry configuration, program flows, and representation. First, I examine how the industrial organization of Chinese television has been influenced by the commercial model that prevails in the West and other parts of the world. Media commercialization, as a universal process applicable to communication systems that assume private ownership, implies the rise of advertising as the major source of revenue and the intensification of competition for audiences.[20] In the context of China, it is a process by which media respond to competitive pressure in order to enhance their market position and to make a profit.[21] Such adaptations are made not just by individual media outlets but also by media sectors as a whole, in the form of policy changes, industrial reconfiguration, and management practices. By the indicators I have identified elsewhere,[22] the state of television commercialization can be portrayed as follows:

1. Market forces: The emergence of the media market signifies a break from the traditional socialist system that never viewed media content as commodities. Instead of subjecting themselves to the ideological dictates of party authorities, media operators now pay conspicuous attention to market considerations. In this commercialized system, the performance of media institutions is evaluated mainly in terms of market success or failure. Ratings are widely used to decide whether a program will be aired or not.

2. Revenue base: A strong indicator of media commercialization is the reliance on advertising and the corresponding withdrawal of state subsidy.[23] With rare exceptions, all television operations have to depend on advertising, subscription, and other nonmedia investment for income. Associated with this change is the rise of the profit motive. Making a profit has become the most important priority for many television operators.

3. Commodification: In a marketized environment, media content is commodified. Money is used to measure virtually all media fare. Although this understanding is commonsensical to capitalist societies, it takes time for the Chinese media to realize this and put it into practice. Currently, media resources such as talent, labor, equipment, and brand names are all commodified.

4. Concentration: The Chinese media system is tied to the administrative system that defines the status, mission, and scope of a media operation.[24] If left to the market, the media are inclined toward concentration and cross-regional expansion. So far, media conglomeration in China is driven not so much by market forces but is rather a result of administrative measures.

5. Privatization: Because it is the most sensitive issue in Chinese communication, private media ownership is still banned. However, nonmedia operations associated with a media outlet are allowed to go public, as in the case of Hunan Television Broadcasting Group, which privatized its advertising and other business operations.[25] Some television ventures such as production houses owned by private or even foreign capital are known to be in operation.[26] Nevertheless, private media ownership in China is far from a reality; state ownership predominates.

6. Market access: Foreign capital, as spearheaded by News Corporation, has been coveting the China market because of its huge population and rapidly growing advertising revenue. As we explore in the next section, while China has been engaging in program trades with the outside world, this is subject to government restrictions. So far, China has allowed some selected transborder television channels such as the Hong Kong–based TVB, ATV, Phoenix TV, STAR TV, and ETV to

land in Guangdong through cable networks.[27] In general, however, the openness of the Chinese television market is rather limited.

Media commercialization in China is an evolutionary process initiated by the marketization of its economy as the country embarked on its course of modernization. Media commercialization took off during the 1990s as advertising rose to replace state subsidies as the primary source of operational revenues. The withdrawal of state subsidies started a chain reaction that created the internal drive for media commercialization, which, fueled by the global political economy of mass media, tended to push the commercial logic forward. The multinational media corporations and the media systems they represent thus became sources of inspiration for Chinese TV institutions.

Media commercialization works both ways. It brings important changes into the country—such as a shift in media functions, the diversification of content, and the multiplication of channels—which may result in cultural homogenization and diversification at the same time.[28] In a commercialized environment, meeting the tastes and needs of audiences has grown in importance, bringing China into line with commercial media systems in other parts of the world. Yet this shift toward a global standard has engendered a diversification of content and the establishment of more channels to meet the diverse needs of the public.

Media commercialization has developed unevenly in China, showing more prominence in urban centers and affluent regions, especially in the spheres of entertainment and nonparty media.[29] An enduring issue that plagues media commercialization is its relationship to the state's desire for ideological control. The Communist Party has dealt with this tension by taking a disjunctive approach that confines reforms to the nonpolitical spheres of television operations while leaving the political sector unchanged. Striking a balance between political control and liberalization is a way of life for media enterprises. This "ambivalence and contradiction" adds up to what may be termed media commercialization with Chinese characteristics.[30] On the one hand, we find that the Chinese television system is getting closer to the global standard of commercial media. On the other hand, the specific ways in which the nation-state, foreign capital, private capital, and consumer markets combine in China are different from what they are in the West. They prevent Chinese television from merely replicating Western television culture and engender a mixed and hybridized culture that matches China's unique social environment.

Program Flow, Cultural Proximity, and Regionalization

Program flows involve the exchange of different types of content that range from news to entertainment. Given that the exchange of entertainment programs is subject more often to economic rather than ideological considerations, it makes sense to focus analysis on television drama and variety shows, as they are more likely to be exchanged, if at all.

Although China has adopted an open-door policy for over twenty years, its door is only partially open in the cultural realm where protectionism still reigns. For entertainment fare, more programs are allowed to cross the national boundary, but they are subject to various limitations. Foreign television drama series, the most popular genre among audiences, are set to make up no more than 15 percent of prime time from 6 P.M. to 10 P.M. and no more than 25 percent of the time dedicated to television drama series as a whole.[31] To reduce their impact, the nonlocal drama series can be carried by no more than three provincial satellite television stations at the same time. There are other regulations on the content of the drama series, setting limits on the importation of content related to martial arts, crime stories, and explicit sex.

Looking back, the inflow of nonlocal television drama series ebbs and flows with regulations and the political winds. When China first opened up to the world, nonlocal programs from Hong Kong, Japan, and the United States were very popular. Such imports increased dramatically in the late 1990s when the cable networks craved more foreign productions to fill up their channels. Nevertheless, PRC productions have become more competitive of late, even when they come into direct competition with nonlocal productions. The cross-border communication between Hong Kong and Guangzhou provides a laboratory for exploring this phenomenon. Since the early 1990s, mainland regulators have looked the other way as Guangzhou cable operators delivered Hong Kong television channels on their local networks. The channels proved quite popular even though they were officially illegal. Their strong performance was a reflection of the metropolitan influence of Hong Kong in southern China. As table 10.1 shows, the market share was overwhelmingly in favor of Hong Kong television, especially in the 1990s. After 2001, China began to officially allow transborder TV channels such as Hong Kong television, Phoenix TV, Entertainment Television Network, and STAR TV to be carried on cable networks in Guangdong. With the official entry of transborder television, one would expect the local players to lose more of their audience. But, after some twenty years of struggle, the local channels finally managed to gain an edge in the ratings war with Hong Kong television in 2005. Although some people may find this turn of events somewhat unexpected, it should be no surprise to anyone who believes in the primacy of cultural proximity in television viewing. Like many other places around the world, domestic programs in Guangdong tend to be more appealing to the local audiences by virtue of their social and cultural relevancy.

Table 10.1. Market Shares of Television Receivable in Guangzhou during Prime Time (Percent)

Channels	2001	2005
Transborder TV		
HK-TVB	39.9	30.1
HK-ATV	22.4	6.9
Phoenix TV	1.8	3.2
Entertainment TV	0.2	2.3
Chinese TV		
Guangzhou TV	10.8	13.5
Guangdong TV	10.2	9.8
Southern TV	6.5	19.0
CCTV	6.2	7.8
Others	2.0	7.4

Source: N. Ou, R. Yu, Z. Zhang, H. Chen, and D. Yang, *Globalization: A TV Game* (Guangzhou: Yangchang Press, 2006) (in Chinese).

Guangdong presents a special case with respect to Chinese television because of its proximity to Hong Kong and its cultural and commercial ties to the city. The rest of China is subject to more restrictive regulations that require the channels to diversify their sources of imported television drama series. Nationwide, statistics for 2002 show that the bulk of imported programs (81.1 percent) are drama series from Hong Kong, Korea, Taiwan, and Japan.[32] The rest are from the United States, Japan, and Europe. Table 10.2 demonstrates that the flow is not dominated by the United States or even the West, but rather by East Asian programming sources (83.2 percent), with Hong Kong leading at 40.7 percent. These statistics point toward the formation of Greater China and East Asian television markets, comprising markets in Hong Kong, Taiwan, and Mainland China.

Table 10.2. Origins of Nonlocal TV Drama Series
in 2002 (Percent)

Origins			
Hong Kong	40.7	Japan	7.0
South Korea	20.5	Europe	3.1
Taiwan	12.9	Singapore	2.1
USA	11.9	Others	1.8

Source: Shanghai TV Festival Organizing Committee,
China TV Drama Report 2003–2004 (Beijing: Huaxia Press,
2004) (in Chinese).

The Greater China television market is at best in the making. The quota limitation in China has led television players in Hong Kong, Taiwan, and elsewhere to form joint production units with Chinese television stations or production houses in order to evade restrictions on imported programs.[33] This also encourages the growth of private or semiprivate production houses that have attracted investment from international corporations. However, the right to broadcast programs remains in the hands of the television stations and the party-state.

The occasional success of television programs in the whole of Greater China demonstrates the strong potential of transborder television as interactions among players from the constituent parts are increasing, resulting in program trades, joint ventures, and other kinds of exchanges.[34] The popularity of some transborder programs, especially those produced in Hong Kong and Taiwan, testifies to the existence of common cultural tastes in Greater China—which constitutes and is constituted by regional television. The audience appears to be socialized to products that try to integrate elements from all three places, including the combination of artists, producers, formats, and stories.

Another notable indicator of the emerging East Asian television market is the rise of South Korean programs. Japanese television drama series, once rather popular in the 1980s and 1990s, were overtaken by South Korean productions in the early 2000s. The number of Korean TV drama series China imported rose from 1 in 1993 to 67 in 2002 and 107 in 2004, epitomizing what has come to be labeled the "Korean tide" in China and Hong Kong. This tide owed its rise to the upgrading of South Korean productions, which paralleled the rapid growth of commerce between South Korea and China. In the thirteen years following the establishment of diplomatic relations, China has become South Korea's leading export market and trading partner.[35] It is no coincidence that one of the most popular shows in Hong Kong, Taiwan, China, and Japan in 2005 was a South Korean costume TV drama series, *Jewel in the Palace*, which depicts the personal struggle of a female doctor in the imperial court. At the same time, the popularity of South Korean programs has aroused some jealousy among local commentators. For instance, in China some commentators slighted the show out of nationalistic sentiments, and some lobbied the central authorities to ban Korean productions in order to make way for local productions.[36] The great success of Korean cultural products—in television, music, and fashion—has caused unease with some Chinese officials, who see it as "cultural domination by a 'lesser' country with a shorter history and a less sophisticated civilization than that of China."[37]

The above account suggests that television globalization needs to be examined at various levels, from the global to the regional, national, and local.[38] Of particular importance in the case of Greater China is television at the national and regional levels. This echoes the call for attention to regional and national television by Straubhaar[39] and by Sinclair, Jacka, and Cunningham.[40] The multilevel perspective is different from the unidirectional flow of the past, with the United States as a dominating center conceived in the theory of media imperialism.[41] It represents increasing flows of capital, programs, and cultures in regions defined by geographical locations and cultural proximity.[42]

The case of Greater China shows that the influence of regional broadcasters far exceeds that of global players, particularly when they make no attempt to offer tailor-made programs. Productions by the constituent parts of Greater China in general also have more popular appeal than their Western counterparts. American television production does not occupy the largest segment of screen time, nor is it the most watched in Greater China. However, the regional influence does not stop here, as there are growing signs that video and television productions from neighboring countries—Korea and Japan—have gained large followings first in Taiwan, then in Hong Kong, and finally in China. These imported programs have eaten up more airtime in China not only because they prove to be very attractive to the middle class and the younger generation but also because there is a strong need for cheap programs to fill up the unlimited airtime. The popularity of these imported programs has also led Taiwanese and Hong Kong producers to imitate their formats. The success of regional productions reinforces the previous emphasis on regionalization rather than globalization in the discourse on international television.

This analysis of program inflows in China demonstrates that its programming menu is hybridizing, offering both local and transborder television. If we take the supply of pirated videos or Internet television into consideration, we will attach even more importance to imported television. As far as the formal programming menu is concerned, local productions still dominate, but the local origin of a production does not guarantee that it is purely domestic. In fact, such programs can be hybrids of various forms that have been successful outside the mainland, attesting to the presence of foreign influence, especially in terms of format.

Transculturation and Hybridization

The diffusion of television formats around the world is generally taken to be an indicator of television globalization because such formats are subject to standardized practices, as in the case of *Who Wants to Be a Millionaire?* These formats are popular because they have been tested in a competitive market and therefore stand a better chance of success in other places. Chinese television practitioners keep abreast of television trends overseas, often learning through observation and exchange, but they seldom purchase the copyrights to foreign formats. Instead they distill the principles from the foreign programs and reinvent them for the Chinese context. To demonstrate how a television format from the West has been adopted and transformed by the Chinese counterparts, I examine the highly successful Chinese program, *Super Girl*, a television singing contest of Hunan Satellite TV that was inspired by *American Idol*, a variation of the talent quest show *Pop Idol* in Britain.

Although *Super Girl* is an imitation of *American Idol*, the producers did not purchase the format copyright but rather invested their time in studying *American Idol*, its British counterpart *Pop Idol*, and other variations. They then made adaptations in order to meet with the specific requirements of the Chinese environment.[43] The resulting hybrid shares both similarities and differences with its Western counterparts.

Most of the similarities lie in the competition rules and procedures. For instance, the competition begins with preliminary auditions, in which thousands of candidates try out but only a few are selected for the regional preliminary rounds. The acrid critiques from judges and relative directness of the feedback to contestants add appeal to the shows. Winners have the opportunity to sign contracts with record companies. Like *American Idol*,

Super Girl emphasizes interactivity. The audience is invited to vote for their favorites by calling or sending SMS text messaging to support their favorite contestant. The strategy of social mobilization was consciously employed by producers to engage the public throughout the broadcast run of *Super Girl*. As the program reached its climax, fans organized themselves and campaigned for their idols with the aid of the Internet, SMS, telephone, and interpersonal persuasion. In the end, the nation was taken by storm, with a total of 3.5 million votes cast in the form of SMS for the winner and 3.2 million for the runner-up.

    American Idol and *Super Girl* exhibit some marked differences as well. *American Idol* restricts the age of its contestants whereas *Super Girl* sets no age limit, thus drawing contestants ranging from four to eighty-nine years of age. *American Idol*'s judges are usually professionals, Hollywood stars, or music producers from big record companies, while judges for *Super Girl* are selected from diverse social backgrounds. In addition to the professional judges, there was a public panel consisting of more than thirty members who were selected from the "rejects" in the former rounds of the competition. In *American Idol*, from the semifinals up, two from each gender with the lowest public votes are eliminated from the competition. In *Super Girl*, when one of the contestants had to be eliminated, the producers staged a contest between the one who earned the lowest score from the judges and the one with the lowest public vote. The winner was determined by the public panel, who then moved on to the next selection process. This mechanism is considered to be a successful innovation because it adds a lot more suspense to the competition.[44] In addition, it resonates with the Chinese tradition of stressing sympathy and sensation over merciless or direct competition. The American judges were found to be highly critical, and sometimes nasty, in their remarks. But for political and cultural reasons, the Chinese counterparts in *Super Girl* were relatively mild and less direct.

    Not only is the format localized to a great extent, its social meanings also appear to be very different from those associated with *American Idol*. To television practitioners, the show represents a watershed event that demonstrates that provincial satellite TV can take on CCTV, the only official national network in the country. And more importantly, *Super Girl* shows how television can be used for entertainment. It amounts to a paradigmatic shift from viewing educational and ideological objectives as an integral part of entertainment programs. As evidenced by online discussions, the program means different things to different people, ranging from personal identification to pure entertainment. To some, it represented the triumph of the citizens at large because they were given the opportunity to define their own taste and aesthetics, in stark contrast to the prevailing practice of having officials and elites defining them on their behalf. After the show, there was an outpouring of discussion regarding the social meanings of *Super Girl*. Some read political implications into the success of the show, attributing the large SMS turnout to the lack of genuine political voting in China and treating it as people's craving for democracy. It is difficult to envision how any of these meanings could be applied to *American Idol* in the United States.

The unprecedented success of *Super Girl* made it an exemplar for making television an entertainment medium. In this sense, it resonates with the idea of media commercialization, which is in line with the direction of global cultural convergence. But any observation that stops here is an oversimplification, since it neglects the ways in which the television format interacted with the local context to produce a hybrid with unique traits and social consequences. In the view of a top manager in research and development at Shanghai Media Group, 98 percent of television formats originate from overseas at this juncture. However, television formats that were imitated without adaptation usually did not work. The formats that worked best were those that had been tried out in East Asia, especially in Taiwan whose culture is akin to China's. This speaks to the importance of cultural appropriation. In the last analysis, we have to make allowance for localization, mixing, and hybridization in the equation of television globalization.

Conclusion and Discussion

The case of Chinese television as a whole, as evidenced in the above review, demonstrates that the cultural globalization thesis requires careful consideration. First and foremost, the nation-state and nationalism continue to play central roles in this age of globalization, not just in news and information but also in entertainment. In order to maintain cultural integrity and to protect the domestic media industry, the nation-state restricts the inflow of television programs. Prime time is reserved for local productions, many of which are made to boost nationalism and mainstream ideology. Nationalism is always used as a peg for criticism of foreign audiovisual influence and in favor of cultural protectionism. Not even Asian productions such as those from nearby South Korea can be spared such nationalistic criticism. This nationalistic sentiment, as a component of regulation and cultural production, helps to tame and complicate the process of cultural globalization.

Cultural resistance may take place at other levels. Domestic and local factors ranging from cultural proximity to local interests to traditional predispositions are always there to require adaptation on the part of incoming cultural forces, thereby creating a mixed or hybridized culture in the course of development. This is especially the case in China, which sets restrictive rules and harbors strong traditions that are often at odds with those of the capitalist West. In the case of *Super Girl*, the format of *American Idol* was significantly changed to respond to the unique local imperatives.

Television culture in no way forms and spreads by pure imitation; it localizes and globalizes selectively in various ways. Although Chinese TV institutions may draw on their counterparts in the West and other parts of Asia for inspiration, they only appropriate what is in their best interest while performing their role as an integral part of the state's propaganda machine. Yet this does not prevent Chinese culture from being Westernized, regionalized, and reinvented at the same time. For transborder broadcasters like STAR TV, there is also a need to localize by offering tailor-made content and repackaging its programs for a given market in China and elsewhere. Hybridization and localization form parts of the equation of transborder broadcasting, so there is no reason to believe that homogenization is taking place imminently and on a large scale. Rather, hybridization at various levels has become the order of the day.

As structural factors are always there to negotiate with the forces of globalization, the interactions between China and foreign influence always result in cultural hybrids that may differ from the original to varying extents, depending on the balance of the contending forces. The sense people make of imported or hybridized culture is even more volatile. While they may vary with the social locations and predispositions of viewers within a society, they also tend to change across societies as well. The meanings of *Super Girl*, for instance, are different from those of *American Idol* in the American context.

The case of Chinese television points to the importance of regionalization as a link between cultural globalization and localization. This is most clearly shown in the pattern of television flows between China and other regions of the world. Hong Kong, dubbed a media capital by Curtin,[45] coupled with Taiwan, form the region from which China imports most of its television programs. Television regionalization at the level of Greater China appears to be more feasible than television globalization. Even here, ideological and political barriers continue to inhibit full regionalization. At the outer layer, television regionalization in East Asia—involving South Korea, Japan, and Greater China—is taking shape. Given that the cultural barriers are much greater between China and the West, the analysis of cultural globalization will miss the point if the regionalization of East Asia television is neglected. Although the cultures of the constituent parts of East Asia share some similarities, they are markedly different in various ways. They are themselves hybridized cultures resulting from various combinations of cultural influences from the West, Confucianism, Buddhism, and local traditions. The cultural globalization thesis tends to assume that cultural influence is directed primarily from the West. It loses sight of regionalization as a greater possibility and of the possibility of having many different cultural combinations and recombinations. The popularity of programs from these neighboring countries of China—South Korea and Japan in particular—reinforces the previous emphasis on television regionalization. It is an oversimplification to conclude that the cultural globalization thesis relies merely on the diffusion of Western audiovisual goods across the globe. In the cultural sphere, although the United States may well be the single most important exporter of television products, this does not amount to a monopoly. Instead, American dominance is challenged by regional, national, and local forces at work in Chinese television culture.

Notes

1. Cees Hamelink, "The elusive concept of globalization," *Global Dialogue* 1 (1999): 1–9.

2. See Anthony Giddens, *The Consequence of Modernity* (Cambridge: Polity Press, 1990); Malcolm Waters, *Globalization* (London: Routledge, 1995); Hamelink, "The elusive concept"; and David Held and Anthony McGrew, *Globalization/Anti-globalization* (Oxford: Polity Press, 2002).

3. Waters, *Globalization*.

4. George Ritzer, *The McDonaldization of Society* (Thousand Oaks, Calif.: Pine Forge Press, 2000).

5. Janet Wasko, Mark Phillips, and Eileen Meehan, eds., *Dazzled by Disney? The Global Disney Audiences Project* (London: Leicester University Press, 2001).

6. Thomas Friedman, *The World Is Flat: A Brief History of the Twenty-first Century* (New York: Farrar, Straus and Giroux, 2005).

7. Joseph Man Chan, "Trans-border broadcasters and TV regionalization in Greater China: Processes and strategies," in *Transnational Television Worldwide: Towards a New Media Order*, ed. Jean K. Chalaby (London: I. B. Tauris, 2005), 173–95.

8. Held and McGrew, *Globalization/Anti-globalization*.

9. Roland Robertson, "Glocalization: Time-space and homogeneity-heterogeneity," in *Global Modernities*, ed. Mike Featherstone, Scott Lash, and Roland Robertson (London: Sage, 1995), 25–44.

10. Monroe Price, *Media and Sovereignty: The Global Information Revolution and Its Challenge to State Power* (Cambridge, MA: MIT Press, 2002).

11. Marwan Kraidy, *Hybridity or the Cultural Logic of Globalization* (Philadelphia, PA: Temple University Press, 2005).

12. Oliver Boyd-Barrett, "Media imperialism reformulated," in *Electronic Empires: Global Media and Local Resistance*, ed. Daya Kishan Thussu (London: Arnold Press, 1998), 157–76.

13. Silvio Waisbord, "McTV: Understanding the global popularity of television formats," *Television & New Media* 5 (2004): 359–83.

14. Robert Holton, "Globalization's cultural consequences," *Annals of the American Academy of Political and Social Science* 570 (July 2000): 140–52.

15. Kraidy, *Hybridity*.

16. Jan Nederveen Pieterse, *Globalization and Culture* (Lanham, MD: Rowman & Littlefield, 2004).

17. Richard Rogers, "From cultural exchange to transculturation: A review and reconceptualization of cultural appropriation," *Communication Theory* 16 (2006): 474–503, 476.

18. Joseph Man Chan and Jack Qiu, "China: Media liberalization under authoritarianism," in *Media Reform: Democratizing the Media, Democratizing the State*, ed. Monroe E. Price, Beata Rozumilowicz, and Stefaan Verhulst (London: Routledge, 2002), 27–47.

19. Rogers, "From cultural exchange to transculturation."

20. John Herbert McManus, *Market-driven Journalism: Let the Citizens Beware?* (Newbury Park, CA: Sage, 1994).

21. See Joseph Man Chan, "Commercialization without independence: Media development in China," in *China Review*, ed. Joseph Cheng and Maurice Brosseau Cheng (Hong Kong: Chinese University Press, 1993), 1–19; and Yuezhi Zhao, *Media, Market and Democracy in China* (Urbana-Champaign: University of Illinois Press, 1998).

22. Joseph Man Chan, "Media commercialization in China: A political-economic and evolutionary perspective," paper presented at the Conference on China's New Media Milieu: Commercialization, Continuity and Reform, Center for Strategic Studies, Washington D.C., June, 2004.

23. Zhao, *Media, Market and Democracy in China*; Zhou He and Huailin Chen, eds., *Chinese Media* (Hong Kong: Pacific Century, 1998); and Joseph Man Chan and Jack Qiu, "China: Media liberalization under authoritarianism."

24. Joseph Man Chan, "Administrative boundaries and media marketization: A comparative analysis of the newspaper, TV and Internet markets in China," in *Chinese Media, Global Contexts*, ed. Chin-Chuan Lee (London: Routledge, 2003), 159–70.

25. Shengming Huang, Yan Zhou, and L. Chen, "On broadcast TV" (in Chinese),

in *A New Century of China Media Markets*, ed. Shengming Huang and Yan Zhou (Beijing: Zhongxin Press, 2003), 3–28.

26. Zhongshi Guo, "Playing games by the rules: Television regulation and China's entry into the WTO," paper presented at the Conference on Transnational Media Corporations and National Media Systems: China after Entry into the World Trade Organization. Bellagio, Italy, May, 2003.

27. Chan, "Trans-border broadcasters and TV regionalization."

28. Guoguang Wu, "One head, many mouths: Diversifying press structures in reform China," in *Money, Power, and Media: Communication Patterns and Bureaucratic Control in Cultural China*, ed. Chin-Chuan Lee (Chicago: Northwestern University Press, 2000), 45–67; Chin-Chuan Lee, "Chinese communication: Prisms, trajectories, and modes of understanding," in *Power, Money and Media, Communication Patterns and Bureaucratic Control in Cultural China*, ed. Chin-Chuan Lee (Chicago: Northwestern University Press, 2000),3–44.

29. Huailin Chen, "On the uneven development of Chinese newspaper market" (in Chinese), in *Chinese Media*, ed. Zhou He and Huailin Chen (Hong Kong: Pacific Century, 1998), 194–211; Huailin Chen and Yu Huang, "Uneven development of mass media commercialization in Mainland China: The case of the press" (in Chinese), *Journalism Studies* (1996): 192–208; Huailin Chen and Zhongshi Guo, "The advertising revenue gap between party newspapers and popular press" (in Chinese), *Mass Communication Research* (1998): 5–26; Chan and Qiu, "China: Media liberalization."

30. Chin-Chuan Lee, "Ambiguities and contradictions: Issues in China's changing political communication," in *China's Media, Media's China*, ed. Chin-Chuan Lee (Boulder, CO: Westview Press, 1994), 3–23.

31. Shanghai TV Festival Organizing Committee, *China TV Drama Report 2003–2004* (in Chinese) (Beijing : Huaxia Press, 2004).

32. Shanghai TV Festival Organizing Committee, *China TV Drama Report.*

33. Chan, "Trans-border broadcasters."

34. Chan, "Trans-border broadcasters."

35. Mark O'Neill, "South Korea considers mainland its Jewel in the Crown," *South China Morning Post*, October 17, 2005.

36. Jian Xun, "New Korean tide vs. anti-Korean tide: Establishing a nation through culture" (in Chinese), *Yazhou Zhoukan* (October 23, 2005): 28–31.

37. O'Neill, "South Korea considers mainland its Jewel in the Crown."

38. Chan, "Media commercialization in China."

39. Joseph Straubhaar, "(Re)asserting national television and national identity against the global, regional and local levels of world television," in *Search of Boundaries: Communication, Nation-states and Cultural identities*, ed. Joseph Chan and Bryce McIntyre (Westport, CT: Ablex Press, 2002), 181–206.

40. John Sinclair, Elizabeth Jacka, and Stuart Cunningham, "Peripheral vision," in *New Patterns in Global Television: Peripheral Vision*, ed. John Sinclair, Elizabeth Jacka, and Stuart Cunningham (Oxford: Oxford University Press, 1996), 1–32.

41. Herbert Schiller, *Mass Communication and the American Empire* (Boston, MA:

Beacon Press, 1969); Oliver Boyd-Barrett, "Media imperialism: Towards an international framework for the analysis of media systems," in *Mass Communication and Society*, ed. James Curran, Michael Gurevitch, and Janet Woollacott (London: Edward Arno, 1977), 116–35; and Annabelle Sreberny Mohammadi, Dwayne Winseck, Jim McKenna, and Oliver Boyd-Barrett, "Editor's introduction: Media in global context," in *Media in Global Context: A Reader*, ed. Annabelle Sreberny Mohammadi, Dwayne Winseck, Jim McKenna, and Oliver Boyd-Barrett (London: Arnold Press, 1997), iv–xxviii.

42. Sinclair, Jacka, and Cunningham, "Peripheral vision."

43. Qing Xia, "SINA's interview with Xia Qing" (in Chinese), July 28 2005, http://eladies.sina.com.cn/nx/2005/0726/1820176901.html (accessed 20 August 2007).

44. Zhengrong Hu, "*Super Girl*: Successfully localized reality show" (in Chinese), *North Media Research* 3 (2006).

45. Michael Curtin, *Playing to the World's Biggest Audience: The Globalization of Chinese Film and TV* (Berkeley: University of California Press, 2007).

ELEVEN

East Asian Pop Culture: Its Circulation, Consumption, and Politics

Chua Beng Huat

In this chapter, Chua Beng Huat offers a Singaporean perspective on transnational cultural flows in Asia. Located at the southern tip of the Malay Peninsula, Singapore is inhabited largely by citizens who claim Chinese ethnic heritage. Although economically prosperous, Singapore is a relatively small city-state of 4.5 million inhabitants, and its media industries are relatively diminutive, aiming much of their output at the domestic audience. Singaporeans therefore reach out to pop culture media from afar. They are big fans of Hollywood movies, but they are even more passionate about Chinese, Japanese, and Korean film, music, and television. Chua argues that this diverse media diet is increasingly common among audiences throughout East Asia and that transnational media circulations are fueling the growth of a shared regional popular culture with a distinctive constellation of stars, genres, and stylistic conventions.

The dense but uneven traffic of pop culture production, circulation, and consumption within East Asia constitutes a loosely integrated regional media market, the totality of which may be loosely designated, both discursively and substantively as an "East Asian pop culture." This chapter delineates its contours and the different processes of regional integration and raises the possibility of a "pan–East Asian" identity engendered by consumption of regional pop culture.[1] Given the unevenness of traffic, not all locations within East Asia are equally positioned to enable empirical observations of the functioning of this totality. Indeed, it is relatively invisible at a location such as Japan, which produces and exports cultural products and imports little from the rest of the region. Conversely, Singapore—without serious media industries of its own, except locally produced television programs—is essentially a location of consumption into which flow pop culture artifacts from around the world.[2] It is, for this reason, a methodologically advantageous place from which to observe empirically the development of transnational flows of East Asian pop culture.

With 75 percent of its population ethnic Chinese, Singapore has always been part of the circuit—including People's Republic of China (PRC), Hong Kong, and Taiwan—of Chinese-language pop culture (within which there are many Chinese languages). This is best exemplified by the history of Shaw Brothers, one of the largest media entertainment companies on the circuit. Set up as a film company in the 1920s in Shanghai, it moved to Singapore during the 1930s and 1940s and then to Hong Kong in 1958. In the 1960s and 1970s, with the PRC embroiled in the Cultural Revolution and Taiwan under repressive Kuomintang military rule, Shaw Brothers was the primary producer of Chinese movies for the global Chinese diasporas.[3] With its stable of actors and actresses, the company set up TVB in the mid-1970s, which rapidly became the dominant station in Hong Kong. Partly as a consequence of government regulations, the company gave up moviemaking in the mid-1980s, concentrating on the television business,[4] where it operates as one of the leading exporters of TV dramas to Chinese markets in Asia. Since the economic liberalization in the PRC and the lifting of martial law in Taiwan, the production, consumption, and flows of pop culture between Hong Kong, Taiwan, PRC, and Singapore have escalated, making it possible for companies like Shaw Brothers to prosper in a sphere that might be loosely designated as "Pop Culture China."[5]

In Singapore, Japanese and South Korean pop culture products also flourish, especially films and television dramas. Japanese products were especially popular from the mid-1980s to the mid-1990s, when they were significantly displaced by Korean pop culture. Since the late 1990s, Korean pop culture has been so influential in the East and Southeast Asian regional markets that it was dubbed the "Korean wave."[6] The popularity of both Japanese and Korean pop cultures in East Asia is mediated through the ethnic-Chinese circuit, as products are dubbed and subtitled into Chinese languages to access the huge regional ethnic Chinese consumer market, including Singapore. Again, these trends make Singapore an especially good vantage point from which to assess regional circulations of pop culture.

Pop Culture Products and Primary Sites of Production

Pop Music

Pop music cannot be dubbed. It can at best be replicated by completely substituting the lyrics with another language, a process commonly undertaken, for example, by Chinese singers with Western pop songs. To Chinese listeners, Japanese and Korean lyrics are nothing short of a string of nonsense sounds with which it is difficult to sing along without the requisite language competence. Consequently, distribution and consumption of Japanese and Korean pop music among ethnic Chinese consumers are far lower than respective films and TV programs, although there are pockets of avid fans of J-pop and K-pop in all locations. Attempts by Korean and Japanese pop musicians to deepen their popularity and increase their market shares in Pop Culture China would require them to sing in English, in a duet with a Chinese singer, or more radically, in Mandarin and to develop complex dance routines in live performances.

Despite the language obstacle, the market for Japanese music in East Asia is economically significant. Otmazgin reports that Japanese music exports to the rest of Asia increased threefold from 1988 to 2002, from 5.5 billion yen to 14.6 billion yen.[7] Of this, Hong Kong, Taiwan, Singapore, and PRC—in descending order of consumption—account for 69 percent and South Korea for 14 percent of Japanese exports, evidence of an East Asian pop culture circuit. Hong Kong accounted for up to 37 percent of the total value of Japanese music Asian exports, which was only 8 percent of total record sales on the island in 2002. In Singapore, Japanese pop music represented only 3 percent of the total music sales for the same period.[8] Obviously, in Pop Culture China, Chinese pop music still dominates.

In the Chinese-language pop music industry, the center of production has shifted from Hong Kong, where Cantonese pop (Canto-pop) prevailed in the 1980s, to Taiwan, where Mandarin pop music is produced with special emphasis on exports to the PRC market. During the 1990s, even the very big Canto-pop stars started switching to Mandarin. For example, Beijing native Faye Wong, who had to sing in Cantonese early in her Hong Kong career, reverted to Mandarin with great success. The emergence of Taiwan as the center of the Mandarin-language music industry has resulted in the prominence of Taiwanese singers such as Jay Chow. Also, Singaporeans who aspire to make it in the Mandarin pop music world sign a contract with a Taiwanese record company, launch a debut album in Taipei, and if they succeed, move their base of operations there and make occasional home visits to Singapore. This route was blazed by one of the most popular Singapore singers of the early 2000s, Stephanie Sun, who won the Best Mandarin Female Vocalist at Taiwan's 2005 Golden Melody Awards. Such a strategy is obviously a reflection of Singapore's small consumer base.

Significantly, the PRC remains largely a consumer of imported Taiwanese and Hong Kong pop music for several reasons. First, the commercial pop music market is in its infancy, lacking companies with the financial means to invest in PRC singers in a highly speculative business. Furthermore, the piracy industry sells increasingly high-quality products at a fraction of the cost of the original, which further discourages such investments. Second, the few PRC rock musicians known to international aficionados during the late 1980s and early 1990s were largely "cultural" heroes known more for their highly ideological lyrics than for their commercial viability. The foremost example in the immediate post-Tiananmen period was Cui Jian, for whom "Rock is an ideology, not a set of musical forms."[9] His lyrics were so deeply laden with local politics and its discontents that they are difficult for pop music consumers outside the PRC to understand;[10] consequently, Cui and other musicians like him have been displaced into at best the "alternative" music category. However, change is afoot in the mainland music scene. The Internet has become a site for penning, performing, and broadcasting one's own music. Some of these efforts have managed to break out of the Internet into commercial popularity; an example is the highly successful 2004 hit *Lao Su Ai Ta Mi* (Mice Like Large Grain Rice), which was recorded by several singers and entered the world of Mandarin *musiak*. With the marketization of the economy and the expansion of consumerism and entertainment industries, PRC singers may come into their own in the near future.

Films

East Asian films now circulate globally in commercial releases, having broken out of their confinement to art house and film festival circuits. However, regional circulation and exhibition of East Asian films is not new. Hong Kong, of course, had been and continues to be a powerhouse of Cantonese- and

Mandarin-language films that are exhibited throughout Pop Culture China.[11] Film production declined after its peak in the 1980s. By early 2000, there were no major production studios; many films are produced by independent filmmakers on low budgets, and the production rate has dropped to half of that of its heyday. Nevertheless, "Hong Kong cinema [remains] a benchmark of achievement, a site of inspiration and cross-cultural borrowing, a model for emulation and a target of rivalry."[12]

Throughout the 1960s Japanese action movies, including the *Blind Swordsman* (*Zatoichi*) series, were highly popular in East Asia. The techniques of their directors were very influential in subsequent Hong Kong Chinese-action (*wuxia*) movies,[13] the genre that is most recognizably culturally Chinese in the world of cinema. The genre evolved in the 1990s, in the hands of practitioners like Stephen Chow and Jackie Chan, into comedies of contemporary urban daily life, in Hong Kong and Hollywood productions, respectively.[14] For the global audience, a spectacular high point for the genre is Taiwanese director Ang Lee's *Crouching Tiger, Hidden Dragon* (2000): "*Crouching Tiger, Hidden Dragon* globalizes the circulation of conventional signs of *wuxia*, rendering them 'international Chinese elements' that appeal to Western eyes. Making Chinese aesthetics, culture, calligraphy and choreography accessible to the global market is the main strategy adopted by Lee. There are practically no untranslatable local data of any sort in the film; the director has made sure that the spectacular action fights are rendered both aesthetically and culturally approachable. The whole point is to popularise a new transnational genre."[15]

The same film, however, had lackluster box-office takings among Chinese audiences, especially in PRC and Hong Kong,[16] who most likely did not take well to the film's explicit subversion of the conventions of the *wuxia* genre. Stoic masculinity common to most *wuxia* heroes was undermined by a "dispirited" Li Mubai (played by Hong Kong actor Chow Yun-Fat) from the very opening scene, in which Master Li made a gift of his sword to a friend-official. To give up one's weapon is tantamount to leaving the *wuxia* world; it is tantamount to death itself. After that, throughout the film, his life was completely dominated by the three female characters—his undeclared love, his enemy, and the young woman who taunts/haunts him—giving the film its overall "feminist" reading, perhaps more in tune with the sentiments of its global audiences.[17]

Nothing breeds imitation like success. Ang's film was followed by efforts from other internationally known Chinese directors: Zhang Yimou's *Hero*

(2000) and *House of the Flying Daggers* (2004), Chen Kaige's *The Promise* (2005), and Feng Xiaogang's *The Banquet* (2006), all hoping to repeat the same global box-office success and recognition in Hollywood's Academy Awards, but none succeeded by either measure.

Prior to so blatantly seeking Hollywood recognition, Zhang and Chen, both members of the so-called Fifth Generation of film directors, had received critical acclaim for domestic PRC-made films. International reception and reading of these directors' early films were often through very particular ideological lenses: First, as the PRC is the origin of "Chinese" traditions, the films were read as critical commentaries on Chinese feudal–rural traditions; second, given the authoritarianism of both the traditional and communist regimes, the films were also read as commentaries on the continuities of authoritarianism, both traditional and communist.[18] Today, however, their films are less concerned with such issues and more strategically aimed at commercial success in transnational markets, both global markets and those in East Asia.

Since the mid-1990s, Korean films have been the latest entries into the global cinema market from East Asia.[19] This is partly a consequence of the Korean government's decision to make pop culture an export industry, after discovering that the successful Hollywood film *Jurassic Park* "generated, with all its spin-off sales, foreign sales worth 1.5 million Hyundai cars," more than two years of Hyundai's car exports.[20] Korean movies made their debut in East Asia, through the Hollywood-style blockbuster action movies *Shiri* (1999) and *Joint Security Area* (*JSA*) (2000). Both films translate the Cold War tension of the North–South Korean divide into personal relations. *JSA* dramatizes illicit friendship and camaraderie between North and South Korean soldiers who police the demilitarized zone. *Shiri* is a tragic romance action movie centered on the relationship between a female secret agent from the North and an unsuspecting male agent from the South. *Shiri* is credited as "heralding a move towards a more market-driven industry and the start of the Korean blockbuster era"[21] and "signalling when South Korean filmmakers finally learned how to compete on the world stage."[22] It was hugely popular with the Korean audience and in 1999 broke the domestic box-office record, a record subsequently overtaken by *JSA* in the following year.

Another genre of Korean films that was popular in its time was the "gangster-action-comedy," such as *My Wife Is a Gangster* (2001) and *Guns and Talks* (2001). In these comedies, "criminals" are humanized by their ineptness or goofiness in other aspects of daily life. These dark comedies played side-by-side with violent action movies, such as *Friend*, a putatively true-life story of three men growing up in Busan in the 1950s. Along with these commercial successes were smaller films that are better known to serious film viewers, such as *301/302*, being the numbers of two apartments in which two neighboring women "act out female symptoms of overeating and under-eating in cleanly modern spaces, haunted by traumas of childhood abuse and a claustrophobic marriage, evacuating the seeming prosperity and stylised success of a well-ordered life,"[23] and *Il Mare* (2000), a fantasy in which two lovers meet across a vast expanse of time, remade in Hollywood as *The Lakehouse* (2006).

Perhaps, as an inevitable consequence of the need or desire to gain ever larger audiences, a new phenomenon became observable by early 2000: films that are produced by a pan-Asian crew and cast. It began with pan-Chinese films, such as *Crouching Tiger, Hidden Dragon*, which has a Taiwanese-American director Ang Lee and lead actors from Hong Kong (Chow Yun Fat) and from PRC (Chang Chen), and lead actresses from PRC (Zhang Ziyi) and Malaysia (Michelle Yeo). This was quickly followed by Zhang Yimou's *Hero*, with Jet Li, Tony Leung Chiu Wai, and Maggie Cheung from Hong Kong, and Zhang Ziyi and Chen Daoming from the PRC. Upping the scale from pan-Chinese to pan-East Asian cast is PRC director Chen Kaige's *The Promise*, which features Japanese actor Hiroyuki Sanada and Korean actor Jang Dong-Kun in leading roles, alongside Nicholas Tze and Cecilia Cheung from Hong Kong. Finally, stretching across the continent to South Asia is Jackie Chan's *The Myth* (2005), with a female lead from Korea, Kim Hee-Seon, and in a supporting role, the Bollywood Indian actress, Mallika Sherawat. From outside the Chinese pop culture sphere, the Korean movie *Musa* (2002) starred Zhang Ziyi in the lead female role.

In these "pan" efforts, the intertwined histories of East Asian nations, of bitter memories of war and colonization, must be suppressed. Thus, in spite of often being period costume dramas, these films are set in historically ambiguous periods or as mythic stories, if not fairy tales, such as *The Myth* and *The Promise*. Yet, even with such devices, the casting of Korean actor Jang Dong-Kun as the slave to Japanese actor Hiroyuki Sanada could provide the space for reading it as a metaphor of the history of colonization of Korea by Japan. Haunted by history, the Hollywood-made *Memoirs of a Geisha* (2005), featuring three ethnic Chinese actresses—Michelle Yeoh, Zhang Ziyi, and Gong Li as geishas—was banned in the PRC because it might cause offense and public disturbance, especially as it was released during the low ebb of Japanese-PRC international relations under Japanese Prime Minister Koizumi's term.

Pan-Chinese and pan-Asian films obviously hope that the stars from different nations will attract the respective national audiences. Stephen Teo further suggests that Hong Kong producers and directors believe such "pan" efforts are financially necessary to survive because the much-anticipated massive consumption capacity of the PRC for Hong Kong films has hitherto not materialized.[24] To date, these expensive productions have not been phenomenal box-office successes; however, such pan-Asian efforts are likely to continue their search for a successful formula.

At mid-2000, the East Asian cinema scene was one of much reduced Hong Kong production, an increasing presence of Korean films, and a few bankable PRC directors financed with foreign investments, all seeking global audiences through a mixture of elements, notably ahistorical narratives of genre-bending *wuxia*, pan-Asian casts, familiar mythologies, romance, and strands of Orientalist tradition. Unlike pop music, whose transnational popularity is constrained by the nontranslatability of the lyric into a different language, East Asian films were aided by the possibility of either dubbing or subtitling or both. However, given the limited screening time, the ability of any film to generate sustained interest and exercise multiple effects—social, cultural, and political—on its audience is quite limited, compared to television drama series.

Serial Television Dramas

As with films, Hong Kong television drama series have been a staple and integral part of Pop Culture China since, at least, the late 1970s.[25] For example, Chow Yun Fat was introduced to the Singapore audience through the extremely popular drama series *Man in the Net* (1980).[26] Meanwhile, Singaporeans were also entertained by Taiwan-produced costume dramas with themes of "traditional" family politics dictated by the Confucian principle of filial piety, often based on the popular romance novels by writer Ziong Yao.

The PRC is, of course, a very latecomer in commercial television drama production. According to Sheldon Lu, "Such top-rated and widely watched dramas as *Yearnings* (fifty episodes, 1990) and *Beijingers in New York* (twenty-one episodes, 1993) marked the maturity of soap opera as a full-blown Chinese genre,"[27] heavily inscribed with local ideology. *Yearnings* told the story of the ups and downs of two Beijing families, one a working family, the other a family of intellectuals, during the Cultural Revolution and the Reform years of the 1980s. One of the scriptwriters was rather forthright and sarcastic about the formula: "We tortured all these characters, making everyone suffer. We made sure all the good guys had a heart of gold, but we made them as unlucky as possible; and the bad guys are as bad as you can imagine—that's the sure way to a good drama."[28]

In spite of the scriptwriter's cynicism, the drama resonated with public sentiment; according to Lu, "it momentarily soothed the viewers, and allowed them to submerge themselves in a drama of love, separation, perseverance, and faithfulness, a personal drama they had all more or less lived through during the years of the Cultural Revolution and the Reform."[29] The state too was pleased. Li Ruihuan, at that time boss of ideology and propaganda, reportedly said after watching the show: "It tells us that an artistic work must entertain first, or it is useless to talk about educating people with it. The influence we exert must be subtle, imperceptible, and the people should be influenced without being conscious of it. In order to make socialist principles and moral virtues acceptable to the broad masses, we must learn to use the forms that the masses favour."[30]

As for *Beijingers*, it is part of what Wanning Sun calls a "Chinese in the New World" genre: "The success or failure of these 'Chinese in the New World' can be read as a symbol of what China needs to do, can do, and will do in the new global economic order. What Wang Qiming [lead male character in *Beijingers*] and other business 'heroes' have lost in transition can be seen as the price China has to pay in order to become a global power. Seen in this light, the link between the production of these Chinese stories of global capitalism and China's eventual entry into the World Trade Organization is not as tenuous as it may appear."[31]

Similar to PRC rock music, such ideologically inscribed dramas are difficult to market outside the country.[32] However, by early 2000, urban dramas of romance among young professionals in big cities, such as Shanghai, are being produced and a few have made it to Singapore in the weekend afternoon slot—for example, *Bourgeois Mansion*. The visual quality has yet to live up to the viewing demands of the regional audience, which is accustomed to much higher production values.

Undoubtedly, the television dramas that are truly popular across East Asia have been the Japanese trendy dramas in the 1990s and Korean dramas since the beginning of 2000. With Japan's ability to finance expensive productions, its television dramas have set the standard for others to follow:

"The Japanese concern with the visual, in combination with their advanced technology, ensures that Japanese television is often very pleasing to the eye. Sets are technically well designed and the photography is excellent. If television is used as a means of relaxation and escape, as opposed to education and enlightenment, it may be very enjoyable to lose oneself among the images without having to bother with the search for ideas."[33]

These are called "trendy dramas" for obvious reasons: The story line is generally about love gained and love lost among urban young professionals, with plenty of agonizing twists and turns.[34] The visual pleasure comes from the fact that the characters, major and minor, are very well-dressed in designer clothes, live in cozy apartments, eat in expensive—usually Western—restaurants in the high-end entertainment district of the city and, above all, the actors and actresses are beautiful men and women. During the euphoric days of the Japanese bubble economy, such series were able to command huge production budgets with up to 50 percent going to pay the beautiful cast.[35] Initially, no thought was given to exporting the dramas. Their subsequent popularity in East Asia was therefore a surprise to the Japanese producers and came as surplus profit when it happened.[36]

These dramas penetrated regional markets through different channels. In Hong Kong, according to Koichi Iwabuchi, promotional efforts of local partners were far more important than those of the Japanese producers. As more than 90 percent of the local audience members were already captured by the two free-to-air television stations, TVB and ATV, Japanese dramas became a significant promotional device for STAR TV, a new cable television provider. Similar arrangements with cable TV stations in Taiwan were established. Such arrangements gave "Japanese TV industries more confidence in the exportability of Japanese TV programs and incentives for forging business tie-ups with Taiwanese [and Hong Kong] media industries."[37] In the PRC, the dramas are most commonly distributed by pirated video compact discs (VCDs) and DVDs. Another important and growing means of circulation is through computer-mediated communication technologies. One fan will often download the episode from a television broadcast, while another will subtitle the dialogue and then upload it for access by other members of the fan community.[38]

In Korea, the importation of all Japanese cultural products was banned for decades as a protest against Japanese colonization. However, the ban did not make Korea impermeable to Japanese pop culture; even the government-owned Korean Broadcasting Station was guilty of illegal importation.[39] With a constant stream of underground importation, Japanese pop culture was "copied," "partially integrated," "plagiarized," and "reproduced" into Korean products.[40] The ban was lifted in October 1998 with the Joint Declaration of a New 21st-Century Korea–Japan Partnership. Subsequently, the volume of Japanese pop culture flows has increased rapidly.

After almost a decade of production and popularity, Japanese trendy dramas lost their vitality. At about the same time, television screens in Hong Kong, Taiwan, and Singapore began to be filled with imported Korean TV dramas. As mentioned earlier, the Korean government began to encourage pop culture exports in mid-1995. Partly as a consequence of the 1997 Asian regional financial crisis, Korean multinational enterprises, the *chaebols*, largely pulled out of the media industry, leaving behind a large group of trained media professionals who subsequently become the backbone of the Korean pop culture industry. The growing tide of Korean pop culture exports quickly came to be dubbed by the PRC media writers as the "Korean wave" or *Hanliu, Hallyu* in Korean.

Similar to Japanese trendy dramas, importation of Korean TV dramas was an industrial strategy for new and smaller television channels to establish their respective audience bases. For example, in 1999, Singapore Press Holdings (SPH), Singapore's monopoly newspaper publisher, ventured into commercial television with two free-to-air stations, one in English (Channel I) and the other in Mandarin (Channel U).[41] The English-language channel failed and shut down its studio within less than two years of its establishment. In contrast, the Mandarin channel was able to carve out a significant audience base through a combination of Korean dramas and local variety shows that look and feel like variety shows in Taiwan, which in turn are very similar to those in Japan. The general formula in these variety shows seems to be high-energy, rapid-fire banter from a team of program hosts whose entire focus is on making fun of, or embarrassing, whoever appears as a guest on the show. The popularity of the Korean dramas in Singapore pushed the established, government-owned, and dominant channel to import them as well. This led to a constant bidding war between the two stations for the dramas such that by the late 2003, there was at least one Korean TV drama on Singapore television every night.

One of the most remarkable dramas, *Jewel in the Palace*, traveled through the entire Pop Culture China circuit. It was first exported to Taiwan in 2004, where it was dubbed into Mandarin. Then it was dubbed into Cantonese and screened on TVB in Hong Kong to record-breaking ratings. As a rule, the

The heroine of *Jewel in the Palace*, Dae Jang Geum, was mentored in culinary and herbal arts, ultimately rising to become head of the emperor's kitchen.

most popular Korean dramas with overseas audiences have been contemporary, urban, romance, or family dramas; historical costume dramas are not exported because regional audiences do not have the requisite knowledge of Korean history to sustain their interest.[42] In the case of *Jewel*, the cultural affinity between the Choson Dynasty period and Chinese history was merely a foil for a tale of court intrigue with a minor romance theme. In addition, the Hong Kong television station made efforts to "indigenize" the Korean drama by providing brief explanations of the narrative before each episode and giving the Chinese-language equivalent of the ingredients in culinary dishes and medical prescriptions that played a central role in the narrative. The Taiwan dubbed and subtitled version was re-exported to Hunan Satellite Television in the PRC and broadcast nationally.[43] Finally, it was also repeatedly broadcast in Singapore on both cable and free-to air-television, completing the Pop Culture China circuit.

By mid-2005, Korean pop culture, Japanese pop culture, and the long-standing Chinese-language pop culture have all become part of the routine pop cultural entertainment diet of East Asians. The unequal flow of products remains. Japan continues to be largely an exporter to the rest of the region, the huge success of Korean TV drama *Winter Sonata* in Japan notwithstanding.[44] Chinese-language materials remain more widely consumed than Korean and Japanese imports within Pop Culture China, with occasional spikes of a very popular singer, film, or drama series.

Transnational Consumption, Audience, and Community

Different pop culture genres impose different demands on an audience member's time. Music requires no more than a few minutes in the case of a song. Film demands usually no more than a couple of hours. In contrast, television drama demands sustained viewing at regular intervals, usually one episode every week; other activities need to be sacrificed or displaced to catch the weekly episode; efforts have to be made to video-record an episode if missing it cannot be helped; and time has to be found to watch it before the next installment is screened. Such sustained and active participation draws the audience into an intimate virtual relationship with the onscreen characters in a drama. Audience interest is further sustained by routine write-ups in local newspapers and entertainment magazines, and by conversations with friends who are always ready to dissect the latest episode and speculate about upcoming developments.[45]

One central question about reception of East Asian television dramas is why audience members identify with the narratives and characters of imported dramas. Previously it has been suggested "cultural proximity"[46] makes imported programs more acceptable. Yet foreignness is often integral to the pleasures afforded by the text and it makes distancing oneself from what is on screen relatively easy. Thus, it could be argued that cultural distance prevails rather than proximity. Empirical studies of audience reception within East Asia bear this out.

Iwabuchi found that Japanese audiences have a tendency to appreciate media products from Hong Kong and other parts of Asia with a sense of nostalgia evoked by their own feelings of having lost the vitality that characterized Japan before the bubble economy of the 1990s. He quotes a report from a weekly magazine: "As we [Japanese] walked around Hong Kong and Bangkok, we found the energy of the people to be overwhelming. It was the same kind of raw vigour that Japan had once during the high economic growth era."[47] Conversely, young Taiwanese fans of Japanese TV dramas express a desire for Japan's capitalist consumerist modernity as their "future." According to Ko, "Japanese idol dramas provide a *real imaginary*, and the imagery is manifested beautifully into a spectacle of modernity. Therefore, metropolitan Tokyo is re-presented as the locus where the individuals pursue freedom, love, and careers; the imagery of 'Tokyo' is a *visual place* that mediates between reality and dreams. These dreams have not yet been realized in Taiwan, but are already present on screen . . . not in Tokyo in Japan, but the 'Tokyo' on screen."[48]

Another persistent question is whether consumption of East Asian pop culture leads to an emergent pan–East Asian identity. The process of individual identity formation is one of unending cultural knowledge acquisition, layering, and interacting. In the constellation of inputs, leisure activities such as pop culture consumption are largely residual and voluntary, enjoyed only after the necessary routines of everyday life are done. No social institutions enforce compliance and provide payoffs to consumption. In addition, consumer or fan affection for a star, a musician, or a particular drama is, with few exceptions, ephemeral, changing rapidly with the latest trends and icons, in both objects and artists, reflected in the short shelf life of pop culture products. All these features seem to suggest low impact on individual identity formation. Nevertheless, ex-consumers and ex-fans can readily recall fond nostalgia for a time when such consumption was an important part of their daily lives. The pop culture of those days has been etched into their memories and has in some ways changed their personalities and their lives.

An artiste or a drama is popular because of large numbers of consumers. The question is, through what processes can this statistical presence constitute itself or be constituted into a "community," however ephemeral? The most conventional mechanism is the fan club, which organizes consumers who share affections for a particular performance artiste or a particular pop culture program into a community. Indeed, fan clubs are often established by artistes or production companies themselves, as means of sustaining consumer affections to extend the longevity of what would essentially be an ephemeral phenomenon. Such fan clubs can, of course, be pan–East Asian organizations, especially via the Internet. Indeed, even without formal organizing efforts, the Internet has become an instrument for pan–East Asian connections among avid fans. For example, savvy consumers are constantly doing the painstaking work of downloading, translating, and subtitling their favorite dramas and then uploading them for the benefit of other members of the cyber fan community. They do this beyond the reach of profit-oriented market players and the legal constraints of the nation-state.[49]

However, avid fandom participation requires greater passion than that of a merely residual leisure activity that fills out the day for the larger population of consumers. It is therefore necessary to conceptualize the idea of a "community of consumers" beyond the limited numbers of avid fans. The potential members of this larger community of consumers are as widely dispersed geographically as the distribution radius of the pop culture products; it is therefore necessarily a transnational and transcultural potential community. Membership is simply by the act of consumption itself; individual consumers need not be aware of or consciously seek out other consumers.

Relative to the almost hyperactive avid fans, most pop culture consumers are passive consumers but not without the possibility of realizing they are part of a community of consumers. The popularity of a pop culture item—singer, actor, or drama—is in part produced by the attention and coverage that it receives from constituent members of the media-culture industry, such as newspapers and magazines. Take the entertainment page of any newspaper in East Asia as an illustration. The page can be conceptualized as a community space for the entire East Asian pop culture. Geographically, the boundary is defined by the places that appear regularly in the page; namely, the production and consumption centers of Seoul, Tokyo, Shanghai, Beijing, Hong Kong, Taipei, and Singapore. The space is "peopled" daily with images and information of East Asian artistes. The likes of Bae Yung Joon in Seoul, Faye Wong in Shanghai, Wong Kai Wei in Hong Kong, and Jay Chou in Taipei inhabit these pages at unpredictable intervals, more frequently in the rising phases of their careers and with diminishing presence when they are on the way out.

These pages are read by an unknown number of readers, unknown to each other. A community is instantly manifested should two or more readers happen to be present at an occasion, during which they participate as part of free-flowing conversation in exchanges concerning one of the artistes or events reported in the pages. Such instances demonstrate the community of consumers of East Asian pop culture as an occasioned and occasional community. These practices are characteristic of the overwhelming majority of consumers, where consumption is leisure and entertainment, rather than as a primary focus of everyday life.[50]

Whether through intense involvement or leisurely consumption, different communities of East Asian pop culture consumers exist. However, membership via consumption will always be voluntary and ever changing; as one fan grows out of it, a new one joins in quick succession, following the rise and fall of a constellation of idols or a string of dramas, creating changing and unstable communities. Consequently, while such communities of consumers can be and are constituted transnationally, they are too marginal to be able to have significant influences in the wider society. For example, overseas fans of Korean drama actor Song Seung-Heon held a letter-writing campaign appealing to the Korean government in 2004 to delay his military conscription so that he could complete the filming of a drama series. Although it energized the fans, it had no effect on the government whatsoever.[51]

Conclusion

In the past two decades, there have been very impressive developments in pop culture production, circulation, and consumption in East Asia. With the possible exception of Japan, which has a domestic market large and wealthy enough to sustain its own pop culture industry, most culture products are now produced for regional consumption. In Singapore, Channel U, a free-to-air television station, now carries the tag line "Leading Asian Pop Culture," featuring programs from all points of East Asia. The totality of an East Asian pop culture now stands in juxtaposition with the globalized American pop culture in every medium. This challenges easy and loose talk of American domination and cultural hegemony in the pop culture entertainment world.

Since early 2000, the Korean pop cultural industry has appeared to be most aggressively seeking East Asian markets. Its TV dramas continue to be exported to the region, its pop musicians seek to make inroads into the Pop Culture China market by partnering with Chinese singers, and its films are receiving increasing attention globally. After a decade of unmistakable popularity, Japanese media appear to lack interest in hogging headlines, although their drama series and singers continue to play on East Asian small screens and airwaves. The Japanese case perhaps foreshadows the trajectory of the so-called Korean wave, which is showing signs of becoming a quiet but persistent flow into the rest of East Asia. Meanwhile, within Pop Culture China, Chinese-language pop culture products continue to be dominant.

Finally, admittedly, each performing artist or each TV drama is too ephemeral to contribute much to identity formation. However, each in-

stance of identification with the artists in person or character onscreen may
contribute to cumulative effects on the long process of a pan–East Asian
collective identity formation, building on the different levels of community
among consumers. Thus, with the consolidation of an East Asian pop culture, an opportunity for the forging of an East Asian identity that is based
on the recognition of cultural differences among East Asians may yet be a
long-term possibility.

Notes

1. This attempt to constitute East Asian pop culture is an ongoing effort of a loose
collective of cultural studies scholars in East Asia; earlier publications include Chua
Beng Huat, "Conceptualizing an East Asian popular culture," *Inter-Asia Cultural
Studies* 5 (2004): 200–21; Koichi Iwabuchi, *Feeling Asian Modernities: Transnational
Consumption of Japanese TV Dramas* (Hong Kong: Hong Kong University Press,
2004); Chua Beng Huat and Koichi Iwabuchi, eds., *East Asian Pop Culture: Analysing
the Korean Wave* (Hong Kong: Hong Kong University Press, 2008).

2. Pop culture is also imported from India, especially Bollywood movies; from the
neighboring Malay-speaking nations of Malaysia and Indonesia, particularly television drama series and musical variety shows; and, of course, the United States.

3. For a detailed study of the different phases and activities of Shaw Brothers, see
Liao Kin-feng, Cheuk Pak-tong, Fu Poshek, and Yung Sai Shing, eds., *Shaw: The
Empire of Chinese Cinema* (Taipei: Rye Field, 2003, in Chinese).

4. Michael Curtin, "Hong Kong meets Hollywood in the extranational arena of the
culture industries," in *Sites of Contestation: Localism, Globalism and Cultural Production
in Asia and the Pacific*, ed. Kwok Kan Tam and Wimal Dissanayake (Hong Kong: Chinese
University of Hong Kong Press, 2002), 92.

5. Chua Beng Huat, "Pop Culture China," *Singapore Journal of Tropical Geography*
22 (2001): 113–21. It needs to be stressed that the four locations have their respective
understandings of the idea of "Chinese-ness." Indeed, analysts of "Chinese" films
often refer to PRC, Hong Kong, and Taiwan as transnational rather than national;
see Sheldon H. Lu, *China, Transnational Visuality, Global Postmodernity* (Stanford, CA:
Stanford University Press, 2001). For a discussion on the difficulties in applying
the term *national* to Chinese cinemas, see Yingjin Zhang, *Chinese National Cinema*
(London: Routledge, 2004).

6. Pop is used to designate a commercial, media-generated segment of "popular"
culture, the political arena that encompasses the everyday-life cultural practices of
the masses in contradistinction to the elite culture of a society; Stuart Hall, "Notes
on deconstructing 'the popular,'" in *Cultural Theory and Popular Culture: A Reader*, ed.
John Storey (New York: Harvester Wheatsheaf, 1994), 455–66. Specifically referring
to cinemas, Meaghan Morris suggests, "A popular 'cultural' genre is one in which
people take up aesthetic materials from the media and elaborate them in other aspects of their lives, whether in dreams and fantasies, in ethical formulations of values

and ideals, or in social and sometimes political activities," in Introduction, in *Hong Kong Connections: Transnational Imagination in Action Cinema*, ed. Meaghan Morris, Siu Leung Li, and Stephen Chan Ching-kiu (Hong Kong: Hong Kong University Press, 2005), 1–18.

7. Nissim Kadosh Otmazgin, "When culture meets the market: Japanese popular culture industries and the regionalization of East and Southeast Asia," in *The Rise of Middle Classes in Southeast Asia*, ed. Shiraishi Takashi and Pasuk Phongpaichit (Kyoto: Kyoto University Press, 2008), 262.

8. Otmazgin, "When culture meets the market," 264–65.

9. Quoted in Andrew F. Jones, *Like a Knife: Ideology and Genre in Contemporary Chinese Popular Music* (Ithaca, NY: Cornell University Press, 1992), 115.

10. Jeroen De Kloet, "'Let him fucking see the green smoke beneath my groin': The mythology of Chinese rock," in *Postmodernism and China*, ed. Arif Dirlik and Xudong Zhang (Durham, NC: Duke University Press, 2000), 239–74.

11. The circulation and exhibition of Hong Kong films in Pop Culture China make the films "transnational" in their reception. I will not take up the complex issue of the "non-national/transnational" character of Hong Kong films; see Esther M. K. Cheung and Chu Yiu-wai, eds., *Between Home and World: A Reader in Hong Kong Cinema* (Hong Kong: Oxford University Press, 2004), xii–xxxv.

12. Morris, Li, and Chan, *Hong Kong Connections*, 2.

13. Kinnia Shun-Tin Yau, "Interactions between Japanese and Hong Kong action cinemas," in *Hong Kong Connections*, ed. Morris, Li, and Chan, 39–44.

14. Stephen Ching-kiu Chan, "The fighting condition in Hong Kong cinema: Local icons and cultural antidotes for the global popular," in *Hong Kong Connections*, ed. Morris, Li, and Chan, 63–80.

15. Chan, "The fighting condition," 76–77.

16. Stephen Teo, "*Wuxia* redux: *Crouching Tiger, Hidden Dragon* as a model of late transnational production," in *Hong Kong Connections*, ed. Morris, Li, and Chan, 200.

17. For an attempt to show how Lee has adjusted the genre to an international audience who could not presume to have any knowledge about the "Chineseness" of the *wuxia* genre, see Teo, "Wuxia redux," 200–203.

18. Chen Xiaoming, "The mysterious other: Postpolitics in Chinese films," in *Postmodernism and China*, ed. Arif Dirlik and Xudong Zhang (Durham, NC: Duke University Press, 2000), 222–38.

19. Shin Chi-Yun and Julian Stringer, eds., *New Korean Cinema* (Edinburgh: Edinburgh University Press, 2005).

20. Doboo Shim, "South Korean media industry in the 1990s and the economic crisis," *Prometheus* 20 (2000): 337–50.

21. Anthony C. Y. Leong, *Korean Cinema: The New Hong Kong* (Victoria, BC: Trafford, 2002), 24.

22. Leong, *Korean Cinema*, 26.

23. Rob Wilson, "Spectral critiques: Tracking 'uncanny' filmic paths towards a bio-poetics of trans-Pacific globalization," in *Hong Kong Connections*, ed. Morris, Li, and Chan, 255.

238 / CHUA BENG HUAT

24. Stephen Teo, ARI seminar on National Cinemas and Pan-Asian Productions, 14 February 2006, Asia Research Institute, National University of Singapore.

25. For details on the Hong Kong television industry's global activities, see Curtin, "Hong Kong meets Hollywood in the extranational arena of the cultural industries," 79–109.

26. Eric Ma provides an insightful analysis of how Hong Kong television drama participates in the shifting formation of Hong Kong identity through its anxious portraiture of PRC migrants into the colony in the early 1980s; Eric Ma Kit-wai, *Culture, Politics and Television in Hong Kong* (London: Routledge, 1999).

27. Lu, *China, Transnational Visuality, Global Postmodernity*, 215.

28. Lu, *China, Transnational Visuality, Global Postmodernity*, 205.

29. Lu, *China, Transnational Visuality, Global Postmodernity*, 207.

30. Lu, *China, Transnational Visuality, Global Postmodernity*, 208.

31. Wanning Sun, "Arriving at the city: Television dramas and spatial imagination," in *Leaving China: Media, Migration and Transnational Imagination* (Lanham, MD: Rowman and Littlefield, 2002), 85.

32. The other two categories of television drama from the PRC are the serialization of dynastic histories and the serialization of Chinese classics, such as *The Three Kingdom* and *Shui Hu Chuan* (水浒传, translated into All Men Are Brothers or Water Margin), which—in addition to excessive number of episodes—are also too demanding on audiences' knowledge of history and literature.

33. Bruce Stronach, "Japanese television," in *Handbook of Japanese Popular Culture*, ed. Richard G. Powers and Hidetoshi Kato (New York: Greenwood Press, 1989), 155.

34. Ota Toru, a television program producer with Fuji TV, recalls that he first began producing trendy dramas during the so-called bubble economy of the 1980s, self-consciously targeting female viewers in their twenties. His aim was to eschew serious themes for shows that emphasized fashion, setting, cast, and music. Ota Toru, "Producing (post)trendy Japanese TV drama," in *Feeling Asian Modernities: Transnational Consumption of Japanese TV Dramas*, ed. Koichi Iwabuchi (Hong Kong: Hong Kong University Press, 2004), 71–86.

35. According to Ota, it can cost up to 40 million yen per hour episode; Ota Toru, "Producing (post)trendy Japanese TV drama," 74.

36. According to some observers, the Japanese TV industry continues to be rather reluctant in negotiating and releasing rights to TV stations in the region, in part because of concerns with intellectual property rights and piracy; see Kelly Hu, "The power of circulation: Digital technologies and the online Chinese fans of Japanese TV drama," *Inter-Asia Cultural Studies* 6 (2005): 171–86.

37. Iwabuchi, *Feeling Asian Modernities*, 7.

38. Hu, "The power of circulation."

39. Seung-Mi Han, "Consuming the modern: Globalization, things Japanese, and the politics of cultural identity in Korea," *Journal of Pacific Asia* 6 (2000): 7–26.

40. Kim Hyun-Mee, "The inflow of Japanese culture and the historical construction of 'fandom' in South Korea." Paper presented at the International Conference

in the Age of Informatization: East Asia into the 21st century, Institute of East and West Studies, Yonsei University, Seoul, Korea, 16 November, 2002.

41. "U" sounds similar to the Chinese word "尤," for excellent.

42. In contrast, Chinese historical dramas do circulate quite well within Pop Culture China.

43. Lisa Leung "Mediating nationalism and modernity: The transnationalization of Korean dramas on Chinese (satellite) television," in *East Asian Pop Culture: Analysing the Korean Wave*, ed. Chua and Iwabuchi, 53–70.

44. Yoshitaka Mori, "Winter sonata and cultural practices of active fans in Japan," in *East Asian Pop Culture: Analysing the Korean Wave*, ed. Chua and Iwabuchi, 127–42.

45. Whereas there is an expanding literature on Asian films, these scholarly works tend to focus on the "national" characters of films, especially of the relations between the film text and the historical, political, and cultural contexts from which these films are made.

46. Koichi Iwabuchi, *Recentering Globalization: Popular Culture and Japanese Transnationalism* (Durham, NC: Duke University Press, 2002).

47. Iwabuchi, *Feeling Asian Modernities*, 155.

48. Yufen Ko, "The desired form: Japanese idol dramas in Taiwan," in *Feeling Asian Modernities*, ed. Koichi Iwabuchi, 123, original emphasis.

49. Hu, "The power of circulation," 177–78.

50. This account is an update by Chua Beng Huat, "Gossip about stars: Newspapers and Pop Culture China," in *Media and the Chinese Diaspora: Community, Communications and Commerce*, ed. Wanning Sun (London: Routledge, 2006), 75–90.

51. For discussion on the transnational politics of fandom in East Asian pop culture, see Eva Tsai, "Existing in the age of innocence: Pop stars, publics and politics in Asia," in *East Asian Pop Culture*, ed. Chua and Iwabuchi, 217–42; and Chua Beng Huat, "East Asian pop culture: Layers of communities," in *Media Consumption and Everyday Life in Asia*, ed. Youna Kim (London: Routledge, 2008), 99–113.

TWELVE

Enacting the Family-Nation on a Global Stage: An Analysis of CCTV's Spring Festival Gala

Zhongdang Pan

Chinese New Year, marking the return of spring, is an occasion for family reunions and celebrations. Although very much a tradition from the distant past, the Chinese Communist Party embraces the event as an opportunity to remind audiences that they are part of a great civilization with a long heritage. Each year, CCTV, the government-run national network, telecasts a Spring Festival variety show that portrays the Chinese people as one big happy family. In this chapter, Zhongdang Pan shows how the program tries to reconcile the many differences among Chinese, promoting images of unity, harmony, and the benevolent rule by the Communist Party. More recently, with China's emergence as one of the world's leading economic and political powers, CCTV has grown even more ambitious by telecasting its Spring Festival to a global audience, suggesting that the government in Beijing benevolently presides over a worldwide family of Chinese.

"Reflecting on the past year," said the hostess of the 2002 Spring Festival Gala, "every Chinese can proudly declare to the world: The scenery on our side is uniquely magnificent!" This opening exclamation condenses the cultural significance of the annual Chinese New Year's Eve extravaganza on state-run China Central Television (CCTV). For more than four hours each year, the gala showcases the Chinese family-nation—its unity and its achievements. It serves not only to renew the "family ties" among all Chinese but also to reassert China's place in the world of nations. Although this "live" variety show is in Chinese, it is now beamed to the world via satellites and high-speed Internet cables, making it a global media event by design and reach. It is also a cultural event with strong global features, blending together a variety of cultural forms, both indigenous and imported. By enacting an emotionally charged and myth-filled narrative of the Chinese family-nation, the gala in recent years has displayed an increasingly confident and assertive new China as a rising economic powerhouse in the world. Embedded in the gala's narrative is the claim that, in the global system, China has earned a rightful place as a power player and the agent representing her is the current party-state.

Since its debut in 1983, the gala has routinely attracted hundreds of millions of viewers, enjoying ratings from as low as 38 percent to as high as 67 percent.[1] In recent years, viewers' attitudes toward the show have cooled somewhat, especially in coastal cities. Nevertheless, the gala has transformed the Spring Festival culture in China. Watched closely or not, in most households, the gala plays in the background as families engage in festival activities.[2] In effect, the gala has turned the occasion for family reunion, a traditionally semiprivate rite of passage from the old to the new, into a nationwide carnival-like event. Watching the gala has become "the New Year's Eve cultural feast."[3] The gala, therefore, is an important text for us to see not only how the officially sanctioned nationalist discourse gets articulated in contemporary China but also how such discursive articulation engages with broader globalization processes.

Following this premise, this chapter analyzes the shows from 1997, 1999, 2000, and 2002. These years are chosen because of specific historical events that became key moments for rearticulating the Chinese state with the nation and the present with the past. They include the anticipated handover of Hong Kong and Macao, the beginning of the new millennium, the success in Beijing's quest for hosting the 2008 Olympics, and China's entry into World Trade Organization (WTO). The primary materials analyzed are videos of these shows, supplemented by other materials, including Chinese scholars' writings and key segments of the galas in other years.

Heterotopia and Simultaneity

Right from the gala's inauguration, its function of articulating a nationalist ideology was clear, indicated by the official theme of the very first gala in 1983: "unity, joy, and hope." In the first fifteen years, the word "unity" was used twelve times in the gala's theme statements.[4] The 1995 theme states eloquently the three layers of meaning behind the word *unity*: "family reunion, multiethnic gathering, and coagulation of all descendents of the Yan and Huang."[5] Recognizing the gala's role in displaying a statist nationalism, one Chinese scholar points out, "the country [*guojia*, or the state and family], and only the country, is the main character in this Chinese nation's most ornate gala."[6] Echoing the same thesis, another Chinese scholar describes the gala as a unique Chinese-style "carnival," characterized by celebratory performances of the country and all the families in it.[7]

As a site of such national enactment, the gala uniquely constitutes one of the "other spaces" that Foucault called "heterotopias."[8] As a heterotopia, the gala takes place in a real site in space, but it is also "a kind of effectively enacted utopia in which the real sites, all the other real sites that can be found within the culture, are simultaneously represented, contested, and inverted."[9] It "juxtapose[s] in a single real place several spaces, several sites that are in themselves incompatible."[10] In explaining the theoretical properties of heterotopias, Foucault used a mirror as an analogy. A mirror is located in a real place, but it creates an illusory space for a subject to be there, in the mirror. It reflects and inverts the subject who is located in a place other than "there"—in the mirror—and functions as a "virtual point" through which the subject directs his or her gaze at the self. That is, through its connections with different sites, a heterotopia functions as "a heterogeneous space"[11] in which we project and present ourselves and through which we "view" ourselves and let ourselves be viewed by others.

As such a heterotopia, the Spring Festival Gala reflects the collective subject of the Chinese nation by juxtaposing different places across the country and the globe in the performances that take place in one site, the CCTV studio, and from there, through the performances, these different places are redisplayed on millions of TV screens in various locales. The connections of different sites through the televised gala are made "visible" or experientially "real" by the imagined (to ordinary viewers anyway) physical network through which their TV screens are connected to the studio in

Beijing, the political center of the Chinese state. To reinforce authenticity, the gala uses various means to show the physicality of such connections. The 2000 gala, for example, opens with a montage sequence, which starts with a red dragon flag draped over the CCTV building, juxtaposed with an orchestra playing the background music. This image is followed by images of a passenger jumbo jet flying overhead, visually threading together different scenery from throughout the country. This is juxtaposed with official seals from the many provinces floating onto the screen one after another. When the music ends, the image cuts to the studio stage occupied by a partial but life-sized replica of a passenger jumbo jet. The two directors of the gala are shown to be stepping out of "the plane." From the top of the stairs, they announce the opening of the gala and send New Year's wishes to "all Chinese in the world."

The connections between the site of the gala performance and all the other sites represented in the shows are highly structured. In terms of genres, the performances are organized into three major clusters: singing and dancing (*ge wu*), traditional vernacular operas (*xi qu*), and language plays. The latter is further divided into cross-talk (*xiangsheng*) and comedy routines (*xiaopin*). As for the performers, they are usually a mixture of established stars and promising newcomers, carefully selected from different regions of the country. Performances include local vernacular traditions from different regions of the country and appeal to various demographic segments of the national audience. There is also a mixture of domestic and foreign performance styles.

The shows also pay regular tribute to the armed forces, as performers in military uniforms commonly act out scenes from military life or sing a song praising the brave soldiers of the People's Liberation Army. The host or hostess of each gala reminds the audience "not to forget our brave soldiers who are protecting our borders on this chilly night so that we and their parents can enjoy the festivity together." Equally important are token representations of ethnic minorities. For example, the 1999 gala includes a song-and-dance routine called *Festivity*. Performers wearing traditional costumes of major ethnic groups dance to songs that are sung in the languages of those ethnic groups and subtitled for the mass audience. One song hailed, "Fifty-six stars, fifty-six flowers, and fifty-six ethnic brothers and sisters of one family; fifty-six ethnic languages saying one thing, loving our China!" The organization of these elements projects a preferred image of a national constellation that is broadcast "live" by CCTV and "lived through" by the audience.

As Foucault clearly stated, heterotopias vary by the ways that time is embedded. Time may be in slices, may be in a cumulative form, or may be fleeting or transitory. The last is what Foucault conveyed as "time in the mode of the festival."[12] Reflecting this feature, the Spring Festival Gala is presented as "the New Year's Eve cultural feast" for the whole nation. The root of this image is in the traditional custom of an extended family enjoying a feast together on New Year's Eve, which is a folk ritual in which all family members participate. In such a ritual, they pass the moment by transcending their individuality and differences and enacting their common bonds. The moment is thus bracketed as being special, or even magical; it marks the transition from the old to the new, from one specific phase of life to another. It is a moment for celebrating achievements in the past year and weaving hopes for a new year. It is a periodically occurring and highly structured moment for renewing the common bonds by making them visible and "materialized" in metaphors, symbols, and ritualistic acts, hence, creating a communal memory.

In this sense, the gala performances also function as what the anthropologist Victor Turner called "liminoids,"[13] a rite of passage. In such performances, the regular and structured distinctions, restrictions, and separations that give rise to orders and hierarchies of everyday life are inverted or subverted; common bonds that transcend the structured divisions of the routine order are privileged and enacted, creating a transitory moment in which individuals experience homogeneity and communion that Turner termed *communitas*.[14] The Spring Festival Gala creates such a moment of *communitas* of the whole nation by bringing hundreds of millions of Chinese together for a shared event.

To concretize the "togetherness," gala producers dramatize and mystify "Beijing time" by leading the studio audience and TV viewers across the country and around the world in a ritual countdown toward midnight. With Beijing time as a metaphor and the countdown clock as an icon for simultaneity, each year's host presides over the countdown to midnight as a ritual. Each annual gala synchronizes the start of a new year not only in this vast country but also for all ethnic Chinese around the globe. Simultaneity then becomes a key temporal element that structures the gala as a heterotopia, engendering a fleeting moment experienced *together* by all Chinese. Synchronization thus weaves one of the most fundamental common bonds.

Dragon, Blood, and Myth

As a unique heterotopia, the gala also manipulates time in other ways to enact a historical narrative that essentializes Chinese as a nation and legitimizes the current regime as its only legitimate political representation. Essentialization is a reductionist process. It fixes and universalizes a few presumed canonical attributes of the Chinese nation so that the resulting representation homogenizes the nation and solidifies its differentiation from others at the same time. It involves both "objectivizing" selected cultural symbols and "iconizing" selected objects. For example, familiar images of objects such as the Yellow River, the Yangtze River, the Great Wall, Mount Tai, Mount Everest, and so on are recurrent symbols in each year's gala. Audiences are told that the ancient land comprised by these objects has nurtured and protected a continuous civilization of five thousand years. Similarly, popular phrases such as "descendents of the Yan and Huang emperors," "family reunion," "brothers and sisters of all ethnicities," and so on also appear repeatedly in each year's gala, functioning as highly loaded symbols. These iconic images and family-based symbols compress the long temporal flow of Chinese history into the moment of the gala—a slice of time—and then in turn transform it into enduring ties that stand for eternity in time.

Objectivizing symbols needs myths and mythologizing physical objects. We can see this from the constructed image of the dragon, a mythical animal that symbolizes vitality, strength, and power. The 1985 gala showed a "hot moment"[15] in popularizing the dragon as one of the most potent symbols of the Chinese nation. That year, Daniel K. Wong, a physician elected the mayor of Cerritos, California, was brought to the gala to sing *Descendents of the Dragon*, whose lyrics conjure up ancient mythological roots of the modern state:

> Far in the east, there is a *jiang*,[16]
> Its name is *Chang Jiang*;
> Far in the east, there is a *he*,
> Its name is *Huang He*.
> . . .
> In the ancient east, there is a dragon,
> Its name is China.
> In the ancient east, there is a group of people,

Who are all descendents of the dragon.
At the foot of the dragon I grow,
Growing into a dragon's descendent.
Black eyes, black hair and yellow skin,
Forever a descendent of the dragon.

Wong, a second-generation Chinese American, who, the host notes, has "succeeded in the mainstream America," maintains not only his physical features but also his bonds to China by declaring himself "forever a descendent of the dragon." The blood tie is sacred. It is presented here as the physical foundation not only for the visible attributes of Chinese but also for the enduring emotional connections that are impossible to sever. Many images and symbols appearing in the gala annually are derivatives of such deep structure and are, in Foucault's words, "nurtured by the hidden presence of the sacred."[17]

One particular moment in the 2003 gala is sufficient to illustrate how sacredness is inscribed in specific objects. This is a semireligious ceremony inserted into a secular TV show; it takes place on a theatrical stage rather than in a religious temple, and it switches the emotions of joy and festivity of the gala into that of solemn homage. By presiding over such a ritual, the gala hosts turn themselves into high priests who bring together viewers in solemn communion. The moment begins with images of soldiers in ceremonial uniforms guarding a golden cauldron. The hostess, Ni Ping, tells the audience, "Tonight, the night when Chinese around the globe spend the New Year's Eve together, we turn our gaze to our Motherland." CCTV, she says, has received thirty-four boxes of soil, collected from the thirty-one provinces and autonomous regions plus Hong Kong, Macao, and Taiwan. During her tearjerking narration, the big screen on stage shows a montage sequence of the ritual ceremonies of soil collection in different locales across the country. Ni then announces: "Dear friends, hundreds of millions in the TV audience are going to witness this historical moment: a group of brothers and sisters from thirty-four different regions are going to mix the thirty-four boxes of soil into the cauldron. This is just like our brothers and sisters' blood flowing into the same stream. We are saying that Chinese sons and daughters share the same blood." A powerful tenor then sings, "Mountains extend, waters flow; connections endure, and affections persist. . . . A long blood vein connects us all. . . . In the soil rest our ancestors, thousands of threads are our flesh-blood connections."

Built upon such presumed blood ties, numerous gala moments show family as "the master metaphor of the nation"[18] and home as a spatial anchor for the family. The 1997 gala, in anticipation of Hong Kong's impending handover on June 30th, opens with a song-and-dance routine called *Great Reunion*. The performers sing, "Round is the sky, round is the Earth, round is every family, and round is the country. . . . Every family is united and Chinese sons and daughters are united to eternity."[19] Playing the same theme, the 2006 gala opens with a song-and-dance routine called *A Hundred Family Names*. With various family names flying across a big screen in the background, three performers, one from the mainland, one from Hong Kong, and the third from Taiwan, sing in unison:

The same ancestors are Yan and Huang,
The same roots are in Han and Tang.[20]
. . .
In the hundreds of family names, you're Li and I'm Zhang,
In our blood flows the same Huang He and Chang Jiang;
In the hundreds of family names, you're Zhao and I'm Wang,
In our heart resides the same glory of the dragon nation.

These examples mix the sacred and the profane, the solemn and the frivolous, the grand and the ordinary. They are woven together not only to express but also to solidify relations among different sites across both space and time, and to juxtapose them into the heterotopia of the Spring Festival Gala. Through these images and sounds on TV screens, millions of Chinese, in and out of China's territorial boundaries, are called upon to partake in the same ceremony, to feel the same blood ties, and to refresh the remembrance of the same ancestors. Through this heterotopia each year, audiences not only watch an entertainment show but also witness an enactment of their "essential" collective beings, as well as the "cultural cosmos"[21] that gives birth to, nurtures, and grounds such beings.

Going Global: The Cosmos of a Cultural Empire

Planning, designing, rehearsing, and staging each year's gala are hugely complex activities that involve heavy organizational investment. It takes months of intense work and involves participation of the whole nation. During the months leading up to the show, the entertainment pages of newspapers across the country and commercial news websites are filled with tidbits and gossip about preparation for the event. Intense interest builds as to who will appear, which star is sacked, and what will be the upcoming highlights. The involvement of TV viewers across various social divides makes the gala take on the appearance of a nationwide carnival.[22]

This analogy, however, is very limited. Indeed, the gala invites intense viewer involvement; it offers a communal experience for all those who watch and "live through" the gala, and consequently, this liminality[23] leads people to "feel" a temporary suspension of the hierarchically structured yoke of political and economic power in everyday life. But compared with Bakhtin's conception of carnivals,[24] the Spring Festival Gala has nothing close to subversive power. What generates laughter, joyous acts, creative role-plays, and other performances is not the inversion of the established codes of political and ideological control. Rather, they are generated by creative co-optation of worldly, everyday, and folk customs into an officially sanctioned script. The gala is, more appropriately, a state-sponsored carnival-like event to perform the specific ideological function of official co-optation. The "truth" to be revealed and consecrated through the festivity is one handed down by the party-state.[25]

Simply put, as a state-owned monopoly network, CCTV cannot be an open venue for "spontaneous" performances by the populace. A careful and elaborate censoring system is put in place to winnow and shape the performances for each gala. It is reported that, in addition to the designated gala director, more than seventeen high-level individuals in CCTV, the State Administration of Radio, Film, and Television (SARFT), and the party's Propaganda Department are involved in reviewing and censoring the show. For each performance, it is reported, more than eighty different elements must be considered in the scripting, rehearsing, and reviewing processes.[26] On November 28, 2008, more than two months before the 2009 Chinese New Year, the head of the State Administration of Radio Film and Television held a meeting with the director of CCTV, among other high-level administrators, stipulating the guidelines for the 2009 Spring Festival Gala.[27]

This exercise of state power comes across in the gala's text. In early 1997, for example, carefully guarded information that Deng Xiaoping, the former senior leader, was dying must have trickled down to programmers at CCTV. Prior to the gala, a twelve-part TV documentary depicting Deng's life and legacy was aired on the network. During the gala, the hostess asserted that the documentary had been "well received around the world" and it was time to "share our remembrance of the spring of eighteen years ago" when Deng led the decision to establish the special economic zones. Following this introduction, a singer launched into a song called "A Spring Story":

In the spring of 1979,
An old man drew a circle by the South China Sea,
Where rose, one after another, cities,
Miraculously piling up gold mountains.
Spring thunders woke up both sides of the Great Wall,
Spring sunshine warmed both banks of the Yangtze River.
. . .
1992, another spring,
The same old man wrote a poem by the South China Sea,
Spring thunders rolled between the heaven and earth,
Setting off a journey.
Spring breezes painted green on this land of the orient,
Spring showers nurtured the ancient garden of China.

Such reverence for political leaders is performed in each year's show. In the 2000 gala, after the ritual of countdown to midnight, the host acclaims, "Let me announce a piece of exciting news! The General Secretary of the Chinese Communist Party, the President of the People's Republic of China, and the Chairman of the Central Military Committee, Comrade Jiang Zemin has written a new spring inscription and asked CCTV to send his New Year's greeting to all ethnicities of the country and all overseas Chinese!" Two other hosts open a scroll to display Jiang's calligraphy. The first host then screams, "General Secretary Jiang's inscription shows an affectionate concern for us and is a huge inspiration to us!" The political center's hailing of its subjects in this moment is unmistakable in the formal full identification of the three official titles that Jiang carries.

These examples show that the state—equated to the country and, in turn, the nation—plays the leading role in each year's gala. Hence, as a unique heterotopia, the gala has a clear political structure: The center radiates a gravitational force pulling the other places toward it. In other words, the juxtaposition of spaces that Foucault talked about is not simply piling them up or adding them together without any signifying pattern. Rather, it is structured as a constellation that conforms to the Chinese imagination of an empire-state.[28]

Enacting this embedded structure, each year the hosts of the gala periodically interrupt the performance to read "New Year's greeting" telegraphs or telephone messages from various groups in different locations around the world. These groups include companies or municipalities in other parts of the country, military posts along the Chinese borders, and Chinese embassy staffs and students in different foreign countries around the world.

China as a cultural empire has no hard boundaries limiting its reach; it involves synchronized activities across a vast space, both in China and under heaven (*tian xia*). It also observes a strict system of admission based on blood ties and nurtured by Chinese culture. Within this system, sharp boundaries are drawn between "us" and "them," but where the boundaries lie is to be determined by the political center. Ethnic minorities are admitted into this empire because, as their performances on the national festival stage show, they contribute to the extension of the empire's reach, both geographically and in people's hearts and minds.[29] Even people of different skin colors may be admitted when they transform themselves by engaging in authentic Chinese cultural practices. This is symbolically shown in the 1999 gala in a cross-talk performed by four "foreign friends" wearing the "Tang Dress" and in a comedy routine in the 2002 gala in which a street vender brags that "Chinese green cards are now hot commodities among foreigners." At least, foreigners can be admitted as "friends" of the empire.[30]

The political order of the cultural empire is globally oriented. Repeated invocations of China's "glorious history of five thousand years" and of "the common ancestors" reinforce the narrative of Chinese cultural universalism.[31] And such universalism is embedded with an imagination of Chinese cultural superiority, as China, against all odds, *has won* her role in the world and has the unique capacity of acculturating others into the cultural empire. Reflecting this psyche, international recognition is treated not only as an indication of achievement but also, at a deeper cultural level, as an indication of what China deserves. Therefore, Beijing "won the right" to host the 2008 Olympics. China also has "won" the WTO negotiations, "opening a new chapter for world economic development in the twenty-first century."[32]

The 2002 gala was most explicit in depicting this image of a cultural empire. The theme of the gala was "networking with the world," clearly taking a cue from China's entry of the WTO. Ostensibly, the theme reflected the director's desire to make the gala more dynamic and interactive with audiences due to a steady decline in the show's ratings in recent years and audience complaints that the show had been too formulaic. Compared with prior years, the 2002 gala had more frequent displays of audience participation. But this gala clearly had a stronger message than simply "getting involved in the gala." Repeatedly, by the hosts and through various performances, the preceding year was celebrated as a year of particularly great achievements for China. Even the character of a peasant street vender in a comedy routine was shown telling the audience, "This year has many happy events. Bidding for the Olympics is successful, our soccer team won, and APEC meeting came to Shanghai." Driving home the message in every way possible, a quiz sequence asks the audiences to name three things that "are dreams coming true for all Chinese in 2001."

To bring home the gala's theme, the host introduced another sequence by telling the audience, "For all the achievements of the past year, all Chinese are proud, confident, and unremitting." Echoing this newfound confidence and pride, singers performed *Someone Asks Me*, and replied enthusiastically, "I tell the world in a loud volume, I am Chinese, I am Chinese, I am Chinese!" The hostess, after listing a number of achievements, claimed, "Today's China wants to go to the world, and today's world must get to know China! China goes to the world!" And she said the last sentence in English. Following that was a song-and-dance routine called *Networking with the World*. Featuring a futuristic stage design and energetic dance routine clearly aimed at a young audience, two tenors sang,

> Want to decorate Fujiyama's midsummer with Mount Tai's rosy dawn,
> Want to splash Danube's water with oars from the Yellow River,
> Want to caress the Siberia with the tropical wind of Hainan Island,
> Want the camels on the Silk Road to carry my Hatha,
> Want to use the bricks of the Great Wall to connect to the iron
>   Eiffel Tower,
> Want to kiss the Sahara Desert with the waves of the Yangtze River,
> Want to move Vienna with the music rock from Gulangyu,
> Want to use Niagara Falls to brew my fragrant tea.
> Networking with the world, the west has man-made tales,
> Networking with the world, the east has natural grace.

This bold reordering of spatial relations points to the insatiable ambition of the Chinese cultural empire. It shows a Chinese collective subject that transcends China's territorial boundaries. It is global in reach. It is limitless in self-confidence. It is poised for the new century when China is destined to change the world. The message is clear: China is going to the world on its own terms, and with its marching steps, China is determined to—and should—shape a new order of globalization. Beginning in 2005, the simulcast of the gala via satellite (CCTV Channel 4) and via high-speed Internet (in Chinese, English, French, and Spanish) furthered this conception of globalizing connections.

Enacting the Chinese Nation on a Global Stage

As a unique heterotopia, the CCTV Spring Festival Gala articulates an officially sanctioned, popular, and emotionally charged discourse on the Chinese nation. It is a discursive system structured with the family as the master metaphor. It is a venue through which all Chinese see their collective self, live the magic of being Chinese, and renew their bonds with family members. It also co-opts the everyday idea of home—a space where individuals' activities are oriented, coordinated, and communicated in order to protect and project the common experiences of domesticity[33]—by turning it into a master metaphor for the state. The state not only guards the ancestral roots of the family but also provides shelter and support for the family. It is a place to which all Chinese people are forever bound by blood ties. It is a place they can turn to and return to. The gala, therefore, offers a highly structured rhetorical setting for the political center of the empire to hail its subjects.

But if this is the only story, then the Spring Festival Gala as a television event is only of limited interest outside of China or China studies. This chapter argues that there is more to the annual TV variety show. The gala is a global media event in design and reach, making the enactment of the Chinese family-nation a performance on a global stage. The hailing of the "descendents of the Yan and Huang Emperors" is directed to the whole world rather than only to China proper. More importantly, as Duara points out, "nationalism is . . . a *relationship* between a constantly changing Self and Other"[34] that is constructed discursively. In enacting the collective Self of the Chinese in essentialized terms, the gala also essentializes the Other and the relationship between the two. It displays on stage the cosmos of a cultural empire that transcends the ontologies of the geography and the constellation of states. It is based on a form of cultural superiority in the disguise of cultural universalism. It does so by mixing together official nationalism— which celebrates the achievements of the Chinese state and legitimizes the party-state authority—and informal and popular nationalism,[35] which is experientially based, drawing analogies to family and home and also to various cultural categories typically found in vernacular festivals and rituals.[36]

Seen in this light, the gala is a global event in that globalization both ignites and in part is constituted by numerous dialogical moments of this nature.

Beyond its text, the Spring Festival Gala is also unique in the realm of global TV broadcasting. It has been continuously running for twenty-eight years, enjoying higher ratings than any other show. In the ten years of this century, even with a proliferation of satellite and cable channels in recent years, the show still maintains a rating of around 40 percent and an audience share in the mid-70 percent range. For CCTV, a state-owned national network with the political mission of propagating the will of the party-state and enhancing national integration,[37] the gala is treated as a major vehicle to accomplish this mission. At the same time, it is also carefully guarded as a major vehicle for CCTV to maintain its monopoly in advertising revenue. For example, in 2002, the gala had ten minutes of advertisements but brought in US$304 million (4.69 percent of CCTV's annual total). The figure rose to $478 million in 2005 (4.65 percent of CCTV's annual total).[38] Contributing to making the gala a major cash cow for CCTV are the global conglomerates that are operating in the Chinese market. For example, an industrial report reveals that NEC won the bid for the most valued ten-second midnight ad spot in the 2005 gala with an offer of more than $1.2 million.[39] Such extratextual evidence shows that the gala has increasingly become a valued vehicle in and for the capitalist global economy. Further supporting this interpretation is the observation that CCTV's decision to simulcast the gala globally is celebrated by some industry analysts who have come to accept the neoliberal vision of globalization in wholesale. To them, it is a rightful measure to make the gala "the point of dialogue between Chinese civilization and the advanced international cultures."[40]

Conspicuously absent from the gala is public life that may be, directly or indirectly, associated with the notion of democracy. As a matter of fact, other than celebrating past achievements and praising the political leadership, there is little overt political expression in the gala. It may be argued that the cultural norm for celebrating this festival places an overriding emphasis on harmony, festivity, and unity, relegating the potentially contentious political issues as unsuitable. For example, the 2008 gala's theme was officially set to be "China in Peace and Prosperity, Society in Harmony,"[41] echoing the "unity" with a new buzzword of the present official discourse on building a harmonious society. However, if the gala is a heterotopia for enacting and experiencing the Chinese collective identity across the globe, the total absence of democracy is quite telling. It clearly suggests that a democratic spirit is not part of the Chinese identity. In this discursive system, democracy does not fit into the glorious Chinese cultural tradition, not in contemporary Chinese life experiences, not in the envisioned relationship between China and the world, and not in the hopes and aspirations of the Chinese nation for a better future.

What, then, are the implications of the CCTV Spring Festival Gala with these discursive characteristics? The analysis in this chapter suggests that experiences of globalization may be examined from the angle of how a particular nation or a state views itself in relation to others, how it projects itself to the globe, and how it asserts itself in the world. Understanding globalization can benefit from observing a particular spatial-temporal entity *in relation to* the more transcending trends and forces. Such "local knowledge," to appropriate from Clifford Geertz,[42] can help us to ground the theoretical formulations of globalization, which often reflects a vantage point that is either extraterrestrial in nature or anchored in the West unreflexively.

With this reoriented theoretical gaze, what we can infer from this analysis is not whether China is for or against globalization, nor is it whether China is being transformed by the magical or evil forces of globalization. Rather, what we can infer is that China is determined to join the global system on its own terms. These terms include cultural essentialism and the endorsement of a strong state—communist or not—that speaks on behalf of the nation with vigorous confidence. Much of the ongoing domestic debate—among intellectuals and in popular press—on China's entry into the WTO and China's approach to globalization in general reflects different interpretations of this fundamental principle. It also underlies the gala performances analyzed in this chapter. Consequently, the kind of Chinese nationalism seen in the gala knits a discursive basis not only for the political legitimacy of the current party-state regime in China[43] but also for a stable and strong Chinese state in the current Western-dominated global system.

But adherence to the principle of a strong Chinese state, when coupled with cultural essentialism, may pose a threat to the world order, as well as the basic principles that undergird, or may arise to undergird it. This cultural essentialism is based on a narrative of victimization and redemption,[44] as well as a narrative of cultural superiority, all of which are visible in the galas. Such narratives, as some scholars have pointed out,[45] have contributed to the rise of nationalistic fervor in China, both at the moments of perceived setbacks (for example, Beijing's failed bid for hosting the 2000 Olympics) and at the moments of perceived triumph (such as Beijing's successful bid for hosting the 2008 Olympics), often featuring self-loathing, xenophobia, and militarism.[46]

Such nationalistic fervor has found platforms for expression with the advent of the Internet and the commercialized book publishing industry.[47] For example, articles and books advocate that China return to isolationism or that it develop its offensive military capability to not only protect China's territorial integrity but also project China's rightful influence.[48] Such expressions may not be in harmony with the current political regime, but they pose a danger given their refusal of self-reflexivity and their tendency to assign blame to the equally essentialized Other. Officially sanctioned nationalism shares with the xenophobic popular nationalism this epistemological defect, as clearly indicated by things such as quickly throwing "anti-China" bombshells on anybody who objects to China's demands or criticizes China or its official policies.

Riding on such a discursive current, the Chinese regime must take the posture of asserting China's rightful place in the world. With this discursive current gathering force, however, it is also possible that any perceived weakness of the Chinese government's position could fuel discontent already brewing in Chinese society, further weakening the Chinese state. A weakened Chinese state may be compelled to appease xenophobic and militant nationalism by turning to the cultural empire image of China for its political imagination, encouraging, directly or indirectly, hostility toward the Other, especially Japan, Taiwan nationalists, and the United States. As this chapter shows, the state-controlled enactment of the Chinese nation during the Spring Festival Gala contains the logical roots of such an unlikely (at the moment) but ultimately plausible discursive marriage. It is a scenario whose likelihood can only be reduced by China's integration into the world system, for which China must insist on its own terms, and at the same time, China must further open its media and its people's public life. Only such openness has a better chance to breed the necessary courage among Chinese intellectuals to engage in reflexive battles that would uproot the essentionalizing tendency.

We must recognize that such necessary openness does not come about automatically with China's entry into the global system. Only when the basic discursive environment starts making such a fundamental shift can we expect the Spring Festival Gala to be an enactment of a more reflexive and confident Chinese nation. For such a condition to be fostered, democratic institutions are necessary. Equally necessary is that discursive reflection on the collective self of the Chinese nation take place in a calm and deliberative environment. Neither is present in contemporary China. As a result, the future Spring Festival Gala will continue to be that of a state-sanctioned and self-aggrandizing enactment of the essentialized Chinese nation and, notes one CCTV insider, an event that "will never lose money."[49]

Notes

1. Actual ratings data have only been available since 1994.

2. On February 8, 2008, more than a hundred trained graduate and undergraduate students were asked to turn in ethnographic recordings of their own family activities on the eve of that year's Spring Festival. The records came from around sixty locales across the country, showing that for most families, the TV set was tuned to the Spring Festival Gala on that evening.

3. L. Liu, ed., *New Year's Eve Cultural Feast: Online Discussions on the CCTV Spring Festival Gala* (Beijing: Zhonghua Shuju Press, 2003, in Chinese).

4. Z. Pan and J. M. Chan, "Building a market-based party organ: Television and national integration in the People's Republic of China," in *Television in Asia*, ed. D. French and M. Richards (New Delhi: Sage, 2000), 232–63.

5. In the Chinese mythology, *Yan Di* (Yan emperor) and *Huang Di* (Yellow emperor) are said to be leaders of the two tribes that eventually merged and settled in the midland of China in 2500 B.C.E. In Chinese mythology, they are both regarded as ancestors of Han Chinese. The authenticity of them as historical figures is still in dispute among historians.

6. Z. C. Pan, "Spring Festival Gala: The last supper," *Southern City Daily*, 3 February 2005, in Chinese.

7. W. Geng, *Carnival in China: A Cultural Analysis of the Spring Festival Galas* (Beijing: Wenhua Yishu Press, 2003, in Chinese).

8. M. Foucault, "Of other spaces," in *Diacritics*, trans. J. Miskowiec, 16, no. 1 (1967/1986): 22–27

9. Foucault, "Of other spaces," 24.

10. Foucault, "Of other spaces," 25.

11. Foucault, "Of other spaces," 23.

12. Foucault, "Of other spaces," 26.

13. V. Turner, "Liminal to liminoid in play, flow, ritual: An essay in comparative symbology," in *From Ritual to Theatre: The Human Seriousness of Play* (New York: PAJ, 1982), 20–60.

14. V. Turner, *The Ritual Process: Structure and Anti-structure* (New York: Aldine de Gruyter, 1969/1995).

15. C. Levi-Strauss, *The Savage Mind* (Chicago: University of Chicago Press, 1966), 259.

16. *Jiang* and *he* are two different words for "river" in Chinese. In Chinese, Yangtze River is called *Chang Jiang* ("Long River") and Yellow River is called *Huang He*.

17. Foucault, "Of other spaces," 23.

18. P. Duara, "De-constructing the Chinese nation," in *Chinese Nationalism*, ed. J. Unger, (Armonk, NY: M. E. Sharpe, 1996), 31–55.

19. In Chinese, the round shape represents "reunion" or "unity." It also signifies completeness and perfection.

20. They refer to Han Dynasty (202 B.C.E.–220 C.E.) and Tang Dynasty (618–907 C.E.) respectively.

21. Turner, "Liminal to liminoid in play, flow, ritual," 41.

22. M. Bakhtin, *Rabelais and His World*, trans. H. Isowolsky (Bloomington: Indiana University Press, 1984).

23. Turner, *The Ritual Process: Structure and Anti-structure*.

24. C. Lindahl, "Bakhtin's carnival laughter and the Cajun country Mardi Gras," *Folklore* 107 (1996): 57–70.

25. For a theoretical exposition on revealing and consecrating "the truth" in cultural performances, see J. J. MacAloon, "Olympic games and the theory of spectacle in modern societies," in *Rite, Drama, Festival, Spectacle: Rehearsals toward a Theory of Cultural Performance*, ed. J. J. MacAloon (Philadelphia, PA: Institute for the Study of Human Issues, 1984), 241–80.

26. The information is taken from various news reports on spring festivals. Among the sources are "A report on why two well-known pop stars' song was sacked," *Sanlian Life Weekly* (January 23, 2006), http://ent.people.com.cn/GB/42075/4052448.html (accessed March 20, 2006); and "Gala: A report on the preparation for the 2005 gala," *China News Weekly* (January 24, 2006), http://www.people.com.cn/GB/news/37454/3169873.html (accessed March 20, 2006).

27. "Spring Festival Gala will showcase the Chinese national festivity, the SARFT prohibits lip-synching in the gala," http://media.people.com.cn/GB/8454199.html (accessed May 3, 2009).

28. H. Bockman, "The future of the Chinese empire-state in a historical perspective," in *Reconstructing Twentieth-Century China: State Control, Civil Society, and National Identity*, ed. K. E. Brodsgaard and D. Strand (Oxford: Clarendon Press, 1998), 253–79.

29. D. C. Gladney, "Representing nationality in China: Refiguring majority/minority identities," *Journal of Asian Studies* 53, no. 1 (1994): 92–123.

30. For a typical articulation of such a divide of others into China's foes and "friends," see N. Fang, B. Wang, and L. Ma, *The Growing China: A Study on the Country and National Consciousness among the Contemporary Chinese Youths* (Beijing: People's Press, 2002, in Chinese). Other scholars of China's contemporary nationalism have made a similar observation; see P. H. Gries, *China's New Nationalism: Pride, Politics, and Diplomacy* (Berkeley: California University Press, 2004).

31. Duara, "De-constructing the Chinese nation"; J. Townsent, "Chinese nationalism," in *Chinese Nationalism*, ed. J. Unger (Armonk, NY: M. E. Sharpe, 1996), 1–30.

32. Quoted from a report of the 2002 gala at http://www.cctv.com.cn/news/ttxw/20020227/100001.html (accessed March 20, 2006).

33. M. Douglas, "The idea of a home: A kind of space," *Social Research* 58, no. 1 (1991): 287–307.

34. Duara, "De-constructing the Chinese nation," 39 (italics original).

35. J. Cheng and K. Ngok, "Chinese nationalism and Sino-US relations: The NATO bombing of the Chinese embassy in Belgrade," in *Nationalism, Democracy and National Integration in China*, ed. L. H. Liew and S. Wang (London: Routledge, 2004), 85–104.

36. T. H. Erikson, "Formal and informal nationalism," *Ethnic and Racial Studies* 16, no. 1 (1993): 1–25.

37. See Pan and Chan, "Building a market-based party organ," for a systemic analysis of the Chinese TV broadcasting.

38. Liu Yali, "Spring Festival Gala: One moment is worth a thousand bucks, One hour brings in $120 millions," http://info.finance.hc360.com/2006/01/24120941893 .shtml (accessed March 20, 2006).

39. Immediately after the midnight bell, there is a ten-second spot. It is used to show the logo of the company that has purchased the spot. The voiceover says, "Such and such company sends New Year's greetings to all the people of our country."

40. Both the figure and the quote come from a report, "NEC won the Spring Festival ad bid, more than a million for 10 seconds," (http://info.finance.hc360.com/2005/02/04145622913.shtml (accessed March 20, 2006).

41. "Zhang Xiaohai and Chen Linchu will direct the 2008 Spring Festival Gala, theme is set." http://news.xinhuanet.com/ent/2007–08/08/content_6491435.htm (accessed May 3, 2009).

42. C. Geertz, *Local Knowledge: Further Essays in Interpretive Anthropology* (New York: Basic Books, 1983).

43. For a discussion on the legitimacy function of contemporary Chinese nationalism, see V. Shue, "Legitimacy crisis in China?" in *State and Society in 21st-Century China: Crisis, Contention, and Legitimation*, ed. P. H. Gries and S. Rosen (London: Routledge, 2004), 24–49.

44. Gries, *China's New Nationalism*.

45. Duara, "De-constructing the Chinese nation"; Gries, *China's New Nationalism*; Y. Zheng, *Discovering Chinese Nationalism in China* (Cambridge: Cambridge University Press, 1999).

46. A controversial best-seller by a group of young scholars first articulated these characteristics of the contemporary Chinese nationalism. See Q. Song, Z. Zhang, and B. Qiao, *China Can Say No* (Beijing: China Commerce Press, 1996, in Chinese). A more recent bestseller articulated even more militant nationalistic fervor. See X. Song, X. Wang, J. Huang, Q. Song, and Y. Liu, *China Is Unhappy* (Nanjing: Jiangsu People's Press, 2009, in Chinese). Outside of China, a number of China observers have written about such characteristics. G. R. Barmé, "To screw foreigners is patriotic: China's avant-garde nationalists," *China Journal* 34 (1995): 207–34; Gries, *China's New Nationalism*; L. W. Pye, "What China wants?" *New York Times*, November 26, 1996, A-21.

47. See P. Mooney, "Internet fans frames of Chinese nationalism: Beijing faces dilemma as anti-Japanese campaign in cyberspace hits the streets," *Yale Global Online,* April 4, 2005, http://yaleglobal.yale.edu/display.article?id=5516 (accessed March 12, 2006).

48. Such views are most forcefully articulated by Ning Fang, Xiaodong Wang, and their associates, all young scholars who rose to a public recognition in the mid and late 1990s. See X. Wang, "On splendid isolation," not dated, http://www.boxun.com/sixiang/991117/9911175.htm (accessed February 12, 2006); N. Fang, X. Wang, and Q. Song, *China's Path under the Shadow of Globalization* (Beijing: China Social Science Press, 1999, in Chinese).

49. The quote is from Yali, "Spring Festival Gala."

THIRTEEN

Bound to Rise: Chinese Media Discourses on the New Global Order

Chin-Chuan Lee

Chin-Chuan Lee offers an analysis of commentary essays published in the Global Times, *a newspaper targeted at elite audiences that features the most extensive international news coverage in Mainland China. The* Global Times *is furthermore the primary site for public commentary and discussion of the country's role in global politics, culture, and economy, especially with respect to China's "peaceful rise" to the status of global superpower. Lee's analysis shows that discussions of globalization are most frequently framed with respect to U.S.–China relations. Lee contends that even though these essays seem to represent open deliberation regarding China's future on the global stage, they in fact correlate with the official policy positions among members of the Chinese leadership. Rather than enhancing public discussion of globalization, the* Global Times *echoes the Communist Party line and therefore fails to introduce fresh ideas into important policy debates.*

The Cold War framework provided ideological clarity for political and media understanding: The Western countries were to contain the Soviet Union, to maintain the unity of the "free world," and to foster steady, non-radical political and economic change in the third world.[1] By comparison, the post–Cold War era is more complicated. Herbert Schiller contends that global corporations today may be more powerful than governmental authorities.[2] Global companies have transnationalized U.S. cultural styles and technologies to serve the ideological and marketing needs of capital, further extending their reach into newfound territories of the former Soviet bloc and many parts of the third world, where the "liberation struggles" have largely collapsed. The rising power of global companies does not, however, mean a decline of the U.S. state. President Bill Clinton declared that the United States was "bound to lead" in the post–Cold War global order.[3] President George W. Bush advanced a "transformational policy," which Secretary of State Condoleezza Rice proclaimed as an "answer to a new historic calling" of "building and sustaining democratic, well-governed states" around the world.[4] Some academics promoted "the end of history" or narratives of civilization-based supremacy.[5] No wonder Said described the United States as "adorned with its redolent self-congratulation, its unconcealed triumphalism, and its grave proclamations of responsibility."[6]

The end of the Cold War has sparked a new phase of the "globalization" era, characterized by "the time-space compression of the world" and the "intensification of consciousness of the world as a whole."[7] Globalization is said to loosen symbolic exchanges from spatial referents, but identity politics has paradoxically come to the fore as a point of contention. World knowledge must be filtered through national-cum-local prisms. In the still chaotic international order, the state is the "prime definer" of national interests and perspectives, whereas the media are a "secondary definer," such that media differences within a nation tend to be dwarfed by comparison to media differences between nations.[8] The nation-state provides a "quasi-religious sense of belonging and fellowship"[9] that codifies its visions, interests, and myths in terms of foreign policy. International news making is, in this sense, an "external presentation of the national face."[10] The media tend to essentialize the complex and contradictory reality of a nation into core attributes and histories that reductively contrast "us" and "them." When the media "rally around the flag" to protect national interests, internal partisan rifts are rendered relatively insignificant.[11] The national prism, often in the name of unity, may suppress "local" dissent, differences, or struggles; a local perspective is often derivative of the national narrative, likely to support rather than challenge the established ideological framework. Finally, media prisms are often constructed by recalling and activating symbols of national and cultural tradition to incite a sense of imagined grandeur and common sentiments.

What is the place of China in this new global order? Not long ago, Gerald Segal contended that China was "overrated as a market, a power, and a source of ideas."[12] Since then, especially after China's entry into the World Trade Organization (WTO) in 2001, the vast and rapid growth of China's economic and military power has provoked a paradigmatic debate over "weak China" versus "strong China."[13] This chapter aims to analyze how China's most influential newspaper on foreign affairs, the *Global Times*, presents a national elite discourse among policy advisors and commentators on the new global order. As will be clear, Chinese media's views of globalization hinge largely on whether the United States would stand in the way of China's rise to world importance. The analysis is contextualized in terms of the changing China–U.S. relationship and international political economy.

Global Integration

U.S. foreign policy has always been marked by an extraordinary mixture of idealism, moralism, pragmatism, and imperial impulse. During the Cold War, the United States perceived itself as "a righter of wrongs around the world, in pursuit of tyranny, in defense of freedom no matter the place or cost."[14] The media habitually highlighted communist abuse of human rights while playing down the atrocities committed by U.S. allies.[15] Since the nineteenth century, the United States has been seeking to change China according to America's image. After Nixon's visit to Beijing in the early 1970s, U.S. media representations of the People's Republic of China (PRC) have paralleled the history of the fragile U.S.–China relationship; the oscillating cycles of romanticism and cynicism reflect not only what is going on in China but also what is going on in the United States and what is going on between them.[16]

In the 1980s when Washington allied with China to fight against the Soviet Union, it refrained from criticizing China for the same human rights abuse for which it attacked the Soviet Union.[17] The end of the Cold War undermined the basis for an enduring U.S.–China alliance against the Soviet Union. In lieu of the former Soviet Union, China has stepped in to be a new enemy of the United States. Further complicated by the brutal images of the Tiananmen crackdown, U.S. media turned their focus on China's human rights abuses in the 1990s. During that decade, media discourses corresponded closely to an official policy transition: The United States began by imposing containment to punish China for the Tiananmen brutalities, but when that failed to produce the expected results, President Clinton was prompted to adopt a policy he called "positive engagement" (a balance of carrots and sticks), which was finally concretized in terms of "global integration."[18] As part of the strategy to "dissolve China into the civilized world" and hopefully instigate change from within China itself, the United States endorsed China's accession to the WTO. Clinton's policy was briefly interrupted when George W. Bush tried to redefine China as a "strategic competitor" rather than a "strategic partner," thereby generating tensions that did not abate until the U.S. war on terrorism helped to improve the bilateral relationship. The United States has been employing a "hedge policy," mixing encouragement and intimidation but emphasizing different elements at different times.

On the Chinese side, the post-Tiananmen regime has eagerly embraced nationalism—along with economic growth—as a new fount of legitimacy. Although nationalist sentiments had been widespread in the reconstruction of China's post-Mao identity, nationalism did not come to the fore to provide a new overarching ideological framework until the mid-1990s.[19] Authorities began to revive traditional values that the Maoist regime had tried for decades to eliminate. In the 1990s, China clashed with the United States over a number of difficult issues: human rights, trade, Taiwan, NATO's bombing of the Chinese embassy in Belgrade, and China's alleged nuclear espionage and illegal campaign contributions in the United States. The communist apparatchiks stage-managed nationalist sentiments by drawing on dramatized external events but tried to manage such sentiments within an orbit of control. The media became a "meeting ground upon which these two forms of (statist and populist) nationalism surge, fuse, and converge in portraying China as being encircled by an ocean of potential enemies who are out to destroy it, often mixing collective victimhood and historical memories in seemingly contradictory modes of xenophobia and narcissism."[20] The market-driven media have been particularly active in exploiting nationalist sentiments for profit.[21]

Alongside the rise of nationalism, China has been embracing the global capitalist order—and seeking to elevate its international status in this order—as a new source of regime legitimation. In 2001 China gained accession to the WTO and was granted the right to sponsor the 2008 Olympic Games, symbolizing its coming of age in the international power club. The media portrayed China as a winner in globalization and on its way up, via the WTO, in the world's pecking order. It was noted that the state suppressed anti-WTO voices and mobilized its propaganda organs to sing a chorus of praise for official policy.[22] Equally important, the 9/11 terrorist attacks and the ensuing war on terrorism paved the way to improving the U.S.–China

This *Global Times* headline reads, "Twenty-two scholars debate over China's future: Virtual consensus on 'economic rise,' a new focus on 'uncertainty.'" The secondary headline reads, "Korea gets bogged down in a morass of protests."

relationship. Since 2002, China has decided not to contest U.S. global supremacy, while at the same time its rising economic and military power has given the PRC a newfound sense of pride, confidence, and ambition.

Policy Enunciators in Elite Communication

China has tried to manage the different "faces" of globalization—and its increased integration into the international political economy—selectively. The state is largely unconcerned with media importation of popular culture that promotes a Western-style management system and corporate culture, but under no circumstances are the media allowed to challenge the state's authority and power.[23] The media have been granted economic privileges in exchange for their loyalty to the state; they garner vast wealth because they maneuver within political boundaries set by the state.[24] The state furthermore retains a decisive control over the appointment, editorial mission, and financial management of major media outlets.

In this chapter, I analyze the discourses of foreign policy advisors and enunciators in the *Global Times*. The paper was originally founded in 1993 as a weekly to absorb the unused reports filed by foreign correspondents of the *People's Daily*, China's foremost party organ, but it has gone through various transformations to become a daily paper at the start of 2006. Riding on waves of nationalist sentiment during a series of international crises in the 1990s (especially NATO's bombing of the Chinese embassy in Belgrade), the paper's circulation has now soared to 1.5 million copies nationwide. It is especially popular among intellectuals, professionals, businesspeople, students, and policymakers. While the *People's Daily* relies almost exclusively on post-office delivery to various state institutions, more than half of the copies of *Global Times* are sold to individual readers on newsstands throughout China. As the only paper in the PRC focusing on national security, military, and China-related international issues and events, it has no serious competitors. Insofar as the *People's Daily* remains hesitant to put foreign news or issues on the front page for fear of causing unwanted policy speculation, the *Global Times* is arguably the most important institution for the expression of quasi- or semiofficial foreign policy positions. The paper continues to draw on the pool of the *People's Daily* foreign correspondents to furnish international reports and analyses, while gradually building its own overseas stringers. Its wide circulation is considered rather unusual given the fact that the *Global Times*'s sixteen pages are priced the same (RMB$1 per copy) as the elite-oriented *New Beijing Daily*'s ninety-six pages.

Four significant features of the *Global Times* are noteworthy. First, it closely reflects the views of China's foreign policy, claiming to interpret world affairs for the Chinese people from the "Chinese perspective." It aims to uphold "national interest" as defined by the foreign policy establishment and not to reveal any differences of opinion or interest within state bureaucracies. Hu Xijin, its chief editor, claims that adhering to the propaganda line not only fulfills the "Party's requirement" and the paper's "social responsibility" but also enables the paper to "enjoy long-term prosperity." He chides the exposé-oriented outlets that encounter constant "political problems."[25] Another senior editor disclosed that the paper rarely steps out of the line because it consults the Foreign Ministry regularly and is kept informed of the current state policy by the *People's Daily*. In the event of occasional "mistakes," he said, the paper is usually forgiven for being a subsidiary of the *People's Daily*.[26] The *Global Times*, on its website, prides itself on receiving high praise for political correctness from the authorities and from none other than Liu Zuyu, the chief censor in the central Propaganda Department.[27] Li Xiguang, a journalist-turned-academic, has close ties to officialdom and is renowned for a series of bitter attacks on the U.S. media for "demonizing" China. He lauds the *Global Times* for "unifying" state agendas, media agendas, and public agendas.[28] This praise is tenable only if the vanguard party is assumed, by fiat, to represent public agendas.

Second, the *Global Times* is a prime example of the highly profitable *marketized* party press that caters to elite readers. By contrast, the *Jinghua Times* is the other highly successful market-driven subsidiary of the *People's Daily*, which serves the mass market with more mundane everyday-life topics to the exclusion of "big politics." Even though the *Jinghua Times* is more profitable, the *People's Daily* takes greater pride in the *Global Times*. Enjoying greater leeway editorially than its parent paper, the *Global Times* tends to commodify nationalistic rhetoric with eye-catching headlines, bold pictures, and shocking topics to satisfy the need for "collective therapy," all for a huge profit.[29] It has been at the forefront of peddling "hot" foreign issues, especially major confrontations, skirmishes, and crises with demonized others such as the United States, Japan, and Taiwan. Where is the boundary of critical commentary? A senior editor chuckled, "We can condemn Bush, but not our own leaders. Nor can we criticize North Korea's Kim."[30]

Third, the paper not only incites "populist" sentiments but also cultivates a polished "elite" image. Deputy Chief Editor Wu Jie claims that the paper does not care for trivial advertisers; instead, he boasts an array of global companies as the paper's major clients.[31] Advertising comes primarily from IT (IBM, Dell, Lenovo, Microsoft, Cisco), automobile (Toyota, Daimler-Chrysler, GM, BMW), and communication (China Mobile) sectors to promote corporate images. The paper garners approximately RMB$125 million (or $15.5 million) from ads per year, making it possible for its staff to draw salaries that on average are higher than those of journalists at the parent *People's Daily*.

Fourth, the *Global Times* is a major venue of elite discourse through repeated amplification and reinforcement of China's foreign policy positions. It is part of what Griffith characterizes as "communist esoteric communication," in which the press transmits policy directives to subelites in order to maintain a "myth of unanimity" and to provide "ex post facto justification of policy steps."[32] The paper carries no editorials but created an "International Forum" (*guoji luntan*) page in 1999. The editor-in-chief describes this forum as "marking for the first time that the media are able to discuss China's foreign policy and national security."[33] Writers with privileged access to such foreign policy discourse in the elite press constitute a subgroup of "establishment intellectuals" who play "a key mediating role in coordinating a symbolic exchange of services . . . between rulers and the larger intellectual elite."[34] In the early 1990s, Shambaugh estimated that there were 600 to 700 "America watchers" in China.[35] They were second-echelon international relations specialists affiliated with central government bureaucracies, professional research institutes, the media, and universities.[36] Most writers cited in the present analysis reside in Beijing and one particular coterie of semiofficial writers stands out among all the contributors to the *Global Times*.[37] This small discursive community is articulate in expression, homogeneous in background, orthodox in outlook, and sensitive to shifting party lines.

Constructive Discourse Analysis

To distill the frames of the *Global Times*'s narratives, I take Gamson's constructionist approach to framing analysis that deconstructs and reconstructs the editorials and column articles into elemental frames.[38] The purpose is to uncover ideological underpinnings of the media texts. The media frames serve as an organizing scheme with which writers provide coherence to their commentaries and through which some critical issues can be discussed. I first deconstruct the editorials and column articles into what Gamson calls a "signature matrix," a device that lists the key frames and links them to salient signifying devices. I then reconstruct their major theses into genotypical categories—or what Gamson calls "ideological packages," replete with metaphors, exemplars, catchphrases, depictions, and appeals to principles.

The *Global Times* carried 375 articles in the International Forum page from 2000 (the year to which the Web text is traceable) to 2005. Excluded from analysis were 141 articles (39 related to Japan and Sino–Japanese relations, and others referring diffusely to assorted topics, institutions, and countries). There were 234 articles (62 percent of the total)—ranging from 33 to 50 articles per year—for a total of 600,000 words in the final pool for analysis. Each article averaged 2,500 words, or three times as long as a *New*

Table 13.1. Themes of the Articles, 2000–2005 (Percent)

Category	2000*	2001*	2002	2003	2004*	2005
Globalization						
Rich-poor gap, globalization bad	16	3	6	3	0	2
Economic globalization, modernization	11	3	3	0	0	6
Global integration	8	3	6	3	0	0
(subtotal)	(35%)	(9%)	(15%)	(6%)	(0%)	(8%)
China–U.S. relations						
U.S. hegemony	31	17	15	33	18	8
U.S. "contains & contacts" China, common interest	8	37	55	37	26	46
Taiwan	5	0	3	0	3	0
(subtotal)	(44%)	(54%)	(73%)	(70%)	(47%)	(54%)
The rise of China						
Peaceful rise	3	10	3	3	29	12
Build up great-power image/responsibility	11	3	6	9	12	6
U.S.'s "China threat" theory, security & strength	8	15	3	9	10	10
Promote multilateral diplomacy	0	12	0	3	3	10
(subtotal)	(22%)	(40%)	(12%)	(24%)	(54%)	(38%)
Number of articles $N = 234$	38	41	34	33	38	50

*Exceeds 100% due to rounding.

York Times opinion column. Given their length, these articles may at first strike one as wide ranging, eloquent, and contemplative. Close readings reveal that they are invariably long on rhetoric within a narrow repertoire of themes and weak on evidence; they appear to restate the official position without advancing new substantive arguments or introducing fresh empirical evidence. As table 13.1 reveals, these articles were clustered thematically around (a) general discourses on globalization; (b) China–U.S. relations; and (c) China's "peaceful rise."

A preponderant amount of attention (58 percent) was focused on the United States. In sum, the elite press discourse was narrowly, reductively, and lopsidedly oriented toward the geopolitical implications of the United States to China's rite of passage to great-power status. The rise and decline of various media themes paralleled the official foreign policymaking process in tandem with internal power and ideological struggle over time. Take two examples: (a) General discourses on globalization rose to prominence in 2000 but quickly receded in significance and were replaced by the long-standing concern about "the U.S. factor"; (b) "Peaceful rise" saw a drastic and abrupt upsurge in 2004, only to quickly decline in 2005. "Globalization" was framed almost exclusively in terms of economic, military, and geopolitical considerations of China's rise, virtually to the exclusion of political globalization of human rights and democracy or cultural globalization of diversity and tolerance. In the absence of strong substantive arguments, constant appeals to revitalizing China's past cultural glory rang hallow and ritualistic.

Globalization

The discourse on globalization by the *Global Times* was rather skimpy: negative articles peaked in 2000 and tapered off but never died down (table 13.1). Globalization was first viewed as a stalking horse for strong Western nations and multinational companies to exploit the resources of—and impose harsh environmental standards on—the underdeveloped nations still struggling for basic survival. Writers were fond of quoting familiar Western leftist voices (Noam Chomsky, Immanuel Wallerstein, Andre Gunder Frank, and even the late C. Wright Mills), sometimes out of context, to denounce "globalization" as an instigator of widened North–South gaps, the digital divide, and cultural imperialism in the world. Much criticism was leveled at the U.S. "fallacy" of placing human rights above national sovereignty, thus "undermining China's core interests." Globalization was an "illusion" and "double standard" as Western countries might "light candles to mourn the 2,000 'civilized' lives in New York but would never burn incense for those 4,000 'barbarous' lives buried in Afghanistan."

Even amid the antiglobalization clamor, none of the writers argued that China should turn its back on globalization. "Discussing now whether China should join the process of globalization," a critic of globalization said wryly, "is tantamount to asking whether China should join the globe." Even staunch critics tended to "naturalize" globalization as an "inevitable" process: China has no choice but to be an active participant in order not to be marginalized or "smothered by the wave of globalization." Citing the anti-WTO protests in Seattle, a writer stated that the most formidable opponents of globalization came from the progressive forces within advanced capitalism itself. The *Global Times* held a forum in collaboration with Tsinghua University that concluded that participating in globalization did not amount to kowtowing to the United States, for no single hegemon could decide how things ought to be run and countervailing forces were expected to emerge.

Many writers claimed that globalization is neither a pitfall nor a myth. They argued that only through active participation in the international division of labor could China be expected to upgrade itself on the economic ladder, to capitalize on foreign capital and management, to keep up with the "technological revolution," and to compete successfully in the global market. Most narratives were mindful of the opportunities and challenges posed by globalization but came to conclude that the gains would be greater than the costs. Some writers advocated that China partake in globalization "fully," while others believed that China should enter into this process "creatively" and "selectively." Both sides were equally vague on the details. Once the overall state policy was set, it became rather easy to peg everything to the "globalization" frame. When anti-Japanese protests ran rampant in April 2005, Beijing was worried that the unrestrained spate of mass feelings might hurt other national interests or even turn against the regime itself. Instead of expressing Beijing's explicit disapproval of the protests in ways that contradict its own nationalistic rhetoric, two noted writers (one of whom was Wang Jisi, dean of the College of International Relations at Peking University) came out to call for public "reason and moderation." They argued that a boycott on Japanese goods "in the globalizing age" was not only futile but also damaging to China's external image. Globalization was used to hide the state's intended clampdown efforts.

China–U.S. Relations

Table 13.1 shows that the U.S.–China relationship accounted for at least half of the articles in any given year, even reaching 73 percent and 70 percent in 2002 and 2003. Overall, these articles could be characterized by a mixture of anxiety, anticipation, and deep ambivalence, even though the tone became somewhat moderate after the 9/11 event. In 2000, Wang Jisi urged the United States to abandon its "human rights diplomacy," which was rooted in the concepts of "manifest destiny" and "American exceptionalism." A writer took issue with the *Washington Post*'s accusation that Chinese media had exploited U.S. shortcomings to "prove" China's superiority. There was an abundance of other colorful yet less substantive caricatures of the United States.

During the two years after the watershed 9/11 attacks, the *Global Times* carried about a dozen articles on the topic. Two weeks after 9/11, the first article by Wang Jisi appeared, urging the United States to shed its exceptionalism, but he did not mention the event's implications to China. A second article appeared two months later, hinting that 9/11 reduced the tensions in U.S.–Russia and U.S.–China relationships. It took five months after September 11 for the sixth article to openly acknowledge that the U.S.–China relationship had been transformed from "strategic competition" to what Bush called "constructive cooperation." The slow and tentative reactions to an episode of global significance seemed to have synchronized with the pace at which China took pains to formulate an official position. Once the policy was set, the articles became predictably pegged to the 9/11 tragedy.

China and its media do not have much trust in the U.S.–led global order or the war on terrorism. For a long time, China had always viewed the United States "as a hegemonic power driven by the desire for world conquest."[39] In the post–Cold War era, the United States is—in Chinese media's eyes—intent on maintaining its superpower advantages through military interventions, the global imposition of a neoliberal economic regime, and the diffusion of American-cum-global values and ideologies. This sentiment was prevalent in the *Global Times*. Some writers even blamed terrorism and "hegemonism" as the twin threats to world peace. It was argued that Washington, having consolidated its hegemonic status, used the war on terrorism as an excuse to conduct a "great-power orchestra." But current criticisms were no longer cast in Leninist canons as in the past.

Global Times writers repeatedly proclaimed that the United States, due to its "Western ethnocentrism" and "white supremacy," did not wish to see China emerge as a strong country. Often cited was the "China threat" theme in various U.S. National Security strategy reports. After 9/11, Washington shifted its primary attention away from China to Afghanistan, but U.S. policy on China was said to remain unchanged. Instead, in the name of counterterrorism, it was argued that the United States has extended its sphere of influence into Central Asia, at China's doorstep. To "contain" China, Washington has allegedly tried to sow discord between China and Russia, and between China and India, while fostering military alliances with Japan. Despite these charges, however, the writers cautioned that the PRC should not be trapped by "anti-China elements" into repeating the Soviet mistake of having a full-scale confrontation with the United States, lest it detract from China's pursuit of its own development agendas. Running through all articles were the motifs of restraint and patience. These motifs followed the tone set by Deng Xiaoping after the Tiananmen crackdown. In order to pull China out of international isolation, Deng's policy revolved around three principles: *taoguang yanghui* (lie low and plow ahead), *bu duikang* (don't confront), and *bu chutou* (don't show off to make oneself a target).

Acquiescing to China's inability to alter U.S. superpower status, many writers urged China not to provoke the United States. Some of them argued that the PRC should be "Asia's China" (a regional power) rather than "the world's China" (a global power). Further, a stable relationship with the United States was portrayed as a key to China's "peaceful rise" and its long-term strategic interests.[40] To mute the "China threat" theme, they urged both countries to cooperate broadly on trade and commerce, counterterrorism, regional stability, environmental protection, and the fight against international crime, narcotics, and nuclear proliferation. Among the issues confronting the Sino–U.S. relationship, disputes over human rights have receded while trade and commercial ties have become more prominent in the media discourse. Unlike the Soviet Union's Cold War competition with the United States, the writers argued that China–U.S. ties should be based on practical (that is, economic) and compatible interests rather than ideological rivalry.

The *Global Times* organized several forums, each time featuring a Chinese expert and a U.S. or Western expert. Chinese interlocutors were Wang Jisi, Yan Xuetong, and Shi Yinhong, while noted U.S. China scholars included Harry Harding, David Lampton, David Shambaugh, and Susan Shirk.[41] U.S. scholars all agreed that the Chinese side tended to exaggerate the extent to which the United States seeks to make an enemy of China. Harding added that more Chinese regarded America as an enemy than the other way around. In reply, Wang Jisi said that Chinese perceive the United States as more significant than Americans perceive China; Americans see China as part of the global puzzle whereas the Chinese look to the United States as the key to their global situation. Lampton did not believe any external forces could really change a big country like China, nor would Washington create trouble for itself by antagonizing China. Taking an exception to Shi's complaint, Shambaugh noted that the bilateral relationship was already well institutionalized, but President Jiang Zemin's proposal to "build a just and fair world order allowing for diverse developmental models" was short on details. Shirk defended the United States for having a plurality of media voices. All four American guests were cautiously sympathetic to Taiwan's situation. Another visiting U.S. scholar wrote to criticize the prevailing pessimism among China's academic elite as not conducive to developing a healthier bilateral relationship. These exchanges confirmed Harding's earlier observation: "Through all shifts of mood, the common denominator has been high emotion, unrealistic hopes, exaggerated fears, and a mutual preoccupation verging on obsession."[42]

Peaceful Rise

As noted, the *Global Times*'s discourse on the global order was primarily linked to the legitimacy and prospect of China's "rise" as a great power. Table 13.1 reveals that the theme of "China's rise" was unevenly distributed: most prominent in 2004 (54 percent), rather weighty in 2001 and 2005 (around 40 percent), and modest in 2000 and 2003 (slightly more than 20 percent), but somewhat dormant in 2002 (12 percent). The considerable shifts are believed to reflect the emphasis and uncertainty of official policy over time.

Table 13.2 further summarizes the result of a keyword search in which "peaceful rise" was referenced. Despite the small frequencies, table 13.2 reveals three patterns. First, a dramatic jump from 12 to 194 references to "peaceful rise" in 2004 was followed by a sharp decline to 63 references in 2005, presumably mirroring a struggle among Chinese leaders. Second, the perceived U.S. attempts to suppress China's "peaceful rise" stood out as a major concern. Third, many narratives invoked traditional Chinese civilization and made historical comparisons with U.S., British, Japanese, and German rises, all to bolster the legitimacy of China's rise.

Table 13.2. Keyword Search on "Peaceful Rise" (Percent)

	2000	2001	2002	2003	2004*	2005
A "rising" China	18%	13%	14%	9%	11%	13%
Historical context and legitimacy of China's rise	0%	20%	3%	0%	19%	6%
Weakness in China's "rise"	0%	7%	6%	0%	1%	3%
Can "rise peacefully" as a responsible power	12%	0%	3%	17%	45%	15%
U.S. contains China's "rise"	29%	33%	71%	58%	11%	31%
General references to other national "rises"	41%	27%	3%	16%	14%	32%
N = 336	(17)	(15)	(35)	(12)	(194)	(63)

*Exceeds 100% due to rounding.

A "great power" complex, mixed with 150 years of national humiliation at the hands of foreign powers, has foregrounded all enlightenment and revolutionary movements in modern China. In sharp contrast to the gloom and despair of the late 1980s, China has found considerable self-confidence verging on a self-congratulatory and neurotic search for world greatness.[43] This shift of national psychology was obvious in the *Global Times*. In echoing official rhetoric, many writers declared that never in the past two centuries was the condition or time more favorable for China to rise onto the world stage. It was argued that China must "grab" the unprecedented opportunities to profit from technological progress in an expanded world market, to become a big winner, and to revive Chinese glory. This "rise" was presented as an "inevitable" order of things: it was said that China would "do the world a disservice if it did not rise."

Occasionally sober voices were heard, mindful of the fact that China is a poor big country and will take another half a century to achieve a middle-income status. In view of the Soviet experience, they maintained that China must keep a low profile and avoid overzealous publicity of its own achievements for fear of being made a scapegoat. It was suggested that China continued to face a severe external environment. To allay the "China threat" fear, some writers advocated that China should build its reputation as a "responsible great power" (thus coinciding with Washington's calls for China to become a "responsible stakeholder") by actively participating in the defense of world peace and security. But a somewhat skeptical writer questioned whether China was ready to pay the dues to defend world peace.

Playing the role as a "responsible great power" in the world order was one of the policy themes promulgated by former President Jiang Zemin at the Sixteenth Party Congress in 2002. He himself had previously suppressed opposition from the orthodox left within his party that accused him of "betraying communism." Since 2002 the media have echoed a change of priority in foreign policy agendas, with "managing the great-power relationship" rising to the top, followed by a "good neighbor" policy, and aligning with the third world coming in third. Calls were constantly made in the *Global Times* for "cooperating with big nations." As a far cry from the Maoist revolutionary rhetoric, the paper now paid lip service to China's "responsibility" to "speak for the third world." In this context, China has invested heavily in Western countries and has provided huge aid programs to third-world countries (especially in Africa) without imposing human rights provisions as does the U.S. aid program.[44]

Even though premiers Zhu Rongji and Wen Jiabao continued to condemn "hegemonism, strong-power politics and all forms of terrorism" in their annual government work reports to the National People's Congress, China has refrained from directly challenging the United States since 2002. Wang Jisi similarly argued that maintaining a stable and nonconfrontational relationship with the United States is essential to China's achieving modernization goals.[45] Another writer used "cold peace" to depict the China–U.S. relationship. Many writers emphasized that inasmuch as China did not have the capacity or the intention to challenge the United States' world status or to drive the U.S. influence out of Asia, China should play a "responsible" great-power role *within* the existing global order. They argued that China should navigate a middle course between extreme globalism and extreme patriotism. The "Shanghai Cooperative Organization" comprising China, Russia, and four countries from Central Asia has been cited as a model of the "good neighbor" policy.

"Peaceful rise" suddenly came into vogue in 2004, the term generally credited to Zheng Bijian, a policy advisor to President Hu Jintao. According to Zheng, "Once all of [China's] potential is mobilized, its contribution to the world as an engine of growth will be unprecedented."[46] It is interesting to observe in table 13.2 that there was a nineteen-fold increase in the use of the term from 2003 to 2004, only to abruptly decline by two-thirds from a peak of 194 to 64 references in 2005. The term, seen by some as contradiction in terms, was soon to be replaced by "peaceful development." Wang Gunwu, an overseas historian, characterized the current "rise" as the fourth in Chinese history; similarly, the *Economist* framed it as "reaching for a renaissance."[47] Historical cases of Western powers were invoked in the *Global Times*: Britain and the United States rose through colonial expansion, imperialist wars, plunder, and monopoly capital; postwar Germany and

Japan owed their rises to U.S. protection; but this time China will rely on "globalization" to achieve greatness.

How should China play a vital part in the making of global rules of the game? Many writers suggested that China could uphold the Confucian values of harmony, peace, *dayitong* (grand unity), moderation, and *ren* (benevolence) to make a more enlightened and humane world possible. Without spelling out how, these statements may sound like empty slogans to most outside observers. To essentialize Confucianism as embodying what's best about Chinese civilization risks obfuscating the multifaceted complexity and contradictions of Confucian ethos that have been practiced over the centuries. It also invites questions as to why the communist regime had tried to eradicate the Confucian ethos. It was commented that the current Communist Party leadership seems to take advantage of Confucianism as a tool to teach people "respect for authority" so they would "accept their place" without challenging party rule.[48]

A Fudan University writer claimed in the *Global Times* that China should not only "rise in peace" (by aligning with the international political economy) but also "rise peacefully" (via good great-power ties) and "rise for peace." Another writer argued that opposite to the traditional Chinese strategy of *yuanjiao jingong* (to attack the states nearby by befriending distant ones), China should foster an Asian alliance and regional integration. Hau Yufan, an otherwise calm China-born scholar in America, was as hawkish on Taiwan as any of the establishment intellectuals in China, maintaining that China should maintain strong military deterrence against Taiwan and exert pressure on Taipei through Washington. Uneven development and environmental deterioration were at times broached, but democratic reform was a nonissue. Yan Xuetong, a noted international relations expert, asserted that national security (read: military power) was more important than economic benefits; in a different article, he tried to measure overall national strength in terms of the number of Olympic medals earned. In both cases he was rebutted by other writers.

Pei Minxin, director of the China Program at the Carnegie Endowment for International Peace, wrote an article in the *Global Times* faulting China for its weakness on what Nye calls "soft power."[49] To build up "soft power," he opined that China should capitalize on the extensive network of the Chinese diaspora and draw rich resources from "open-minded Chinese cultural values" to build a compelling political ideology "with Chinese characteristics" that is able to "balance the Western value system founded at its core by 'freedom and democracy.'" Having announced this high principle, he did not say what sort of Chinese ideology he had in mind. Elsewhere, in an English article published in the United States, Pei painted a much darker picture of China's "developmental autocracy" as using economic development to enhance the legitimacy of authoritarianism instead of promoting democracy.[50] Within China, Pei promoted "Chinese ideology" to counterbalance Western "freedom and democracy," but in the United States he criticized China for its poor record in "freedom and democracy." The gap was glaring. His English treatise, if translated, would have little hope of seeing the light of the day in the *Global Times*.

Conclusion

China did not officially attend to globalization until 1997, when the theme was written into the Fifteenth Party Congress report, with the impetus arising from Beijing's enthusiasm to enter the WTO. Analyzing the *Global Times* has thrown light on media discourses among leading members of official think tanks. As a whole, they portrayed China as a winner in the globalization process. If the United States is "bound to lead," then China is "bound to rise." Overseas, there have been some discussions on whether the "Beijing consensus" offers an alternative to the "Washington consensus." Among the protagonists of the Beijing consensus is the Nobel laureate in economics Joseph Stiglitz, while *New York Times*'s Howard W. French is one of its antagonists.[51] The *Global Times* has been virtually mute on this topic.

This chapter shows that the Chinese elite and authorities have been, for the most part, interested only in economic globalization: cultivating foreign capital, markets, and technology. They are determined to keep such "bourgeois thought" as democracy and human rights out of China's media. "The global" seems almost synonymous with China–U.S. ties, "globalization" is reducible to economic and geopolitical opportunities for China to rise as a great power, and "the national" means a Beijing-defined national interest. Wang Jisi represents the official position when he claims that China has everything ready for its rise, except for Washington's cooperation.[52] In contrast, Pei, an overseas scholar, is sharply critical of China's neo-Leninist state as more likely to "experience decay than democracy." He doubts that this flawed system—fraught with crony capitalism, rampant corruption, and widening inequality—can "pass a stress test."[53]

Media discourses in the *Global Times* are state-defined and disregard subnational or subcultural perspectives. "Our nation" is assumed to have a *single* unified position, and no other. The views expressed are incredibly one-dimensional, one-sided, instrumental, and homogeneous. They toe the shifting official line and do not introduce alternative voices into the unauthorized public sphere. While opinion surveys showed that urban Chinese condemned U.S. hegemony but admired its domestic way of life,[54] media discourses in this analysis concentrated on the hegemonic aspect. Seldom do they raise issues about the enormous problems and costs associated with China's rise. Speaking among elites and to other subelites, these policy enunciators are highly articulate, loquacious, and repetitive. They absorb, comply with, and reproduce the official line. They thus reinforce one another's views and sentiments as insiders of a semiofficial elite circle, fitting aptly into what Wu describes as "one head, many mouths."[55]

Many writers have tried to promote President Hu's proclaimed policy to build "a harmonious society" (*hexie shehui*) and "a harmonious world." A harmonious world may mean "smile diplomacy."[56] If traditional or Confucian values are to be privileged as a tool for maintaining regime stability at home and advancing "soft power" abroad, the regime has not faced up to its Maoist persecution of Confucianism as a "feudal" totality. It was, above all, crucial to know that Confucius took pains to differentiate the gentleman's (*junzi*) way of "agreeing without being an echo" (*he er butong*) from the little man's (*xiaoren*) way of "echoing without being in agreement" (*tong er buhe*).[57] If Confucianism preaches the virtue of consensus and tolerance (*he*), Beijing's promulgation of a "harmonious society" and a "harmonious world" seems to call for ideological conformity (*tong*). While the writers demand a multilateral and more "democratic" global order, they make no mention of the need for a more diverse and more democratic domestic order.

All articles tend to be declarative, not expository or argumentative—long on general rhetoric but silent on the specific modus operandi. Assuming away historical continuities and ruptures, they do not explain why China embraces global capitalism and breaks away from its socialist past. They tend to play up and generalize the policy influences of think tanks, media talks, academic reports, or popular writing in the United States, especially when China is unfavorably portrayed. They take pride in and yet feel insecure about China's future. As a whole, they are preoccupied with the "American threat." While making globalization a culprit of world injustice, they overlook its negative impact on China's stratification and environment. They intersperse the themes of counterhegemony and antiunilateralism with those of "lying low" as a "responsible great power." They have never answered why China supports oil-rich "rogue countries."

In sum, economic growth and nationalism have been the main sources of regime legitimacy for China since the 1990s. What is different in the current turn of events is that vast and rapid economic growth has further fueled China's nationalistic yearnings for a rise to greatness in the era of globalization. As the only marketized elite foreign-news paper, the *Global Times* has thrived by constructing state-approved discourses that regard China as one of the winners of globalization, albeit with the mixed blessing of the United States. From time to time, with the *Global Times* as an instrument and a partner, the state has also highlighted the United States as "the Other" to divert public attention away from domestic discontent. They have colluded to take advantage of nationalism while trying to contain it within an official trajectory. The *Global Times* owes its success to its ability to strategically fill the foreign-news vacuum with commentary that is more vividly and emotionally written than that of its domestic-news peers. It plays a key role in cultivating elite consciousness and shaping popular consensus in China. The newspaper also serves as an important platform that articulates and reveals the will and wishes of China's foreign-policy makers before the global community of nations.

Acknowledgments

This chapter is part of the larger project, "Negotiating with Media Globalization: The Impact of China's Accession to WTO on its Media and Telecommunications Industry," supported with funds from the Research Grants Committee of Hong Kong (CityU 1246/03H). Further support from the Center for Communication Research at the City University of Hong Kong is also gratefully acknowledged. Thanks are due to Dr. Yinjuan Yang for her assistance in data collection and to Professor Yu Huang and Professor Michael Curtin for their feedback on an earlier version of this chapter.

Notes

1. Immanuel Wallerstein, "Geopolitical strategies of the U.S. in a post-American world," in *Beyond National Sovereignty: International Communication in the 1990s*, ed. Kaarle Nordenstreng and Herbert I. Schiller (Norwood, NJ: Ablex, 1993).

2. Herbert I. Schiller, *Mass Communication and American Empire*, 2nd ed. (Boulder, Colo.: Westview, 1992).

3. Joseph S. Nye, *Bound to Lead: The Changing Nature of American Power* (New York: Basic, 1990).

4. Condoleezza Rice, "Transformational diplomacy," http://www.state.gov/r/pa/prs/ps/2006/59339.htm, dated 18 January 2006 (accessed 11 March 2006).

5. Francis Fukuyama, *The End of History and the Last Man* (New York: Free Press, 1992); Samuel Huntington, "The clash of civilizations," *Foreign Affairs* 71, no. 3 (1993): 22–49.

6. Edward W. Said, *Culture and Imperialism* (New York: Knopf, 1993), xvii.

7. John Tomlinson, *Globalization and Culture* (Chicago: University of Chicago Press, 1999); Roland Robertson, *Globalization* (London: Sage, 1992).

8. Chin-Chuan Lee, Joseph Man Chan, Zhongdang Pan, and Clement Y. K. So, *Global Media Spectacle: News War over Hong Kong* (Albany: State University of New York Press, 2002).

9. Mike Featherstone, *Undoing Culture* (London: Sage, 1995), 108.

10. Featherstone, *Undoing Culture*, 111.

11. Edward W. Said, *Covering Islam* (New York: Pantheon, 1981); Lee et al., *Global Media Spectacle*.

12. Gerald Segal, "Does China matter?" *Foreign Affairs* 78, no. 5 (1999): 24–36.

13. David M. Lampton, "Paradigm lost: The demise of 'weak China,'" *National Interest* 81 (2005): 73–80.

14. Said, *Culture and Imperialism*, 5.

15. Edward Herman and Noam Chomsky, *Manufacturing Consent* (New York: Pantheon, 1988).

16. Chin-Chuan Lee, "Mass media: Of China, about China," in *Voices of China: The Interplay of Politics and Journalism*, ed. Chin-Chuan Lee (New York: Guilford Press, 1990), 3–32.

17. Harry Harding, *A Fragile Relationship: The United States and China since 1979* (Washington, D.C.: Brookings Institution, 1992), 201.

18. Chin-Chuan Lee, "Established pluralism: U.S. media discourse about China policy," *Journalism Studies* 3 (2002): 383–397.

19. Guangqiu Xu, "Anti-Western nationalism in China, 1989–99," *World Affairs* 163 (2001): 151–62; Suisheng Zhao, "Chinese nationalism and its international orientations," *Political Science Quarterly* 115, no. 1 (2000): 1–33.

20. Chin-Chuan Lee, "The global and the national of the Chinese media: Discourses, market, technology, and ideology," in *Chinese Media, Global Contexts*, ed. Chin-Chuan Lee (London: Routledge-Curzon, 2003), 2.

21. Yu Huang and Chin-Chuan Lee, "Peddling party ideology for a profit: Media and the rise of Chinese nationalism in the 1990s," in *Political Communication in Greater China*, ed. Gary Rawnsley and Ming-yeh Rawnsley (London: Routledge-Curzon, 2003), 41–61.

22. Yuezhi Zhao, "Enter the world: Neo-liberal globalization, the dream for a strong nation, and Chinese press discourses on the WTO," in *Chinese Media, Global Contexts*, 32–56.

23. Yunxiang Yan, "Managed globalization: State power and cultural transition in

China," in *Many Globalizations: Cultural Diversity in the Contemporary World*, ed. Peter L. Berger and Samuel P. Huntington (New York: Oxford University Press, 2000), 19–47.

24. For recent analyses, see Chin-Chuan Lee, Zhou He, and Yu Huang, "Party-market corporatism, clientelism, and media in Shanghai," *Harvard International Journal of Press/Politics* 12, no. 3 (2007): 21–42; Chin-Chuan Lee, Zhou He, and Yu Huang, "Chinese Party Publicity Inc. conglomerated: The case of the Shenzhen Press Group," *Media, Culture & Society* 28 (2006): 581–602.

25. Xijin Hu, "lajin 'quanqiu' he 'yanqiu' de juli" (Bring "globalization" and "eyeballs" closer). *Qingnian jizhe zazhi* (Young Journalists Magazine), http://www.xinwenren.com/Article_show2.asp?ArticleID=6515 (accessed 11 March 2006).

26. Interview (anonymous), Beijing, 12 April 2007. The informant disclosed that the Foreign Ministry subscribes to 600 copies of the *Global Times* every day.

27. Zuyu Liu, "jianchi yulun daoxiang, zhengqu zuijia xuanchuan xiaoguo" (Stick to the correct opinion orientation, strive for the best propaganda effect), http://www.china.com.cn/chinese/zhuanti/hpdl/1099446.htm, 10 November 2004 (accessed 11 March 2006).

28. Xiguang Li and Yanan Lu, "huanqiu shibao de yicheng shezhi" (The *Global Times* sets the agenda), http://www.people.com.cn/GB/14677/21963/22063/2978344.html, 10 November 2004 (accessed 11 March 2006).

29. Huang and Lee, "Peddling party ideology for a profit."

30. Interview (anonymous), Beijing, 12 April 2007.

31. Jie Wu, "quanqiu shibao de 2006" (*Global Times 2006*), http://media.people.com.cn/GB/35928/36356/3880092.html, 22 November 2005 (accessed 11 March 2006).

32. William Griffith, "Communist esoteric communication: *Explication de texte*," in *Handbook of Communication*, ed. Wilbur Schramm and Ithiel de Sola Pool (Chicago: Rand McNally, 1973), 512–520.

33. See note 26.

34. Carol Lee Hamrin and Timothy Cheek, eds., *China's Establishment Intellectuals* (Armonk, NY: Sharpe, 1986), 3–4.

35. David Shambaugh, *Beautiful Imperialist: China Perceives America, 1972–1990* (Princeton, NJ: Princeton University Press, 1991).

36. Among the fifty-nine writers in 2005, 68 percent came from four leading universities (Peking, Tsinghua, Renmin, and Fudan) or major think tanks (particularly, the Chinese Academy of Social Sciences and the College of International Relations), and 14 percent were identified as senior journalists.

37. Among them were Jisi Wang (dean, College of International Relations, Peking University), Xuetong Yan (director, Institute of International Problems, Tsinghua University), Yinhong Shi (director, Institute of American Studies, Renmin University of China), Shulong Chu (Tsinghua University), Feng Zhu (professor of international relations, Peking University), and Yufan Hau (professor of political science, Colgate University, Hamilton, N.Y.).

38. William A. Gamson, "A constructionist approach to mass media and public

opinion," *Symbolic Interactionism* 11 (1988): 161–74; William A. Gamson and Andre Modigliani, "Media discourse and public opinion on nuclear power: A constructionist approach," *American Journal of Sociology* 95 (1989): 1–37.

39. Shambaugh, *Beautiful Imperialist*, 301.

40. Jisi Wang, "China's search for stability with America," *Foreign Affairs* 84, no. 5 (2005): 39.

41. Harding-Yan, 9 August 2002; Lampton-Wang, 22 October 2002; Shambaugh-Shi, 12 December 2002; Shirk-Wang, 16 January 2004.

42. Harding, *A Fragile Relationship*, 358.

43. As a historical footnote, the "peaceful rise" discourse recalls and contrasts with the "global membership" (*qiu ji*) debate that occurred in 1988 (only to be suffocated in 1989). Both media instigators were closely allied with the ruling authorities. Although the *Global Times* is a favored barometer of Beijing's foreign policy climate, the *World Economic Journal* was tied with the political fortunes of the reform bureaucracy under Premier Zhao Ziyang. "Peaceful rise" promotes national pride in a post–Cold War world order, whereas the "membership" debate warned that China might be "expelled from global citizenship" for lack of political and economic reform. The latter admired the United States as a model of good society, while the former is feeling good about China but ambivalent about the United States.

44. "The great game: A 14–page special report on China and its region," *Economist* 31 March 2007.

45. Wang, "China's search for stability with America."

46. Bijian Zheng, "China's 'peaceful rise' to great-power status," *Foreign Affairs* 84, no. 5 (2005): 18.

47. "The great game," *Economist*, 3.

48. "Confucius makes a comeback," *Economist* (19 May 2007): 36.

49. Nye, *Bound to Lead*.

50. Minxin Pei, "The dark side of China's rise," *Foreign Policy* 153 (2006): 32–40.

51. Joseph Stiglitz, "Development in defiance of the Washington consensus," *Guardian* 13 April 2006; Howard W. French, "Is it a 'peaceful rise'? U.S. shouldn't bet on it," *International Herald Tribune*, 20 April 2006. Joshua Ramo of the Foreign Policy Center, who first coined the term "Beijing consensus," argued that China has a ruthless willingness to innovate, a strong belief in sovereignty and multilateralism, and a desire to accumulate the tools of "asymmetric power projection." It is intent on projecting enough "asymmetric power" to limit U.S. political and military action in its region.

52. Wang, "China's search for stability with America."

53. Pei, "The dark side of China's rise."

54. For an analysis of a large-scale survey dataset, see Chin-Chuan Lee, Charles Man, Francis Lee, Wan-ying Lin, Mike Yao, and Zhou He, "Imagining the United States as the 'ambivalent other': The impact of nationalism and media use in China," Center for Communication Research, City University of Hong Kong; Stanley Rosen, "Chinese media and youth: Attitudes toward nationalism and internationalism," in *Chinese Media, Global Contexts*, 97–118.

55. Guoguang Wu, "One head, many mouths: Diversifying press structures in reform China," in *Power, Money, and Media: Communication Patterns and Bureaucratic Control in Cultural China*, ed. Chin-Chuan Lee (Evanston, IL: Northwestern University Press, 2000), 45–67.

56. "The great game," *Economist*, 6.

57. Confucius, *The Analects*, trans. D. C. Lau (London: Penguin, 1976): 122.

FOURTEEN

Chinese Techno-Nationalism and Global Wifi Policy

Jack Linchuan Qiu

China is widely perceived as the "workshop of the world," home to factories that produce more than 25 percent of the world's textiles and some 90 percent of the toys. The growth of such industries fueled the country's transformation from a largely agrarian society into an increasingly modern and urban society that is heavily dependent on international trade. Most of the industries driving this transformation tend to employ relatively unskilled workers who are paid low wages. Yet if China is to continue to improve its economy, it must begin to compete in high-wage industries, like media, computers, and telecommunications. To do so, China must begin to develop innovative technology standards that will be adopted by others around the world. Chinese policymakers and high-tech companies are avidly pursuing these goals, argues Jack Qiu, driven in part by economic necessity and in part by nationalist passions that imagine China as a global leader in technologies of the future.

Computer, electronics, and telecommunications—often known collectively as the information technology (IT) industry—form a crucial component of globalization. In addition to providing a basic infrastructure fundamental to processes of international and global communication,[1] they also engender highly globalized networks of financing, designing, manufacturing, and distributing IT goods and services. These networks constitute a "global

Advertisements for wireless Internet services in Shenzhen, Guangdong Province (photograph by Jack Linchuan Qiu).

assembly line"[2] built on a largely hierarchical set of relationships between core players (for example, those in Silicon Valley) and relatively more peripheral players (such as low-wage electronics factories in China or low-end call centers in India). Will this traditional international division of labor persist? Will it be transformed with the rise of Asian economies, especially with China as an "engine of growth"[3] for the global IT industry?

For more than a decade, China has led the world in labor-intensive electronics manufacturing, but in recent years rising wages and burgeoning techno-nationalism have encouraged Chinese policymakers and executives to reposition the electronics industry toward a higher, more strategic position in the global assembly line. According to policy discourse, China can no longer afford to be simply a low-cost workshop for the world; it must also become a designer and initiator of new IT products. This means China must begin to establish global technological standards of its own, ones that work to China's advantage.[4] Toward this end, tremendous resources have been invested in the research and development (R&D) of new IT standards. This chapter focuses on a particular example of this larger process, concerning a Chinese Wifi (wireless-fidelity) security standard called WAPI (WLAN Authentication and Privacy Infrastructure), which spurred a major dispute in the global wireless Internet industry in 2003–2006, resulting in outbursts of techno-nationalist sentiments among Chinese "netizens" and strained relations between China and the United States.

Before examining the specifics of this case, it is important to note that this dispute is by no means an isolated development. In recent years, China has rolled out a series of high-tech standards that have caused transnational "standards wars" in many markets including video discs, home networking, and 3G mobile communication.[5] Another example is digital television, as the Chinese standard was developed to create distinctive products for its huge domestic market. Instead of licensing technology from outside, this move is believed to be a crucial step in developing a television system that is financed and designed in China, as well as manufactured and assembled there. In the long run, it is hoped that the domestic market for digital television equipment might serve as a springboard for further innovation and for the adoption of the Chinese system in other countries.[6]

Similarly, with respect to wireless Internet, China has been searching for innovations and standards that might elevate Chinese technology to a higher status in the global hierarchy. This chapter explores the struggles and debates surrounding the WAPI standards because Wifi is among the most rapidly growing technologies worldwide, opening doors to many new applications and creating considerable market opportunities. With so much riding on the fortunes of Wifi, companies and countries are angling for technical standards that will work to their advantage. Unlike ten years ago, China is now one of those competitors. As this chapter will show, a variety of Chinese players promoted the development of a distinctive set of Chinese standards to pursue a techno-nationalist agenda. As a result, despite the highly globalized nature of the IT industry, we see in this case a peculiar persistence of national culture and national politics. Just as importantly, the controversy over technical standards also blossomed online, where thousands of Chinese netizens, especially bloggers acting as opinion leaders, debated the virtues of Chinese standards and of techno-nationalism itself. As this seems to indicate, the top leadership of PRC no longer monopolizes the power to define national interest with respect to IT industries. In other words, cultural and structural change triggered by globalization is not only antecedent but also integral to the formation of techno-nationalism itself.

This chapter begins with a discussion on techno-nationalism and its evolution in Chinese history. It then describes the dispute over the Chinese Wifi standard, explains the logic behind the policy and the trade struggles that ensued, and shows why this case is a key to understanding China's active role in the transnational IT industry. Finally, it discusses how online deliberations became an important driver in the policy process, indicating one of the ways in which the Internet is becoming a new site of public engagement beyond the direct control of the Chinese Communist Party (CCP) and the Chinese government. In so doing, this chapter argues that one of the most important changes in the global economy during the twenty-first century will be the emergence of countries like China and India as central players in technology innovation and development. It further suggests that if China is to truly play a role, the Chinese government must encourage the growth of public deliberation while also seeking to temper the fires of nationalism that are now emerging in the global IT industry.

The Evolution of Techno-Nationalism

Techno-nationalism is the pursuit for the technological prowess of a nation, which is culturally rooted in the traditions of nationalism and institutionally expressed through concrete political economy structures and processes.[7] It is a common phenomenon among modern nation-states but has escalated in recent decades due to a general sense of crisis triggered by globalization, thus constituting yet another instance of what Castells calls "the power of identity."[8]

Historically, techno-nationalism has long been an integral part of modern nation-building, for example, since the time of Alexander Hamilton in the United States.[9] But as an explicit concept, it was a creation of the 1980s when the rise of Japan posed an unprecedented challenge to U.S. dominance in high-tech sectors.[10] In other words, the concept of techno-nationalism was invented in the first place to address a particular mode of friction in the global high-tech market. According to McDougall, the concept means "the institutionalization of technological change for state purposes, that is, the state-funded and -managed R&D explosion" and the articulation of the critical importance of the technological prowess in international competition.[11] Green identifies three basic stages of techno-nationalism in Japan: first, "import-substituting indigenization," meaning key foreign technologies need to be acquired and produced domestically through different manners of technology transfer; second, newly acquired technology and technical know-how being diffused throughout the economy; and third, the creation of policies to build domestic capacities to innovate and manufacture better technological products beyond the initial imported prototypes.[12]

Techno-nationalism is, of course, not a unique Japanese development. Although the concept is commonly linked to the rapid rise of Japan as a global technology leader in the 1980s, Ostry and Nelson contend that it is a common response for all modern powers to address "market failure" in the high-tech sector.[13] Although specific forms vary, techno-nationalism has taken shape under the different institutional circumstances in the United States and Japan, as well as the United Kingdom, France, and Germany. Through their account of techno-nationalism in these various countries, Ostry and Nelson find that (a) public institutions, especially universities, play a fundamental role; (b) each of these countries relies on "a diverse collection of government agencies" rather than "a central government office" in pursuing its high-tech policies; and (c) techno-nationalism is often closely connected with military institutions.[14]

China was once the most advanced technological power in the world,[15] but it went into a prolonged period of stagnation until the Opium War (1839–42) woke it up to the painful reality of technological inferiority. As a result, there is a very strong historical connection between China's technology policy and its military programs. The first Chinese-owned telegraph line, for example, was built in Taiwan in 1877 by the Qing government in order to mobilize troops against Japanese encroachment to the island.[16] State-led technology initiatives continued through the Republican era (1911–49) and reached further heights after the founding of the PRC in 1949. After tasting the bitterness of technological inferiority again during the Korean War, PRC leaders gave priority to the development of "strategic weaponry."[17] They exploded a nuclear bomb in 1964, launched a satellite in 1970, sent a man to space in 2003, and destroyed an obsolete satellite with a China-made missile in January 2007, all causing surprise to much of the world.

But is techno-nationalism the only formation here? Like elsewhere, the prominence of techno-nationalism in China results primarily from the dominant role of the modern nation-state in allocating power and resources. But national sovereignty has been eroded by what Ostry and Nelson term "techno-globalization," as multinational corporations (MNCs) set up branch offices around the world. Meanwhile, at least equally important are regional formations both below and beyond the national level that have become increasingly central to high-tech industries around the world. Although the importance of subnational regions like Silicon Valley or Shanghai and the Yangtze River Delta is obvious, techno-nationalism remains the most prominent cultural and institutional formation. "Techno-regionalism" may in some cases be influential, but in countries like China, the central government in Beijing still tries to insist on the principle of national planning and national sovereignty.[18]

Nevertheless, Chinese techno-nationalism is shaped by subnational forces and by transnational regional dynamics in Asia Pacific, especially with respect to Japan and the Asian "tiger" economies.[19] Despite their differences, these countries all have state-led policy environments designed to foster high-tech industries, and the effects of these policies have spilled over to the PRC. It is against this backdrop that we observe the continued centrality of the national government in China's high-tech sector in the aftermath of the Asian financial crisis and the global IT slowdown at the turn of the century.

The developmental state provides tremendous support to domestic enterprises in the form of R&D, financing, and the market structuring of domestic commerce and international trade.[20] But why should the national government extend its visible or invisible hands to the domestic IT companies? Why cannot firms, local governments, or supranational organizations play a larger role in dealing with "market failure"? The rationalization necessarily draws upon and feeds back into techno-nationalism, particularly with regard to the issue of national security because, after all, military systems are almost exclusively national.[21]

As Feigenbaum demonstrates through historical analysis, there has been "a powerful set of ideas about the relationship between the state, technology, and national power in China" since the founding of the PRC.[22] Two of the most fundamental themes during and after Mao's age include "technology as a matter of grand strategy" and "self-reliance as a strategy of technological development."[23] The idea of self-reliance (*ziligengsheng*) is particularly crucial to justifying indigenization policies and providing a basis for China's long-standing attempts to establish itself as an independent technology power. Through this analysis, Feigenbaum finds that China's high-tech achievements, even during Mao's era, have less to do with the traditional Stalinist-style system of command and control and more to do with a structure of "innovative management institutions" that are "more akin to those in contemporary Silicon Valley, based on initiative, personal incentives, risk-taking, and networks of cooperation among experts."[24]

Feigenbaum's argument is consistent with Ostry and Nelson's finding that techno-nationalism does not have to be centered on a single state agency that controls the high-tech sector in a hierarchical manner. Rather, it is often based on a relatively flexible network linking multiple players in government, research institutes, and the military. This has become even more salient in China since 1978, when actors in the business sector, especially nongovernmental enterprises, started to play a notable role.[25]

In recent years, a consensus emerged from discussion among Chinese policymakers, entrepreneurs, and researchers that the country cannot continue to be just a manufacturer and subcontractor in the global IT industry.[26] It needs to move up the value chain and establish its "own" intellectual property rights over the process of production and profit allocation. Hence the popular saying: "Third-rank firms make products; second-rank firms make brands; first-rank firms make standards (*sanliuqiye zuochanpin, erliuqiye zuopingpai; yiliuqiye zuobiaozhun*)."

On the issue of "standards wars," Kennedy offers a structural analysis of the various Chinese initiatives that lie at the heart of China's techno-nationalist ambition.[27] Through this analysis, he concludes that the industrial coalition behind WAPI is "narrow and weak relative to the coalitions formed by their foreign competitors," but some other attempts "such as those in home networking, have attracted a broader base of support and as a result show genuine commercial promise."[28] This may be a sound conclusion because, after all, coalition building is always vital to success in political economy processes. But, as will be shown in the following, Chinese techno-nationalism needs to be construed not only as structures of coalition and competition relationships but also as a complex set of historical and discursive formations that shape the dynamic process of China's integration into the global IT marketplace. WAPI advocates may exhibit a relatively "narrow and weak" web of connections, as Kennedy contends, but the cultural and communication processes behind the WAPI standards dispute are certainly of much larger relevance when the issue at stake is techno-nationalism rather than the outcome of any particular dispute. With much malleability, techno-nationalist discourses reflect, reinforce, but also transform coalition structures, which is crucial to our understanding of emerging IT powers such as China and India in the twenty-first century.

The Rise and Fall of WAPI

WAPI is a wireless Internet communication standard developed in China. It is supposed to work on top of Wifi, although compatibility is disputable according to the Institute of Electrical and Electronics Engineers (IEEE). The IEEE is incorporated in New York and its Wifi 802.11i standard, also known as WPA2, is the main competitor against WAPI.

The development of WAPI has gone through three phases: (1) incubation phase from early 1990s to spring 2003, (2) national launch phase from May 2003 to fall 2004, and (3) the global competition phase from November 2004 to March 2006. First, during the incubation period, the central player was IWNComm (Xidian jietong), a company in China's northwestern city of Xi'an, whose members have been conducting research on mobile Internet since the early 1990s. During the Maoist era, Xi'an was a key base for military R&D, including telecommunications, which left a legacy of high-tech research in the city.[29] In particular, IWNComm is a spinoff from Xi'an Telecommunications University (Xidian), which enjoyed grants from China's high-tech 863 Plan and the National Natural Science Foundation.[30]

In July 2001, the Ministry of Information Industry (MII) formally assigned the task of designing a national wireless Internet protocol to IWNComm, Xidian, and several IT companies and research institutes. The group was named China Broadband Wireless IP Standards Working Group (BWIPS), which is the most crucial organization to the fostering of WAPI. BWIPS has ten founding members, including six firms and research institutes based in the inland cities of Xi'an, Wuhan, and Guilin, while the other four are located in Beijing, including three national-level state agencies. All leading IT players in Shanghai, Guangzhou, or Shenzhen were conspicuously missing from this coalition. Given the fact that most of China's IT industry is geographically concentrated in its southern and eastern coastal regions, the overwhelming representation of inland firms and institutes in the initial setup of BWIPS signals a peculiar geography of techno-nationalism in China.

BWIPS expanded to comprise twenty-seven new members such as Tsinghua University, ZTE, and Lenovo in just a few years. In addition to MII, three key state agencies formed alliances with the BWIPS, including the Standardization Administration of China (SAC), State Encryption Management Committee (SEMC), and State Council Information Office (SCIO). Yet, BWIPS still had not incorporated telecom operators such as China

Mobile and China Telecom, probably because the telecom operators were already providing mobile Internet services using the Wifi standard. At this point, BWIPS also failed to include China's largest Internet equipment manufacturer, Huawei, or any of the MNCs like Intel.

Three months after the establishment of BWIPS, China entered the WTO in November 2001. The Chinese government subsequently adjusted its high-tech policy, attaching more importance to the R&D of technical standards.[31] With increasing support from the government and additional member organizations, BWIPS finished drafting the two standards—GB 15629.11 and GB 15629.1102—in November 2002. Collectively known as the WAPI standards, the draft went out for a short period of public consultation between December 2002 and January 2003. An evaluation session for WAPI was held on January 8, 2003, when a team of Chinese IT experts endorsed the new standards.

The WAPI standards were formally issued on May 15, 2003, marking the beginning of the national launch phase. On July 9, it was announced that the new standards would be mandatorily implemented starting on December 31, 2003. The right to use the standards in manufacturing wireless Internet equipment was granted exclusively to twenty-four domestic companies for free.[32] Dismayed by the promulgation of WAPI with such a short notice and the perceived discrimination against foreign firms, the MNCs protested against WAPI. After all, they had developed a wide range of Wifi products that would have been "outlawed" in China due to their lack of access to the new standards. This also appeared to be a technical barrier to market entry, which generated concern that China was not operating in the spirit of the WTO. Responding to these complaints, Chinese authorities issued a new deadline, postponing the mandatory implementation of WAPI standards to June 1, 2004.

This compromise by the Chinese government marked the beginning of the end for the proposed standard. The MNCs and their Chinese supporters (many in the coastal region) began to campaign vigorously against WAPI. Through the Wifi Alliance and trade organizations like the U.S. Information Technology Office (USITO), their complaints continued to be channeled to high-level Chinese and U.S. officials. Soon the Chinese and American media began taking sides as well. On March 2, 2004, the Bush administration expressed its concern through a letter signed by U.S. Secretary of State Colin Powell, Secretary of Commerce Donald Evans, and U.S. Trade Representative Robert Zoellick, which was sent to Chinese Vice Premiers Wu Yi and Zeng Peiyan. Before long, Intel formally announced that it was unable to adopt the WAPI standards before the June 1 deadline, a stance soon adopted by other members of the Wifi Alliance.

The national launch of WAPI was stalled while the debate in China reached its pinnacle. MNCs as well as some domestic Chinese media outlets, most notably *Caijing* (*Finance*) magazine, leveled critiques at WAPI and at China's standard-setting procedures.[33] First, they argued that there was no need for distinctive Chinese national standards, especially ones that were incompatible with the existing Wifi standards. Moreover, the security design of Wifi was already being updated into WPA2. Critics furthermore charged that too little consideration had been given to the implementation of WAPI, which could impose high costs on service providers and consumers. Even if technically sound, the establishment of this national standard meant that Chinese businesspeople would be unable to roam outside China using the same wireless Internet devices. Critics also charged that the new standards would harm Chinese equipment manufacturers and service providers with their international export and expansion efforts. Most seriously, the MNCs and U.S. trade officials charged that the standard-setting procedure was unfair, closed, and discriminatory against foreign companies, constituting a violation to China's WTO commitment.

While the MNCs, the Wifi Alliance, and USITO focused their attention on state officials in both countries, the above critiques of WAPI were also articulated and circulated by Chinese financial and commercial analysts, but this triggered a tide of rebuttals in Chinese popular media with techno-nationalists heatedly referring to the WAPI critics as "traitors" (*hanjian*). Interestingly, although IWNComm and other BWIPS members offered their counterarguments on multiple occasions, the most systematic rebuttal of the WAPI critiques came from Chinese intellectuals utilizing IT-oriented publications (such as *Internet Weekly*) and weblogs (such as *Blogchina*). Jointly they argued that WAPI was technically feasible and that many companies in the PRC and Taiwan were already prepared to launch products using the WAPI standard. The most fundamental justification for WAPI was neither the fostering of domestic industry nor the global monopoly of American companies but rather China's national security needs. This should, argued WAPI supporters, overrule fair trade and international commerce concerns because matters of national security were not within the scope of WTO jurisdiction.

In a typical populist manner, China's market-driven journalists appealed to the masses to muster support for WAPI: Why should China rely on foreigners? Why can't it have its own technology standards? Aren't the anti-

WAPI arguments all part of a U.S.-inspired conspiracy to thwart China's rise as a global IT power? This nationalist rhetoric seemed to have been well received. An online survey conducted by Sina.com, China's largest Internet portal, showed that 64.1 percent of the 6,196 survey participants responded favorably to the question "Can China implement this national standard?"

Although techno-national sentiments intensified in commercial media, the top leadership of China seemed ready to compromise. On April 21, 2004, during her trip to the United States, Vice Premier Wu Yi agreed to postpone the mandatory implementation of WAPI indefinitely as part of a Sino–U.S. trade agreement. This decision by the Chinese government immediately triggered an outpouring of commentary and criticism. On May 9, 2004, *People's Daily Online* published an article, "Postponing WAPI Is Not to Appease the US," justifying the government's position. Meanwhile, the National Bureau of Asian Research (NBR), an American nonprofit institution, released a report criticizing China's "neo-techno-nationalism" for its attempt to achieve "national interests by leveraging globalization."[34] The *People's Daily Online* article and the NBR report prompted a new round of debate among China's IT policy analysts, for example, Jiang Qiping, who utilized both print media and weblogs in his rebuttal.[35] Chinalab, the IT policy research organization behind *Blogchina*, also released *Neo-Globalism: Research Report on China's High-Tech Standards Strategy*. Shortly thereafter, in August 2004, two leading analysts in Chinalab published *Challenge Intel*, arguing that the IT industry in China and the global market are suffering from the dominance of Intel; that the monopoly has to be undermined to achieve China's full ascendance as a technology power; and that the implementation of WAPI is a necessary strategic step towards that end.[36]

Before the polemics subsided, the BWIPS initiated a new offensive, this time at the global level. In November 2004, WAPI was submitted to the ISO/International Electrotechnical Commission (ISO/IEC) to be considered as a new global wireless Internet standard. Concrete efforts were taken to broaden the alliance of BWIPS beyond its initial core. After a series of negotiations, the WAPI Industrial Union was established in early 2006 with twenty-two members including Huawei, Datang, and all four of China's national telecom operators.[37] Foreign firms were also welcomed to join the WAPI Industrial Union, although few accepted the invitation. In January 2006, the encryption algorithm of WAPI was declassified to win support from members of the ISO/IEC subcommittee.

The application process was, however, full of bitterness for the Chinese. Facing WAPI challenge, the IEEE and the Wifi Alliance submitted their improved WPA2 standard. Consequently, the ISO/IEC subcommittee needed to consider both WAPI and WPA2 as candidates for global mobile Internet standards. To do so, two meetings were held in Orlando, Florida, and Frankfurt, Germany. Before the Orlando conference in November 2004, however, the American embassy denied entry visas to four members of the six-person Chinese delegation. When the Frankfurt meeting was convened in February 2005, the WAPI proposal was deleted from the agenda, prompting the Chinese representatives to stage a walk-out in protest of the subcommittee's action.[38] As soon as the news reached the PRC, commercial media and the blogosphere exploded with criticism.

Discussions were held in Beijing in August 2005 on the possibility of combining WAPI and WPA2 into one standard, which ended in failure. The ISO/IEC subcommittee then proceeded to let its members vote on the two standards on separate ballots from October 2005 to March 2006. The votes were overwhelmingly for WPA2, while WAPI was only endorsed by five member states (China, the Czech Republic, Iran, Kenya, and Spain) and three observer states (Cuba, Luxembourg, and Russia). Subsequently, WPA2 became the new international standard, and WAPI was rejected. BWIPS responded strongly to this outcome, accusing IEEE and the Wifi Alliance of using "deception, misinformation [and] confusion" during the selection process, "thus seriously violating the ISO/IEC code of ethics and procedural rules and principles, and creating an unfair ballot environment dominated by prejudice and discrimination."[39]

Ironically, a few years earlier, it had been the MNCs and the Wifi Alliance who felt the pain of discrimination in the making of China's new national standard, but now it was the turn of BWIPS and its techno-nationalist supporters to cry foul, using the very same allegations of unfairness and improper procedures. Is this simply a historical coincidence or another indication that the specific definition of national interests is always contingent on the institutional context in which it is articulated?

Defining National Interests

The battle for WAPI was fought and lost at the national and global levels. Researchers such as Kennedy have rightly argued for the importance of coalition building in standards wars from a structural perspective,[40] but this section will examine the discursive process by which techno-nationalism was constructed through patterns of communication that have a much wider scope of application beyond this specific case. Although there are many ebbs and flows, a typical example of techno-nationalist discourse can be extracted from a report released by the State Council Development Center (SCDC) entitled *2004 China Market Development Report*. In the midst of WAPI's national launching period in 2003–2004, the authors argued: "The promulgation of this standard marks the future direction of the wireless LAN and wireless IP networking industry in China. From now on, our country is on par with Europe, Japan, and the United States in the R&D of key technological innovations and the issuing of new standards. This not only clears the way for the take-off of the wireless LAN market in China but also indicates that, on the basis of autonomous intellectual property rights, the promulgation of national standards is beginning to support the core competitive capacity of domestic firms as a major channel for upgrading the IT industry" (author's translation).

This clearly reflects the ambition of the techno-nationalist program because the SCDC is an in-house think tank of the PRC central government. It reflects the continuing role of state-led initiatives in not only the R&D of high-tech programs but also institutionalized advocacy of techno-nationalism through official reports like this. Although the policy discourse remains elite based, which has been a basic feature of post-Mao China,[41] there is a crucial widening of the social scope in terms of players participating in the WAPI controversy.

As suggested by Feigenbaum, from the 1950s until fairly recently, the PRC's techno-nationalist discussion had been primarily led by a small group of strategic weaponry experts including top military leaders and leading scientists.[42] However, after the market reform and the globalization of the Chinese IT industry, particularly following China's entry into the WTO, we have observed a rapid descent of the WAPI advocacy from a top-down official verdict to a more inclusive and multidimensional debate involving governmental, commercial, and public opinion leaders.

In the policy circle, these included not only specialized standard-setting organs in the Chinese government such as MII, MST, and SAC but also the Ministry of Commerce and Vice Premier Wu Yi, whose mandate had more to do with trade than the building of China's innovative capacity. High-ranking U.S. officials like Colin Powell also played an unprecedented role in pressing the Chinese government to back down on its techno-nationalist ambitions during bilateral trade negotiations in 2004. A more crucial role was played by trade organizations and industry organizations like the USITO and the Wifi Alliance, which served as crucial forces in coordinating lobby activities on both sides of the Pacific. The Chinese techno-nationalists tried to emulate this by founding the WAPI Industrial Union in early 2006. Albeit too late in the game, this showed a consensus between the two sides of the dispute regarding the key importance of using organized discursive strategies to influence policymaking.

This widening scope of deliberation also means that a growing number of IT firms—large or small, domestic or multinational—could now take part in the dispute. Commercial entities such as IWNComm and Intel played an increasingly crucial role. Despite their competition with each other, these firms shared the main goal of occupying the emergent wireless Internet market. Thus different definitions for China's national interests were proposed based on each company's status as well as its marketing and public relations strategy. Meanwhile, telecom operators like China Mobile and device manufacturers like Huawei, who distanced themselves from the dispute in the beginning, ultimately were absorbed into the WAPI camp toward the end of the controversy.

Most intriguing in this process is the overwhelming involvement and partisanship among China's commercial media outlets. As Yuezhi Zhao contended, China's new commercial media have played a major role promoting WTO accession, arguing that it would be in the best interests of China to take part in neoliberal globalization.[43] But on the particular issue of techno-nationalism, two opposing camps quickly took shape. A key advocate of WTO entry is *Caijing* magazine, a finance magazine founded by the leading Beijing journalist, Hu Shuli, representing the interests of transnational capital, corporations, and China's new "stockizens."[44] Taking a techno-globalist view, articles in *Caijing* contend that China's national interests are best served if consumer interests in the wireless Internet market are met at low cost and with high compatibility to the existing Wifi system. Consumers, especially high-end business users, should be able to roam internationally using the standards. The most fundamental national interest is to prevent arbitrary state intervention and respect the "natural" selection of the marketplace. Although using the national interests as an argument, this is indeed an attempt to undermine techno-nationalist advocacy of a strategic domestic IT industry.[45]

On the other hand, techno-nationalist sentiment was pervasive in China's traditional and online media during WAPI's national launching stage, especially during spring–summer 2004, as well as the phase of its global competition (November 2004–March 2006). This included numerous newspapers, TV programs, and Internet portals like Sina.com, as well as books like *Challenge Intel*. The center of the discursive action, however, was *Blogchina*, the Beijing-based platform for China's high-tech bloggers. It was on this blog site that the influential essays by Jiang Qiping were published. Although some of his writings first appeared in print magazines and were only republished by *Blogchina*, this site provided a crucial function of escalating nationalistic sentiment by hosting and sharing responses to the articles by Jiang, his proponents, and adversaries. Generally speaking, public opinion in this camp regarded WAPI as a rare chance to foster domestic R&D in high-tech intellectual property, which would then push China's IT industry beyond pure manufacturing and subcontracting for the MNCs to a high level of independence and power. The need for China's own standards was also emphasized as a matter of national security.

Despite their differences, media on both sides collectively created a larger discursive environment in which the actual policies were framed and debated, away from the traditional state-centered approach in defining China's national interests. It is, however, incorrect to exaggerate this tendency of decentralization. For one thing, it does not suggest a demise of state power. Policy decisions made by Chinese government agencies, be they the initiation of R&D for the new standards or the suspension of WAPI, remain critically important. The network of MNCs would also have been less effective without direct and indirect support from the U.S. government.[46] Although in China the new WAPI standards got much support through the media, it was Vice Premier Wu Yi who vetoed the mandatory implementation of WAPI. It was not Intel or Colin Powell, nor any of the articulate members of China's upper and middle class, however magnified their voices were through outlets like *Caijing*. Increasing pluralism in the discursive domain therefore does not necessarily lead to a more open and democratic system of national policymaking, especially when there is a lack of parallel development within the political institution itself.

Although many media organizations were involved in the controversy, online and offline, the influential voices were still concentrated in a small number of publications, in particular *Caijing* and *Blogchina*. Within a bipolar structure, both sides were characterized by an inclination to make grand generalizations, both of them drifting away from productive consensus making. This deepened the communication gap with policymakers and may have undermined the perceived value of public input.

Despite the transnational scale of this dispute, much of the discursive action remained paradoxically concentrated in the coastal region of China, especially Beijing. As discussed previously, the genesis of WAPI owed much to the Maoist legacy of military R&D in inland cities and the low levels of incorporation of these places into China's new transnational IT industry. The unusually active role played by IWNComm in Xi'an and similar players in Wuhan and Guilin during the incubation phase and early phases of WAPI diminished, however, once the dispute received more public attention and became a media event. The center of discussion then moved decisively to Beijing, where both *Caijing* magazine and *Blogchina* were headquartered. This was certainly anything but a coincidence, for Beijing is the center of not only political power but also media power within the market for information and communication technologies (ICT) services and products, including both MNCs and domestic firms, as well as China's mass media industry. As the center of a complex system of production, trade, and competition, Beijing served as the nexus for relations among research institutes, subcontracting factories, PR and advertising agencies, and the stock market, all around the central issue of WAPI and the shaping of China's techno-nationalism.

Concluding Remarks

The rise of China as a "pole of market growth" in the global economy[47] is reorienting research attention from the "core" of Western industrialized nations to the traditionally more "peripheral" Asian regions. This is more than a shift in the geographical sense; more importantly, it is a process of reconsidering and reassessing the basic historical parameters and key cultural dynamics underlying the issues at stake facing the world's IT market. Only through this latter process can we map out the uncharted waters of the ongoing policy debate and the subsequent intellectual geopolitics of the new century.

The main phenomenon being analyzed in this chapter is China's growing ambition to reposition its IT industry toward the higher end of the "global assembly line." This requires a certain level of domestic innovative capacity among Chinese R&D personnel as well as state-led initiatives aiming at technological independence and control over intellectual property rights. Thus, in this context, the key concept of techno-nationalism matters greatly, much more so than in the liberalized IT industries of Western societies after the period of deregulation and privatization since the 1980s. The substantive reorientation in this case is therefore not simply about the growing power of China internationally but more precisely about the evolving patterns of techno-nationalism *within* the Chinese system. As we have seen, historical factors such as the Maoist legacy of the high-tech divisions of the People's Liberation Army (PLA) are crucial to explaining the cultural and institutional frameworks surrounding China's techno-nationalist ambition today. Besides historical continuity, there is also uneven geographical development that provided fertile ground for the fostering techno-nationalist programs like the WAPI. It was thus not a coincidence that inland cities like Xi'an, being less absorbed into the global economy compared to coastal cities, played a major role in this standards dispute.

Most important, we can see several trends in the discursive construction of Chinese techno-nationalism that provided arguably the crucial basis for state policy and corporate strategy during the WAPI controversy, both for the Chinese players and for multinationals in China. These include (1) the broadening of the social scope in terms of the actors involved, (2) the intensification of conflicts and the polarization of public opinion among various interests groups in China, and (3) the increasing importance of commercial mass media and new media outlets vis-à-vis formal institutional politics. In other words, what we are observing is a decisive drift away from the statist mode of techno-nationalism, and centered structurally and discursively on a tiny segment of China's ruling elite, which had played a dominant role throughout the Maoist era and until fairly recently. But during the WAPI controversy, the MNCs, USITO, and the U.S. government became key players as well. So did domestic commercial media like *Caijing* magazine. A huge number of nongovernmental techno-nationalists have also emerged using *Blogchina* as their rallying point. Although official state discourse usually avoids direct clashes with transnational capital, these nonstate actors tended to be deliberately provocative and confrontational.

Another reorientation resulting from the above analysis is that one must go beyond the usual allegation of China being the main aggressor in the global system or even a threat to the world. The rise of China—and of India as well—also presents tremendous opportunities. Whether one can seize the opportunities depends to a significant degree on our grasp of issues related to techno-nationalism. As we have seen, the rapidly developing global IT industry is equally a challenge to China as much as it is China's challenge to the world system. Leading actors of Chinese techno-nationalism came from the inland cities and the depth of the military apparatus, far away from the more globalized cities of Beijing and Shanghai. Because these people were excluded from the policy and market processes due to their geographical and institutional location, they see little hope for restoration back to the historical position they once enjoyed. The real "aggressor" is, in this sense, the encroachment of global capitalism that erodes the nation-state, resulting in uneven development, which also partially explains the polarization of opinions during the dispute. In other words, before China caused instability in the transnational system by challenging the Wifi establishment, there had already been internal domestic instability caused by globalization. The resulting uneven development after China's WTO accession became a pivotal condition for the WAPI controversy. The political economic disruption caused by global capitalism then reverberated—culturally, institutionally, and technologically—back into the web of bilateral ties between China and the United States, and back into the global system of IT development and standard setting.

Finally, if we take uneven development as the ultimate source of instability, the discursive construction of techno-nationalism would be indeed worrisome because the logic of exclusion is still alive and well. Once the controversy escalated beyond the core circle of policymakers and R&D personnel, Beijing again became the center of action due to its centrality in the political, commercial, and media systems of the country. The majority of the population, especially the working class in China's burgeoning IT industry, was uninformed and uninvolved, for the overall concern was intellectual property rights for the propertied upper class and the powerful authorities behind them. Will techno-nationalism increase social equality? Will WAPI create decent jobs and make China's economic growth more sustainable? One has to wonder if the silence of the working class and the continued exclusion of the majority of the society from IT policy discourses might become the most menacing source of instability for China and the world system in the long run. Techno-nationalism, as we've seen with the WAPI dispute, ultimately could contribute significantly to that instability.

Notes

1. D. K. Thussu, *International Communication* (Oxford: Oxford University Press, 2001).

2. T. G. McGee, ed., *Industrialization and Labor Force Processes* (Canberra: Australian National University, 1986), 35.

3. Organisation for Economic Co-operation and Development, *Information Technology Outlook 2006* (Paris: OECD, 2006), 16.

4. Y. Zhao, "China's pursuits for national sovereignty and technological developments in the network age," paper presented at Beijing Forum, Beijing, November 2–4, 2007.

5. S. Kennedy, "The political economy of standard coalition," *Asia Policy* 2 (2006): 41–62.

6. C. Buckley, "China's homegrown technology vs. the establishment," *International Herald Tribune*, March 14, 2005.

7. R. J. Samuels, *Rich Nation, Strong Army* (Ithaca, NY: Cornell University Press, 1994); M. J. Green, *Arming Japan* (New York: Columbia University Press, 1995).

8. M. Castells, *The Power of Identity* (Oxford: Blackwell, 1997).

9. R. Reich, "The rise of technonationalism," *Atlantic Monthly* (May 1987): 62–71.

10. W. A. McDougall, *The Heavens and the Earth* (New York: Basic Books, 1985); Reich, "The rise of technonationalism"; Samuels, *Rich Nation*.

11. McDougall, *The Heavens*, 5.

12. Green, *Arming Japan*.

13. Sylvia Ostry and Richard R. Nelson, *Techno-Nationalism and Techno-Globalism* (Washington, DC: Brookings Institute Press), 28–61.

14. Ostry and Nelson, *Techno-Nationalism*, 48–49.

15. J. Needham, *Science in Traditional China* (Hong Kong: Chinese University Press, 1981).

16. Y. Zhou, *Historicizing Online Politics* (Stanford, CA: Stanford University Press, 2006), 23–33.

17. E. Feigenbaum, *China's Techno-Warriors* (Stanford, CA: Stanford University Press, 2003).

18. Zhao, China's Pursuits.

19. C. Johnson, *Japan, Who Governs?* (New York: Norton, 1995).

20. Samuels, *Rich Nation*.

21. Samuels, *Rich Nation*.

22. Feigenbaum, *China's Techno-Warriors*, 2.

23. Feigenbaum, *China's Techno-Warriors*, 4.

24. Feigenbaum, *China's Techno-Warriors*, 3.

25. A. Segal, *Digital Dragon* (Ithaca, NY: Cornell University Press, 2002).

26. Zhao, China's Pursuits.

27. Kennedy, "The political economy."

28. Kennedy, "The political economy," 42.

29. Segal, *Digital Dragon*.

30. "Can IWNComm recover from the indefinite postponing of WAPI?" *21 Century Economic Report* (Beijing) (*21 shiji jingji baodao*), June 9, 2004.

31. "Chinese S&T minister plans to launch research into 12 key technologies," *Xinhua News Agency*, January 9, 2002.

32. Y. Wang and F. Zhang, "Rediscovering the WAPI dispute," *Caijing* (April 5, 2004): 82–83.

33. Wang and Zhang, "Rediscovering the WAPI dispute."

34. R. P. Suttmeier, X. Yao, and A. Tan, *Standards of Power?* (Seattle, WA: NBR, 2004): 18.

35. See, for example, Q. Jiang, "Face the failure of the 'new Westernization movement' (*zhengshi 'xinyangwu yundong' de shibai*)," *Blogchina*, May 14, 2004, http://www.blogchina.com/new/display/31007.html (accessed March 28, 2006); Q. Jiang, "The rise of 'neo-techno-nationalism,'" *eNews*, June 7, 2004, http://www.blogchina.com/new/display/33444.html (accessed March 28, 2006).

36. X. Fang and X. Fang, *Challenge Intel* (*Tiaozhan Intel*) (Beijing: China Customs, 2004).

37. W. Li, "Nation pushes forward own encryption standard," *China Daily*, March 8, 2006, 9.

38. Buckley, "China's homegrown technology."

39. M. Clendenin, "WAPI battle exposes technology Rifts with China," *EE Times*, March 17, 2006, http://www.eetimes.com/showArticle.jhtml?articleID=183700631 (accessed April 15, 2009).

40. Kennedy, "The political economy."

41. R. Kluver and J. H. Powers, ed., *Civic Discourse, Civil Society, and Chinese Communities* (Stamford, CT: Ablex, 1999), 11–22.

42. Feigenbaum, *China's Techno-Warriors*.

43. Y. Zhao, "Enter the world," in *Chinese Media, Global Contexts*, ed. C.-C. Lee (London: Routledge, 2003), 32–56.

44. Y. Zhao, "Underdogs, lapdogs, and watchdogs," in *Chinese Intellectuals between the State and the Market*, ed. X. Gu and M. Goldman (London: Routledge Curzon, 2004): 60–61.

45. Ostry and Nelson, *Techno-Nationalism*.

46. Thussu, *International Communication*, 231.

47. D. Schiller, "Poles of market growth?" *Global Media and Communication* 1, no. 1 (2005): 79–103.

Contributors

JOSEPH M. CHAN is currently a professor at the School of Journalism and Communication, the Chinese University of Hong Kong, where he served as a former director. He is also the Changjiang Chair Professor in the School of Journalism, Fudan University, People's Republic of China. He has published numerous articles and book chapters on international communication, political communication, and media development in Greater China. His books include *Mass Media and Political Transition: The Hong Kong Press in China's Orbit* (coauthor), *Global Media Spectacle* (coeditor), *In Search of Boundaries: Communication, Nation-States and Cultural Identities* (coeditor). He served as a president of the Chinese Communication Association and as visiting scholar at Harvard, Oxford, and University of California–Berkeley. He is the editor-in-chief of the Chinese journal *Communication & Society*.

MICHAEL CURTIN is a professor in the Department of Communication Arts at the University of Wisconsin–Madison and director of the Global Studies program at the UW International Institute. His books include *Redeeming the Wasteland: Television Documentary and Cold War Politics*, *Playing to the World's Biggest Audience: The Globalization of Chinese Film and TV*, *The American Television Industry* (coauthor), *Making and Selling Culture* (coeditor), and *The Revolution Wasn't Televised: Sixties Television and Social Conflict* (coeditor). He is currently writing *Media Capital: The Cultural Geography of Globalization*. With Paul McDonald, he is coeditor of the International Screen Industries book series for the British Film Institute.

CHUA BENG HUAT is concurrently leader, Cultural Studies in Asia Research Cluster, Asia Research Institute, and convenor, PhD Program in Cultural Studies in Asia, National University of Singapore. His publications on cultural studies include *Life Is Not Complete without Shopping*; *Consumption in Asia: Lifestyles and Identities* (editor), *Inter-Asia Cultural Studies Reader* (coeditor), and *East Asian Pop Culture: Analysing the Korean Wave* (coeditor). He is founding coexecutive editor of the journal, *Inter-Asia Cultural Studies*.

SHANTI KUMAR is an associate professor in the Department of Radio-Television-Film at the University of Texas–Austin. He is the author of *Gandhi Meets Primetime: Globalization and Nationalism in Indian Television* and the coeditor of *Planet TV: A Global Television Reader*. He has also published book chapters in edited anthologies and articles in journals such as *Television and New Media*, *Jump Cut*, *South Asian Popular Culture*, and the *Quarterly Review of Film and Video*.

CHIN-CHUAN LEE is the chair professor of communication and director of the Center for Communication Research at the City University of Hong Kong, and is also professor emeritus of journalism and mass communication at the University of Minnesota.

MADHAVI MALLAPRAGADA is an assistant professor in the Radio-Television-Film Department of the School of Communication at the University of Texas–Austin. Her current book project, *Home, Homeland, Homepage: Indian American Networks in the Digital Age*, examines the role of the Web in creating new networks of capital, culture, and community between India and the United States since the 1990s.

DIVYA C. MCMILLIN is an associate professor of international communication and cultural studies at the University of Washington–Tacoma. She is author of *International Media Studies*, which is a postcolonial critique of the field. Her second book, *Media Globalization and Youth Identity*, explores the conditions of globalization that produce youth labor and consumer identities. She has published articles in the *Journal of Communication*, *International Journal of Cultural Studies*, *Continuum: Journal of Media and Cultural Studies*, and the *Indian Journal of Gender Studies*, among other journals.

SREYA MITRA is a graduate student in the Department of Communication Arts at the University of Wisconsin–Madison. Her research interests include globalization, culture industries, gender, and sexuality in the context of contemporary Indian film and television. She has presented on popular Indian cinema and television at several media studies and area studies conferences.

SUJATA MOORTI is the author of numerous journal articles on diasporic media and explores the intersections of race, sexuality, and gender in U.S. media representations. She is the coeditor of *Global Bollywood: The Travels of Hindi Song and Dance* as well as *Local Violence, Global Media: Feminist Analyses of Gendered Violence*. She teaches at Middlebury College in Vermont.

ZHONGDANG PAN received his PhD in communication from University of Wisconsin–Madison in 1990. He has taught at Cornell University, University of Pennsylvania, and Chinese University of Hong Kong. He is now a professor in the Department of Communication Arts at University of Wisconsin–Madison and Changjiang Scholar Chair Professor in the School of Journalism at Fudan University in China. He has conducted research on public opinion and China's media changes.

ASWIN PUNATHAMBEKAR is an assistant professor in the Department of Communication Studies at the University of Michigan–Ann Arbor. His research and teaching revolve around globalization, cultural industries, new media and media convergence, and public culture with a focus on South Asia. He is coeditor of *Global Bollywood* and is currently writing a book that examines the operations of film, television, and dot-com companies in Mumbai as they grapple with the challenges of imagining Bollywood as a global cultural industry.

JACK LINCHUAN QIU is an assistant professor at the School of Journalism and Communication, Chinese University of Hong Kong. He researches information and communication technologies (ICTs), class, globalization, and modern capitalism in the contexts of China and the Asian Pacific. He is coauthor of *Mobile Communication and Society: A Global Perspective* and author of the forthcoming *Working-Class Network Society*, as well as more than a dozen research articles, chapters, and review essays, some of which have been translated into multiple languages and circulated among media policymakers globally through such organizational channels as UNESCO and UNITAR. Dr. Qiu also cofounded and moderates the China Internet Research Network.

HEMANT SHAH is a professor in the School of Journalism and Mass Communication at the University of Wisconsin–Madison. His research and teaching areas include global media, diaspora, and culture; media images of race and ethnicity; and media and development. He is coauthor of *Newspaper Coverage of Interethnic Conflict: Competing Visions of America*. His research has appeared in *Communication Theory, Journalism Monographs, Journalism Quarterly, Media Asia*, and *Howard Journal of Communication*, among other journals.

LAKSHMI SRINIVAS is assistant professor in the Department of Sociology at the University of Massachusetts–Boston. Her research lies at the intersection of sociology, anthropology, media, and globalization studies. She has published multiple articles on cinema and spectatorship, public culture, leisure, and consumption and is completing a book manuscript based on ethnography of movie-going in India.

EMILIE YUEH-YU YEH is a professor in the School of Communication and director of the Centre for Media and Communication Research at Hong Kong Baptist University. Her books include *Taiwan Film Directors: A Treasure Island* (coauthor), *Chinese-Language Film: Historiography, Poetics, Politics* (coeditor), and *East Asian Screen Industries* (coauthor).

YUEZHI ZHAO is a professor and Canada Research Chair in political economy of global communication at the School of Communication, Simon Fraser University, Canada. Zhao has written extensively on China's media and communication industries during the reform era, including the commercialization of China's media industries, the political economy of Chinese telecommunication developments, and the role of communication and culture in China's global integration. She is the author of *Media, Market, and Democracy in China*, coauthor of *Sustaining Democracy? Journalism and the Politics of Objectivity*, and coeditor of *Democratizing Global Media: One World, Many Struggles, The Political Economy of Communication: A Reader*, and *Global Communications: Toward a Transcultural Political Economy*. Her newest book, *Communication in China: Political Economy, Power, and Conflict*, explores China's rapidly evolving polity, economy, and society through the prism of its communication system.

Index

transculturation, 204. *See also* hybridization
transnationalism: in Chinese cinema, 173, 175–76, 183, 189–90, 195; in Indian cinema, 19–21, 22, 24–25, 49, 54, 55–58; in Indian television, 119–20, 122–24, 132–33, 134
trendy drama (Japanese TV genre), 228–29, 230
Turner, Victor, 244. See also *communitas*; *liminoids*

Vande Mataram ("Hail to the Motherland"), 53, 55, 127, 137n31
Varma, Ram Gopal, 145, 149, 150–51

WAPI (Chinese wireless Internet standard): competing for global standards, 293–95; controversy over, 292–93; launch of, 286, 290, 291–92; mandatory implementation of, 292, 294; technonationalism triggered by, 293–94, 296, 298, 300
Warlords, The (Chinese film), 195–97, 198. *See also* pan-Chinese cinema
Web, Indian-American: beauty as cultural

consumption on, 67–68; forging of, 61; notions of family and nation on, 63, 66, 71, 78–79; politics of "home" on, 61–62, 68, 66, 71–72, 74; transnational discourse of banking on, 69–71
wedding, Indian: as ability to reconcile Indian and Western practices, 90; connecting India with immigrant communities, 83–84; diasporic subjectivity of, 91–95; industry, 86–88; as invented tradition, 85, 98; media outlets, 88–89; in women's lives, 84–85
Westernization. *See under* globalization
World Trade Organization (WTO): China's globalization and, 262, 263, 270, 277; Chinese film industry and, 161, 169, 173, 175; Chinese television regulation and, 218n26; Spring Festival Gala and, 250, 254
wuxia genre, 224, 227. *See also* pan-Asian cinema

Zee TV, 3, 9, 45, 119, 120, 124–25
Zhang Yimou, 163, 165, 167–70, 176, 178. See also *Curse of the Golden Flower*; "Fifth Generation" filmmakers; *Hero*

Popular Culture and Politics in Asia Pacific

The University of Illinois Press
is a founding member of the
Association of American University Presses.

Composed in 10/13.5 Janson Text
with Electra display
by Jim Proefrock
at the University of Illinois Press
Manufactured by Integrated Book Technology

University of Illinois Press
1325 South Oak Street
Champaign, IL 61820-6903
www.press.uillinois.edu